ADVOCACY & OBJECTIVITY

Published for the
Organization of American Historians

Mary O. Furner

ADVOCACY &
OBJECTIVITY *A Crisis in the*

Professionalization of

American Social Science,

1865-1905

The University Press of Kentucky

H 53
.U5
F87

Publication of this book was assisted by
the American Council of Learned Societies
under a grant from the Andrew W. Mellon Foundation

ISBN: 0-8131-1309-1

Library of Congress Catalog Card Number: 73-86403

A statewide cooperative scholarly publishing agency
serving Berea College, Centre College of Kentucky,
Eastern Kentucky University, Georgetown College,
Kentucky Historical Society, Kentucky State University,
Morehead State University, Murray State University,
Northern Kentucky State College, Transylvania University,
University of Kentucky, University of Louisville, and
Western Kentucky University

Editorial and Sales Offices: Lexington, Kentucky 40506

for my mother & father

Contents

Preface

This book is the result of a desire to find out what would happen if historians and social scientists, themselves recognized professionals, examined the history and present influence of the professions with something like the imagination, diligence, and zeal for objectivity that scholars have long devoted to political parties, business leaders, and labor organizations. The professions have seldom raised their leaders to prominence as folk heroes, nor have individuals identified primarily with the professions appeared as major combatants in those legendary struggles between the people and the interests or the masses and the classes that have fixed so much attention on revolutions, reform movements, and wars.

Yet it can hardly be denied that at least since the latter part of the nineteenth century a large measure of control over the complex, routine, day-to-day workings of vital economic, social, and political processes has been delegated to people with professional credentials as the source of their authority. With few exceptions, professionals in key positions are anonymous as far as the general public is concerned. They are neither publicly elected nor reviewed. But the multiplication of functions requiring a level of technical expertise that can only be acquired through highly specialized training has made professionals indispensable to modern life, often in performing services and making judgments that they themselves have helped to make essential. Such power deserves scrutiny.

Attempts to probe the workings of the social science professions have a special significance, for professional social scientists, through their extensive control over formal education and publication in the social sciences, have developed enormous power to influence the content and extent of social criticism in the United States. Until recently, however, most studies of social science professionalization have been done by people in the individual disciplines, not by historians. Too often such studies have been designed to justify a particular discipline or school rather than to add to our understanding of the developing social science professions as institutions in which flesh-and-blood human beings, with normal biases and animosities as well as high ideals and special skills, have assumed primary responsibility for the scientific study of society. Just as historians have begun to recover the history of American education from its glorification of the public school, students of the professions are discarding filiopietistic approaches in favor of tough-minded inquiries into the character of relationships between social scientists and other powerful groups in government, industry, and the educational establishment.

Some of the best studies of American social science have traced the growth of basic knowledge in the disciplines (Joseph Dorfman's impressive treatment of *The Economic Mind in American Civilization* is a good example) or explained the influence of major idea systems such as evolutionary naturalism or the welfare state on the attitudes and inquiries of social scientists. These studies, along with a number of excellent intellectual biographies, have done much to fill in the intellectual history of American social science.

By contrast, this study is an effort to develop an important aspect of the social history of American social science. I first became interested in the history of the professions when I was investigating the reaction of American intellectuals to charges made against them in the McCarthy era. An individual's response often seemed to depend to a large extent on his position in the social institutions that facilitated his work and guaranteed his continued influence. Professionals, and academics in particular, often found themselves in circumstances quite different from those of intellectuals who worked through more independent institutions. Older sociological definitions that projected an image of unswerving unity within professions seemed to need revision. The social science professions were obviously not monoliths that imposed a uniform set of behaviors on all their members. Rather they were complex social groups with recognizable elites and opposing factions organized formally or informally to defend various points of view on professional and wider social questions.

Before long it became clear that a deeper understanding of the role of professional social scientists in American life depended on a close examination of internal developments within the social science professions. It seemed logical to carry the study back to the professionalization period in the late nineteenth century, there to attempt to discover what alternatives had existed for American social scientists in those more fluid circumstances, what motives and forces had helped to shape the dominant institutions and ways of behaving, what hopes and ambitions had been eliminated or discarded, and how American social scientists ultimately came to perceive themselves and be perceived by their fellow citizens.

The Gilded Age is an exciting time to study the professions. Although the classical professions of theology, law, and medicine had always exercised sway, especially through the leadership of Puritan divines and in the Revolutionary generation, the middle years of the nineteenth century were a time of general deprofessionalization. A quick acceleration of industrial and urban growth after the Civil War reversed that trend and provided a seedbed for dozens of specialized roles that required professional training. As Robert Wiebe has suggested, traditional values and habits which had organized Americans into geographical communities began to be replaced by forces that created new communities of people who were united primarily by their occupations. Authority based on status in a stable social hierarchy gave way to recognition won by effectiveness in dealing with fluid situations that required constant supervision. Rapid social change created a demand for continuous, efficient social services based on sound theory, and that need provided a strong impetus to the development of professionalism in the study of society. The rise of the modern university in the same period was a historical coincidence of overwhelming significance. While the new research orientation in higher education probably did not cause professionalization, the university was certainly a potent catalyst in fields where academic credentials could serve as universally recognizable symbols of professional competence.

Professionalization in social science to 1905 is the story of emerging dominance by academics. I have concentrated in this study on the early development of economics, sociology, and political science. My major emphasis is on economics, for that discipline professionalized earliest and its members experienced the process more self-consciously than others. For a time the lines between these three disciplines were quite fluid. All three had origins in antebellum moral philosophy and amateur social science. As the field of economics was defined more narrowly around market concerns, people who were attracted by an interest in either reform or social dynamics migrated into sociology, while those who were intrigued by constitutional and administrative problems developed the field of political science. In these formative years at least relations between the disciplines and their connections with the preacademic social science which preceded and for a time paralleled academic social science cannot be ignored. But the questions debated, the roles created, the methods developed, the disagreements explored, and the power struggles played out in economics were the most crucial in the development of an image that dominated American social science when the formative period ended.

Neither historians nor anthropologists belonged in this study. In the formative years of the historical profession, academics who styled themselves as scientific historians were absorbed with separating themselves from their nonacademic predecessors. Though the best of the patrician historians cared as much about accuracy as their professional successors, the so-called amateur typically considered history a branch of literature. Under German influence, the new academic historians wanted to pursue more specialized inquiries that might yield explanatory generalizations about the past. Either preacademic or early professional historians might favor a particular social class or political position, but their work lacked the immediate policy applications that tied economics, sociology, and political science into current social development. When a historian took a post as an ambassador, he stopped doing the work—full-time research and writing about the past—that characterized him professionally, while an economist in the Interstate Commerce Commission, a political scientist administering an agency in the Philippines, or a sociologist working in the Bureau of Labor Statistics continued to function as a social scientist.

The case with anthropologists was also different. In their emergent period, which really fell largely in the twentieth century, anthropologists were primarily concerned with establishing a field distinct from physical science by ridding themselves of concepts and generalizations derived from biological models. They attempted to organize inquiries around the idea of culture, to create a unique terminology, and to develop field techniques of research.

After marking out what seemed to be sensible boundaries for this study, I tried to find out how emerging groups of American social scientists envisioned their role. Instead of concentrating on the development of knowledge as a professionalizing force, I examined how social scientists thought they ought to behave, what they thought their responsibilities were, how they hoped to perform a vital social function as they fulfilled their own ambitions, and what restraints they recognized. To gain perspective, I compared the motives of nonacademic with academic social scientists by analyzing the power struggles within organizations. Throughout, I tried to combat the almost irresistible urge in professionalization studies to deal with an inferior past as preface to a superior present.

As this study grew, the concept of academic freedom emerged as a uniquely helpful device for understanding professionalization. The academic freedom cases of the 1880s and 1890s have been described by others as important events in the development of academic freedom and analyzed for the light they shed on the growth of the modern university. The cases involving social scientists were also critical incidents in the professionalization of social science, for each case called the emerging social role of the social science professions into question. Using some celebrated and some less familiar cases, I examined the discussion that each crisis provoked *within* the disciplines to discover the dominant and minority views of the emerging profession's mission at the time and tried to determine how mechanisms that were developed for defending academic freedom actually influenced the direction of professionalization.

A great many people have helped me with the preparation of this book. For years, as teacher and friend, Professor Robert Wiebe has hovered on the fringes of my intellectual life, stepping in at critical moments to provide exactly the advice and encouragement I needed to overcome an obstacle or find the courage for a more difficult endeavor. His critical reading helped me immeasurably in sharpening the focus and tightening the argument of this study. I am also grateful to George Daniels for helping me to understand professionalization. My colleagues Alfred Young, J. Carroll Moody, and Carl Parrini found time to read the manuscript and to make useful suggestions. As chairman of my department at Northern Illinois University, Emory Evans encouraged scholarship by taking a sincere and friendly interest in each person's professional activities, while the department as a whole administers a steady dose of intellectual stimulation. For another kind of sustenance I turned to my family and close friends and was never disappointed.

One learns, by doing a study that requires a great deal of manuscript research, to be utterly dependent on the highly skilled and dedicated staffs of libraries and archives. Though I cannot name here the many individuals who showed me personal kindnesses, I gratefully acknowledge the assistance of archivists and librarians at Columbia University, the Concord Free Public Library, Cornell University, the Detroit Public Library, Duke University, Harvard University, the Johns Hopkins University, the Library of Congress, Michigan Historical Collections,

Northwestern University, the Pennsylvania Historical Society, Stanford University, Tulane University, the University of Chicago, the University of Illinois, the University of Nebraska, the University of North Carolina (Chapel Hill), the University of Washington, and the Wisconsin Historical Society.

Other generous people helped me with the preparation of the manuscript. I am indebted to Avis Johnson Turrel, Lois Wesolowski, and Gwen Cannon, my student assistants, for their care in typing various versions of the manuscript. I owe special thanks to Sarah Mason, whose scrupulous checking of most of the notes saved me from numerous errors.

Introduction

The industrial America that grew up after the Civil War made people conscious of society in new ways. The factories, the corporations, the railroads, the burgeoning cities—those powerful totems of a modern age had seemed so promising one by one. Considered together, they had a more ominous look. First around the great cities and then across the whole country they knit people up in interdependent systems where everyone prospered or suffered more or less together. People had trouble justifying the old conviction that poverty and prosperity were the just rewards of individual merit. In an era of unprecedented opportunity, there were also alien, impersonal, seemingly uncontrollable social forces that a person could not fathom by the old maxims. Out of the confusion a host of questions rose. Finally they congealed into one great "social question," and for a moment in the 1880s the future seemed to depend on finding the answer.

No one was quite prepared to answer the social questions posed by industrialization. Reformers concentrated at first on trying to regain the simplicity of a preindustrial era and restore lost virtues. Politicians cautioned against expecting much direction from government. Ministers and moral philosophers still taught people how to behave ethically in their personal and civic affairs, but they seemed no better equipped than their fellows to explain the baffling new economic relationships. In an age that honored science above other sources of wisdom, it became clear that people who established their ability to study society scientifically would command attention and influence the course of events. The modern social science professions were the product of that need and opportunity.[1]

The first postwar social scientists were concerned citizens from various walks of life, brought together by a common interest in helping people who became casualties of industrial society. In 1865 they formed the American Social Science Association (ASSA) to gather information and develop techniques for ameliorating bad social conditions. As long as these amateur social scientists devoted most of their energy to humanitarian causes, they added little to basic social science knowledge. When some ASSA leaders gradually shifted their attention from the unfortunate victims of social change to processes affecting society as a whole and then embarked upon empirical studies to discover how society worked, they took the first tentative steps toward professionalization as social scientists.

In the new universities, meanwhile, another group of social scientists was taking shape. Unlike the antebellum colleges, which placed primary emphasis on transmitting a cultural tradition and developing the civic morality of students, the emerging universities developed an ethos of their own which stressed the creation of new knowledge above everything else. University-trained economists, political scientists, and sociologists were expected to engage in a highly intensive type of research, even as they accomplished the secondary goals of teaching the results of their investigations to students and training a new generation of inquirers. Because these professional academics made social

1. Two different conceptions of the structure of a profession have been useful in this study. One, typified by William J. Goode, "Community within a Community: The Professions," *American Sociological Review* 22 (April 1957):194-200, suggests that all members of a profession are bound by a common sense of identity, share values in common, have the same role definitions for members and nonmembers, share a common professional language that is only partly understood by outsiders, produce a homogeneous next generation through recruitment and training to established standards, and judge achievement internally but refuse to pass judgment on colleagues for the larger society. A contradictory view advanced by Rue Bucher and Anselm Strauss, "Professions in Process," *American Journal of Sociology* 66 (January 1961):325-34, rejects the unity theme and stresses the importance of different levels and specialties within a profession. Professions are conceived as loose coalitions of "segments" or interest groups, each with its own distinctive identity, sense of the past, and goals for the future. Delicately aligned under a common name at a given point in history, these contending segments may break apart at any time when their conflicting sense of mission, different ideologies or methodologies, and diverging interests and associations prove too divisive. Both the static community theory and the dynamic segment theory are useful in analysis, as are the functional and process approaches.

science their sole career, they had an even deeper interest than the amateurs in establishing their ability to study society scientifically, and their full-time dedication to a common intellectual enterprise made it easier for them to define and project an authoritative image.

Among nonacademic and academic social scientists alike, the tension between reform and knowledge provided an impulse to professionalization.[2] Both groups faced a common problem: how to reconcile the reform interests that attracted them to social science in the first place with their need for recognition as objective, dispassionate scientists capable of providing disinterested guidance for society. Establishing scientific authority was especially difficult for the so-called amateurs[3] because many of them were publicly connected with controversial political posi-

2. In this study professionalization means simply the process by which a group of people moves toward acquiring the attributes of a profession: a unique social mission, a systematized body of knowledge that provides the basis for practice and becomes increasingly esoteric, authority to perform a vital social function which is recognized and sanctioned either legally or informally by the community, a code of ethics to govern behavior toward colleagues and clients, and a unique professional culture. Basic works such as A. M. Carr-Saunders and P. A. Wilson, *The Professions* (Oxford, 1933), and Robert K. Merton, *Some Thoughts on the Professions in American Society,* Brown University Papers, 37 (Providence, R.I., 1960) develop a similar definition in detail. Academic professionalization also involves the separation of specific academic disciplines from larger bodies of knowledge, the creation of academic departments, professional organizations, and specialized journals. For a discussion of this distinction, see Hamilton Cravens, "The Abandonment of Evolutionary Social Theory in America: The Impact of Academic Professionalization upon American Sociological Theory, 1890-1920," *American Studies* 12 (Fall 1971):7-9.

3. The use of the term amateur in this study is not intended to imply an invidious comparison with professionals. Instead, the terms amateur, nonacademic, preacademic, and preprofessional are used—with the slight but useful variations in meaning that they allow—to distinguish social scientists who were not the graduate-trained, full-time academics that ultimately became the typical professional scientists from those who were. These four terms also communicate something about how the individuals or groups in question conceived of themselves. I recognize the limitations of such categories, particularly if they suggest that there was one, linear, almost predestined path to professionalism, instead—as I believe—of various viable alternatives in competition for ultimate recognition and dominance. It is equally unfortunate when such labels imply that practice outside the universities was somehow inevitably inferior to the work of academics. Of course, the problem arises from describing nonacademic groups in part by comparing them with academics. Yet the academic-nonacademic distinction was one vital difference. Readily available alternatives such as "genteel reformers" or "the best men" emphasize characteristics and concerns that are not central to this study and may sound even more disparaging. The generic categories that I have invented so far simply impose more order than ever existed, though a grouping of bureaucratic social scientists was promising. Hopefully

tions. No matter how hard preacademic social scientists tried to change their image, indeed no matter how successful some of them were in concentrating on the pursuit of knowledge and leaving practical applications to others, anyone who resented their findings or disagreed with their social views could easily cast doubt on their objectivity by hurling the reliable epithet, "reformer."

Academic social scientists were in some ways more vulnerable. Even in higher education professors were expected to uphold the values of the community, not to challenge accepted traditions. Yet modern research training imbued its recipients with an iconoclastic spirit that compelled them to examine every assumption and inquire into every social problem. When historical economists investigated accepted economic laws as they actually functioned in the real life circumstances of factory, marketplace, or treasury they almost inevitably drew some conclusions which threatened vested economic interests. In general, the research facilities that scholars needed were provided by private philanthropists with conservative social opinions or public officials who were subject to political pressures. Yet scholarly investigations often yielded recommendations for reform that jeopardized those very sources of support.

As long as the ASSA remained the only social science association, there was little open rivalry between amateurs and professors in the emerging social science disciplines. Though certain professionalizing academics might be passionately interested in reform, they usually based their claim to public support on their ostensibly nonpartisan endeavors in research and teaching. The ASSA amateurs wanted to gather social science data so that they could apply it directly to social problems; thus they came to teaching only after other efforts to affect policy had failed. There were no clear ideological tests that separated academics

---

better terms and concepts to describe these various types of social scientists can be developed as their motives are more fully understood. The best solution might be simply to rehabilitate the term amateur so that it would suggest not less accomplishment but instead different institutional affiliations, motives, and work routines.

from nonacademics. Liberals or conservatives in one group often had more in common with like-minded counterparts in the other movement than with political or philosophical opponents in their own. Supporters of laissez-faire were prominent in both groups, and it was also true, in the 1880s at least, that humanitarians among the amateur social scientists and ethical statists among the historical economists in the universities evolved reform programs that nearly converged. In other words, the range of political and social views articulated in both the ASSA and the emerging academic professions could be located along fairly similar spectrums.

But the differences in the two patterns of professionalization —and consequently in the way people in each group envisioned their roles—eventually proved to be unbridgeable. Though ASSA members developed scientific methods of investigation, most of them continued to seek the sort of professional status usually associated with the classical learned professions of theology, law, and medicine. In that venerable tradition, professionals were regarded as men and women of broad general culture and wide-ranging ability. They were knowledgeable and reliable model citizens who could be trusted to manage affairs. Essentially their competence was the product of individual character and class privilege, not esoteric knowledge or technical skill beyond the reach of laymen. They conceived problems in practical terms and communicated their findings to ordinary people in everyday language.

By contrast, academics quickly developed a professional subculture. They created sophisticated concepts, a technical vocabulary which required special knowledge, and a private network of communication through their own journals and associations. As proof of their special competence, they sought authority for their disciplines by attempting to gain recognition of the advanced degrees that they alone dispensed and the professional connections that they controlled.[4] Lacking such hallmarks,

4. For a similar distinction between traditional and modern concepts of professional status, see A. M. Carr-Saunders, "Metropolitan Conditions and Traditional

social scientists of the ASSA type gradually lost status. Professionally trained academics eventually gained control of social science. With control, they won a right to rationalize social institutions and to answer social questions—a right that persists, with very important consequences, today.

Eliminating external competition was only one of the problems involved in the academic professionalization of social science. Disputes within the academy proved even more troublesome. Social scientists inevitably treated controversial questions. In the early 1880s a small group of reform-oriented, professionally trained economists began attacking the premises of classical economics that an older generation of economists had used to explain and justify the American economic system. United by common experiences, a shared opposition to laissez-faire, and a keen sympathy for labor, the young revisionists succeeded in breaking down a number of old certainties in the field. As these ethical economists challenged such fundamental institutions as private property, competition, and capitalism, traditionalists reacted defensively at first, working out new arguments to protect old theories.

For several years in the mid-1880s economists aired their differences loudly, bitterly, and far too publicly. At stake were not only the answers to questions of cosmic importance to society but also the emerging institutions of economics as an academic profession. In some ways the conflict was fruitful, for it exposed the limitations of outmoded concepts as well as the fallacies in utopian schemes. It opened up new fields of inquiry that were responsive to the needs of an industrial society, and it raised the level of methodological sophistication in economic research. On the negative side, the economic controversy made social scientists even more vulnerable than usual to attacks from interest groups outside the profession.

Professional Relationships," in *The Metropolis in Modern Life,* Robert Moore Fisher, ed. (New York, 1955), pp. 286-87. A convenient compilation of various approaches to the process of professionalization is Howard M. Vollmer and Donald L. Mills, eds., *Professionalization* (Englewood Cliffs, N. J., 1966).

Direct interference in public affairs taught academic social scientists the most painful lessons of the professionalization process. Tenuous at best, the scholar's claim to authority weakens dangerously when battles within the scholarly community become public. If experts disagree, then who can claim the sanction of science for dissenting views? In order to survive professionally, economists had to find ways of repressing partisanship and presenting an appearance of unity and objectivity to the public. Gradually moderates forged a kind of working alliance that sacrificed extremists in both schools to scholarly values that highly self-conscious professionals considered more important: professional security and the orderly development of knowledge in their disciplines.

In the 1880s and 1890s, a series of academic freedom cases profoundly affected the direction of social science professionalization. These cases have usually been presented as episodes in the history of anti-intellectualism, demonstrations of how reformers fared at the hands of conservative trustees and politicians, or as chapters in the development of the American idea of academic freedom. Actually the academic freedom cases contributed as much to internal discipline in the social science professions as they did to the external image of the social scientist. When trouble struck, the reaction of a scholar's professional colleagues could determine the outcome of the case. Between 1886 and 1900 economists, political scientists, and sociologists experimented with various ways of handling attacks on fellow social scientists. Gradually mechanisms evolved that gave a fairly small group of prominent leaders informal but nonetheless effective authority to determine who would be defended and how. If official or quasi-official action on the part of an organized scholarly profession could save a threatened colleague, the absence of such intervention could mean professional doom. Thus the academic freedom cases helped to spell out limits of permissible dissent within the emerging social science professions. By logical extension—depending on who controlled the organizations—a conservative, liberal, or radical consensus could predominate, a subtle orthodoxy could be imposed. As organized efforts succeeded in saving people's jobs and established some clear immunities for scholars, they also homogenized behavior and narrowed the territory that academic social science covered.

As professionalization proceeded, most academic social scientists stopped asking ethical questions. Instead they turned their attention to carefully controlled, empirical investigations of problems that were normally defined by the state of knowledge in their fields rather than by the state of society. Professional social scientists generally accepted the basic structure of corporate capitalism. Abandoning their pretensions to a role as arbiters of public policy, they established a more limited goal: recognition as experts with extraordinary technical competence in a highly specialized but restricted sphere.

The tension between scholarship and reform has nevertheless persisted in the social sciences. At various times in the twentieth century, notably, for example, when professors opposed American involvement in World War I and again during the McCarthy period, social scientists faced charges of subversive activity which forced them to reevaluate their professional goals. In the 1960s radical caucuses attempted to control the meetings of social science associations and to commit their professions officially to policy positions against American involvement in Southeast Asia or in favor of increased opportunities for minority groups in American society. The resulting ferment within the professions closely resembled the chaos in economics in the mid-1880s. As then, one side insisted that social scientists must take a moral stand on controversial issues of overwhelming importance to the peace and security of the society. With equal vehemence the other side protested that politicization only subverts important academic values and diminishes the contribution that scholars can make to society if they confine themselves to their special fields of competence. There was a rough but decidedly imperfect correlation between people's political views and their membership in the dominant or insurgent factions. Scholars wrestled with the difficulty of separating professional and substantive questions. While this dispute, which approached theological intensity, raged within the professions, external pressures mounted, job screening by political identification apparently increased, and public and private support for social science research declined.

To understand these problems better, it is important to go back to their source in the nineteenth century. It is the purpose of this study to describe how rival patterns of professionalization developed in social science, how dedication to reform and commitment to objective scholarship clashed and were integrated, what kinds of social scientists prevailed, to what ends, and at what cost to the society they claimed to serve.

1   *Reform versus Knowledge*

From 1865 to 1885, a single, comprehensive organization represented the diverse interests of American social scientists. Though academic specialists of a later time have described the American Social Science Association as little more than a coalition of reformers, contemporaries looked to the ASSA as a major source for guidance in adjusting to modern industrial society.[1] Many of the most distinguished figures in literary, academic, social, industrial, political, and professional circles joined the ASSA. As this diverse group of inquirers searched for ways to solve social problems, they also moved gradually toward a clearer conception of the social scientist's role in society.

Unlike the university professors who would eventually dominate the academic social sciences, early ASSA members were united by no common pattern of training, guided in their efforts by no full-formed code of ethics, inspired by no traditionally recognized social mission. Even as they cooperated in reform ventures, groups with varied interests and diverse perceptions of themselves as social scientists competed for control of the association. By the mid-1880s several professionalizing impulses had developed in the ASSA. But for the timely competition of university-based social scientists, these impulses might have led social science professionalization in some very different directions. Thus the ASSA, important enough for its own achievements, also provides a useful basis of comparison for the study of professionalization within the academic social science disciplines.

The amateur social scientists in the ASSA approached professionalization in an unorthodox manner. Their history demonstrates the difficulty of using conventional models to understand the academic professions and their antecedents. According to traditional canons, a profession invariably begins as an occupation and moves along a continuum toward professional status as its members, acting more or less in unison, begin to perform a vital social function, develop a body of knowledge to guide practice, create a code of ethics to govern their conduct as professionals, and win formal recognition from society for their authority in the field. The limitations of that model for analyzing the ASSA are obvious. ASSA members followed dozens of different occupations and traditional professions.[2] A shared interest in alarming social conditions drew people together from different walks of life, but their mutual concern did not define one common mission for the social scientist. Depending on their backgrounds and interests, these early social scientists saw different missions. Because there was no clearly defined body of knowledge that could explain the origin of social welfare needs and no recognized body of specialists or set of procedures for coping with dramatically increased dependency, the ASSA provided a laboratory for theoretical and practical experimentation. Progress toward professionalization in the ASSA never followed a straight line. It began bravely, faltered, shifted direction, surged forward, branched, and finally faltered again as different kinds of leaders and different philosophies held sway.

Though ASSA activity reached in many directions, two definite impulses were always present: the urge to reform and the quest for knowledge. At the beginning reform was the dominant theme. Many members worked as volunteers in humanitarian societies or as officials in government bureaus that dealt with the needy. The avalanche of information which their efforts generated sensitized ASSA leaders to the need in industrial

1. For an example see J. Franklin Jameson's diary entry of 8 December 1882 in Elizabeth Donnan and Leo F. Stock, eds., *An Historian's World: Selections from the Correspondence of John Franklin Jameson* (Philadelphia, 1956), p. 36, n. 116.

2. In a paper read at the November 1972 meeting of the Southern Historical Association, Thomas Haskell attributed the unique character of the ASSA to the association's professional origins. Citing the presence in the organization of doctors, lawyers, ministers, and teachers, he argued that the internal structure and operation of the ASSA reflected the existing division of labor among traditional professions.

society for standardized, scientific procedures to use in gathering and evaluating social data. Until American political realities thwarted such dreams, there was momentum in the ASSA toward a professional civil service which would operate at the policy level, especially in social service agencies that extended the assistance of government to the people.

Gradually, however, progressive members realized that effective, broad-gauged social criticism required both a systematic program of organized research and the appearance of objectivity. As their desire to understand society transcended their devotion to special issues, some ASSA leaders dedicated themselves primarily to rational scientific values. They wanted to know how society worked and to communicate their knowledge directly to the people, leaving the direct implementation of reform to others. Some ASSA leaders believed in disseminating knowledge through the popular media and the common schools. Others, recognizing a need for more specialized knowledge and authoritative status, tried to build a base for their version of the social science movement in higher education. Finally, in an attempt to clarify their image and fulfill what they had come to perceive as their professional mission, a group of these pre-professional, preacademic, still so-called amateur social scientists attempted to establish a general social science curriculum in the colleges and universities. But the professionalization of academic social science, with its more specialized disciplines and research ethos, was too far advanced for effective competition.

The development of theoretical social science could hardly have been foreseen at mid-century. Unlike the utopian social theorists of the 1840s and the 1850s, the founders of the American Social Science Association were practical, even conventional Americans who confronted a host of unfamiliar welfare problems in mid-century New England. Faced with a rising tide of Irish immigration, Massachusetts established in 1851 a Board of Alien Commissioners whose members found themselves dealing with the problems of illness, indigence, poverty, and crime. Rural migration to growing cities and wartime population mobility strained private welfare resources even further. In 1862 Samuel Gridley Howe proposed the creation of a Board of State Charities to coordinate the efforts of separate relief agencies. Howe wanted to replace hit-and-miss philanthropy with a rational approach to welfare, which would begin by collecting information on the size and nature of the problem. When Howe's union of relief agencies attracted the attention of philanthropists and reformers, it grew into a grander organization with a loftier purpose. Members of the Boston Social Science Association, a new society modeled on the British National Association for the Promotion of Social Science, suggested that the Massachusetts Board of State Charities provided the ideal basis for a national social science movement in America. In 1865 the American Social Science Association was established.[3]

The ASSA attracted people who sensed a new dimension in the human problems created by industrial society. As they saw fresh evidence of individual need and helplessness, they defined social science existentially. "Our attention has lately been called," an ASSA circular read, "to the importance of some organization in the United States, both local and national, whose object shall be the discussion of those questions relating to the Sanitary Conditions of the People, the Relief, Employment, and Education of the Poor, the Prevention of Crime, the Amelioration of the Insane, and those numerous matters of statistical and philanthropist interest which are included under the general head of 'Social Science.' " So little seemed to be known. Frank B. Sanborn, one of the founders, later recalled that it was "the scarcity of material for the investigation of social questions which suggested the importance of bringing together in this way the persons interested in the development

3. Luther Lee Bernard and Jessie Bernard, *Origins of American Sociology: The Social Science Movement in the United States* (New York, 1943), pp. 530-31; Board of State Charities of Massachusetts, *First Annual Report* (1864), pp. iv-v; American Social Science Association, *Constitution, Address, and List of Members* [1865], pp. 10-11; Howe to Governor John Albion Andrew, quoted in Bernard and Bernard, *Origins,* pp. 531-32.

of civilization here, and in setting forth its results, and its unresolved problems, for the information and guidance of each other." Not knowing quite how to proceed, welfare workers hoped by comparing data from various situations to develop a better understanding of the problems they and their clients faced.[4]

Gradually, as they worked together to rationalize welfare procedures, ASSA members began to think more consciously of themselves as social scientists. Some may have hoped to dignify otherwise irksome duties by adding the aura of science to their charity work, but they also turned to science for a model to use in organizing the chaotic mass of data that overwhelmed them when they pooled their records. When a group of untrained investigators vowed "to gather all information within reach" and to "diffuse this information through and beyond our country," they faced problems far more perplexing than the perennial financial worries of charity organizations. None of them had formal training in social science (for none existed in America), but educated men and women of the mid-nineteenth century had common access to a Baconian model for scientific analysis. It was only natural that they turned first to the Baconian tradition for guidance.[5]

To some extent the Baconian model determined not only what the amateurs did but how they envisioned their role in society. As it had been popularized over time, the Baconian method demanded three simple steps in problem solving: the collection, classification, and interpretation of facts. To mid-nineteenth-century Americans, the existence of absolute truth was an undiminished reality. Though advanced thinkers were beginning to describe natural processes through theories of evolutionary change, most people clung simultaneously to the more conventional model of a universe governed by immutable laws. As surely as iron laws held planets rigidly on course, ASSA

4. ASSA, *Constitution*, pp. 10-11; Board of State Charities of Massachusetts, *Second Annual Report* (1866), pp. xii-xiii; Frank B. Sanborn, "Aids in the Study of Social Science," *Journal of Social Science* 19 (1885):14 (hereafter cited as *JSS*).
5. "Introductory Note," *JSS* 1 (1869):1-2.

members reasoned, there were equally binding principles to guide human conduct.[6]

There was no contradiction between a Baconian approach and humanitarian intentions. As George Daniels has explained, "Bacon had said that knowledge was power, and he hoped to use science to elevate the condition of man beyond his wildest dreams and give him a control which he had never known before. This was one Baconian idea that was adhered to rigorously by all scientists . . . ; the dominant theme was still that science was the great hope for mankind, and that any progress that was made would be by virtue of the revolution begun by Lord Bacon."[7] The philanthropists, bureaucrats, reformers, and educators who joined the ASSA hoped to make a social revolution by developing a social science.

The simplicity of Baconian procedure made it convenient for amateurs. Baconian method required no consciously articulated theory of causation, no theoretical questions to guide research, not even a hypothesis. ASSA members were accustomed to dealing with results, not causes. But suddenly old formulas that ascribed poverty and crime to individual wickedness seemed useless. Americans were no longer even remotely homogeneous in national origins, social class, intellectual heritage, values, customs, or aspirations. Huge cities, great factories, and strange unassimilated populations compounded the problems of poverty and dependence. Some general response was obviously needed. At first ASSA members hoped to find the new causes of social problems by looking hard at the combined results. Like earlier Baconians, many of them believed that science was "the knowledge of many methodically arranged so as to become attainable by one." So simple a faith waned quickly among evolutionary theorists. Yet even very talented amateurs clung to the fiction that piling up enough data would lead to the dis-

6. The view was pervasive. For widely separated examples, see ASSA, *Constitution*, p. 67; "Introductory Note," *JSS* 1 (1869):1-2; Frank B. Sanborn, "Society and Socialism," *JSS* 33 (1895): 20-21.

7. George Daniels, "Baconian Science in America, 1815-1845" (Ph.D. diss., University of Iowa, 1963), pp. 62, 257-58.

covery of self-evident truths. Those truths in turn would show how men should live.[8]

Because facts were the key to discovery in a Baconian system, amateur social scientists were intensely preoccupied with machinery for handling data. The structure of the ASSA illustrates their passion for classification. They divided their concerns among four departments—Education, Public Health, Social Economy, and Jurisprudence—and made a graphic list of the evils each department should study:

1. Under the Department of Education will come everything relating to the interests of Public Schools, Universities, and Colleges; to Reformatory, Adult, and Evening Schools; to Instruction in the useful Arts; to Systems of Apprenticeship, to Lyceums, Pulpits, and the formation of Societies for the purpose of Public Instruction. In this department will be debated also all questions relating to Classical, Linguistic, and Scientific Studies, in their proportion to what is called an English Education; and the bearing of National and Patriotic Memorials upon Popular culture.

2. Under the Department relating to Public Health, a very large proportion of the popular interest will naturally be fixed. All Sanitary and Hygienic matters will come before it; and what the Sanitary Commission has learned in the last four years will be made available, through its action, to the people at large. The subject of Epidemics, of the origin and spread of Cholera, Yellow Fever, and Eruptive Diseases, will be legitimately discussed here. It will consider all questions of Increase of Population, Vaccination, Ventilation of Public and Private Buildings, Drainage, Houses for the Poor, the Management of Cemeteries, Public Baths, Parks, and Public Gardens, Places of Recreation, the Management of Hospitals and Insane Asylums, the Adulteration of Food and Drugs, all questions relating to the Duration of Human Life, Sanitary Regulations of the Army and Navy, and all Matters of popular interest connected with medical science. We shall look to our ablest physicians and surgeons for contributions to this department.

3. Under the head of Social Economy, we shall consider Pauperism, actual rather than legal, and the relation and the responsibilities of the gifted and educated classes toward the weak, the witless and the ignorant. We shall endeavor to make useful inquiries into the causes of Human Failure, and

8. This view was reaffirmed twenty years after the ASSA was founded by Carroll D. Wright, "The Scientific Basis of Tariff Legislation," *JSS* 19 (1885):14.

the Duties devolving upon Human Success. We shall consider the hours of Labor, the relation of Employers and Employed; the Employment of Women by itself considered; the relation of Idleness to Female Crime, Prostitution and Intemperance; Workhouses, Public Libraries and Museums, Savings Banks and Dispensaries. Here, too, will be discussed National Debt; the subjects of Tariff and Taxation; the Habits of Trade; the quality of our Manufactures; the Control of Markets; the Monopolies in the Sale of Food, or the Production of articles of common use; the Value of gold; and all questions connected with the Currency.

4. In the Department of Jurisprudence we aim to consider, first, the absolute science of Right; and second, the Amendment of laws. This department should be the final resort of the other three; for when the laws of Education, of Public Health, and Social Economy, are fully ascertained, the law of the land should recognize and define them all. Under this head shall be considered all questions of the justice, the expediency, and the results of existing statutes, including their bearing on Suffrage, Property, Privilege, Debt, Crime, and Pauperism. Here, then, will come up the vexed questions of Prison Discipline and Capital Punishment.[9]

Bleak as the catalog of human weaknesses was, the optimistic charter members of the ASSA hoped to discover the scientific principles that could eliminate such evils and then change the civil laws accordingly.[10]

Experience was as important as scientific theory in shaping the amateur ethos. For many amateur social scientists, social responsibility was a habit reinforced by family tradition and New England ethical teaching. The sentiments of people attracted to the movement ranged from hard-core Yankee abolitionism to a milder evangelical reformism. Samuel Gridley Howe had been a frequenter of revolutions. As a young man he joined the Greek rebellion against Turkish rule. In both France and Poland he supported the 1830 risings against autocratic regimes. He was the editor of the antislavery *Commonwealth,* a supporter of John Brown, and a surgeon on the bloody battlefields of the Civil War. Abolitionists William Lloyd Garrison, Wendell

9. ASSA, *Constitution,* pp. 15-16; "The American Social Science Association," *JSS* 6 (1874):1; Bernard and Bernard, *Origins,* pp. 543-44.
10. "Principal Objects of the American Social Science Association," *JSS* 1 (1869):3-4.

Phillips, and Thomas Wentworth Higginson joined the ASSA;
Henry Villard, the association's first secretary, was Garrison's
son-in-law. General John Eaton led a Negro regiment—as did
Higginson—and then served in the Freedmen's Bureau. Edward
Atkinson helped freed Negroes to become Sea Island cotton
producers. Charles F. Dunbar ran a Boston antislavery newspaper. Francis Lieber left his professorship at South Carolina
College so that he could oppose slavery openly. Charles Sumner
was a radical abolitionist and a Radical Republican. As young
Union officers, Francis Amasa Walker and Carroll D. Wright
both viewed the Civil War as a righteous crusade against evil.
John Bascom and Francis Wayland were moral philosophers
who consistently advocated ethical judgments on public issues.

The antislavery experience united the ASSA founders in
common enthusiasm for specific, practical reforms accomplished through direct involvement. As Baconian science provided a model for their thought, the abolition movement gave
these nascent social scientists a convenient pattern for their actions. Frank Sanborn recalled "the warmth and eagerness with
which we launched for the voyage, and anticipated noble results
from our venture. It was at the close of a long and sharp civil
war, by which the national authority had been vindicated, and the
Republic restored, as we believed, to its auspicious birthright."
The institution of slavery had been eliminated by direct and
sensible, if novel, measures, such men believed; later their approach to other reforms was a replica of the strategy they
believed had achieved abolition. Slavery was repugnant to
natural law. Data showing the unnatural evil of the system had
been gathered, classified, analyzed, and publicized by men and
women whose sole interest was the amelioration of society.
United to press a common noble cause, people from all walks of
life had educated the opinions of the better part of society. The
necessary war had preserved a righteous Union while correcting
its deviations from natural goodness. Abolition was finally confirmed through legislation and supervision. The system had not
been fundamentally changed; rather a specific evil had been

discovered and rooted out in an eminently practical way.[11]

If there was a typical amateur social scientist it was Frank B. Sanborn, ASSA secretary for more than half a century. Born in 1831 in Hampton Falls, New Hampshire, Sanborn traced his ancestry back to a Puritan reformer who had reached New England in 1640. Sanborn's education followed the classic pattern for the intellectual elite: Phillips Exeter and Harvard. He attended the sermons of Theodore Parker and, in 1853, made the ritual journey to Concord to meet Ralph Waldo Emerson. The transcendentalists influenced Sanborn greatly, but his life was even more profoundly affected by a childhood sweetheart, Ariana Walker. She encouraged him to believe in his intellectual ability and became, he told Parker, "so interwoven into my being that I cannot think of life without her." Their relationship demonstrated Sanborn's romantic idealism. In young womanhood Ariana developed tuberculosis. Though her health grew progressively worse she and Sanborn became engaged and a deathbed marriage followed. When his young wife died Sanborn returned to Cambridge, desolate and in need of some emotional outlet, to finish his Harvard degree under Parker's sympathetic tutelage. With Emerson's help, he opened a preparatory school in Concord and made a place for himself among the Concord philosophers. In the Radical Club, Boston's leading intellectual center, he shared the companionship of Emerson, Garrison, Phillips, Howe and his wife Julia Ward Howe, Higginson, and John Greenleaf Whittier in discussing universal suffrage, peace, the education of women, and, inevitably, abolition.[12]

Though Sanborn lacked the fine creative mind of the transcendental philosophers, his talent with practical affairs made him a useful abolitionist. Touring as secretary of the Massachu-

11. Frank Sanborn, "The Work of Social Science, Past and Present," *JSS* 8 (1876):23.

12. George Harvey Genzmer, "Franklin Benjamin Sanborn," *Dictionary of American Biography*, 16:326-27 (hereafter cited as *DAB*); Sanborn to Theodore Parker, 24 July, 1 September 1854, Sanborn MSS, Concord Free Public Library; Van Wyck Brooks, *New England: Indian Summer, 1865-1915* (Boston, 1940), pp. 122-23.

setts Free Soil Association, he met John Brown and was fascinated by his powerful personality. Soon Brown asked Sanborn to become his New England agent. "What an inconceivable amount of good you might so effect," Brown persuaded, "by your counsel, your example, your encouragement, your natural & acquired ability for active service. . . . Certainly the cause is enough to live for if not to [die] for." Sanborn knew of Brown's intention to raid Harper's Ferry, tried to dissuade but eventually assisted him, and then refused to testify before a United States Senate investigating committee. When an order was issued for his arrest Sanborn fled to Canada, returned on the advice of friends, was arrested, obtained release on a writ while a posse of supporters chased the arresting officers out of town, and finally was discharged by a friendly court. Sanborn cared for Brown's children, educated his daughters in the Concord school, and comforted his wife. The same intense commitment enlivened Sanborn's Unionism during the Civil War and his support for radical measures during Reconstruction.[13]

An almost restive civic activity characterized Sanborn, as it did many of the amateurs. In 1863 he became secretary of the newly created Massachusetts State Board of Charities and began introducing a system of collecting and reporting data which was copied nationwide. He drafted several bills for improvements in welfare services. In the 1870s and 1880s, while he was secretary of the American Social Science Association, he was also an officer of the National Conference of Charities, the National Prison Association, the Clarke School for the Deaf, and the Massachusetts Infant Asylum. He lectured on social science at Cornell, Smith, and Wellesley. He maintained literary interests,

13. John Brown to Sanborn, 2, 26 February 1858; Sarah Brown to Sanborn, 12 July 1881; S. G. Howe to Sanborn, 8 February 1860; Sanborn to "My Dear Friend," 28 December 1862 (detailing his views on political and racial questions), Sanborn MSS, Concord. In Sanborn to Ralph Waldo Emerson, 10 November 1859; 26 January, 3 February 1860, Sanborn MSS, Manuscripts Division, Library of Congress, Sanborn describes his feeling for Brown and his flight to Canada. On Brown's daughters in his care, see Elizabeth S. Miller to Sanborn, 26 February 1860, Sanborn MSS, LC. His abolitionist views and his actions in the Brown case are further detailed in several letters from Gerrit Smith (1857-1860), also in Sanborn MSS, LC.

writing biographies of Thoreau, Brown, Howe, Bronson Alcott, Emerson, and Hawthorne, while sending off a steady flow of ascerbic political comment and literary criticism to newspapers and literary journals. At social science meetings Sanborn spoke on topics that ranged from disease, drunkenness, and postal savings to the tariff and race relations. Through a long and unusually active life Sanborn maintained the breadth of interests and talents, the variety of contacts, the comprehensiveness of view, and the practicality of approach that characterized amateur social scientists but were frequently lacking in their more specialized professional successors. The workhorse of the ASSA, he was always present, always active, always accommodating to change, and always ready to make another attempt at defining social science.[14]

A fundamental aspect of Sanborn's definition of social science—one that he repeated passionately and moderated only reluctantly—was its intrinsic connection with reform. Other social scientists shared Sanborn's humanist perspective. If the ASSA completed the work it proposed, Daniel Coit Gilman promised, it would produce "an earthly paradise—an enchanted ground." George William Curtis agreed that "all advance from barbarism" was due to "the development of social science." Carroll D. Wright called social science "the science of the age,—the science which was to attract the attention of men of benevolence, of broad charity, and of philanthropic motives,— men and women who were willing to aid in the cause of humanity for the sake of humanity." Even William Graham Sumner, far removed from Sanborn and Wright in his view of what was good for humanity, agreed that social science must save men from the folly of their own deviations from natural law.[15] The reform tendencies of amateur social scientists in the

14. "Sanborn," *DAB*, 16:326-27. See also William B. Rogers to Sanborn, 1 February 1864; Sanborn to W. T. Harris, 26 April 1866; Sanborn to Samuel Eliot, 29 January, 4, 10 February 1869; Charles Francis Adams, Jr., to Sanborn, 23 October, 9 November 1869, Sanborn MSS, Concord.

15. Daniel Coit Gilman, "Opening Address," *JSS* 12 (1880):xxiii; George W. Curtis, "Opening Address," *JSS* 6 (1874):33; Carroll D. Wright, "The Growth and

1870s reflected a conception of knowledge in which thought and action were inseparable, but their reformism also revealed a keen awareness that something fundamental was lacking in the American response to industrialism—a realization that dawned more slowly on other groups.

The social problem that seemed most serious to many ASSA members was the development of a permanent working class. Though they seldom overtly admitted it, a strong class consciousness informed the humanitarianism of the amateur social scientists. Carroll D. Wright, Francis Amasa Walker, and Sanborn were among the first Americans to conclude that industrialization had produced a class of permanent wage workers who could not reasonably be held responsible for many of their own misfortunes. Workers who owned or controlled no productive instruments except their labor were extremely vulnerable in the periods of industrial depression which seemed inevitable in the Gilded Age. Yet when privation struck a huge class of laborers all at once, the sources of private charity that had cushioned individual calamities in a simpler society were painfully inadequate. Urban and industrial growth had attracted Americans fresh from isolated farms or small towns and immigrants from different cultural and linguistic backgrounds. Some of these people were unable to cope with urban life; away from customary restraints, they fell prey to a pattern of idleness, drunkenness, and crime which they would not have chosen in a healthier environment. Such disadvantaged Americans constituted the "social question" that received increasing attention. ASSA members believed that people in unfortunate straits deserved the compassionate assistance of more affluent Americans. The ASSA response to the social question was motivated by a complex mixture of decency, guilt, and fear. If the lower classes were ignored, they would turn the cities into raging infernos.

Purposes of Bureaus of Statistics," *JSS* 25 (1888):2-3; William G. Sumner, "American Finance," *JSS* 6 (1874):181-89. Gilman, Curtis, and Wright were all ASSA presidents and long-term active members. Sumner dropped out as his interests settled more specifically on academic economics.

Not surprisingly, while ASSA members sought ways to ameliorate the conditions of lower-class life, they tried simultaneously to condition the laboring class to accept what could not be changed.[16]

Most ASSA members accepted the emerging industrial system as fundamentally desirable. The need, they thought, was for people to learn to live with certain necessarily harsh realities and to make the most of vast new opportunities. At first the amateur social scientists expected to reach poor people and working-class people directly through the association's educational activities. At public lectures and open meetings specialists told how to improve the ventilation of city houses, combat disease through better sanitation, and provide more nutritious meals by installing Alladin ovens in the kitchens of the poor. Others worked out detailed plans for improvements in factory conditions, industrial insurance, profit sharing, and cooperative buying.[17] Some programs were aimed at developing sentiment among the "better sort" of people for voluntary welfare measures and support for regulatory social legislation. Annual meetings laid the sordid details of factory labor and slum life before the influential citizens who were always invited to attend.[18] Two assumptions were implicit in these educational efforts: first, that illness and crime were social pathology, curable by measures that promoted physical and moral health; and second, that voluntary, collective efforts to reduce the economic insecurities of the industrial system were vastly preferable in almost every case to basic changes in the system.

16. See, for example, Lorin Blodget, "Waste of Existing Social Systems," *JSS* 4 (1871):8-18; Frank Sanborn, "The Work of Social Science, Past and Present," *JSS* 8 (1876):31-37; Sanborn, "Past and Present in Social Science," *JSS* 43 (1905):1-21. There is a constant preoccupation with the social question in the meetings and journals.

17. "Introductory Note," *JSS* 1 (1869):3; "Progress in Economic Education," ibid., p. 139; "Current Record of the Association," *JSS* 2 (1870):vii-xi.

18. Between 1869 and 1884 articles in the *JSS* fell into the following categories: health and medicine, 29; charity, 26; law, 23; lower education, 22; laboring classes, 22; economics, 19; prisons, 15; government, 14; purposes of social science, 10; civil service, 9; finance, 8; southern question, 6; higher education, 5; business, 3; farm problems, 3; immigration, 2.

Time, experience, and the apparent failure of voluntary programs eventually turned the ASSA toward greater interest in
formal education as a means of uplift and control. There was
sporadic talk of a national university to train civil servants, but
most of the early plans focused on the lower schools. Ameri-
canization was a recurrent theme. The ASSA designed programs
to mold both native-born and immigrant children into useful,
peaceful, patriotic, and self-sufficient citizens. "Experience
demonstrates to me," the head of the Illinois Social Science
Association told Sanborn, "that the pioneer work of the social
scientist is to arouse the people to the suffering and oppression,
the starvation and crime which are the direct results of the bad
methods now universally employed. . . . Can we work in any
more effective way, at present, than by educating the children
in regard to their duties as citizens?" William Torrey Harris,
head of the ASSA Department of Education, listed influences
that corrupted children's morals and specified duties that they
should be taught in school. Members sponsored clubs to inculcate patriotism and encourage health habits, school savings
banks to teach children thrift, and kindergartens for the youngest members of working families. To inspire immigrant children,
one industrious group provided busts of famous Americans at
low cost for public schools. And the association heartily endorsed vocational training to provide the skills and habits
needed for industry.[19]

Throughout the 1870s ASSA leaders approached higher education largely by recommending additions to various existing
curricula. They expressed their dissatisfaction with the social
consciousness of conventional religion by suggesting a large dose
of social science in the training of ministers. Sometimes a
professional avant garde used the ASSA to promote higher
standards. A member of the Department of Jurisprudence

19. Samuel Eliot, "An American University," *JSS* 5 (1873):162-77; Elizabeth
Boynton Harbert to Sanborn, *JSS* 11 (1880):103-4; W. T. Harris, "Moral Education
in the Common Schools," *JSS* 18 (1884):122-34; "Current Record," *JSS* 2
(1870):vii-viii; "Report of the Secretary," *JSS* 20 (1886):14-26.

favored law schools over legal apprenticeships because the schools could offer theoretical training in "all the branches of Social Science which are yet in shape to be usefully taught in the class-room." The Health Department recommended innovations in medical education which were favored by leaders in the professionalization of medicine. As the head of an institution introducing a new type of graduate education in America, President Daniel Coit Gilman of the Johns Hopkins University was eager to see the ASSA organize and finance large-scale research projects.[20]

When education seemed too slow or the task too large, the amateurs turned to legislation for reform. From the beginning of the social science movement those leaders who were engaged in new and significant knowledge-gathering ventures had realized the potential value of their surveys and conclusions to lawmakers. "I look with great expectation to the newly formed Social Science Association for light to guide our legislators in their efforts to reduce the burdens and alleviate the miseries of Pauperism," Sanborn had declared. "Hereafter may our lawgivers have the opportunity, as in Europe, of calling upon the wisdom and accumulated experience of persons who have made the welfare of their fellow men a special and long pursued study." Supporters of government projects for gathering data promised that an expanded census or a permanent bureau of labor statistics would guide legislators as they tried to improve existing laws and meet new responsibilities.[21]

ASSA leaders agreed that conventional politics produced a hodgepodge of unscientific legislation based on the principle of appeasing vested interests, not on social science. Before the full corruption of Grantism and its state and city imitators was

20. For an example of the first type of program see W. G. Hammond, "Legal Education and the Study of Jurisprudence," *JSS* 8 (1876):170; Daniel Coit Gilman, "Address," *JSS* 11 (1880):xxiii.

21. Board of State Charities of Massachusetts, *Second Annual Report* (1866), pp. xii-xiii, 213; "Current Record," *JSS* 3 (1871):199; James A. Garfield, "The American Census," *JSS* 2 (1870): 31-55; Carroll D. Wright, "The Growth and Purposes of Bureaus of Labor Statistics," *JSS* 25 (1888):2-3.

revealed, it was still possible to believe that a paucity of reliable data, not the lack of decent intent, prompted legislators to act like criminals. As shrewd an observer as E. L. Godkin blamed the lack of a scientific approach to legislation on devotion to outworn habits. Through the ages political thinkers had relied on a priori theories, using moral rather than empirical justifications for the measures they wrote into law. No one had advocated scientific methods for the improvement of government. Long after inductive methods were widely used in natural science, men had gone about their political business in the old selfish way, never bothering to perfect machinery for collecting data and applying it to social problems. At last, Godkin avowed, there was a social science in the making that would provide a truly objective basis for legislation.[22]

The development of a civil service system was a natural extension of the amateur's conception of social science. Not only would objective testing place intelligent officials in the appropriate jobs, but the results of this procedure would be a government equipped to serve its citizens scientifically. Well before the Progressives, these reformers recognized the critical importance of experts in government. An apparent deterioration in the quality of government added to the attraction of civil service reform.[23]

As legislators continued to ignore their advice, more social scientists channeled their energies into specialized reform agencies that sought to force changes in public policy. For some—such as the Reverend Enoch Cobb Wines, secretary of the New York Prison Association; Thomas Gallaudet, advocate of education for the deaf; and George William Curtis, crusader for civil service reform—the ASSA served primarily as one more agency to advance their favorite causes. Others with a similar

22. Samuel Eliot, "Civil Service Reform," *JSS* 1 (1869):117; E. L. Godkin, "Legislation and Social Science," *JSS* 3 (1871):120.
23. Ari Hoogenboom, *Outlawing the Spoils: A History of the Civil Service Reform Movement, 1865-1883* (Urbana, Ill., 1961), and John G. Sproat, *"The Best Men": Liberal Reformers in the Gilded Age* (New York, 1968).

discontent turned away from a corrupt government and concentrated upon private, voluntary programs.

The relationship between the ASSA and the National Prison Association illustrated a pattern of cooperation and separation that would be repeated in the coming years. Agitation for reforms in criminal justice had attracted prominent supporters before the Civil War. At the founding meeting of the ASSA, some proposed a separate department for crime prevention and the treatment of prisoners, but instead those subjects were placed under the Department of Jurisprudence where the humanitarian interests of prison reformers conflicted with the professional motives of judges and lawyers. Under the auspices of the ASSA, Wines and Professor Timothy M. Dwight of the Columbia University Law School toured prisons in the United States. Wines then served as a leader in the National Prison Congress at Cincinnati and in 1870 represented the ASSA at the International Congress on Prison Reform. That same year Wines helped to found the National Prison Association, an extension of the ASSA which maintained close ties with the original association. In comparable fashion the organization of the National Conference of Charities, the National Conference of Boards of Health, and the American Public Health Association, all in 1874, absorbed many of the practical functions of the ASSA's Departments of Social Economy and Health, leaving only the Department of Education relatively undiluted.[24]

At the same time the ASSA was undergoing a general crisis. Attendance at its meetings dwindled and membership shrank. There were no general meetings in 1871 and 1872. After the resignation of Henry Villard the association was without a permanent secretary for almost two years. The organization seemed about to die. Sanborn recalled later the "period of comparative stagnation, when our activity was in abeyance, until in the autumn of 1872 the late James Barnard of Boston

24. American Social Science Association, *Constitution,* pp. 15-16; Sanborn, "Work of Social Science," p. 34; "Current Record," *JSS* 2(1870): vi-vii.

and some of his friends came to the rescue, and the local work in this city was reorganized, with Professors Agassiz and Peirce of Harvard University, and others who had not been actively interested before."[25]

Academics suddenly emerged as new leaders. The Barnard group solicited letters of advice, five of which were printed in the ASSA journal. Three Harvard professors—Emory Washburn, Benjamin Peirce, and Louis Agassiz—recommended greater decentralization with local meetings around the country, a more professional approach to their subjects, and a more dynamic, imaginative leadership. J. W. Hoyt of Madison, Wisconsin, an active member of the Western Social Science Association, and Daniel Coit Gilman, then a professor at the University of California, described potential interest outside the Northeast and underlined the importance of a broad base and a more welcoming attitude toward Westerners and Southerners.[26] Action on the proposals followed immediately. When officers were elected in 1873, Agassiz, Peirce, Barnard, and Harvard president Charles W. Eliot joined Samuel Eliot and Samuel Gridley Howe as directors. Curtis, a New Yorker, became president, but four western vice presidents—Hoyt, Gilman, George Davidson of California, and W. T. Harris of Saint Louis—were elected. Nevertheless, Easterners continued to dominate the departments. Charles Eliot headed the Department of Education, David Ames Wells the new Department of Finance, and William B. Rogers, the first president of the ASSA, the Department of Social Economy, while a Boston judge and physician were in charge of the Departments of Jurisprudence and Health. Sanborn became permanent secretary and editor of the *Journal*.[27]

In April 1874 the Executive Committee turned to the prob-

25. "Affairs of the American Social Science Association," *JSS* 6 (1874):16; "Acting Secretary's Report," *JSS* 7 (1874):342.

26. Agassiz to the American Social Science Association, *JSS* 8 (1874):375-76; Hoyt to the ASSA, *JSS* 8:377-78; Gilman to the ASSA, *JSS* 8:378-79.

27. List of Officers, *JSS* 5 (1873):206.

lem of branch associations. Some local organizations already existed. The Boston Social Science Association had been instrumental in rescuing the ASSA from possible oblivion, and the membership of an active Philadelphia branch outnumbered the national. In addition, some state organizations had been formed. Now a campaign emerged to build a variety of branches with strong ties to the ASSA. The presidents of those already being organized in Saint Louis, New Haven, San Francisco, Galveston, and Detroit were made ex-officio vice presidents of the ASSA. The chairmen of local branches, usually government agencies such as the Boston Department of Health, became ex-officio directors. Finally, a network of Committees of Correspondence was established to exchange publications with other societies and generally broaden the foundation of the ASSA. As if to satisfy Hoyt's plea for fairness to the West, Detroit was the site of the general meeting of 1875. The following year membership reached four hundred.[28]

The full meaning of the revival and reorganization unfolded in some confusion. Officers spoke with an unaccustomed caution about their field and their purpose. In reply to the need for a definition of social science, President George William Curtis hedged in 1874: "If I say that by social science we mean the science of society, you will truly reply that I move without advancing; nor, indeed, could I assert that the relations of social phenomena, modified as they perpetually are by the human will, and by almost incalculable conditions, have been reduced to the laws of an exact science." Sanborn, the organization's weather vane, spoke just as evasively: "I have never seen or heard of a person who could concisely define . . . social science, or state wherein it differs from other branches of human knowledge. It seems, indeed, to be neither a science [n]or an art, but a mingling of the two, or of fifty sciences and arts,

28. "American Social Science Association," *JSS* 6 (1874):2-4. The reorganization is described in detail in Sanborn to W. T. Harris, 10, 16 October, 18 November 1873 (with copies of resolutions voted); 2 February, 22 March, 10 April 1874, Sanborn MSS, Concord Free Public Library.

which all find a place in it. Whatever concerns mankind in their social, rather than in their individual relations, belongs to this comprehensive abstraction, and social science shades off easily and imperceptibly into metaphysics on one side, philanthropy on another, political economy on a third, and so round the whole circle of human inquiry."[29]

These were the statements of people groping toward a more respectable scientific sense of their work. An assertive self-confidence was giving way to a more orderly quest for knowledge. Contrary to the interpretation common among historians, the urge to reform waned as specialized interest groups moved apart from the ASSA. If the desire to teach and correct remained, the standards of academic science increasingly outweighed it.[30] Probably a number of members recoiled from the rough ridicule that reformers received from professional politicians and businessmen, especially after the failure of Liberal Republicanism. By turning for guidance to active academics, and especially to scientists in well-established disciplines, the ASSA had broadened its leadership and also diluted the peculiar reforming zeal of New Englanders.

With specific reform activities delegated to single-purpose organizations, the ASSA was free to devote more energy to the development and dissemination of knowledge. In the midst of the reorganization, Sanborn sounded the new note of prudence and in the process a revised rationale: "In this infinite variety of need and opportunity for research and practical work, the special place of the American Social Science Association is that of uniting all and communicating with all who may wish to do so. It does not assume to direct, scarcely to advise or recommend, but to bring those who are striving for the same end into friendly relations with each other, and to furnish a common

29. George W. Curtis, "Opening Address," *JSS* 6 (1874):33; Frank B. Sanborn, "The Work of Social Science in the United States," *JSS* 6: 36.

30. For the standard interpretation see Bernard and Bernard, *Origins,* esp. chapt. 40, "The Struggle of the Association for a Clarification of Its Objectives"; Irwin Unger, *The Greenback Era: A Social and Political History of American Finance, 1865-1879* (Princeton, N.J., 1964), p. 139.

center from which influence may radiate and in which unity may be found."[31] In rudimentary form, he was describing a professional organization.

As the Social Science Association turned away from reform and rededicated itself to objective knowledge, a new scientific force threatened to discredit the effort. Most professional scientists had long since rejected the union of knowledge and practical application that many ASSA members desired. Using the dramatic catch phrases of Darwinian theory to capture public attention, evolutionists who rejected even the desirability of reform proclaimed themselves the only legitimate social scientists. Herbert Spencer and John Fiske were their idols. Their American agent and popularizer was Edward L. Youmans, the editor of the *Popular Science Monthly,* while the prominent naturalist Agassiz, new leader of the ASSA and bitter opponent of the Darwinian concepts that undergirded Spencerian sociology, was their archenemy.

Hoping to discredit both Agassiz and reform, the *Popular Science Monthly* began attacking the ASSA. "Recognizing that the aim of this organization is excellent, and much of its work highly commendable," an editorial announced in 1874, "we are of the opinion that it falls short of what should be its chief duty. . . . So far from promoting social science, we should rather say that social science is just the subject which it particularly avoids. It might rather be considered as a general reform convention. It is an organization for public action, and most of its members, hot with the impulses of philanthropy, are full of projects of social relief, amelioration, and improvement. Of pure investigation, of the strict and passionless study of society from a scientific point of view, we hear but very little. . . . The Association seems to be but little in advance of an ordinary political convention." As if to prove his point, Youmans started

31. Criticism of reformers is described in Sproat, *"The Best Men,"* chapt. 3 and passim; Richard Hofstadter, *Anti-Intellectualism in American Life* (New York, 1962), particularly chapt. 7, "The Fate of the Reformer." Sanborn, "The Work of Social Science in the United States," pp. 37-44.

the serial publication of Spencer's *Principles of Sociology* in the same issue.[32]

Even though the ASSA program of the following year was the association's most academically respectable effort to date, the *Popular Science Monthly* still accused the social scientists of flying false colors. "We miss (as we did a year ago) any thing in the proceedings answering to the definite object of the organization as put forth in its title," Youmans charged. He outlined a definition of science which was exactly what the ASSA had proposed for a decade—collection and classification of data leading to the discovery of general social laws—and then denied that the ASSA had any real interest in such a goal. He accused the amateur social scientists of deliberately attempting to deceive the public by cloaking their reformist schemes with the dignity of science. "So long as the term 'social science' is employed to characterize the heterogeneous and discordant opinions of unscientific men upon the most intricate and refractory problems of civilized life, it will be discredited in its true application," Youmans concluded.[33] Laissez-faire evolutionists had learned the tactic of dealing with opponents by branding them charlatans.

No doubt many members of the ASSA remained as eager for reform after 1874 as before. Implementation of the new emphasis on objective investigation was gradual. In the late 1870s, however, a shift away from practical humanitarian subjects toward more theoretical questions in economics and political science was obvious. A typical program included papers on the silver question, taxation, the tariff, banking, municipal economy, the Southern question, and city and state government. ASSA presidents such as Woolsey, Wells, Gilman, and Dean Francis Wayland of the Yale Law School were distinguished specialists in established disciplines, not reformers identified with a single cause. A new publications committee which super-

32. "The Social Science Association," *Popular Science Monthly* 5 (July 1874):367-69.
33. "Under False Colors," *Popular Science Monthly* 7 (July 1875): 365-66.

vised the contents of the journal also reflected the ASSA's evolution. Two members, Sanborn and Thomas Wentworth Higginson, were still best known as humanitarian reformers. But two more, Horace White and Hamilton Hill, were prominent economists, and two others, Wayland and Gilman, represented respectively the traditional and the dramatically new in university leadership.[34]

In the early 1880s there were signs that the ASSA was actually beginning to function as a scientific society. Influential members taught practical social science courses in colleges, and a few of the earliest professionally trained economists and historians sought ASSA membership. The association still considered responsible social reform the ultimate motive for social science, but these professionalizing amateurs had realized the need to draw a line between reform and knowledge in order to establish their authority. While people who were mainly interested in specific humanitarian causes shifted their energies to single-purpose reform societies, nearly all ASSA leaders in the 1880s placed primary emphasis on the orderly pursuit of organized investigations.

But professionalization in the ASSA was moving in two conflicting directions. In the mid-1880s some ASSA leaders decided that higher education was the best means of placing social science at the disposal of society. These academically inclined professionalizers threatened the integrity of a parallel effort on the part of another important group of amateurs to make the scientific study of society the province of important government bureaus. Within the ASSA, in other words, people who supported the scholarly goal of scientific objectivity were in conflict with people mainly interested in advancing the service goals espoused by high-level bureaucrats. Furthermore, ASSA members who wanted to build a comprehensive curriculum for teaching practical social science in the colleges ran headlong into resistance outside the amateur movement. Am-

34. "Contents," *JSS* 8 (1876); 9 (1878); 10 (1879); 11 (1880); "Report of the General Secretary," *JSS* 12 (1880):2.

bitious, highly self-conscious, professionally trained social scientists were in the process of establishing their own authority in
academic institutions by building a claim for scientific objectivity and theoretical competence in special fields. From the
mid-1880s on, the career of the ASSA can best be analyzed in
comparison with developments in those emerging academic
disciplines, especially in economics.

2

Scientists of Wealth & Welfare

Both in the colleges and in public affairs economics took on great importance in the Gilded Age. In antebellum colleges economics had been political economy, with all the mercantilist overtones its name implied. It was taught as a part of moral philosophy, and in cultivated circles adherence to its maxims was something of a test of character. By the mid-1880s economics had nearly everywhere been converted to a separate discipline with pretensions to the status of hard science.[1] Emphasis had shifted from commercial to industrial questions, following at a respectful distance an identical change in the economy.

Given the obvious relevance of the subject to current problems, the attention paid to economics in the era of rapid industrialization was neither inordinate nor surprising. The transition in economics affected many conflicting interests, and it was not accomplished without controversy. Because economic doctrine buttressed social position and political power, the price of authority was high. In order to establish their authority, economists were forced to keep asking the same troublesome questions: what is economics, how should an economist work, and what is the limit of the economist's social mission?

Three separate groups of economists participated in the conflicts and cross-conflicts that shaped both the discipline and the profession. They were distinct enough in membership, training, and motives to be considered separate generations along a continuum that led from amateur to professional status. At mid-century a group of college professors joined with some progressive businessmen to liberate economics from moral philosophy and redefine it as a normless science of wealth. In the

1870s and early 1880s a small transitional group of professionalizing economists tried—with dramatically contrary results—to
reconcile classical theory with their own observations and experiences. Finally the first wave of professionally trained academic economists took charge of the discipline, organized it,
and resolved much of its internal controversy by the end of the
century.

As each of the three generations of economists attempted to
establish its authority, similar disagreements broke unity within
each group—first between the moral philosophers and the business economists, again within the transitional group, and eventually within the first group with professional training. One
point of contention was the familiar product of conflicting
American values: on the one hand accepting economic inequal-
ity as natural, and on the other demanding the realization of
promised political and social equality. Another division reflected an increasing specialization of knowledge that called for a
separation of science from social action developing alongside an
awareness of what such knowledgeable specialists might do to
transform human existence if they applied their skills to life.
People pitted the value of looking at society organically against
the utility of breaking it down into component institutions.
Beneath these specific polarities ran the constant tensions in
Western thought between induction and deduction, art and
science, liberty and security, anomaly and order. Each economist made these choices according to individual experience.

The mid-century economic synthesis was the joint creation of
academics who domesticated English classical economics as a
scientific substitute for moral philosophy and American businessmen who needed just such a rationale for the developing
industrial economy. In the 1830s Francis Wayland, a Baptist
minister who became president of Brown University, and Henry
C. Carey, an Irish political refugee with enormous interests in

1. Wilson Smith, *Professors and Public Ethics: Studies of Northern Moral Philos-
ophers before the Civil War* (Ithaca, N.Y., 1956), pp. 3-4; Gladys Bryson, "The
Emergence of the Social Sciences from Moral Philosophy," *International Journal of
Ethics* 42 (April 1932):304-8.

Pennsylvania mining and manufacturing, seemed strange bed-fellows. Yet each man represented a substantial segment of economic opinion and in spite of their differences on money and the tariff they agreed on the fundamental correctness of unregulated competitive enterprise.[2]

After the Civil War the alliance of minister's sons and moral philosophers with spokesmen for commercial and industrial interests continued. Members of the so-called clerical school of academic economists such as Francis Bowen, John Bascom, and Arthur Latham Perry worked closely with a group of wealthy and prominent men of affairs that included Amasa Walker, David Ames Wells, Edward Atkinson, Horace White, Gamaliel Bradford, Charles F. Dunbar, John Murray Forbes, and Joseph Ropes. Their common goal was the installation of laissez-faire as an American system of economics. Walker, Perry, Bascom, and Bowen wrote the standard economics texts of the 1860s and 1870s. Though Walker and Bowen were older, most of these economists were New Englanders born in the late 1820s who had been weaned on John Stuart Mill and participated in the rapid commercial expansion of the Middle Period. When the Civil War ended, they wanted industry unleashed. Walker, Atkinson, Bradford, and Forbes had interests in commerce and banking. Other laissez-faire advocates held positions in journalism that enabled them to control financial policy in the *North American Review,* the *New York Evening Post,* the *Boston Daily Advertiser,* the *Springfield Republican,* and, as allies of Edwin Lawrence Godkin, in the influential *Nation.* Together these academics and publicists taught the American people economic lessons which endowed laissez-faire with strong supporting sanctions.[3]

2. For the background on Wayland, Carey, and later laissez-faire economists, see Joseph Dorfman, *The Economic Mind in American Civilization,* 5 vols. (New York, 1949), 2:752-55; 3:5-8, 16, 49-65, 81; Michael J. L. O'Connor, *Origins of Academic Economics in the United States* (New York, 1941), p. 174; John Fred Bell, *A History of Economic Thought* (New York, 1953), pp. 487-95. Sidney Fine, *Laissez Faire and the General-Welfare State,* paperback ed. (Ann Arbor, Mich., 1964), provides useful background information on all the laissez-faire economists.

3. Amasa Walker, *The Science of Wealth: A Manual of Political Economy*

To make economics a science of wealth, it was necessary first to establish it as a science. Instead of emphasizing a Baconian model as the ASSA social scientists did, laissez-faire economists relied on Newtonian analogies as a more powerful support for their a priori doctrines. Though these economists never absolutely rejected inductive methods, they accepted certain controlling assumptions about human nature which made deduction seem more reliable as a method of reasoning. A man who had faith in a physical universe governed as one magnificent system by immutable natural laws found it almost as easy to believe in an industrial system kept in harmony by the natural balance that resulted when freely competing individuals sought their economic advantage. Left free from legislative meddling, the economic machine would work as perfectly as the celestial one.[4]

Scientific analogies absolved laissez-faire economists from moral responsibility for their teachings. Giving up the humanist perspective of moral philosophy was harder for some than for others, but to facilitate the rationalization of developing practice there was obvious value in converting economics to a normless science. If economists restricted their mission to discovering and explaining economic laws, they could applaud the successes of the industrial system without bearing blame for the suffering it caused.[5]

(Boston, 1866); Arthur L. Perry, *Elements of Political Economy* (New York, 1866); John Bascom, *Political Economy* (Andover, Mass., 1859); Francis Bowen, *Principles of Political Economy* (Boston, 1856); Bowen, *American Political Economy* (Boston, 1879). For an excellent sketch of Walker, see Joseph Jansen Spencer, "General Francis A. Walker: A Character Sketch," *Review of Reviews* 15 (1897):159-61. On Bowen, see Robert Church, "The Economists Study Society: Sociology at Harvard, 1891-1902," in *Social Sciences at Harvard, 1860-1920,* ed. Paul Buck (Cambridge, Mass., 1965), p. 24; also Harold F. Williamson, *Edward Atkinson: The Biography of an American Liberal, 1827-1905* (Boston, 1934); Roswell Cheney McCrea, "Edward Atkinson," *DAB,* 1:406-7.

4. For their views on the relation of ethics and economics, see Francis Wayland, *The Principles of Political Economy* (Boston, 1850), pp. iii, 15; Bascom, *Political Economy,* pp. 9-16; Bowen, *Principles,* pp. v, 22-24; Walker, *Science of Wealth,* pp. 1-4.

5. Unger, *Greenback Era,* pp. 125, 127; Wayland, *Principles,* pp. iv, 140-41; Bowen, *Principles,* pp. v, 13; Bowen, *American Political Economy,* pp. iv, 11, 15; Perry, *Elements,* p. 26; Walker, *Science of Wealth,* pp. vi-ix.

Though they dropped their claim to moral authority, the laissez-faire economists never intended to give up their influence on economic affairs. They envisioned the new, free-standing economics as a policy science and themselves as policy consultants. When they spoke, they wanted legislators to listen. The economists charged that selfish politicians would cheerfully legislate against the welfare of the people if someone made it worth their while. Yet when the same economists gave expert testimony at legislative hearings, served on government commissions, or commented on tariff, trade, and money questions in the popular press, they frequently represented special economic interests themselves. It became common practice for both colleges and journals to hire economists for the purpose of defending a specific point of view on economic questions. Occasionally new editors or trustees found it necessary to change economists. Yet even as they worked in reform societies or as political appointees, laissez-faire economists kept up their claims of scientific objectivity in order to defend their right of advocacy and add weight to their opinions. Because their livelihoods were not dependent on holding clients or remaining in office, laissez-faire academics were often freer than businessmen and journalists to participate in the free-for-all of interest politics.[6]

By the mid-1870s laissez-faire economists had consolidated their control of the discipline in the colleges. Economics had become a science of wealth and a useful justification for entrepreneurs who were reaping the fruits of an expanding economy. Prominence as an economist depended on faithfulness to the laissez-faire system, not on training or demonstrated scientific ability. As Richard T. Ely noted with studied cynicism, a person who wanted to teach economics in one of the best

6. On the political activity of members of this group, see Fine, *Laissez Faire*, pp. 48-51; Dorfman, *Economic Mind*, 3:49-56, xiii; Unger, *Greenback Era*, pp. 139-44; Sproat, *"The Best Men,"* pp. 182, 187, 191-96; Williamson, *Atkinson*, pp. 78, 92. Even though Francis Bowen was relieved of his economics classes when his views on protection and his support for funding the national debt below par became intolerable to Boston mercantile interests, he was not fired.

colleges in 1876 (he referred to Columbia) had only to "buy
Mrs. Fawcett's *Political Economy for Beginners;* see that your
pupils do the same; then assign them once a week a chapter to
be learned; finally, question them each week on the chapter
assigned the week before, using the questions found at the end
of the chapter." According to Ely the recitation system gave
students "an imperfect comprehension of certain great fundamental facts . . . with not a very high opinion of political economy." But it was also sufficient preparation for "the degree of
A.B. first, and afterward for that of A.M." Francis Amasa
Walker agreed that laissez-faire was more than a mere test of
economic orthodoxy. "It was used," he insisted, "to decide
whether a man was an economist at all."[7]

Though laissez-faire economists established no separate scientific society in the 1870s, they used the Finance Department
of the ASSA as a focus for their claims to scientific status. By
providing a common meeting place and a forum for exchanging
ideas, the ASSA did much to unite laissez-faire advocates.
Though Francis Wayland died the year the ASSA was chartered,
two of his sons became presidents. Bascom, Perry, Walker,
Carey, Atkinson, White, Godkin, Bradford, Ropes, and Dunbar
were all energetic members. In 1874, when the ASSA adopted a
more professional outlook, Wells, Forbes, Bradford, Francis
Amasa Walker (Amasa Walker's son and co-author of *Science of
Wealth*), and William Graham Sumner took over the Finance
Department. Over the next few years Wells served three terms as
ASSA president, and the closely knit group of laissez-faire
economists contributed significantly to the association's increased interest in serious, scholarly debate. As meetings took
on a more professional tone and the journal improved, the
quality of economic discussions was also noticeably higher.

7. Frank A. Fetter, "The Early History of Political Economy in the United
States," *Proceedings of the American Philosophical Society* 87 (1944):60; Ely, "On
Methods of Teaching Political Economy," in *Methods of Teaching History*, Heath's
Pedagogical Library, ed. G. Stanley Hall (Boston, 1898), pp. 61-62; Walker, "Recent
Progress of Political Economy in the United States," *Publications of the American
Economic Association* 4 (1889):254.

Emphasis shifted from political issues to theoretical questions. Without the usual coordinating features of a common educational background and occupation, laissez-faire economists in the 1870s had still developed enough self-consciousness, awareness of the value of scientific authority, and unity of purpose to approach professionalization.[8]

Yet certain steps that the mid-century laissez-faire economists might have taken to consolidate their authority seem not to have occurred to them. Except for joining the ASSA, they made no move to establish machinery to separate economists from noneconomists by objective, nonideological standards. Without uniform qualifications themselves, these amateurs demanded no more of others. Apparently they saw no conflict between their claims to scientific authority and their open partisanship on policy matters. Their sense of mission was limited topically to specific issues, temporally to the current situation, and socially to the business interests whose activities they rationalized. No doubt in part unconsciously, they were clients of the business class and supporters of its ethos. In effect, they were agents of modernization. Scholars in more advanced sciences were inspired by a sense of dedication to the pursuit of new knowledge with ultimate utility for humanity. The laissez-faire economists of the 1860s and 1870s merely favored one class over others.

A smaller group of economists who matured in the 1870s advanced the transition from amateur to professional status. Two of them, William Graham Sumner and Simon Newcomb, were a logical extension of the laissez-faire tradition. Both men adhered to the economic orthodoxy of their predecessors, but they were also theoretical innovators who achieved a professional quality of original scholarship. Two more, Francis Amasa Walker and Carroll D. Wright, reached a professional level by perfecting ideas and techniques that challenged laissez-faire. In established professions, the professionalization of individuals occurs through a uniform socialization process designed for the

8. Based on lists of officers, members, and records of ASSA activities in *JSS*.

purpose of transmitting skills and values to novices. Breaking new ground, these four prototypes created their own avenues to professionalism from the circumstances of their lives.

Behind the orthodoxy of Newcomb and Sumner and the revisionism of Walker and Wright lay a fundamental difference in the value these men placed on individualism. Though the four were contemporaries—Newcomb was born in 1835 and the other three in 1840—experience took them in different directions. Both Sumner and Newcomb came from working-class families. As children they sometimes endured privation, but they also learned the conservative creed: pull yourself up in the world by hard work. Both looked to education as an avenue of upward mobility.

Newcomb came to economics from physical science. After running away from an intolerable apprenticeship and teaching in various places, he presented himself to Joseph E. Henry of the Smithsonian Institution. As Henry's fortunate protégé, Newcomb was put to work for the Coast Survey and educated at the Lawrence Scientific School at Harvard, where he studied under Benjamin Peirce. Newcomb's first interest was astronomy; with his brilliant studies of the motions of celestial bodies he soon established a distinguished international reputation. As head of a government scientific office in Washington during the 1870s, Newcomb became involved in the economic debate that permeated Gilded Age political rhetoric. The scientific symbolism of laissez-faire economics held a natural attraction for him, and his own work made the Newtonian analogy to immutable economic laws even more binding than it was for amateur social scientists who had not been trained in physical science. For Newcomb economics was a body of eternal truths or it was not a science. When the mathematical economics of Stanley Jevons came to his attention, Newcomb made his own original contribution to the field by using statistical methods to develop a quantity theory of money.[9]

9. "Simon Newcomb," *Proceedings of the American Philosophical Society* 49 (1910):iii-iv; Charles G. Abbot, "Simon Newcomb," *DAB*, 13:452-54.

Unfortunately Newcomb's innovative energy was diverted when new economic theories placed him on the defensive. In 1884 he joined the Johns Hopkins faculty, where economics was taught by Richard T. Ely, a German-trained historical economist. The young Ely boisterously denied the existence of immutable laws in economics, challenged most of the assumptions of laissez-faire, and advocated positive state action in behalf of the poor. Newcomb lashed out in righteous fury against an approach so alien to both his background and his scientific reputation. His easy access to laissez-faire journals made him a formidable enemy of anything new in economics, but his anger paralyzed him. He stopped doing original work in economics and gradually slipped back to amateur status.[10]

By comparison, William Graham Sumner's influence was far more significant. Initially Sumner studied for the ministry, first at Yale College and then at the University of Göttingen. In Germany, working under the guidance of a group of gifted theologians who had revolutionized biblical scholarship by applying the most rigorous critical methods, he grasped the meaning and spirit of modern scholarship. By comparison, he found German social scientists hopelessly dogmatic and subjective. Sumner was ordained an Episcopal minister and actually preached for a few years in a stylish New York church; yet he found the cautious, quasi-political role of a minister in upper-class institutional religion totally uncongenial. His real calling was scholarship. Like many of his educated contemporaries, Sumner wanted to study the economic and social problems of his day scientifically, but American social science seemed so hopelessly unscholarly that it discouraged him. Suddenly, in Herbert Spencer's *Study of Sociology* (1870), he found the model for an organic study of society which he had been seeking. Resigning his clerical post, Sumner became the first occupant of a chair in political and social science at Yale.[11]

10. J. F. Normano, *Spirit of American Economics* (New York, 1943), p. 138; Dorfman, *Economic Mind*, 3:84-86.
11. "Sketch of William Graham Sumner," *Popular Science Monthly* 35 (June

Without professional training in social science, Sumner brought the critical methods of German theology and the moral lessons of his own experience to the study of economics. He recalled his artisan father's contempt "for demagogical arguments and for all the notions of labor agitators, as well as for the entire gospel of gush." His own life experience confirmed the value of industry and independence and made him suspicious of government interference in the lives of the people. As reform movements that called for government action multiplied in the 1870s and 1880s, he adopted laissez-faire as a scientific justification for a negative state. Sumner was certain that tampering with natural forces such as free competition and individual enterprise would unhinge society. From the mid-1870s on, in the ASSA and other organizations, he dedicated himself to teaching people to accept laissez-faire. When Darwinian mottos provided scientific support for the survival of the fittest through each individual's struggle for existence, Sumner adopted Social Darwinism too. Against government regulation, public welfare, tariff protection, and soft money, he was as active in political controversy by the mid-1880s as any of his enemies on the other side of the question.[12]

Circumstances placed Francis Amasa Walker and Carroll D. Wright on the other side. The social class and educational backgrounds of these two men were as important as those of Sumner and Newcomb in determining their perspectives on economics. Walker and Wright were both New Englanders born to prominent families and educated for lives of social and moral responsibility. Both entered the legal profession with the intention of using law as a background for careers in public service.

There was a striking contrast in the way these four transition-

1889):261-66; Harris E. Starr, *William Graham Sumner* (New York, 1925), pp. 18-19, 30, 66-69, 129-34, 151, 159, 169-70; Sumner, *Earth-Hunger and Other Essays*, ed. A. G. Keller (New Haven, Conn., 1913), pp. 3-4; Richard Hofstadter, *Social Darwinism in American Thought*, rev. ed. (Boston, 1955), p. 51.

12. "Sketch," p. 261; Sumner, "The Challenge of Facts," in *Sumner Today*, ed. Maurice R. Davie (New Haven, Conn., 1940), pp. 67-92; Sumner, *Earth-Hunger*, p. 4; Sproat, *"The Best Men,"* pp. 56, 91-92; Starr, *Sumner*, pp. 188-94, 231-32.

al economists responded to the Civil War. Neither the moral issue of slavery nor the constitutional question of states' rights versus national sovereignty attracted Sumner and Newcomb. Sumner found friends who were willing to buy him a substitute; he spent the war years studying in Germany. Newcomb avoided service by using Washington connections to obtain a commission as mathematics instructor in the United States Naval Academy. But the two New Englanders, sons of a prominent abolitionist and a Universalist minister with a habit of challenging orthodoxy, heard the shots fired on Sumter as a clarion call to duty. Both enlisted immediately. Wright was elected lieutenant of his regiment, served for a time as assistant adjutant general, and ended the war with the rank of colonel. Walker won even greater distinction as adjutant general with three successive commanding generals of the Second Army Corps. Wounded, captured, imprisoned, and paroled, he finally achieved the rank of brevet brigadier general.[13]

Their wartime responsibilities gave Walker and Wright administrative experience and an understanding of human suffering that Newcomb and Sumner never duplicated. Even more important, Wright and Walker identified themselves with a movement whose meaning at two different levels profoundly affected their later careers. First, though their social and religious backgrounds emphasized the moral value of individualism, they saw a great moral evil, slavery, ended by the collective action of a gallant people. Second, in supporting the Union cause on the constitutional level, even the son of a leading laissez-faire economist found himself attracted to the more rational, centralizing tendencies of the industrializing North as against the more

13. For biographical data on Walker, see Davis R. Dewey, "Francis A. Walker as a Public Man," *Review of Reviews* 15 (1897):166-67; Joseph Jansen Spencer, "Francis A. Walker: A Character Sketch," ibid., pp. 162-64; Jeanette P. Nichols, "Francis Amasa Walker," *DAB*, 19:342; J. Laurence Laughlin, "Francis Amasa Walker," *Journal of Political Economy* 5 (March 1897):228-32. On Wright, see James Leiby, *Carroll Wright and Labor Reform: The Origins of Labor Statistics* (Cambridge, Mass., 1960). Their military careers can be traced through numerous indexed references in *The War of the Rebellion: A Compilation of the Official Records of the Union and Confederate Armies,* 128 vols. (Washington, D. C., 1880-1901).

localized, tradition-ordered patterns of the agrarian South. For a time both men continued to espouse laissez-faire, but the Civil War prepared them psychologically to conceive of government as the prime educational agency for correcting social evils.[14]

Their subsequent careers reflected the difference. Initially Walker and Wright followed the nonacademic professionalization pattern which characterized the bureaucratic wing of the ASSA. Both men occupied unique positions in the development of statistical methods used by state and federal agencies to gather the demographic and economic data needed for modern government. Walker served President Grant's administration in the Revenue Commission and then as Chief of the Bureau of Statistics. As superintendent of the ninth and tenth censuses in 1870 and 1880, he made improvements which won him international acclaim as a statistician. Wright followed a similar pattern when his pioneering work in establishing the first state Bureau of Labor Statistics in Massachusetts led President Garfield to make him head of the newly established United States Bureau of Labor Statistics. Over the next twenty years Wright's fact-gathering innovations, especially his extremely valuable reports on industrial conditions, earned him an international reputation second only to Walker's.[15]

Working as government appointees required a degree of nonpartisan objectivity that made it impossible to defend any ideology openly. Furthermore, the kind of work that both men did made them receptive to an inductive emphasis in economics which was beginning to challenge laissez-faire. Empirical findings did not always agree with neat deductive formulas. In 1874 Walker became professor of economics and history at the Sheffield Scientific School at Yale. As he began to study the timely

14. Spencer, "Francis A. Walker," pp. 161-62; Wright, "War, God's Missionary," *Reading News and Chronicle* (11 February 1871), quoted in Leiby, *Carroll Wright*, p. 14.
15. Dewey, "Francis A. Walker," pp. 167-68; Nichols, "Francis A. Walker," *DAB*, 19:342-43; Joseph Dorfman, "The Role of the German Historical School in American Economic Thought," *American Economic Review* 45 (May 1955):22; Leiby, *Carroll Wright*, pp. 29-34, 55-63.

problem of wages, he found a doctrinaire approach impossible. "I can't swallow a great many things which have been treated by the economists of the hypothetical school as axiomatic," he told David Wells. "It is high time for us to review the fundamental assumptions of pol. econ." Although Walker continued to presume in favor of noninterference by government, he challenged laissez-faire doctrines on the beneficence of competition and the wages fund. Realizing the hopelessness of competition as a safeguard for individual laborers in large industries, he was the first academic economist to express open sympathy for unionization. By 1876, rather than face a labor revolt, he was ready to endorse government regulation of working conditions and limitation of immigration in order to give labor an even chance in competition with big business.[16]

Wright lagged behind Walker in his acceptance of direct government regulation, but he too doubted the prevailing business ethic. He conceived of the new government information bureaus as educational agencies whose investigations would enlighten public opinion and bring about voluntary, piecemeal reform in the conditions of industrial labor. Both men worked diligently in the ASSA, but Wright in particular attempted to foster the association's commitment to a blend of scientific objectivity and professional responsibility. Eventually, as a lecturer in various colleges and as head of the Carnegie Institution, he completed the transition to academic social science.[17]

Walker and Wright were key figures in the professionalization of social science. Though neither had professional training, they acquired technical and theoretical skills which made them valuable in new scientific enterprises. Yet they retained the traditional style of professionalism, operating as well-known public

16. Walker to Wells, 29 June 1874; 8 February 1875, David Ames Wells MSS, Library of Congress; Francis Amasa Walker, *Wages Question* (New York, 1876), pp. 163-64; Dewey, "Walker," pp. 168-70.

17. Leiby, *Carroll Wright*, pp. 77-78, 92, 139, 169-79; Wright, "Popular Instruction in Social Science," *JSS* 22 (June 1887):28-36; Wright, "The Growth and Purposes of Bureaus of Statistics of Labor," pp. 1-14.

figures with broad-ranging competence rather than strictly as technical experts. Both men were influential and at the same time noncontroversial enough to be valuable figureheads for organizational movements in social science. Walker was president of the American Economic Association and the American Statistical Association. Wright served as president of the ASSA, the American Statistical Association, and the American Association for the Advancement of Science. On the spectrum between laissez-faire and welfare capitalism they occupied a middle point. By combining the bureaucratic and academic patterns of professionalization, they also served as a bridge between the amateur and professional social scientists who questioned laissez-faire.

In the 1870s the first generation of American economists trained by professional economists appeared. Because no graduate training was available in America, these men followed a procession of American scholars in older disciplines who had found instruction in Germany. At the time German economics was dominated by the evolutionary and ethical views of Wilhelm Roscher, Karl Kneis, Adolph Wagner, Johannes Conrad, Bruno Hildebrand, and Gustav von Schmoller: the so-called historical school. At the peak of their influence in Bismarck's Germany, these men had replaced the laissez-faire premises of English classical economics with a grand conception of the positive role the state could play in guiding the evolution of an economic system capable of spreading the benefits of industrialism to all classes. They described themselves as historical economists because they believed that a nation's economic system was the product of history, not natural law, and that people could shape their economic institutions to suit their social goals.[18]

Because a number of Americans adopted a similar historical and ethical approach to economics and also endorsed the concept of the positive state, German training has received great

18. Fine, *Laissez Faire,* pp. 198-99; Dorfman, *Economic Mind,* 3:87-98; Normano, *Spirit of American Economics,* p. 133.

emphasis in explanations of the rise of professional economics and the decline of laissez-faire. One study has concluded that "the concept of the social organism, the rejection of speculative theories, the reliance on empirical data, the practice of the higher criticism, the search for limited generalizations, the use of the comparative method—all these characteristics of the German historical science were to mark the work of the 'new' economists in America, and were to be the cause of conflict with those of the old school."[19] But modernization was occurring in the United States as well as in Germany, and amateur social scientists who knew little or nothing of German models were gathering empirical data as they searched for ways to soften the impact of industrial conditions on the working class. Furthermore, some Americans trained in Germany failed to respond to the treatment. Class backgrounds, preparatory education, earlier experiences, and individual goals seem to have affected the impact of German training and thus influenced the professionalization process for this generation of economists about as much as it did their predecessors in the laissez-faire and transitional groups.

Americans who responded affirmatively to the ethical content of German economics were already strongly motivated by evangelical religion. Edmund J. James, Richard T. Ely, Simon Nelson Patten, and Henry Carter Adams, all prominent exponents of the new economics in the 1880s, provide a good sample. James was the son of a minister's daughter and a circuit-riding Methodist preacher who through a long and distinguished career moved his family from place to place as his services were needed in establishing Methodist churches and schools in the Mississippi Valley. Ely's father, an orthodox Presbyterian descended from a line of Congregationalist preachers, set so rigid a moral example that his son regretted his inability to experience conversion and later sought to fulfill his ethical obligation in scholarship. Patten's ancestors conformed to a classic model: Puritans who

19. Jurgen Herbst, *The German Historical School in American Scholarship: A Study in the Transfer of Culture* (Ithaca, N. Y., 1965), p. 134.

started in New England, moved westward into eastern New York, on—as Congregationalists or Presbyterians—into western New York and Ohio, further west into Illinois, and finally on to Iowa or beyond. His father, stern like Ezra Ely and equally unwilling to let his children play cards or other games, was a ruling elder in the United Presbyterian Church of Sandwich, Illinois, for forty years. Adams's father graduated from Andover Theological Seminary and moved to Iowa in the 1840s as a Congregationalist missionary.[20]

Growing up in the 1850s, all four boys saw adults treat political, social, and economic problems as ethical questions. In southern Illinois, where James was learning social values, sentiment was bitterly divided over slavery and people considered the fate of black people decidedly a moral issue. As a youth in New Hampshire Adams's father had been one of the celebrated fifty who walked out of Phillips Exeter Academy when they were not allowed to form an antislavery society. He made a lifelong habit of applying ethical tests to public questions. Bitter doctrinal controversy between Baptists, Methodists, Presbyterians, and Episcopalians spilled over into other disputed areas in western New York, where Ely's father often wrote moralistic editorials on political issues. Simon Patten's father sat in the Illinois legislature throughout the controversy-ridden 1850s, supported Lincoln, and raised a regiment when the Civil War began. Later Patten witnessed tariff debates, which the people of Illinois conducted with the same moral intensity.[21]

20. Richard Allen Swanson, "Edmund J. James, 1855-1925: A 'Conservative Progressive' in American Higher Education" (Ph.D. diss., University of Illinois, 1966), pp. 5-7; Minutes of the Illinois Conference, 1878, 1888; W. N. McElroy to E. J. James, 28 November 1910, Box 14, General Correspondence, Edmund J. James MSS, University of Illinois; Richard T. Ely, *Ground under Our Feet: An Autobiography* (New York, 1938), pp. 13-16; Benjamin G. Rader, *The Academic Mind and Reform: The Influence of Richard T. Ely in American Life* (Lexington, Ky., 1966), pp. 4-6; Rexford Tugwell, "Notes on the Life and Work of Simon Nelson Patten," *Journal of Political Economy* 31 (April 1923):153-58; Roswell C. McCrea, "A Biographical Sketch of Simon Nelson Patten," *Annals of the American Academy of Political and Social Science*, Supplement, 107 (May 1923): 347; Marvin B. Rosenberry, "Henry Carter Adams," in *Michigan and the Cleveland Era*, ed. Earl D. Babst and Lewis G. Vander Velde (Ann Arbor, Mich., 1948), pp. 23-25.

21. Swanson, "Edmund J. James," pp. 9-10; W. H. Webster to James, 23

None of the four ethical economists in this group had youthful experience with commerce or industry. As sons of farmers and ministers, they absorbed those traditional rural and spiritual values that were most directly challenged by the impersonal, centralizing trends of the postwar era. They all had the inspiration to serve society, but the roles they might have entered seemed somehow passé, irrelevant to the problems of their age. Men who understood the new social and economic patterns seemed more likely to play a part in determining how people would behave toward one another in industrial society. What was needed, it seemed, was a new kind of specialist: one who could analyze and guide social policy from the comprehensive, disinterested, ethical perspective which the ministry had once maintained and speak with the authority which ministers had once commanded, but with a modern, scientific voice.

In hope of finding training for a role that barely existed, each of the four embarked on an educational quest. They already possessed some of the attributes that professions cultivate—altruism, faith in knowledge as the source of progress, and eagerness to serve—but they hardly knew which profession to choose. James had the clearest sense that his future lay in social science. With impatient dispatch, he sampled what Illinois Normal University, Northwestern University, and Dunbar's Harvard had to offer, found them all wanting, and set out to obtain the much admired German D. Phil., or doctor of philosophy degree. At Halle he studied with Johannes Conrad, one of the younger historical economists who in 1872 had formed the Verein für Sozialpolitik with the deliberate purpose of cementing the economist's role in guiding the development of German industry in an ethical direction. As Conrad defined it, economics provided exactly the kind of springboard to influence which James had been seeking.[22]

December 1910, Box 14, General Correspondence, James MSS; Rosenberry, "Henry Carter Adams," pp. 23-25; Ely, Ground, p. 13; Tugwell, "Patten," pp. 160-64.

22. W. H. Webster to James, 23 December 1910, Box 4, General Correspondence, James MSS; Swanson, "Edmund J. James," pp. 15-26.

Ely's pattern was different. At first moral philosophy satisfied his ethical interest, so he transferred from Columbia to Halle still seeking graduate training in philosophy. A brief acquaintance with Conrad convinced Ely that the new economics was both more ethical than German philosophy and more likely to lead to reform. He went on to Heidelberg, where his work with Karl Kneis prepared him to treat economics as a science capable of defining and achieving a just society. Shy Simon Patten made the same transition. His father sent him to Northwestern to study law, but philosophy was more congenial to his reflective, introspective nature. When he was permitted to follow James to Halle, the ethical dimension of historical economics captured Patten too.[2][3]

In Adams's case, the initial connection between ethics and economics was even more obvious. As a sickly, sensitive child whose introspection was encouraged by a doting mother, he identified completely with Jesus, revering him not so much for his death as for "his life, his willingness to be misunderstood, his calm confidence in himself, his rage at the privileged thieves of his day, and his renunciation of love." Adams planned to continue his education until he was thirty years old "for no other reason than that Jesus had not begun his work till 30." At Andover, however, he found his father's faith sterile and unresponsive to current social problems. Organized religion seemed at best oblivious to the suffering of the working class and at worst culpable in its willingness to defend the greedy employers who caused the suffering.

At some cost to his conscience Adams abandoned hereditary beliefs and left the seminary to accept an assignment as the first graduate fellow in social science at the new Johns Hopkins University. Even before he was aware of the German historical school, he had concluded that "no study . . . comes so directly into contact with daily life—affecting the conditions and hap-

---

23. Rader, *Academic Mind*, pp. 9-13; McCrea, "Patten," pp. 349-51; Tugwell, "Patten," pp. 172-73; Henry R. Seager, "Address," *Annals of the American Academy of Political and Social Science,* Supplement, 186 (May 1923): 336.

piness of men—as much [as] Political Economy." In Baltimore, observing firsthand the conditions of the poor, Adams grew even more confident that he could ease human suffering and fulfill his own missionary inclinations through the study of economics. At President Gilman's suggestion, he went to Berlin for advanced study.[24]

If anything, German study dimmed Adams's faith in the possibility of reforming industrial society through sound economics. Whereas Ely and the others had been impressed by the efficiency and vigor of German government, Adams was skeptical. He had a high regard for German universities, but the showy grandeur and aristocratic wastefulness of the Wilhelmian court repelled him. Socialist criticisms of industrial society seemed humane and valid. Yet the socialist's faith in state action rather than individual regeneration as a way of reforming evil conditions appeared both naive and dangerous to important values. At the end of a year at the University of Berlin, Adams confessed his confusion. "The more one studies this problem of society," he mused, "the more he is impressed with the idea or rather the truth that nothing can do it any good until universal love reigns . . . and what Christ taught is accepted as . . . the guiding principle of men's lives. Evil cannot be repressed. When the law puts its hand down in one place it may effect what it endeavors in one particular instance, but it only changes the form of the evil. That which is bad breaks out in another way, in another place."[25]

As Adams neared thirty he decided, with some embarrassment, to build his reputation by studying the "hard, selfish subject" of finance. "It will give me confidence," he explained, "with the men whom I wish to meet in this country, the

24. Ephraim Adams to H. C. Adams, 15 September 1878; Adams to "My Own Dear Mother," 16 May, 27 January 1878; [?] November 1888; 7 April 1884; 22 October 1877; Adams to Bertha H. Wright, 30 December 1889; n. d. [late 1889 or early 1890]; F. A. Walker to Adams, 30 August 1877, Henry Carter Adams MSS, Michigan Historical Collections, University of Michigan.

25. Adams to "My Dear Mother," 23 November, 1, 8 December 1878; 2 March 1879; Adams to "Dear Father," dated 20 June 1878, but actually written 20 June 1879, from Paris, Adams MSS.

moneyed men and the lawyers." Though his sympathy with the
working class was by no means dead, a new careerism had begun
to erode his religious idealism.[26]

Careerism was also a dominant note among professionally
trained economists who resisted the new economics. Arthur
Twining Hadley and Frank William Taussig, two contemporaries
of Ely, James, Patten, and Adams who also studied in Germany,
provided the most illuminating contrast. Neither Hadley nor
Taussig was strongly motivated by evangelical religion. Both
men had urban origins. Both were connected by family tradition with social roles which the post-Civil War expansion of
business and its secular ethos did not threaten as they did the
ministry or the farm.

Hadley was the only member of the new generation of
professional economists to come from a long line of professors.
In 1856 he was born on the edge of the Yale campus, where his
father was a distinguished classicist and philologist. As student,
professor, and president, he spent most of his scholarly life at
Yale, constantly engaged in defining the special quality of the
academic vocation. His entire experience was in a conservative,
genteel, and cultivated segment of the upper middle class, where
the emotional fervor of ethical economics seemed out of
place.[27]

Taussig might have thought that his background actually
proved the beneficence of classical economics. His father was an
educated Bohemian who settled in the Saint Louis community
of "forty-eighters" led by Carl Schurz and quite literally made
his fortune by taking advantage of the opportunities that mid-
century expansion provided. As a doctor, a teacher, a suburban
mayor, and an antislavery Unionist in a border state, he developed political connections which brought him a patronage
appointment as collector of internal revenue in the Saint Louis
district during the Civil War. After the war Taussig became
treasurer of a company organized to bridge the Mississippi River

26. Adams to "Dear Mother," 10 May 1880, Adams MSS.
27. Morris Hadley, *Arthur Twining Hadley* (New Haven, Conn., 1948), pp. 1-15.

at Saint Louis and monopolize the business of hauling loco-
motives through the city. With House of Morgan money, an
ideal location, and railroad fever working for it, the company
reaped a substantial return which made it possible for the elder
Taussig to give his son every cultural and educational advantage.
Frank Taussig was proud of his father. His childhood experience
convinced him that an energetic and enterprising man could ride
the shifting tides of economic boom and recession to prosperity.[28]

The beginning of professional education only confirmed the
attitudes toward economics and academics which Taussig and
Hadley had developed earlier. Hadley's reaction to the new
economics he found in Adolph Wagner's seminar at the University of Berlin was a striking revelation of the extent to which
a dose of Sumner could fortify an already conservative youth
against teachings that contradicted laissez-faire. Ely had
credited Wagner with a profound influence on his thought.
Hadley noted instead that it was "astonishing how nearly impossible it is for a German scholar to keep his head straight
when he gets hold of such a subject as political economy."
Though Hadley was less hidebound in his economic thinking
than Sumner was, German training never shook his habitual
presumption in favor of laissez-faire or convinced him that
economics was a science of welfare. He left Berlin without
taking a degree and returned to Yale. At Harvard Dunbar's
influence on Taussig was probably less profound. Taussig eventually became a master of historical method, but the ethical
mission which German economics preached held no attraction
for him. His postgraduate sojourn in Europe was for the conventional grand tour, not for study. Though he spent "three un-
forgettable months" in Wagner's Berlin, he simply ignored the
German historical school. Without attending Wagner's seminar,
without even meeting the great master, Taussig returned to

28. J. A. Schumpeter, A. H. Cole, and E. S. Mason, "Frank William Taussig,"
Quarterly Journal of Economics 55 (May 1941):337-40; F. W. Taussig, "My Father's
Business Career," *Harvard Business Review* 19 (Autumn 1940):177-83; Redvers Opie,
"Frank William Taussig," *Economic Journal* 51 (June and September 1941):347-49.

Harvard and finished a Ph.D. in economics under the conservative guidance of Charles F. Dunbar.[29]

Taussig and Hadley found the industrial age they entered as young scholars as natural and acceptable—though not ideal—as the four reformers found it alien and sordid. James left Germany determined to find a teaching job and start agitating for a society of economists to plan social legislation. When Ely landed in New York in 1880 and compared the filth and graft he saw with the efficiency and cleanliness of Berlin, he swore that he would devote his life to improving such conditions. Patten thought of the economist as a public servant with a duty to develop a national economic plan. If Adams was more cautious than the others, his religious conviction was also more profound.[30]

Between the extremes represented by these six young professionals, others in the same generation found their places according to their own lights. Two, Edwin Robert Anderson Seligman and J. Laurence Laughlin, fit no particular pattern. Though Seligman studied in Germany after Columbia and largely accepted the evolutionary, relativistic, reconstructionist ethic of the historical school, he drew on a background more like Taussig's than Ely's. Seligman's father was a wealthy New York Jew with large financial interests, but he was also a philanthropist who respected education and supported both humanitarian and good government causes. His children acquired not only a cosmopolitan cultural outlook but a keen sense of civic responsibility and an inclination toward activism which contradicted laissez-faire. As an economist drawing on that Jewish tradition of liberal humanism, Seligman accepted the validity of social reform, but he remained more moderate in expression than his colleagues in the evangelical tradition.[31]

Laughlin was another kind of blend. From rural Ohio, he

29. This account of Hadley's reaction to German economics relies on letters published in Hadley, *Hadley*, pp. 32-35, 45-47. For contrast, see Ely, *Ground*, p. 146. On Taussig, see Schumpeter et al., "Taussig," pp. 340-42; Opie, "Taussig," p. 349.

30. Ely, *Ground*, pp. 134, 56-63; Tugwell, "Patten," pp. 172-75.

31. Joseph Dorfman, "Edwin Robert Anderson Seligman," *DAB*, 22 (Supplement 2):606-9.

matured in a Scotch-Irish Presbyterian family, but his father was neither farmer nor minister. Instead he was an ambitious lawyer who eventually moved his family to a larger town and became mayor. The self-made son of a self-made father, Laughlin financed his own education at preparatory school and worked as a teacher while he earned a doctorate in history under Henry Adams at Harvard, where he learned to doubt the motives of reformers. Training in classical deductive economics under Dunbar started the already conservative Laughlin on an ultraconservative career.[32]

In the early 1880s these first-generation professional economists began to take their places in the colleges and new universities of the United States. Employment was uncertain in the formative years of graduate education, and that insecurity told on some of them. Ely found his first job at Johns Hopkins quickly, but the prominence of the country's first graduate school made competition for tenured positions frightfully keen. Though Adams found work immediately, he had to spend several years teaching half-year stints at three different schools. Taussig quickly established himself as Dunbar's protégé at Harvard and earned tenure, but Laughlin was never so secure. Hadley taught classes outside his field and waited seven years for a permanent appointment at Yale. James spent several years in high school work while he wrote enough economics to be employed by the new Wharton School at the University of Pennsylvania. Patten might never have found a position without the help of his friends. In 1878 he returned to the Illinois farm, as isolated and unhappy as ever. Nearly desperate, his father sent him back to law school, but his eyesight failed and he returned home to suffer long months of near blindness in defeated silence. On a visit to James, Patten discovered a treatment that improved his vision, and he too began to write a treatise in economics. In 1888, a full decade after Patten's German D. Phil. had been awarded, James was finally able to

32. Alfred Borneman, *J. Laurence Laughlin* (Washington, D. C., 1940), pp. 1-3; Herbst, *German Historical School,* p. 106; Henry Adams, *The Education of Henry Adams* (New York, 1931), pp. 301-3.

bring his brilliant friend to the University of Pennsylvania, where he stayed the rest of his life.

In order to establish their reputations the young professionals busied themselves with research. Their scholarship burgeoned beyond anything earlier generations had imagined. In no time each one had claimed a major economic subject. They started applying professional techniques to the study of railroads, money, the tariff, finance, labor, socialism, and the discipline of economics itself. When their books and articles began to appear, a new era of economic knowledge opened. Suddenly the opinions of professional social scientists began to matter. As their work attracted the invidious attention of powerful interests, the conflicting claims that ethical and traditional economists made to authority grew in importance. Given the vitality of economic debate in the 1880s, confrontation was certain.

3 *Battle of the Schools*

As the first generation of professionally trained economists took charge of the discipline in the early 1880s, substantial differences in training and social philosophy divided them. In some respects their disagreements were rooted in the same tension between reform and knowledge which persisted in amateur social science, but there were also questions of method, social philosophy, and mission which pertained specifically to economics. Some social purpose was to be served by airing the divisions among economists widely, for eventually those issues bore on policy decisions that faced the nation. Yet in order to establish themselves professionally as authorities on economic policy, it was imperative that the economists demonstrate at least outward unity on basic issues. Instead, for a time, economists paraded their ideological and methodological divisions while a group of ethical revisionists tried to discredit laissez-faire and capture the emerging profession.

Between 1884 and 1886 laissez-faire and new school economists engaged in a public debate that became increasingly acrimonious as insults and accusations were exchanged. The furor they created added to the general uncertainty of the mid-1880s. While the economists' controversy helped to expose deeper divisions that had developed in America, it also robbed the rapidly changing society of a source of stability and understanding. It delayed the reasoned application of scientific economics to the technical problems created by modernization; yet it led to a definition of economics which confined the economist's ultimate competence largely to technical questions.

The differences between old and new economists might not have seemed so great if both factions had not allowed their most recalcitrant members to define the terms of the argument. Newcomb and Sumner were committed to a level of economic conservatism that was far more restrictive than most laissez-faire economists demanded. Ely was a much more outspoken reformer and less scientific in his approach than other ethical economists. From opposite ends of the ideological spectrum, these three seized the initiative in establishing the character of the debate. They polarized issues needlessly and for a while they managed to force others to make choices on their terms. As a result they slowed the process of professionalization in economics.

The public debate began in 1884 when Ely published an account of the differences between the old and the new in political economy. Because he was the first into the fray, Ely was able to choose a strategy to fit the desired outcome. He decided to attack the old economists on ideological and methodological grounds. In calling the two sides old and new, he adopted the classic tactic of professionalizing groups: to discredit the purveyors of a competing social mission by branding them as charlatans whose skills, if they were ever sufficient, had grown hopelessly out of date.

Thus Ely's analysis was a study in exaggerated opposites. The old economists were English, hypothetical, and deductive. The new economists were German, realistic, and inductive. Old economists believed in the existence of a priori laws which could not be changed, no matter who suffered, while new economists recognized what everyone of ordinary sense could see—that economic policies changed with the times. The old economics was a science of wealth which glorified the baser human emotions, justified selfishness, and raised competition to the level of divine ordinance. The new economics would serve all mankind, the laboring masses as well as the capitalist classes, and try, as industry changed, to guide the development of humane economic practices that subordinated wealth to welfare. The old economics mistrusted government, but the new economists saw no reason to refrain from using the power of the state to safeguard the vital interests of the people.[1]

1. Richard T. Ely, "Past and Present of Political Economy," *Johns Hopkins*

If a professional economist of moderate views had subjected Ely's model to careful analysis, much of its oversimplification might have been exposed. Instead the orthodox economist least qualified by training and temperament to defend scientific economics identified himself as Ely's archopponent. Simon Newcomb's motives were partly scientific and partly personal. As a mathematician and an astronomer, he depended on the existence between phenomena of relationships which were regular and consistent, unaffected by time or sentiment. As a member of the faculty of the Johns Hopkins University, he was outraged by what amounted to a public attack on his intelligence by a junior professor in his own university. In his eagerness to set the record straight, Newcomb misjudged both the character of Ely's argument and the vulnerability of his own case.[2] If Ely had intended to create two battling schools of political economy out of whole cloth, he could not have done so unaided. In Newcomb, he found a willing accomplice.

Newcomb made grave tactical errors. By recognizing Ely as the leader of the revisionist school, he greatly enhanced his opponent's importance and made it easier for other revisionists to fall into a similar pattern of deference. In accepting Ely's interpretive framework, he endorsed the argument that two diametrically opposed schools of economists in fact existed. At a time when inequities in the distribution of wealth were beginning to seem unjustifiable even to many conservatives, Newcomb defended the absolute primacy of self-interest in economic activities and baldly denied that economics had anything to do with welfare. By logical extension, he placed opponents of positive state action in league with the most exploitative capitalists.

University Studies in History and Political Science 2 (March 1884): 143-202. On charlatanism, see William J. Goode, "Encroachment, Charlatanism, and the Emerging Profession: Psychology, Sociology, and Medicine," American Sociological Review 25 (December 1960):902-14.

2. Newcomb to Daniel Coit Gilman, 3, 14 May; 1, 4 June 1884, quoted in Hugh Hawkins, Pioneer: A History of the Johns Hopkins University, 1874-1889 (Ithaca, N.Y., 1960), p. 180; Benjamin G. Rader, The Academic Mind and Reform: The Influence of Richard T. Ely in American Life (Lexington, Ky., 1966), p. 32.

On scientific questions Newcomb was just as unwise. Though the static Newtonian analogies which sanctioned laissez-faire economics as a science had lost some of their former authority when the evolutionary concepts associated with Darwinism were popularized, Newcomb still clung to the dogma of universally applicable laws as the only true test of science. Yet he had to admit that the abstract laws of classical economics often failed the test of practical application to the actual conditions of a particular time and place. That contradiction added force to the historical economist's contention that economics, an evolving, social, human science, should never have been judged by the standards of the exact, inhuman sciences in the first place. Many of the younger, professionally trained economists were already using empirical methods to study conventional subjects such as the tariff, railroads, and money. But Newcomb tried to make deduction another test of the scientific quality of an economist's work. There was no need to juxtapose the two methods. If he had accepted induction and then differentiated economics from history by insisting that prediction was an essential part of economic reasoning, he might have clarified an issue. Instead he identified the use of inductive, historical, and statistical methods as irresponsible relativism and expanded the area of disagreement.[3]

The dispute between Ely and Newcomb quickly spread to include other antagonists on both sides. Ironically, neither of the principal figures accurately represented sentiments on either side of the controversy. Ely was often motivated largely by personal ends which were external to the field of economics. Newcomb had no real stake in economics beyond the reputation he had established before the controversy began, but it was in his interest to do all he could to oppose a pattern of professionalization that would leave him out, no matter what its scientific character. Unfortunately each man's argument struck responsive chords.

3. Simon Newcomb, "The Two Schools of Political Economy," *Princeton Review,* n.s., 14 (November 1884):291-301.

The Ely-Newcomb controversy quickly degenerated into an academic free-for-all of classic proportions. Newcomb's wounded dignity was matched by Ely's ambition and his growing fear for his academic life. Newcomb insisted that Johns Hopkins President Daniel Coit Gilman arbitrate the dispute, and friends of laissez-faire began pressuring Gilman to fire the young troublemaker. Then the ultraconservative *Nation* printed a review that accused Ely of deliberately misrepresenting the orthodox school. While Ely squirmed, friends counseled moderation. His wily colleague Herbert Baxter Adams urged him, having stirred up the animals, to get over the fence and aggrandize himself by behaving discreetly. But Ely ridiculed Newcomb before campus gatherings and got his former students to repeat the charges in their journals.[4]

As tempers flared, a new dimension was added with the publication, nearly simultaneously in early 1885, of Ely's major study of "Recent American Socialism" and a collection of essays by Sumner designed to discredit the new economics by refuting revisionist arguments on such fundamental questions as bimetallism, wages, and protection. Suddenly Ely faced an adversary far more awesome than Newcomb. Sumner was just as determined to prove that there were two schools in economics. Observing the new school had stiffened his resolution to keep the profession under the judicious control of economists who upheld what he considered to be legitimate scholarly standards. Sumner was not nearly so much concerned about technical questions of method and proof as he was about policy. Anyone who claimed to be an economist and still recommended massive state intervention in economic affairs must be quickly exposed as a charlatan. First in a discussion of ethical economics and now in a treatise that commented sympathetically on socialism,

4. Herbert Baxter Adams to Henry Carter Adams, 27 April, 23 August 1884, H. C. Adams MSS; H. B. Adams to Ely, 9 August 1884, Richard T. Ely MSS, Wisconsin Historical Society; "Notes," *Nation* 39 (24 July 1884):74; Hawkins, *Pioneer,* pp. 180-81; Rader, *Academic Mind,* pp. 31-32. Hawkins's account of the controversy within the Hopkins faculty is based on the papers and recollections of Albert Shaw, an Ely student who had become editor of the *Dial.* Rader's account relies on Hawkins's and on the Gilman papers.

he believed, Ely had committed the unpardonable sin. Unless the price for such recklessness was set very high, other ethical economists would follow his scurrilous example.[5]

Clearly Sumner was aware that nothing less than control of the emerging profession was at stake. Lining up beside Newcomb as a defender of scientific economics, he tried to demonstrate how dangerously nonprofessionals, with their vague, sentimental, unscientific thinking, could confuse economics questions. For the sake of truth and social order, Sumner insisted, serious consideration of the economic questions that faced Americans had to be confined to the only place where there was any hope of a sensible outcome: "the forum of academic discussion." Only in a protected atmosphere where external political pressure was slight could responsible scholars reduce the relentless operation of economic forces to scientific laws and provide a sound basis for limited—severely limited—state action. The political arena was no place for scientific judgment. Thus the gravest error an economist could commit was the deliberate politicization of the discipline.[6]

Sumner brought the issue subtly around to advocacy. As if he had never expressed himself on a controversial issue, Sumner explained that he had finally decided to defend orthodox doctrines against their detractors only after concluding that the unscientific pronouncements of such agitators were contributing dangerous misconceptions to an already near critical situation of class antagonism. When men who claimed scientific authority tried to teach people that they could escape the inexorable pressure of economic laws, they committed an act of incitement. Ordinarily competent scholars were in control of scientific disciplines and able to "repress presuming ignorance and charlatanism." Such was not currently the case in economics. Instead, as economists bickered among themselves, they were in danger of losing the influence they had once possessed

5. Richard T. Ely, "Recent American Socialism," *Johns Hopkins University Studies in Historical and Political Science* 3 (April 1885):231-304; William G. Sumner, *Collected Essays in Political and Social Science* (New York, 1885).

6. Sumner, *Collected Essays*, pp. 3-6, 15.

among responsible people. The only hope that Sumner could see of making economics a constructive force again was to defeat this new school of social reformers with all its pretensions to moral superiority, to reinforce the irrefutable premises of classical economics, and to purge the profession of irresponsible elements once and for all.[7]

Ely had no intention of waging a lone campaign against foes as powerful as Newcomb and Sumner. If any purging was to be done, Ely wanted to do it. Friends who had access to journals kept up a steady flow of criticism against the laissez-faire economists, calling them either hopelessly outdated as scholars or clients of the unscrupulous rich. Meanwhile Ely began laying plans for an organization to unite revisionist economists against such threats of reprisal as Sumner had made. To capture influential support Ely turned first to Francis Amasa Walker, where he found a friend. Walker had been favorably impressed by Ely's indictment of the orthodox school, at whose ungentle hands he too had suffered an unbearable amount of "supercilious patronage and toplofty criticism." It was easy for Walker to appreciate "the need of such moral support from fellow workers in political economy as might come from formal association and concerted action." Even so, Walker was scientist enough to wonder whether anything but destructive consequences could come from an organization that deliberately divided economists along ideological lines. "Whether the formation of a society composed of economists who repudiate laissez faire as a scientific doctrine is desirable, or whether, on the other hand, we shall not do better to assert ourselves aggressively within the Political Economy Club already formed," remained for Walker in the spring of 1884 "a question fairly subject to discussion."[8]

The Political Economy Club (PEC) was hardly a suitable location for the mission Ely had in mind. In 1882 J. Laurence

7. Ibid., pp. 36-38.
8. For example, see Albert Shaw, "New Studies in Political and Social Science," *Dial* 6 (July 1885): 72-73; Hawkins, *Pioneer*, pp. 181-82; Walker to Ely, 30 April 1884, Ely MSS.

Laughlin had called upon his friend Edward Atkinson to help him bring together a group of leading economists in a small, manageable organization that might be "authoritative and useful in many ways." The result was a hybrid congregation of academics, journalists, industrialists, legislators, government officials, and lawyers who held regular dinner meetings in New York, Boston, or Washington for what was often mainly social discourse. At Laughlin's urging, Simon Newcomb was the perennial president. Prominent members included Charles Francis Adams, Atkinson, David Wells, Abram Hewitt, former Secretary of the Treasury Hugh McCulloch, E. L. Godkin, and Horace White; Sumner and Hadley of Yale; Dunbar, Taussig, and Laughlin of Harvard; Perry of Williams, and the Careyite Robert Ellis Thompson of the University of Pennsylvania. Since membership was by nomination and blackballs were possible, the PEC was a gentlemen's private club.

Despite the fraternal trappings, there is some evidence that Laughlin envisioned the PEC as a quasi-professional association. His unsuccessful endeavors to avoid party politics are the best proof. At one point two nonacademic members, White and Wells, proposed dropping a scheduled discussion of the effect of machinery on wages in order to devote the session to the more exciting project of determining what policy the Democratic party should follow regarding the tariff. Laughlin appealed to Newcomb to help him "gently but firmly . . . repress the tendency to make our Club a body for free trade agitation . . . and point it steadily to discuss the really difficult and unsettled questions in P.E. wh. all recognize as important in their effect on the whole fabric of our science." Unfortunately for Laughlin, the nonacademic members generally disliked theoretical discussions and the older academic contingent in the PEC was almost as committed to political questions, especially free trade. To improve appearances, one or two known protectionists were invited to join, but the association developed a reputation for partisanship.

For a time there were efforts to strengthen the academic

influence. As economists trained in the historical school acquired academic positions, several of them were invited to join. Seligman, Henry Carter Adams, James, and Ely were members at least by 1887. Yet the balance of power remained with the businessmen and journalists, and clashes between the old and new members made some meetings so tense that moderates took steps to keep the strongest partisans apart. Despite Laughlin's efforts, the PEC never functioned as a professional association. Because the group was organized on a social basis, without platform or regular elections, there were no institutionalized ways of dealing with conflict between academic and nonacademic members or between laissez-faire devotees and reformers. The dominance of laissez-faire thinkers in the PEC was a fair reflection of economic orthodoxy in the early 1880s, not only among influential business and professional leaders but in the majority of academic positions as well. If Ely wanted an organization to destroy laissez-faire, this was not the one to choose.[9]

One organization to promote the concept of the positive state had already been attempted. Originally Edmund James may have been motivated to create an organization of liberal economists in support of state action partly in the interest of professionalizing American economics along German lines. As the most ardent American disciple of Johannes Conrad, the founder of the German Verein für Sozialpolitik, James had a

9. From the scant information available, A. W. Coats has pieced together the story of the PEC. See Coats, "The Political Economy Club: A Neglected Episode in American Economic Thought," *American Economic Review* 51 (September 1961): 624-37. (The quoted material here is from pp. 628-29.) See also Dorfman, *Economic Mind,* 3:272; Alfred Borneman, *J. Laurence Laughlin* (Washington, D.C., 1940), p. 9; Harold F. Williamson, *Edward Atkinson: The Biography of an American Liberal, 1827-1905* (Boston, 1934), pp. 53-54; Rader, *Academic Mind,* p. 34; Laughlin to Newcomb, 9 September 1885, Simon Newcomb MSS, Manuscripts Division, Library of Congress; Laughlin to Seligman, 29 December 1887, E. R. A. Seligman MSS, Columbia University Special Collections; H. C. Adams to Bertha Wright, 13 April 1890, Adams MSS. The Wisconsin Historical Society Book Collection contains a dinner program entitled "Political Economy Club, 1889, By-Laws and Members," which lists the people named here and a few more. Coats attributes part of the animus between Laughlin and Ely to the fact that Ely succeeded in forming a professional association, thus preempting Laughlin's initiative.

compelling model to follow. "If economic students were to
have any influence whatever upon the course of practical politics," Conrad had told him, "it would be necessary to take a
new attitude toward the whole matter of social legislation." As
soon as he arrived at the University of Pennsylvania, James
began talking with associates about the possibility of founding
an organization to involve economists in state planning. Early in
1885 he and Patten circulated a draft platform for the Society
for the Study of the National Economy. Few economists responded. Though the platform called for extensive federal initiative in education, transportation, conservation, and industry,
the University of Pennsylvania's devotion to protectionism may
have discouraged as many economists as James's explicit rejection of laissez-faire.[10]

Profiting by James's example, Ely planned a professional
organization with a broader base. If economics had been a
professionalizing occupation, what he wanted to do would have
been easy enough. He could simply have proposed that everyone admitted to the profession be required to meet certain
prescribed standards for entrance, follow a prescribed pattern of
training, possess specified skills and attitudes, identify clients by
their need for certain services, and conceive of the profession's
responsibility to society in a specified way. Ely hoped to
accomplish all those goals, but his situation was more complicated than the usual model presupposes. Prominent positions
were already occupied by people with advanced training whose
ideas he abhorred. Instead of drawing a line horizontally across
a group of people performing the same function with varying
degrees of skill, he wanted to draw a vertical line down through

10. Richard Allen Swanson, "Edmund J. James, 1885-1925" (Ph.D. diss., University of Illinois, 1966), pp. 94-95; Richard T. Ely, *Ground under Our Feet* (New York,
1938), p. 134; Ely, "The Founding and Early History of the American Economic
Association," Papers and Proceedings of the American Economic Association, Supplement, *American Economic Review* 26 (March 1936):144; "Report of the Anniversary Meeting, 28 December 1909," *Publications of the AEA*, 3d ser., 11
(1910):107-9; James to President Theodore Roosevelt, 4 March 1905, Edmund
James MSS; Dorfman, *Economic Mind*, 3:205-6. The original of the platform is in the
James MSS. It is published in Ely, *Ground*, pp. 296-99.

an amorphous body of self-designated economists and separate them into two distinct factions according to their social philosophies. The economists Ely intended to exclude were "men of the Sumner type." In fact, the original purpose behind the whole organizational scheme was to create standards, endorse methods, and establish a social mission which would eliminate the "Sumner crowd" from the profession of economics.[11]

Mere professionalism was not the object. Ely hoped to shape the character of the profession according to his own personal ethical and scientific standard by differentiating people with a given set of attitudes and competences from the total group of social scientists. He wanted his special group to be considered authoritative in certain areas. The simplest way of defining groups would have been to differentiate all academic economists from the rest of the academic profession, since professors were already considered professionals and granted certain privileges because of their professorial role. But obviously there were people teaching economics in 1885 whose authority Ely hoped to destroy. Conversely, some of his most valuable allies in economics were not professors. At this stage of professionalization Ely evaluated a person's credentials as an economist according to what he advocated, not by what he did for a living.

The ultimate objective of Ely's plan was more effective advocacy for economists interested in reform. Yet in order to succeed he had to define the commitments of the proposed American Economic Association (AEA) broadly enough to attract a majority of all practicing economists. Otherwise he would only manage to isolate himself. During the summer of 1885 he drafted a platform designed to be progressive enough to appeal to young liberals who were anxious to rectify the social evils of industrialism and yet cautious enough to satisfy many older moderates as well.

11. Ely to Seligman, 9, 23 June 1885, Seligman MSS. For an excellent earlier treatment of the formation of the American Economic Association which addresses itself to somewhat different questions than this one does, see A. W. Coats, "The First Two Decades of the American Economic Association," *American Economic Review* 50 (September 1960):555-74.

To strike that delicate balance, Ely consulted with a few carefully chosen associates and gathered their reactions. His confidants were Seligman, Henry Carter Adams, James, Patten, Richmond Mayo-Smith, John Bates Clark, Andrew Dickson White, Charles Kendall Adams, Washington Gladden, and a few of his own former students: Albert Shaw, Woodrow Wilson, and Charles Levermore.[12] In every case Ely had reason to expect a receptive attitude. With Seligman, H. C. Adams, James, Patten, Mayo-Smith, White, and C. K. Adams, he had the common bond of German education. As ambassador to Germany and president of Cornell University, White had helped Ely to publish his first article and get his first job. The German-trained historian C. K. Adams had sent the *Nation* a favorable review of Ely's article on the two schools of political economy and protested the critical review that was printed. With H. C. Adams, Clark, James, and especially Gladden, Ely shared a deep concern for the absence of Christian principles in economic life. Shaw and other students had been his trusted allies during the Newcomb controversy.[13] By gaining the support of such people, Ely attempted to combine in his movement the powerful strands of modern science, reform activism, and social Christianity.

Because his own views were extreme, Ely had to make compromises even with sympathetic colleagues in order to win enough support. First, to eliminate the issue that might prove most divisive, he proposed that the AEA take no position at all on the tariff. It supported Ely's view of the nature of economics to have the tariff question recognized as an evolutionary problem in which government policy needed to be adjusted as the nature of the economy gradually changed. Though Patten pro-

12. Ely to Seligman, 9, 23 June 1885, Seligman MSS; Ely to H. C. Adams, 18 June 1885, Adams MSS; Ely to Mayo-Smith, 18 July 1885, Richmond Mayo-Smith MSS, Department of Special Collections, University of Chicago Library; White to Ely, 24 June 1885, Ely MSS; Ely to White, 2, 30 November 1881; 16 January 1882, Andrew Dickson White MSS, Cornell University Collection of Regional History and University Archives.

13. Ely, *Ground,* pp. 56-63; Rader, *Academic Mind,* p. 17; C. K. Adams to Ely, 4 August 1884, Ely MSS.

tested, other historical economists cared less about the trade controversy than they did about other potential areas of state action. The major focus of the new economics was shifting to the conflict between labor and capital. Ely ranked economic issues in a new hierarchy of importance which may not have satisfied many amateurs who were accustomed to dealing with the typical concerns of classical, liberal economics; but Ely's emphasis on the problems of modernization no doubt appealed to the interests of most professionally trained academics.[14]

Another compromise emerged on the role of the state. A few of the positive statists would have preferred to enumerate categorically the areas of industrial and social development which the state should supervise in the interest of social welfare. Patten, for example, wanted to "give in some specific form our attitude on all the leading economic questions where state intervention is needed." Ely only described the state as "an ethical agency whose positive aid is an indispensable condition of human progress." In a subtle way, Ely's version was more radical, for it committed a professional organization of scholars to making ethical, not merely scientific judgments. It specifically rejected laissez-faire as a doctrine "unsafe in politics and unsound in morals," but it proposed no concrete state action that could immediately alienate the defenders of special interests. Instead of leaving too much initiative with government, Ely reemphasized the pluralism of the proposed economic association and the varied origins of its support by pronouncing the solution of the labor question "impossible without the united efforts of Church, state and science."[15]

Even among close associates there were suspicions of Ely's motives which he had to allay. Their concerns differed according to whether their major interests were in the scientific, religious, or statist aspects of the new economics. Seligman was

14. Ely, *Ground*, p. 137; Ely, "Report of the Organization of the American Economic Association," *Publications of the AEA* 1 (March 1886):6-7; Ely to H. C. Adams, 8 July 1885, Adams MSS.

15. Patten to Ely, 13 July 1885, quoted in Ely, *Ground*, p. 137; Ely, "Report," pp. 6-7.

mainly attracted by the possibility of extending scientific analysis to new economic questions and increasing cooperation among scholars. Though a liberal, he was much less enamored of ethical judgments than the evangelical Protestants. He wondered whether Ely's allegiance to Christianity and socialism might subvert the scientific standards of the new association. To convince Seligman of his fundamental conservatism, Ely assured him that he accepted only a few of the ideas of the Christian Socialists and looked upon Christianity "simply as a social influence." The state should never interfere where free competition and individual initiative would suffice. "As to laissez faire," Ely added, "the idea is to combat the influence of the Sumner crowd." Seligman was persuaded. He assured Mayo-Smith, who had shared his skepticism, that Ely's purpose was simply to advance the scientific development of economics along modern lines and "to work on public opinion only through the results of scientific work in the centres of learning."[16]

With Henry Carter Adams, on the other hand, Ely appealed to a religious background similar to his own. Here his tactic was to reveal the interest in the AEA plan shown "by a large and influential body of Christians." Counting on Adams's support, he suggested that the AEA might benefit from the good offices of the *Christian Union,* the *Congregationalist,* and the Christian public generally if sympathetic people were made aware of the new relationship between economics and Christian ethics.[17]

With equal vigor Ely affirmed or denied all other troublesome reports. The AEA was to be nothing like the German Verein. But it was to be an association of "pure scientists—like the unions in Italy and Germany—and to keep out all 'cranks,' admitting only men whose opinions will serve as a source of strength, not weakness." It was to expose the unscientific character and oppose the pernicious influence of laissez-faire, but it was to encourage perfect freedom in economic discussion. Though economists who used all legitimate research methods

16. Ely to Seligman, 9 June, 8 July 1885, Seligman MSS; Seligman to Mayo-Smith, 7 August 1885, Mayo-Smith MSS.
17. Ely to Adams, 8, 18 July 1885, Adams MSS; Ely, "Report," p. 11.

were welcome, the AEA would encourage people to look "not so much to speculation as to an impartial study of actual conditions of economic life," making use of "statistics in the present, and of history in the past" to reach scientific conclusions.[18]

No wonder an outsider like Simon Newcomb could charge that the Ely platform was designed to make the AEA "a sort of church, requiring for admission to its full communion a renunciation of ancient errors, and an adhesion to the supposed new creed." When the AEA was safely established, Ely admitted that there was no such thing, as far as he could see, as an economic society without advocacy, either open or secret. In the final analysis, he argued, "it is essential that intelligent men and women should distinguish between us and certain economists in whom there is little faith."[19] The trick was to cast the net widely enough.

When the organizational meeting of the AEA was held in September 1885, it was clear that Ely had put together a workable combination of people, qualifications, and circumstances. Holding the meeting in conjunction with the American Social Science Association created a conservative impression and at the same time attracted other critics of laissez-faire. In advance of the session Ely had dealt with individual objections successfully. At the meeting, however, his hold on the decision-making process weakened somewhat. When academic economists with similar reservations on the platform came together, they were able to force some modifications.

The most common concerns regarding the platform centered on the impression that might be created by a formal rejection of laissez-faire. Though no one objected to isolating Sumner and Newcomb, several professional economists drew back from an implied denunciation of the entire heritage of classical economics. Adams found it strangely untenable for men who called

18. Seligman to Mayo-Smith, 7 August 1885, Mayo-Smith MSS; Ely to Adams, 18 June 1885, Adams MSS; Ely, "Report," p. 7.
19. Simon Newcomb, "Review of Ely's Outlines of Economics," *Journal of Political Economy* 3 (December 1894):106; Ely, "Report," pp. 16-19.

themselves historical economists to crusade against economic principles that must have been appropriate when they originated, even if they were out of place in industrial society. Alexander Johnston of Princeton wanted to make it clear that the AEA was not a mere rebellion against classical economics but a larger movement intended to prevent the formation of any orthodoxy that might slow the advance of scholarly work in the field. With a slightly tarnished record to clear, James proposed that the AEA acknowledge the useful work of the classical school and guarantee to honor truth, no matter who might discover it. Elisha Benjamin Andrews, newly arrived in economics from the ministry, agreed that no "earnest economist" should be excluded by his beliefs.[20]

Behind all the protests against Ely's platform lay a single fear: that people would get the idea the so-called new economists were all socialists. Seligman complained of an exaggerated reaction among certain economists against the principle of free competition. In itself, he argued, competition was neither good nor evil except as it operated in a particular situation to help or harm mankind, and economics was not yet so well developed as a science that it was safe to advocate unlimited government action. No economist who wanted to work in a truly scientific spirit should be deterred from joining the AEA "through fear of any imagined Katheder-Socialist tendencies." Always critical of German statism, Adams shared Seligman's fear that a formal rejection of the principle of nonintervention might be mistaken for adoption of "the German view of social relations." The new economists ought to guard against creating the impression that they favored an ever enlarging role for the state, James concurred, and to give "no justification for the charge that we are 'state socialists' or 'professorial socialists.' "[21] It was a fear that was to follow social scientists for generations.

Eventually most of the criticisms raised by new economists

20. Ely, "Report," pp. 21-29.
21. Ibid.

who were less radical than Ely found a place in the platform. Herbert Baxter Adams, Washington Gladden, Alexander Johnston, and John Bates Clark prepared a new draft. Though they were hardly an anti-Ely committee, they eliminated the objectionable reference to laissez-faire as an unsafe and immoral doctrine and deemphasized the role of the state in economic and social action. They toned down the language and made respectful mention of the contributions of earlier economists. Finally a codicil was added which described the platform as nothing more than a general indication of the views of the founders, in no way binding on individual or prospective members. On September 9, 1885, the revised platform and constitution were accepted and the American Economic Association took its place among a growing number of professional organizations.[22]

For many observers, a few minor changes in the wording of the AEA platform failed to eliminate Ely's stamp from the organization. To one pundit, the significance of the new society was clearcut: "The long controversy between the economists and human beings has ended in the conversion of the economists." Francis Amasa Walker was honored with the presidency, but Ely was elected to the vital post of secretary, where he would effectively run the organization. Of the fifty people who joined the AEA at the Saratoga meeting, more than twenty were either former or practicing ministers, including leading Social Gospel spokesmen such as Gladden, Lyman Abbott, and R. Heber Newton. By contrast, though the two groups met jointly, only thirteen members of the ASSA joined the AEA. Nearly half that number were young professional economists who had only joined the ASSA within the preceding two years, and several more were older representatives of the pre-1874 ASSA, which had also placed great emphasis on reform.[23]

22. Ibid., pp. 29, 35-36. Herbert Baxter Adams's presence indicates his brief but serious interest in getting the historical economists to ally with the American Historical Association and develop their academic identity as historians, not social scientists. See H. B. Adams to H. C. Adams, 12 March 1885, H. C. Adams MSS.

23. Elisha Mulford to Ely, n.d. 1885, quoted in Ely, "Report," p. 31. The figures

There were a few encouraging signs for academic economists who hoped that the AEA might serve a serious scholarly purpose and eventually unite a badly divided profession. Moderates among the historical economists had located each other. A few had begun to see inconsistencies in their methodological and ethical positions. In the heat of the platform debate, Seligman had even noted that "there is much less difference between the followers of the historical school and the present moderate adherents of the orthodox school, than is generally imagined." Though the membership included nonprofessionals of all sorts, four academically trained economists—Seligman, Adams, James, and Clark—held important advisory positions.[24]

In 1885, however, the signs of compromise were only distant promises. Moderates may have pressed for continuity in economic scholarship and unity in the discipline, but they were momentarily unable to resist the pressure for an ideological offensive. The AEA was committed to advocacy, no matter how the fine print of its platform might read. As industrial tension increased and turned violent, critics of the prevailing social and economic systems flocked to the new standard. Even moderate professionals took more radical stands in the turbulent succeeding year. True to Ely's plan, the AEA became a haven for reformers.

Reaction among laissez-faire economists was predictably negative. Not a single laissez-faire spokesman from the colleges, liberal journals, or business joined the AEA. Neither influential amateurs such as Atkinson and Wells, academic free-traders such as Perry, nor protectionists of the old Carey school sent any representatives to test the character of the AEA firsthand. Ely had intended to exclude his most bitter rivals, Newcomb and Sumner, but antipathy to the new association cut further into the ranks of less extreme conservatives and younger, professionally trained traditionalists than even he desired.

and comparisons here are based on membership lists for 1886 in "American Social Science Association," *JSS* 22 (June 1887):172-80; Ely, "Report," pp. 43-46. The first year membership of the AEA was reported at 182.

24. Ely, "Report," pp. 28, 40-41.

The total absence of any response from Harvard or Yale was the most conspicuous indication of conservative sentiment. Dunbar's reaction was easiest to explain. As a member of the American Social Science Association and the Political Economy Club, he was already associated with economists whose amateur backgrounds and opinions on policy issues coincided with his own. Any platform that excluded Sumner was almost certain to alienate Dunbar, and with Dunbar disapproving, Taussig could hardly join.

Like Dunbar, Laughlin stayed out of the AEA because he differed with its members on theoretical grounds. His convictions made it impossible for him to condone a positive role for the state in economic or social affairs. Shortly before the AEA was formed, Laughlin had defined his view of the legitimate sphere of economic inquiry. In the process of preparing a student's edition of Mill's *Principles*, he deleted every reference to the role of the state in solving social problems. He was merely removing a corrupting influence, he explained. "The omission of much that should properly be classed under the head of Sociology, or Social Philosophy, would narrow the field to Political Economy alone." His reaction to the AEA platform had exactly the same tone. "Your description of subjects seems to speak of matters lying outside of Political Economy," he responded, "and I feel that I ought to keep within the limit of that study,—at least for the present."[25]

Laughlin and Ely differed almost absolutely on the kinds of questions which economists should be asking. For Laughlin, economics was still about the wealth of nations. Economists ought to be engaged in discovering the universal laws that governed trade and industry, so that the nation could follow them in developing a strong economy. No reformers, economists simply wanted to know how things worked in the

25. J. Laurence Laughlin, ed., *Principles of Political Economy*, by John Stuart Mill (New York, 1884), pp. iii-iv, noted in Robert Church, "The Economists Study Society: Sociology at Harvard, 1891-1902," in *Social Sciences at Harvard, 1860-1920*, ed. Paul Buck (Cambridge, Mass., 1965), p. 30; Laughlin to Adams, 17 October 1885, Adams MSS.

market and the workshop. Economics had no more to do with right and wrong than theology had to do with supply and demand. Yet the very questions that meant so much to Laughlin, Ely branded hackneyed or inconsequential. What Ely cared about were the ethical questions of minimum welfare for all people and a decent return for labor. Each could see the bias in the other's view of economics; neither could see the value judgments in his own.

Historical economists who were worried about creating too radical an image made an effort to bring a few conservative academics into the AEA. At least as a gesture, they elected Laughlin to the council, though he was not in attendance. With stony disapproval he announced his unwillingness to join "a class of disciples" or support an organization of scholars with "any constitution save love of truth." An association that deliberately rejected Sumner must also want to exclude him. To anyone who inquired, Laughlin explained that he had no wish to be "another rag tied on to Ely's kite to steady his erratic movements." Not until 1904, long after the economic controversy had been settled, did Laughlin join the AEA. In the meantime, at Harvard and later at the University of Chicago, he remained a bitter critic of ethical economists and their missionary tendencies.[26]

Although Hadley's reaction was less vitriolic than Laughlin's it was probably even more damaging to the AEA. When Adams and Ely invited him to become a member, Hadley wanted to join. More than any substantive reservation, more than any irrevocable conflict of views, it was the association's reforming image that prevented him. Hadley's response was an important test, for he was perhaps the most thoroughly attuned to traditional scholarly values of any of the younger economists. He was just the sort of academic who would ordinarily cooperate enthusiastically with attempts to advance the professionalization of his discipline.

26. Edward W. Bemis to Ely, 29 September 1886, Ely MSS; Laughlin to Seligman, 11 July 1890, Seligman MSS.

Nevertheless, the original objectives of the AEA had appalled him. Even after the platform was amended, he doubted that the radical image of the movement had been expunged. "The worst elements of the old platform have been omitted," he told Adams, but it "still retains its character, and gives the public the decisive impression of the whole. The newspapers continue to treat the Association as standing on its old platform, and consider this as simply an abbreviation." The historical economists had done nothing significant to convince the literate and responsible public of their moderate intent. No mere shifting of words could erase the earlier impression.[27]

If the revisionists had offered Sumner an office instead of ignoring him, Hadley suggested, they might have proved that the revised platform indicated a real moderation in policy. The exclusion of Sumner was a more important factor in Hadley's decision than any economic principle. Being offered a position in an organization that was widely believed to be a deliberate conspiracy against his senior Yale colleague placed Hadley in an extremely awkward position. To Adams he confessed that he had indeed "rejected a large number of the views of the 'orthodox' economists," but he had not yet "approached the positions of that platform." To join a group that publicly rejected laissez-faire in favor of state interference in social and economic activities would be, he explained, "to place myself in a false light." Perhaps the widely circulated stories of Sumner's attempt to hound Walker out of Yale had some influence. In the end, though Hadley's feelings of comradeship with a number of the AEA's younger professional economists inclined him to join, caution persuaded him to refuse. "I differ with Mr. Sumner on a great many points," he concluded, "but the reasons why he *received* no invitation are probably reasons why I should not *accept* one."[28]

The AEA formally divided economists. "We have mortally offended both Yale and Harvard," Adams commented, "but

27. Hadley to Adams, 18, 26 September 1885, Adams MSS.
28. Ibid.; Hadley to Ely, 26 September 1885, Ely MSS.

that can't be helped. They are the orthodox economists."[29] It was a vast oversimplification. When Yale and Harvard boycotted the AEA, they put pressure on those who had joined. By training, by the academic positions they held, and by the nature of the research they were doing, Hadley, Taussig, and Laughlin were prepared for positions in the vanguard of professionalization. The rapid evolution of higher education toward almost exclusive responsibility for specialized research and advanced training of experts in various fields placed a premium on the skills and knowledge such men possessed. Their absence from an organization that claimed to represent the discipline of economics called the whole movement into question. When responsible academics refused to join a professional society because of what it advocated, they pointed up an issue that would have to be settled before the professionalization of economics was complete. The battle of the schools, culminating in the formation of the AEA, posed a serious question for all economists: what sort of advocacy, within what limits, was compatible with the professional social scientist's role?

29. Adams to "My Dear Mother," 21 September 1885, Adams MSS.

4   *Patterns of Professionalism*

In the months following the formation of the AEA, debate focused more sharply than ever on what it meant to be an economist. To a degree the exploration of the role followed familiar patterns. Debate over doctrine continued to be couched in terms of what was considered orthodox and what was innovative or revolutionary. But there were also new ingredients in the discussion, novel ways of behaving, emerging expectations and institutions that changed the nature of an economist's activity and altered his patterns of communication both with other economists and with the public. The existence of a unique professional status had been acknowledged, partly because the traumatic birth of the AEA had called attention to it, but there were still no clear guidelines for professional activity. Especially in the academic milieu, economists experimented almost feverishly with various ways of perceiving their professional obligations and defining their prerogatives—so feverishly, in fact, that their behavior often seemed contradictory. All this testing and trying took place against a background of acute social unrest that challenged conventional values throughout society and profoundly affected the economists' quest for a secure and effective position.

Among representatives of the two extremes in economic thinking, patterns of confrontation remained stable. When Newcomb's *Principles of Political Economy* and Ely's *Labor Movement in America* appeared in 1886, for example, the dialogue which followed showed that little had changed in those quarters since the Ely-Newcomb controversy of 1884.

Their views on economics had changed hardly at all. The first new textbook in more than a decade, Newcomb's volume was largely a reiteration of the consensus reached by laissez-faire economists at mid-century. Universal law, beneficent self-interest, and the negative state remained conceptually intact. In chapters on wealth, production, consumption, price, value, rent, taxation, and money, all the conventional topics received their standard treatment, but there were no chapters on the conditions of labor in industrial society, the increase in poverty, or the possible socialization of welfare even to hint that Newcomb shared the humanitarian concerns of new school economists. All those philanthropic problems were relegated to sociology or morals.[1]

As if to inflame his critics, Newcomb gave a vivid example of the distinction between disciplines: Given a laborer who works hard all day and then squanders his pay on hard liquor every night, the sociologist studies the man's heredity, his childhood experiences, his companions, and the effect of exhausting work on his morale. The moralist seizes upon the evil effects of the drinking habit on the man and his family, trying to persuade the sinner to stop drinking. But if the economist knows his proper business, Newcomb concluded, he simply "looks at the pile of earth thrown up by the man's shovel, shows that love of strong drink was one of the moving forces that inspired him, and reckons how much less work would have been done if he had not expected the tavern to be open that night." Economics was simply a science of wealth as it had always properly been, and the economist was obligated merely to predict what would happen under certain economic circumstances, not to reform anything or anyone.[2]

Newcomb's outraged critics descended. Though they actually differed with him on ideological grounds, they supported their disagreement by criticizing his credentials. A tactic that had been foreshadowed in the earlier Ely-Newcomb clash was perfected. Taking advantage of his access to the *Dial*, Ely had Newcomb publicly dismissed as a rank amateur. It was "not a

1. Simon Newcomb, *Principles of Political Economy* [1886], Reprints of Economic Classics (New York, 1966), pp. iii, 4, 31-40.
2. Ibid., pp. 11-13.

little noteworthy," Ely's friend Shaw wrote, "that there should have come forth from the naval observatory at Washington the most ambitious treatise on the *Principles of Political Economy*" to appear in recent years. It was almost as though an "astronomical mathematician and a maker of nautical almanacs" had rushed into print before his manufactured credentials were completely invalidated by the advance of science. With cutting sarcasm, Shaw showed how the organization of chapters in Newcomb's economics text exactly paralleled the arrangement of his earlier book on astronomy. Newcomb might believe he was a universal genius, Shaw concluded, but "in matters of social organization, his astronomical bias is vitiating."[3]

Another historical school critic dealt with Newcomb on similar guild terms. In a journal published by the American Association for the Advancement of Science, an organization where Newcomb's standing as a scientist should have been almost impervious to slur, Edmund James protested the "absurd notion" that a man who was an expert in one field should automatically be considered competent in another. "If a man who had given the best years of his life to political economy should wander over into the field of astronomy and physics 'to bring order into the reigning confusion,' " James suggested, "Professor Newcomb would be just the man to administer a severe and deserved castigation. The offense is none the less serious because in this case we have a great and successful astronomer and physicist wandering over into the economic field and undertaking to set things to rights." James was able to support his criticism by pointing to recent works in economic theory which Newcomb had apparently overlooked, and that charge was corroborated by an otherwise friendly review in the *Nation*. Obviously the *Nation* did not share James's conclusion: that Newcomb was guilty of fomenting social unrest by promulgating "a kind of political economy which, regarding the case as

3. Ely to Shaw, 19 November 1885, quoted in Hugh Hawkins, *Pioneer: A History of the Johns Hopkins University, 1874-1889* (Ithaca, N.Y., 1960), pp. 181-82; Albert Shaw, "Recent Economic Works," *Dial* 6 (December 1885):210-13.

closed in favor of the existing order in its present form, has done and is doing more to promote the most dangerous type of communistic and socialistic spirit and doctrine than all the vaporings of so-called professorial socialism of the last generation."[4]

James might have been predicting the tone of conservative criticism when Ely's *Labor Movement* appeared a little later in 1886. The book was a product of Ely's social philosophy. As in earlier works, he romanticized labor. He attributed motives to labor organizations that were far more altruistic than objective evidence supported. Instead of defending unions and strikes as labor's legitimate weapons in an unequal conflict with employers or praising the laborer's attempt to escape permanent working-class status, Ely traced the motivation of the labor movement to Christianity. Laborers organized as much for the good of mankind as for their own benefit, he argued. In his eyes struggling workers were the unconscious apostles of Christian brotherhood. Frightened upper-class conservatives and industrialists whose interests were threatened by labor's increasing resort to forceful measures looked upon Ely as a disciple of the devil.[5]

At a time when the phenomenal growth of the Knights of Labor caused unprecedented alarm among businessmen, Ely eulogized the Knights. His sympathies were so involved that his research lacked sophistication and objectivity. When he defined the Knights' goals and judged their tactics, he relied uncritically on letters from close friends in the organization. He admonished employers to be open and Christian in their dealings with the Knights; yet he defended the Knights' secrecy. If violence came, Ely concluded, it would be the result of capitalist greed and intransigence, not labor's understandable determination to improve working conditions through collective action. The funda-

    4. Edmund J. James, "Newcomb's Political Economy," *Science* 6 (27 November 1885):470-71; "Newcomb's Political Economy," *Nation* 42 (14 January 1886):38-39.
    5. Richard T. Ely. *Labor Movement in America* (New York, 1886), pp. 1-6.

mental theoretical question, whether wages could in fact be raised through strikes, Ely avoided entirely.[6]

The book demonstrated Ely's conception of appropriate professional behavior. One of the earliest and most comprehensive treatments of labor organization, it appeared at precisely the right moment to provide information and a point of view for many Americans who were confused by the drastic change in labor-management relations during the 1880s. The book explained socialism at a simple level, distinguishing between evolutionary or peaceful socialism, which sought gradual reforms that Ely approved, and revolutionary socialism, whose violence he condemned.[7]

Ely's volume on labor also broke precedent in the force of its advocacy. Instead of addressing himself to economists Ely dedicated his book to the working class. He made no effort to conceal his warm sympathy with the labor movement. Picturing himself as labor's adviser, he adopted the paternalistic approach that working men might have encountered in the institutional churches. He cautioned them against strong drink, for it might undermine the sympathy of the better sort of people; against "demagoguery, especially political partyism"; against envy and "every thought of leveling down"; against impatience and violence. He also encouraged labor to resist injustice and demand a fair share of the product of their labor. "If your demands are right," Ely promised, "if they are reasonable, then you will win and hold your gain. The world will listen even to socialism, if properly presented."[8]

If the world would listen, laissez-faire economists would not. In no time Newcomb attacked Ely in the *Nation*. "Dr. Ely seems to us to be seriously out of place in a university chair," he wrote. "His worst defect is an intensity of bias, and a

6. Ibid., pp. 76-91; Benjamin G. Rader, *The Academic Mind and Reform: The Influence of Richard T. Ely in American Life* (Lexington, Ky., 1966), pp. 68-69, 78-79; Nicholas Murray Butler, "Ely's Labor Movement in America," *Science* 8 (15 October 1886):353-55.

7. Ely, *Labor Movement*, pp. 110-18, 277, 94.

8. Ibid., pp. v-xiii.

bitterness toward all classes of society except one, to which it would be hard to find a parallel elsewhere than in the ravings of an Anarchist or the dreams of a Socialist." Even as the climax of a bitter personal feud, Newcomb's words were strong. As professional criticism, they exceeded emerging standards of propriety which the Ely-Newcomb debacle helped to shape.[9]

In 1886, besides the Haymarket affair, there were more strikes and other clashes between laborers, capitalists, and police than in the entire previous history of the United States. It was no time to make charges of anarchism or socialism lightly. Such criticism seemed to hold economists partly responsible for cataclysmic events that threatened public order, alienated classes, endangered life, and destroyed property. Thus the extremism of Ely and Newcomb created a crisis situation. For the moment it forced economists to judge individual colleagues by the impact of their actions on the entire profession. The peculiar urgency of the situation accelerated efforts to arrive at some consensus on the rights, duties, immunities, and responsibilities of social scientists in American society.

Eventually these deliberations defined professionalism in a way that stripped both Newcomb and Ely of their former influence. At first, however, some of the more advanced professional economists reacted to the second phase of the Ely-Newcomb controversy with sympathy for Ely. Their own positions on economic questions seemed to make little difference. What mattered was the immediate effect of a dangerous attack upon the security of a fellow professional.

Taussig provides the best example of this kind of reaction. Though he had criticized Ely's reforming tendencies many times, his support went to Ely, not Newcomb. Three days after the disastrous review appeared, Taussig wrote to Ely requesting membership in the AEA. The reason he gave was a personal one.

9. Simon Newcomb, "Dr. Ely on the Labor Movement," *Nation* 43 (7 October 1886):293-94. For Newcomb's authorship see Ely to John Bates Clark, 14 October 1903, Ely MSS. For Newcomb's analysis of the impact the incident had on his career, see Newcomb to Peirce, 3 January 1894, Newcomb MSS, quoted in Hawkins, *Pioneer,* p. 185.

"It is now settled," he explained, "that I am to adopt a scholar's life, and to remain in Cambridge as a teacher of political economy." But the timing of the move suggests that Taussig was motivated as much by professional considerations. "I saw with much regret the savage attack on you in the *Nation* this week," he told Ely. "One may suspect the source from which it comes. Its tone is certainly quite unjustifiable."[10] Taussig chose to support Ely not because he condoned his advocacy but because he considered Ely—for all his pro-labor sentiments—more professional in training and aspirations than Newcomb. If Ely was unable to publish controversial views without being subjected to irresponsible charges from within the profession, all economists would suffer. Nothing explains the timing cf Taussig's decision to join the AEA better than his determination to take a stand against such coercion.

Economists from varied points on the ideological and professional spectrums followed suit. As president of the University of Wisconsin and promoter of social sciences there, John Bascom had discarded his mid-century devotion to laissez-faire for a more interventionist social philosophy. In another year his sympathy for labor would lead to his resignation from Wisconsin under pressure from hostile business interests, but at the moment he encouraged Ely to continue his reform advocacy. "The censure of the *Nation* goes but a very little way with me," Bascom told Ely. "I believe there is a very important work to be done on this labor question, and every man who enters the contest on the right side, well equipped to sustain the better reason, has my earnest sympathy." Edmund James assured Ely that "a blow from that source should be considered a compliment."[11]

The weaknesses in Ely's scholarship made it extremely difficult for some economists to defend him, especially if his advocacy conflicted with their own opinions. Franklin Henry Giddings, a New England-born minister's son who advanced from

10. Taussig to Ely, 10 October 1886, Ely MSS.
11. Bascom to Ely, 14 October 1886; James to Ely, 15 October 1886, Ely MSS.

amateur status as a writer for the *Springfield Republican* through an active interest in economics in the 1880s to become the first American full professor of sociology, was always a defender though not a fanatic supporter of laissez-faire. In 1886 he edited a journal designed to expand public knowledge of the labor question. Reacting to *The Labor Movement*, Giddings told Ely: "It has interested me greatly, and has removed some misconceptions that I had held concerning the drift of your teaching. I had formed the impression, which seems to be general, that you had strong socialistic leanings, but your book has set me right." Giddings's comment to his friend John Bates Clark probably reflected his appraisal of Ely's scholarship more accurately. Amidst the "wash and swash and fog of recent historical economics," Giddings found Clark's *Philosophy of Wealth* a delightful change. "There are a dozen pages in one of your chapters that are worth more than all the padded books and monographs that Ely has produced put together."[12]

At Yale a professional economist condemned Ely's advocacy totally. Over Ely's protests, Seligman sent *The Labor Movement* for review to Henry Farnam, one of the younger traditionalists who had not joined the AEA. Professional scruples like Taussig's did not deter the junior colleague of William Graham Sumner. Farnam's review scourged Ely for bias, faulty research, foolish gullibility, and outrageous partisanship. In Farnam's view, crediting labor organizations with advancing Christian brotherhood even though they beat or intimidated workers who refused to join, practiced arson against employers, and condoned the murder of police was incomprehensible as professional behavior. Ely had condemned as class legislation laws that were intended to preserve order and whitewashed union activities; in so doing, he had further inflamed an already critical situation, despite his professed abhorrence of violence.

Farnam's extreme disapproval of Ely's position led him to support Newcomb's charge of socialism. "Dr. Ely says—and he

---

12. Giddings to Ely, 2 November 1886, Ely MSS; Giddings to Clark, 24 October 1886, John Bates Clark MSS, Columbia University Special Collections.

certainly ought to know—that he is no socialist," Farnam wrote. "Yet much that he says sounds so much like what a good many of the socialists say, that he ought hardly to complain, if people occasionally mistake him for one. If a man should march in a socialist procession, bearing a red flag with the inscription 'I am no socialist,' he could hardly pick a quarrel with the newspapers for reporting him a socialist. Neither should Dr. Ely complain, if the color he gives to many statements leads people to call him a socialist in spite of his emphatic protests to the contrary." Farnam's criticism showed how uneasy conservative economists were with Ely as their most publicized professional colleague.[13]

Once more Ely was reduced to fearing for his academic life. When he learned that the furor over his book had revived the pressure on Gilman to fire him, Ely turned for help to influential friends. No matter how popular his works were with labor leaders and Christian socialists, he realized that the support of leading economists had become vital to his academic security. He asked John Bates Clark, whose *Philosophy of Wealth* had recently appeared and commanded excellent reviews, "to take more than usual pains just at the present time to strengthen me in public opinion . . . if you feel that I am doing a good work and would dislike to see the instruction in economics in J. H. U. given to a man like Newcomb." Ely fully realized the damage that charges of socialism might do him, but he hoped to convince even conservatives that they also stood to lose influence and the security that free scholarship required if liberals were restrained with their connivance. "I should like to see something," Ely ventured, "perhaps an editorial on honorable methods of criticizing in economics."[14]

13. Ely to Seligman, 25 October 1886, Seligman MSS; Henry Farnam, "Review of Richard T. Ely, The Labor Movement in America," *Political Science Quarterly* 1 (December 1886):683-87; Farnam to Munroe Smith, 14 November 1886, *Political Science Quarterly* MSS, Columbia University Special Collections.

14. John Bates Clark, *The Philosophy of Wealth* (Boston, 1886); Henry Carter Adams, "Review of Clark's Philosophy of Wealth," *Political Science Quarterly* 1 (December 1886):687-90; Ely to Clark, 1 December 1886, Clark MSS. Hugh Hawkins (*Pioneer*, p. 184) concludes that Ely believed "the danger was past" after Shaw's and Abbott's reviews and H. B. Adam's earlier favorable recommendation to Gilman. Hawkins cites a letter from Ely to Shaw written on the same date as the letter to

Ely's plea for the development of a professional consensus on freedom of advocacy fitted into a more general reassessment of the economist's role that had been maturing among thoughtful professionals throughout the year. Since 1885 the major concern of an increasingly self-conscious group had centered on the advocacy institutionalized in the platform of the AEA. Shortly after the organizational meeting, responsible members of both schools had started searching for a common ground on substantive and procedural questions. Henry Carter Adams was the focus of overtures from the laissez-faire side. Adams was in the process of evolving a conception of the role of the state in industrial society which lodged in government the responsibility for raising the level of competition to eliminate exploitative practices. At one point Hadley confessed to Adams that he too was quite willing to admit privately that state action was indispensable in certain circumstances. Yet he feared that many people, economists included, could turn a valid generalization about the role of the state into a dangerous practical maxim. "The statement of principles of the A. E. A. may do a great deal of harm in precisely that way," he added. "The fact that the principles are true only makes the danger of misinterpretations more serious."[15]

Conservative economists estimated the impact of advocacy by the reputations of the economists involved. "It makes a great deal of difference whether the authorized interpreters are you and Walker and Richmond Smith on the one hand," Hadley told Adams, "or James and Ely on the other." As long as Ely remained prominent in the AEA, his version of the efficacy of state action would represent the whole profession. "I am seriously desirous of coming to an understanding," Hadley hinted, "but I was afraid, and am still afraid, of getting into a position which would do practical harm to me and to others, where I should seem to be made an advocate of measures and

Clark. At least on 1 December 1886, Ely wanted Clark to believe that he was still in danger at Johns Hopkins.
15. Hadley to Adams, 1 May 1886, Adams MSS.

maxims which I cannot but regard as dangerous in the extreme." Adams's more cautious demeanor and sounder scholarship appealed to Taussig too. Like Hadley, he perceived Adams as a promising alternative on the revisionist side and tried to cultivate agreement in an area where Adams differed decisively from Ely. "We must look to the Germans for suggestions," Taussig remarked to Adams, "but must work out our own salvation in our own way,—a fact which some of our friends are apt to overlook."[16]

Finally Ely's problems brought Adams and John Bates Clark to an understanding. Both men were critical of the injustice that an unregulated capitalist industrial system produced. Yet as they began to achieve scholarly recognition both also began equating moderateness of opinion with objectivity, and objectivity with scholarly worth. Because of the insecurity of his position at Cornell, Adams in particular had reason to be spelling out his standards. From the beginning of his career he had identified wealthy industrialists and the bureaucrats who served them as the greatest potential threat to free scholarship. "Plutocracy is in the saddle and is bound to unhorse everybody who does not ride behind," he told Clark. Yet Adams blamed Ely's troubles mostly on Ely's own limitations. "To speak frankly and between ourselves," Adams added, "I think it is a lack of scholarly analysis, and a tendency to depend too much on exhortation, that stands in the way of Ely's promotion [to the rank of associate professor at Hopkins] rather than his views on social questions."[17]

Clark's judgment was even more critical. "I agree with your views as to our friend Dr. Ely," he replied. "He was last year writing rapidly for money (a great deal of it) and the result was not favorable in several respects." A scholar simply had to consider the consequences of his actions. "When personal attacks are impending we do not need to precipitate them," Clark concluded. "That would be the opposite of tactful. We

16. Ibid.; Taussig to Adams, 4 July 1886, Adams MSS.
17. Adams to Clark, 16 December 1886, Adams MSS.

can speak our minds on scientific questions without giving excuse for personal thrusts." Simply because Ely's reputation was a matter of general concern, Clark hoped to find "some way to put New School Economics as represented by Dr. Ely in a right light."[18]

What started as a tentative confidential accommodation between a few economists in the vanguard of professionalization developed into a public analysis of the potential for broader agreement among professional economists. Between March and July 1886 selected spokesmen of traditional and revisionist views in economics conducted a debate through a series of articles in *Science,* the journal of the respected American Association for the Advancement of Science (AAAS). The *Science* "Economic Discussion" has been considered the high point of conflict between the old and new schools. Actually the exchange served a dual purpose. It clarified the differences between the two schools, but it also identified some issues on which agreement could be reached. The *Science* debate prompted some of the same people who were concerned about Ely's image to think seriously about the image of the profession as a whole. Through the intemperance of some of the rhetoric it produced, the debate dramatized the danger of public controversy and reemphasized the desirability of developing a unified position wherever the potential for community existed. Thus it was not only the climax of opposition between the old and new schools but a prologue to compromise as well.

How *Science* happened to be the vehicle for a symposium of such critical importance to economists is not quite clear. The journal was founded in 1883 by Alexander Graham Bell and Gardiner Hubbard to report on developments in American science. Both Daniel Coit Gilman and Newcomb held places on the board of directors. At first the editorial policy was directed toward popularization. When success proved elusive the founders appointed a new publisher, Charles L. Condit, and

18. Clark to Adams, 10, 29 December 1886, Adams MSS.

experimented with various other emphases, trying to find a combination of offerings which would attract a stable clientele in the scientific community and pay the bills. Condit was an aggressive, petulant, combative sort of man who had gained experience in journalism on the staff of the *Nation*. His ambition, he reported, was to "give this country a grand journal representing not like 'The Nation' one man's power and the very unequal results of one man's thinking, but a broad, comprehensive and developing body of scientific opinion." Condit's zeal soon brought him into bitter conflict with the editors of *Science*. When his judgment was questioned by Bell and Hubbard, he relied for protection on a close relationship with Newcomb. Condit was well aware of Newcomb's interest in economics.[19]

When economists began making vigorous claims to scientific status in the early 1880s, they lacked the rudiments of organization and publication. Briefly the AAAS responded with a somewhat condescending inclination to include the social sciences in its operation. A separate section for economics and statistics was established, and space in the journal was allocated. In 1884, seeking scientific sanction for his heretical views, Ely asked Charles Condit to read his paper on changes in political economy. Condit found Ely's analysis naive and his economic opinions objectionably far from conventional business lore, but the paper gave the enterprising journalist an idea. In February 1886, one of the editors of *Science*—probably Condit—took five members of the AEA Council, including a reluctant Henry Carter Adams, to a fancy lunch at Delmonico's and sought their approval for his plan "to get up a public discussion" of economics in *Science*.[20]

At first the plan included only new school economists, but

19. "To the Patrons of 'Science,' " April 1884; "To the Directors of the Science Company," 13 February 1885; G. G. Hubbard to the Directors, 8 January 1886; Condit to Newcomb, 9, 14 January 1886, Simon Newcomb MSS, Box 38, Manuscript Division, Library of Congress; "The American Association Meeting at Philadelphia," *Science* 4 (July-December 1884):189-90.

20. Condit to Ely, [?] November 1884, Ely MSS; Adams to "My Dear Mother," 1 March 1886, Adams MSS.

eventually the list was expanded to include the laissez-faire side. The result was a colloquium between the most prominent representatives of major institutions: Hadley of Yale, Taussig of Harvard, James of Pennsylvania, Seligman and Mayo-Smith of Columbia, Ely and Newcomb of Hopkins, and Adams, who then taught at both the University of Michigan and Cornell. Thus a better cross section of economists participated in this neutral forum than in the debates at the founding of the AEA, and the range of topics was considerably wider. Two preliminary discussions—one on the role of government in creating and enforcing contracts and another on the silver question—whetted the economic appetites of regular *Science* readers. In the main series participants addressed themselves to questions sharpened by two years of lively controversy: the nature of economics, the role of the state in economic affairs, and the character of the economist's mission.[21]

As the debate progressed, changes in the makeup of the economic community became evident. Spokesmen for the extreme reformist and conservative positions persisted, but their voices no longer drowned out more moderate views. Several years of professional activity in the field had rooted out some oversimplifications, raised the intellectual level of the argument, and tempered the quality of criticism that was considered appropriate for professional discourse.

One of the major changes was the way in which the new school was defined. At the extremes there were no significant concessions. Ely continued to defend approximately the same position he had advanced when he first outlined the characteristics of the two schools in 1884. As he perceived it, the uniqueness of the new school lay in the determination of its adherents to use economics as a basis for social reform. It was no longer necessary for economic thinking to be governed by assumptions that doomed most men to poverty. If the unbreakable imperatives of a preindustrial system had made an equitable distri-

21. *Science* 7 (January-June 1886):221-28, 265-71, 375-82, 485-91, 529-33, 538-42; 8 (July-December 1886):3-6, 14-19, 25-26, 46-48, 81-87, 103-5.

bution of wealth and comfort impossible, Ely argued, no such a priori arrangements rationalized injustice any longer. Machines and new sources of power made it possible to transcend the grim Malthusian realities which may have existed in primitive societies. People could establish goals designed to place the welfare of the whole people above the customary privilege of any dominant class and then consciously direct society's various enterprises toward the achievement of those goals. Because advances in the economic system made a new social ethic possible, the obligation of designing a more humane system of economic relationships fell heavily on economists. Ely argued that the responsibility for making those ethical judgments and articulating "what ought to be" defined the role of the new school economist.[22]

Though Ely's social philosophy remained the same, he recognized the vulnerability of the ethical and scientific relativism that formed the basis for his conception of the new economics. Attacks on his moral and scholarly soundness had made him sensitive to the need for providing new justifications when he scoffed at old certainties. Unsure of the most effective way to defend the new ethical role, Ely moved on a number of fronts. Both the laissez-faire system he considered so inequitable and the economists who still defended it found their most telling rationalizations in an argument from natural law. To undermine that static concept and to support his own evolutionary relativism, Ely argued that the entire structure of economics was relative. The discipline could be anything or nothing, depending on what economists wanted to make it. Economic theories had always changed with the times. Economists determined their priorities by looking to the problems of the society in which they lived. In view of the fact that the economic questions of the day had inescapable ethical overtones, progressive economists in the 1880s had responded by orienting their investigations toward ethical questions. In so doing, they had reshaped

22. Richard T. Ely, "Ethics and Economics," *Science* 7 (11 June 1886): 529-33; Ely, "The Economic Discussion in Science," ibid., 8 (2 July 1886):4-6.

economics in a legitimate and entirely conventional manner.[23]

At the time of the *Science* debate, Ely was only beginning to realize the dilemma that historical economists had created by rejecting natural law. Even so, he sensed the need for some new source of authority and began experimenting with alternatives. Not surprisingly, one of his arguments was moral. If capitalists who profited enormously from an unjust system were excluded, he contended, a consensus for a new, humane social ethic had already developed among fair-minded people. In adopting it, ethical economists only followed the dictates of enlightened opinion. To guard against seeming to concede that economists should regularly draw their authority from the opinions of others, Ely also presented a rudimentary argument for authority based on professional competence. His sense of the problem was so limited that he failed to grapple with the difficult task of showing how evidence of an economist's analytical ability—the outgrowth of time and experience in studying economic conditions—could be converted into proof of his competence to make judgments on ethical questions, where he might be influenced by personal values and social attitudes that had nothing to do with economics. Even so, by shifting the basis for professional authority from qualities inherent in the science itself to the special habits of the practitioner, Ely confronted questions that many other economists had yet to recognize.[24]

In 1884, when new school economists had first challenged the assumptions of the prevailing economic system, the initial reaction of old school economists had been to exalt the principles of laissez-faire to a system of absolute certainties. Newcomb's thinking had progressed no further by 1886. Once more his answer to Ely defended the entire system of Newtonian conceptions that ethical economists attacked. Instead of ridiculing Ely's moral elitism or exposing his ethical relativism, Newcomb conjured the horrors of a science that produced no reliable generalizations. Without exact relations between cause

23. Ibid.
24. Ely, "Ethics and Economics," p. 530; Ely, "Economic Discussion," p. 6.

and effect to form a basis for prediction, he argued, "it is no use to talk about questions of economic policy, and the safest course is to frown upon all social movements as productive of results which no man can foresee, and which are as likely to do harm as good."[25]

If Ely and Newcomb had learned nothing since 1884, economists between the two extremes were prepared to compromise. Eager to play down the ethical side of new school economics, Seligman defined the uniqueness of the new school by emphasizing the importance of its historical perspective. He reaffirmed the new school's belief in an evolutionary, nondogmatic economics, but he avoided making exaggerated claims for the superiority of their views. Instead of evaluating the economic institutions of a society by measuring them against a set of absolute moral standards, Seligman explained, new school economists simply proposed relating a country's economic system to its historical development. Instead of damning earlier economic systems as unjust and evil, historical economists merely placed them on an evolutionary continuum.[26]

Seligman's historical emphasis formed the basis for a less controversial view of the economist's mission. Whereas Ely believed that economists could devise a just economic system and show how to put it into operation in society, Seligman assumed that the economic theories of an age did not precede and shape its systems of production and distribution but rather followed and rationalized what the historical development of industry brought into being. The rudiments of his economic interpretation of history were already apparent. "It is given to no man to be original," he wrote; "every one is a product of his times, of the *zeitgeist*, and the ideas of the period are unconsciously reflected in the individual." On that basis earlier economists, even devout believers in laissez-faire, had been neither

25. Simon Newcomb, "Aspects of the Economic Discussion," *Science* 7 (18 June 1886):538-43; Newcomb, "Can Economists Agree upon the Basis of Their Teaching?" ibid., 8 (9 July 1886):25-26.
26. E. R. A. Seligman, "Changes in the Tenets of Political Economy with Time," *Science* 7 (23 April 1886):375-82.

sinister conspirators with greedy capitalists nor their unwitting dupes. They had simply looked at the social problems created by rapid industrial expansion, discerned the inadequacies of mercantile theories developed at an earlier stage, and reacted, perhaps too zealously, by trying to envision an economic system more suited to the needs of modernization. Though Seligman dealt more harshly with economists like Malthus and Ricardo, who had been able to justify wretched conditions for most of mankind, he defined economics as a continuous, cooperative venture for men of learning, not a battleground for contending schools. Like other schools before it, he admitted, the new school was a product of its times, not a sudden revelation.[27]

As Seligman described it, the distinguishing characteristic of new school economics was its interest in the condition of labor. Once more he was able to make the difference seem historical, not moral. Laissez-faire economists opposed measures designed to alleviate unbearable working conditions because they were still attuned to the conditions of early industrialization. They concentrated on the problems involved in increasing production and failed to realize that the key historical element in the economic system of the Gilded Age was a huge class of workers who depended for survival almost entirely on forces beyond their individual control. "The paramount question of political economy to-day is the question of distribution," Seligman explained, "and in it the social problem (the question of labor, of the laborer),—how, consistently with a healthy development on the lines of moderate progress, social reform may be accomplished; how and in what degree the chasm between the 'haves' and the 'have-nots' may be bridged over; how and in what degree private initiative and governmental action may strive, separately or conjointly, to lessen the tension of industrial existence, to render the life of the largest social class indeed

27. Ibid. See also E. R. A. Seligman, "Review of Henry Sidgwick's The Scope and Method of Economic Science," *Political Science Quarterly* 1 (March 1886):143-45, for an even more direct rejection of the extremism of early proponents of ethical economics.

worth living." In the spring of 1886 many people reacted to the social question in anger and fear. By contrast, Seligman accepted organized labor as a permanent fixture of industrial society, responded compassionately as an individual, and urged economists to recognize their obligation to find a solution to labor's pressing problems somewhere between "quiescent conservatism" and "the vagaries of radicalism."[28]

By cutting the tie between historical method and ethical judgment, Seligman provided a promising rationale for agreement between historical economists in both schools. Taussig made a similar effort to identify a moderate position in his exchange with James on the role of the state. James prepared the ground by advocating extensive state action. Expanding the role of government in economic affairs had been his single most important objective as a new school economist. His abortive attempt to organize economists for that purpose had drawn fire from conservatives, but in 1886 his study of the gas works in Philadelphia persuaded the city fathers to retain public ownership in the face of determined pressure from private interests who sought the lucrative franchise. Flushed with success, James took a vehement stand in favor of government ownership of all natural monopolies. When society reached an advanced stage of development, he argued, certain vital economic functions could be performed by the state alone. Individual enterprise in utilities, transportation, and the management of natural resources was bound to sacrifice community interests to the profit motive. Certain other functions were too distasteful or demanding to attract individual investment at any but exploitive cost. Like Ely, James divided economists into two distinct groups on the question of state action and insisted that those who presumed in favor of laissez-faire were the agents of vested interest.[29]

28. Seligman, "Changes," p. 382.

29. Edmund J. James, "Relation of the Modern Municipality to the Gas Supply," *Publications of the AEA* 1 (1886):80-122; James, "The State as an Economic Factor, Part 1," *Science* 7 (28 May 1886):485-88; Sidney Fine, *Laissez Faire and the General-Welfare State,* paperback ed. (Ann Arbor, Mich., 1964), pp. 225-27.

In his response, Taussig tried to identify James as an extremist and himself with a moderate, historical approach. James had
argued that every advance in the level of a people's economy
was accompanied by an increase in the economic activity of the
state. Taussig showed that more increase in production had
occurred in the nineteenth century, when the prevailing mood
opposed state action, than in the seventeenth and eighteenth
centuries, when the state had been expected to foster and
supervise economic activity. Though Taussig had concluded
from his own research that interests other than the smooth flow
of trade were usually served when governments imposed tariffs,
he ignored all the inducements that national governments had
offered in the nineteenth century to encourage the expansion of
industry.

In some ways Taussig's argument was only a restatement of
traditional views. At times he relied on ultra-laissez-faire rhetoric to define the function of the state as a question economics
simply should not try to answer. But his main thrust was to
establish an alternative to extreme old and new school positions. Taussig was ready to grant the propriety, even the necessity of state ownership under certain conditions, but he branded
a presumption in favor of state interference as dangerous as a
laissez-faire bias against it. "If economists of the old school
belittled the importance of the state," he concluded, "those of
the new school are in danger of succumbing to a temptation to
exaggerate it."[30]

The question of advocacy was most prominent in the final
phase of the *Science* debate, a dialogue between Adams and
Hadley on the connection between economics and policy. Their
exchange further softened the polarity between old and new
school economists. Adams was the catalyst. He had doubted the
wisdom of a public debate from the start and agreed only
reluctantly to contribute a minor paper on property. But the
events of 1886, including the increased bitterness of the Ely-

---

30. Frank W. Taussig, "The State as an Economic Factor, Part 2," *Science* 7 (28
May 1886):488-90.

Newcomb controversy, Adams's own professional insecurity, unprecedented labor violence, and vicious capitalist retaliation, caused him to reconsider. For the first time in his career he placed professional considerations clearly foremost. As an antidote for Ely's dangerous insistence on a union between ethics and economics, Adams proposed what he thought might be a workable compromise: a safer and less controversial liaison between economics and jurisprudence.[31]

Giving up the right to make ethical judgments was a significant reversal for Adams. The tie between ethics and economics had drawn him to the discipline in the first place. He had become an economist instead of a minister because economics seemed to offer more hope of reconstructing society to provide equity for all classes. But he had always been skeptical of the efficacy of state action, critical of the German statist model, and more cautious than Ely in claiming moral authority for economists. As the AEA was being planned, Adams had attempted to restrain Ely's idealism. When the *Science* discussion drew Ely into another dangerously exposed position, Adams again tried to moderate his colleague's influence. Both men agreed that the nature of economics and the role of the economist, not method or the role of the state, were the fundamental issues dividing professional economists.

By the summer of 1886, however, Adams drew the conclusion that his own experience taught. Professional economists were not going to be permitted to make ethical judgments that challenged basic values or threatened entrenched interests. To avoid catastrophe for his emerging profession, Adams proposed giving up any claim to moral authority. Hoping to devise a more defensible mission and yet maintain influence, he outlined an advisory role for specialists in economic policy. Economists would limit their public advocacy; but in accord with what Adams argued was a natural link between economics and jurispru-

31. Henry C. Adams, "Another View of Economic Laws and Methods," *Science* 8 (30 July 1886):103; "Comment and Criticism," ibid., (23 April 1886):361. A full discussion of Adams's troubles at Cornell and Michigan in the mid-1880s follows in Chapter 6.

dence, they would continue to make policy recommendations through channels to legislators.[32]

To justify the connection between economics and jurisprudence, Adams retraced the evolution of social science. He believed that society was an organism capable of change and growth. There were no iron laws which the desires and abilities of men could not shape to their special needs. Institutions such as capitalism and competition were simply products of historical evolution, supported by tradition and vested interest but neither good nor bad in themselves. A theory of natural law had replaced divine justification as a support for science in the eighteenth century. Now the time had come for a consciously human law to take precedence over natural law. Society could do more than respond dumbly to the laws of evolution, Adams reasoned. Instead of accepting the survival of the strongest or cruelest as inevitable, society could determine an artificial environment and create a set of rules to guarantee the survival of people with qualities that were judged to be socially fittest. Guided by intelligence and purpose, humanity could establish humane social goals and control its own movement toward them.[33]

For a time Adams had hoped that economists would play a major role in determining social goals. In the *Science* debate he conceded that a more likely role for economists was to wait until social goals were determined by society as a whole. Then, where adjustments in economic institutions were needed, economists could provide the specialized knowledge required to implement them.

Adams's treatment of competition was a good example of the change in his thinking. As late as the middle of 1886 Adams had advocated a reevaluation of the entire economic system, with all its traditional Malthusian assumptions. He had hoped that every traditional practice would be forced to justify itself

32. Henry C. Adams, "Economics and Jurisprudence," *Science* 8 (2 July 1886): 15-19.
33. Ibid.

against society's chosen goals. After the Haymarket affair and subsequent events, however, Adams concluded that certain fundamental institutions were too deeply entrenched to be eliminated by anything short of revolution. Yet those key values could be altered gradually. In a laissez-faire system, for example, the entire community might favor avoiding some sharp, unethical competitive practice. But each individual's resolve to be fair would weaken when he became convinced that others would take advantage of their neighbors even if he did not. Adams was certain that people would gladly obey regulations which restrained everyone equally. "The only way in which the social purpose can influence the practice of individuals is for law to establish uniformity of action," he explained. Regulatory legislation could raise the level of permissible competition. With their expert knowledge of the economic system, economists could show government how to amend the laws.[34]

The connection between economics and jurisprudence was a rationale for compromise that some of the younger professional economists could easily accept. Richmond Mayo-Smith of Columbia was pioneering the field of statistics in an attempt to develop scientific methods for assessing the impact of various laws and customs. When the state contemplated an action, Mayo-Smith believed that economists with high technical competence could predict whether the results would be good or evil. Especially where economists were developing sophisticated methods of gathering and analyzing data, they seemed increasingly willing to concentrate on rather specific technical problems instead of making generalizations about the entire economic and social system.[35]

Even so, the advisory role that Adams defined still went beyond the limits which some conservatives could accept.

34. Ibid., pp. 15-17. Compare Adams to "Dear Mother," 10 May 1880, Adams MSS. Henry C. Adams, "Relation of the State to Industrial Action," in *Two Essays by Henry Carter Adams,* ed. Joseph Dorfman (New York, 1969), pp. 57-133.
35. Richmond Mayo-Smith, "Methods of Investigation in Political Economy," *Science* 8 (23 July 1886):86-87; Adams, "Another View of Economic Laws and Methods," pp. 103-5.

Hadley was no more comfortable with Adams's conception of economists as policy scientists than he had been with Ely's vision of himself as a moral arbiter. In fact he saw little difference between the two. Though Hadley respected Adams, he was convinced that a contrived relationship between economics and jurisprudence was "likely to lead to grave mistakes in thinking and action." Behind the link between the two processes lay the historical and scientific relativism that Hadley still rejected. The only mission he could really accept for economists was the strictly scholarly one: discovering the laws that govern economic relationships. Economists could accomplish that primary task only if they assumed rigid hypotheses and developed causal relationships without regard for local or historical variations. Hadley never denied that there were connections between economic theory and law, but putting those connections into practice was a job for legislators. "Industrial activity is limited by legal conditions; legislative activity, by economic conditions," he wrote. "The attempt to confuse the two, and to merge them in a crude science of sociology, seems for the present likely to check scientific progress, and to involve us in serious practical dangers." If economists began dabbling in policy, even at the level of implementation, the systems they helped to create would co-opt them. They would become involved in the outcome and lose the very objectivity that made their scientific work worthwhile.[36]

On substantive issues, however, the *Science* debate showed grounds for agreement even between Adams and Hadley. Throughout 1886 Adams was engaged in developing an analysis of the role of the state in industrial action. Eventually he arrived at a position that accepted the basic capitalist institutions and placed the state in a regulative role, mainly to make sure that organized labor was able to compete on roughly even terms with consolidated industry. In opposition to the well-known convictions of his mentor, Sumner, Hadley arrived at a

36. Arthur T. Hadley, "Economic Laws and Methods," *Science* 7 (16 July 1886):46-48.

similar position. Early in 1886 he rejected unregulated competition as an outmoded and immoral system that discriminated in favor of the more unscrupulous competitors. Before Adams published his justification of state regulation to raise the level of competition in industry, Hadley had condemned entirely free competition as a doctrine that favored "the unfittest rather than the fittest." Hadley still feared the results of extending government activity, but he had accepted the principle that a complex industrial economy could not be considered self-regulating. "To enjoy industrial liberty, it will be necessary to resign the claim to industrial lawlessness," he conceded; "the alternative is socialism." Either through voluntary cooperation or state initiative, Hadley and Adams agreed, laissez-faire must give way to regulation.[37]

As the *Science* debate unfolded against a background of bitter social conflict, it disclosed a potential for accommodation among moderates on both sides of the economic controversy. On substantive and methodological issues, the lines between the two schools were blurring. Among the younger professionals, some traditionalists were giving up their passionate, unswerving commitment to laissez-faire while interventionists modified their extravagant claims for the role of the state. Identification strictly according to method was impossible when deductive economists like Patten favored a positive state while Taussig, who used inductive, historical methods, envisioned a much less active role for government.

Even more important, the *Science* debate heightened awareness of the desirability of compromise. When Adams's article on jurisprudence appeared, Taussig wrote to agree—"There is nothing in it that I should dissent from"—but also to question the usefulness of further debate. "How far it is desirable to

37. Arthur T. Hadley, "How Far Have Modern Improvements in Production and Transportation Changed the Principle That Men Should Be Left Free to Make Their Own Bargains? Part 1," *Science* 7 (5 March 1886):223-25. Adams sent Hadley a copy of his paper on the role of the state in industrial action on 20 April 1886, more than a month after Hadley had published this article as part of a pair on the topic, the other written by Sumner. See Hadley to Adams, 1 May 1886, Adams MSS.

bring prominently before the public such discussions of the connection between political economy and other branches, I am not so sure," he added. "I sometimes think it more important to insist on simple fundamental principles, so as to get rid on the one hand of such stuff as [Arthur Latham] Perry lately gave us in the Nation, and on the other hand of such attempts at legislation as [Congressman John] Reagan's rail-road bill typifies." Hadley agreed. "You were right in thinking that the 'Science Economic Discussion' would do harm rather than good," he told Adams. "It makes a great show of differ-ence when practically no corresponding chasm exists. I have not changed my mind on the points at issue, but I have changed my mind on the desirability of saying anything about them."[38] Thinking in both groups was converging on similar patterns of professionalism.

38. Adams, "Another View," p. 103; Taussig to Adams, 4 July 1886; Hadley to Adams, 21 November 1886, Adams MSS.

5 *Compromise*

As discussions among economists progressed in 1886, it became clear that adequate bases for compromise between the schools in economics were emerging. Partly the sentiment for compromise arose from developments within the discipline. Professionalism increased and economic investigation moved toward new paradigms. Similar patterns of graduate education were appearing in leading universities, and there were signs that greater uniformity in training and experience might produce a more homogeneous view of the discipline. The advance of the science was clearing away outmoded doctrines such as the wages fund, while expanded application of flexible analytical devices such as the concept of marginalism gradually reduced the rigidity of older economic principles and helped to narrow the gap between theory and practice. As professional economists practiced full-time scholarship, their commitment to ideology decreased somewhat while careerist activity increased. Economists who had once desired wide public recognition began to wonder whether steady advancement in the profession might not be preferable. Where achievement was judged by internal, scholarly standards, scientific objectivity was the one test of merit that could be applied impartially; thus it grew in importance.

Other pressures for compromise were external. For two years prior to the *Science* debate economists had exposed their internal disagreements through noisy public controversy. In 1886, when unprecedented social divisions frightened Americans of every political persuasion, economists finally succeeded in scaring themselves. Pressed by their own vulnerability and the general tempo of events in the mid-1880s, the economists had reached a turning point. To influential leaders like Taussig and Adams, the orderly development of a desirable professional role seemed to depend on creating at least the appearance of unity.

Yet until economists who had been connected with both schools could unite in a common professional organization, the appearance of division would prevail. As the foremost ethical economist, Ely was a symbol of disunity. The move toward compromise culminated in a joint effort by representatives of both schools to terminate Ely's influence in the AEA.

In the developing profession, a number of factors which counteracted polarization had already appeared. Within a few months of each other in 1886, Columbia and Harvard launched journals, the *Political Science Quarterly* and the *Quarterly Journal of Economics,* which ended the one-sided dominance of scholarly publication outlets that Elyite new school economists had enjoyed in the *AEA Publications* and the *Johns Hopkins University Studies.* To a degree this proliferation of journals was designed to enhance the prestige of the parent universities, and those rapidly growing, highly self-conscious institutions provided a set of alternative loyalties that drew some attention away from ideological squabbles.

In the beginning each new journal had trouble enough filling its pages and making ends meet. Editors tried to avoid alienating a whole class of potential authors or subscribers. Increasingly reviews called attention to the common regard among both schools for achieving high scholarly standards. New school moderates made a special effort to recognize the contributions of laissez-faire economists who made use of inductive or historical approaches, sometimes to the consternation of those who received their favors. Laughlin, for example, was "utterly disgusted that the Pol-Science Quarterly reviewer classed his BiMetallism and Hadley's book on railroads as unconscious examples of the use of the so-called historical method." Probably rightly, Laughlin perceived such praise as a new school tactic to separate younger traditionalists from some of the methodological stereotypes that had characterized laissez-faire. Even so, such conciliatory gestures softened the lines of controversy.[1]

1. Munroe Smith, "The Domain of Political Science," *Political Science Quarterly*

Laissez-faire economists responded. When the prospectus of Columbia's *Political Science Quarterly* promised a balanced and objective treatment of all questions, Hadley was delighted. "Something of the kind has been much needed," he replied. "It is a rare piece of good fortune to have it taken up by men who have no 'isms' to forward. There is a group of younger economists who cannot accept the extreme views of the orthodox school, but who distrust yet more the socialistic tendencies at the other extreme. I hope that your quarterly will furnish them the means of making their work public without identifying themselves with any school of thought."[2]

Columbia's initiative actually contributed more than Harvard's to the spirit of compromise. Some support for the *Political Science Quarterly*'s moderate image came from the presence on its editorial board of social scientists who were interested in fields other than economics. Neither the founder of the Columbia Faculty of Political Science, John William Burgess, nor younger political scientists such as Frank Goodnow and Munroe Smith had much interest in the niceties of economic theory. As Columbia's leading economist, Seligman found the role of compromiser particularly congenial. Five years earlier, on joining the Columbia faculty, he had emphasized progress in scholarship as the most viable basis for reform. "The true aim of Economical Science today is to supplant idle vagaries and fanciful crudities with free theories which shall be generalizations in accord with the historical sequence and observed actuality of facts, and—much more important—to discuss the feasibility and means of many much needed reforms," he had written in 1882. "In other words the practical applications of true Political Economy must be clearly set forth, & the chasm which exists in vulgar prejudice between theory and practice—those two much abused words—must be bridged

1 (March 1886):1-8; Richmond Mayo-Smith, "Review of Hadley's Railroad Transportation and Laughlin's History of Bimetallism in the United States," ibid., pp. 141-43; Edward W. Bemis to Ely, 29 September 1886, Ely MSS.

2. Hadley to Munroe Smith, 17 February 1886; Ginn and Co. promotion letter to Columbia alumni, 8 April 1886, *Political Science Quarterly* MSS, Office File, Columbia University Special Collections.

over." But by 1886 Seligman insisted on historical rather than ethical judgments. Combined with initiatives from other competitors of Harvard and Hopkins, Seligman's leadership and Columbia's ambition helped to create a new balance of power in economics which provided alternatives between the two extremes.[3]

Without some overt sign of willingness on the laissez-faire side, however, compromise efforts were stymied. The necessary signal came from Charles F. Dunbar, head of economics at Harvard and well-known proponent of classical economics. In the first number of the *Quarterly Journal of Economics*, Dunbar reviewed the issues and made it clear that Harvard was ready to offer concessions. To play down conflict, he placed the old and the new in political economy on a continuum instead of in opposition. Revisionist economics was "no revolution, but a natural reaction, probably salutary, and destined to promote ultimately a rapid but still orderly development of the science, upon the lines laid down by the great masters of what is called the deductive school."[4]

Basically Dunbar went over the same ground that the younger professionals had covered in the *Science* debate: method, the substantive concepts of laissez-faire, and the ethical competence of the economist. His treatment of the method question coincided remarkably with Seligman's earlier comments. Like Seligman, Dunbar simply threw the issue out. He argued that it was entirely useless to distinguish between schools on the basis of induction and deduction. Economic proofs could be demonstrated just as well by either method, and members of both schools used both, according to the nature of the investigation at hand and the dictates of individual taste. Dunbar even conceded the new school argument that economic laws arrived at deductively applied perfectly only

3. George A. Plimpton to R. M. Smith, 6 May 1886; Seligman to Munroe Smith, 1, 16 July 1886, *Political Science Quarterly* MSS; Seligman to H. C. Adams, 30 November 1882, Adams MSS.
4. Charles F. Dunbar, "The Reaction in Political Economy," *Quarterly Journal of Economics* 1 (October 1886):1-27.

when conditions remained exactly the same as those that had been assumed in the model. He admitted the necessity of considering the variables in each individual situation when applications were made. By softening the line on deduction, Dunbar delivered traditional economists from the embarrassing extreme that Newcomb had more or less forced on them when he chose to defend laissez-faire almost entirely on grounds of method.[5] It was a feat a younger economist could not have performed nearly as well.

Giving up on the method argument freed Dunbar to maintain selective support for some of the theoretical premises of laissez-faire economics. Even here his tone was conciliatory. It was not so much that laissez-faire economists had been wrong about such tenets as competition and self-interest, he explained. They had simply failed to carry their investigations far enough. Lulled into lethargy by a science that seemed so nearly complete, they had fallen behind the times and failed to discover all the "derivative laws" that would alter the operation of great economic forces under the new circumstances of an industrialized economy. If those who revered the tenets of classical economics had fallen mistakenly into a defensive posture, however, their failure was neither a failure of the science nor a negation of the fundamental importance of competition and self-interest in the economy. In scientific reasoning economists had to assume certain determinants. Unfortunately, by arguing for totally unregulated competition and completely unbridled self-interest, a few intransigent laissez-faire supporters had driven more perceptive students to the inevitable, necessary reaction. With a more moderate, constructive outlook, old school economists could redeem themselves.[6]

Even on the role of the state Dunbar offered a compromise

5. Ibid., pp. 9-14. Actually Seligman had rejected the methodological interpretation of the dispute as early as 1883. See his "Sidgwick on Political Economy," *Index*, 16 August 1883, pp. 75-76. In 1936 Ely finally agreed, reporting that his German professors had hardly mentioned method. See Richard T. Ely, "The Founding and Early History of the American Economic Association," *American Economic Review* 26 (March 1936):145.

6. Dunbar, "Reaction," pp. 9-14.

position. He couched his explanation of the old school position in disarmingly modern, historical terms. At an earlier state of economic development people had clamored against state supervision, he argued, while in the present generation history produced a desire for state interference. The classical economists' habit of assuming an absence of restriction when reasoning about trade, or a freely competing individual when reasoning about wages and profits, had never implied that they regarded laissez-faire as a maxim. They had simply adopted a useful mode of reasoning. In practice old masters such as Smith and Malthus had in fact encouraged state interference in selected cases, while "Mill, first or last, suggested legislation as the cure for pretty nearly every evil not deemed positively incurable."

Actually Dunbar's argument was disingenuous. By taking most of his examples from the trade question instead of dealing with the critical labor issue, Dunbar skirted the area where most new school economists thought the state should interfere. He confessed that a majority of old school economists had probably acquired a strong presumption in favor of laissez-faire by studying the trade question, where the evidence in favor of noninterference seemed so clear; then he could still maintain that it was possible to "adopt the most critical points of doctrine from the English school, and yet demand an increase of the State's activity."[7]

Having apparently yielded so much, Dunbar could refuse to concede one vital point: the ethical competence of the economist. While he claimed to understand the sympathy that new economists felt toward labor and to respect their faith in Christian love as a motivating force, Dunbar resolutely opposed any "infusion of emotion into economics." No scientist was expected to harden his heart to human suffering, but no science could proceed in an orderly manner if scientists allowed their hearts to rule their heads. Economists should not be pressured by reckless advocates into avoiding conclusions—even those that recognized the inevitability of poverty—if objective investigation

7. Ibid., pp. 19-23.

led to such results. However harsh the truth might be, no true reform could be accomplished unless it was based on a thorough understanding of the way economic systems operated. The advocate, by slowing the search for truth, merely prolonged the course of hardship.

Dunbar denied any objection to reform on its own merits. If the search for truth could be kept free from the contaminating influence of ethical aspirations, he saw no reason why economic laws should not be used to alleviate human suffering. But the economist's responsibility was to discover the laws, and it was up to others to put theory into practice. Any attempt to merge science and ethics would quickly destroy the integrity of the science.[8]

As a signal of willingness to compromise on the laissez-faire side, Dunbar's message was skillfully concocted. He combined traditional principles with enough new conceptions to satisfy moderates in both schools. On some laissez-faire assumptions he actually yielded; in other instances he merely conceded points that deductive economists had already abandoned. When Dunbar finished explaining the continuities and congruities between the old and the new economics, only one irrevocable disparity remained, and it separated traditionalists only from new school economists who insisted on a union of ethics and economics. Dunbar never opposed the connection that Adams proposed between economics and jurisprudence. He never objected to economists in the role of technical experts. In return for a retreat from laissez-faire by the older and more conservative economists, he simply asked younger liberals to stop making moral judgments. From a bargain framed that way, the only economists clearly excluded were Ely and his disciples.

As pressure mounted, Ely tried to defend himself. The major point at issue was whether an economist could hold sympathies, take positions, and advocate policies that challenged the prevailing social and business ethic. One of Ely's main contributions to the *Science* debate had been a rudimentary defense of advocacy

8. Ibid., pp. 23-26.

on the same ground that others were using to deny it: the economist's professional expertise. In February 1887 Ely again insisted that academic economists had not only the right to complete freedom of advocacy but the moral obligation to use it. Criticism by influential opponents was not enough to prove reformers wrong. In the nature of things, economists would constantly be questioning conventional assumptions and opposing the cherished prerogatives of powerful interest groups. But specialized knowledge validated their opinions. "If the science of economics is not a humbug," Ely insisted, "[the economist] must know more about industrial society than others." As he moved ahead of current consensus and marked out new directions for the future, the economist would inevitably perceive society's proper course more accurately than others for the very reason that he was a specialist.[9]

Ely tried to turn the argument for scientific objectivity to his advantage by branding his opponents as partisans. Americans had trouble getting used to economists audacious enough to support reforms that business interests opposed mainly because such economists played a new social role connected with the rise of modern social science. Until some time after the Civil War, Ely explained, political economists "were not appointed, like professors of chemistry, as searchers after truth, but as advocates—chiefly of free trade or protection." Because such economists had been the lackeys of vested mercantile and industrial interests, able scholars had avoided the field. Businessmen had naturally despised their economic apologists, even as they bought and controlled them. Workers had simply realized that economists would never support their causes and considered them enemies.

But great industrial changes and an upsurge of dissatisfaction among the masses had finally generated economic questions so pressing they could not be ignored. Responding to social necessity, Ely argued, "truly scientific men" were ready to take great

9. Richard T. Ely, "Political Economy in America," *North American Review* 144 (February 1887):115.

risks. Instead of pandering to dropsical wealth, professional economists were turning to independent inquiry. The new economists had succeeded against enormous odds in challenging the myths that supported economic exploitation. While industrialists and their apologists reacted violently, public opinion was responding favorably. "People value the searcher for truth more than formerly," Ely observed triumphantly, "the mere advocate less."[10]

But the battle was not yet won. "A small clique of men" had set themselves up as guardians of economic orthodoxy and, "still maintaining that position, even now attempt to exercise a sort of terrorism over the intellect of the country." The AEA had been formed to resist an imposed orthodoxy, Ely claimed, but defenders of business interests still harassed deviants. When new economists opposed them, supporters of laissez-faire resorted to the ultimate weapon, "that never-failing refuge of incompetence and malignity, the epithet 'socialism.' " At such times, Ely suggested, economists who prized their right to seek the truth and publish their findings, no matter whose interests were affected, had to rely on their universities to resist interference, on the people to demand justice, and especially on their professional colleagues to support their claims to freedom of advocacy, even on ethical questions.[11]

The more Ely protested, the more other professional economists worried about his influence. In April 1887 several of the most prominent new school economists began making plans to unite the profession by expanding membership of the AEA to include representatives of Harvard and Yale, as well as other traditional economists who had refused to join. As a member of the AEA council, Seligman contacted other members and proposed enlarging the association to include economists of every opinion. Obviously the association could not be expanded under a platform that had been designed to exclude the advocates of laissez-faire.

10. Ibid., pp. 116-17.
11. Ibid., pp. 114, 118.

Ely's former support began to crumble. Francis Amasa Walker was perfectly willing to admit that the platform was "the real stumbling block." He believed that the content of the statement deterred some economists from joining, while others simply objected on the principle that any platform at all was contrary to freedom of inquiry. "It should never have been adopted," Walker conceded; "it should be repealed at our next meeting. . . . If my stepping down from the presidency would promote harmony and extend the usefulness of the Association, I shall cheerfully yield to any one who may be named—even Sumner."[12]

It was a dark proposal for Ely, the man who had organized the AEA to drive "men of the Sumner stamp" out of economics. The fact that Ely was under consideration for tenure at Hopkins made the situation even more precarious. Too much eagerness for compromise would reveal disunity among Ely's supposed followers at exactly the time when he needed a demonstration of support. Accordingly, he pleaded with Seligman, Clark, James, Adams, and others to move cautiously. "You are quite right in your feelings about unity of our efforts," Ely told Seligman. But victory in the effort to change economics was near. Of the important economists in major colleges and universities, only Sumner, Farnam, and Hadley of Yale, and Dunbar and Laughlin of Harvard remained outside the AEA. Taussig had joined, and the others had been invited more than once. "If we introduce discordant elements will we not endanger our existence—especially just now?" Ely asked. "When we are a year older, it will not make so much difference. But is it not best to be very conservative for the present?"[13]

At first consideration, prominent early proponents of ethical

12. Walker to Seligman, 25 April 1887, Seligman MSS. This letter is published, incorrectly dated as 24 September [1887] in Joseph Dorfman, ed., "The Seligman Correspondence, Part 1," *Political Science Quarterly* 56 (March 1941):108-10.

13. Ely to Seligman, 25 April 1887, Seligman MSS, published in part in Dorfman, ed., "The Seligman Correspondence, Part 2," *Political Science Quarterly* 56 (June 1941):281. On his own Ely was busy inviting former students and others who might support him to join. See Charles B. Spahr to Ely, 29 October 1887; Edward Atkinson to Ely, 29 April 1887, Ely MSS.

economics supported Ely. Though Clark approved of expanding the AEA, he emphatically opposed dropping the platform in 1887. "I had not anticipated so radical a move," he told Adams, "though I have from the first thought that the platform would ultimately cease to be necessary. It does a certain work by giving character to the association during its earlier years. My proposal [to Ely] was that we agree not to oppose abolition of the platform a year hence, providing the measure be not pushed this year." Though Clark wanted to soften divisive issues, he hoped to avoid letting economics slip all the way back to its former status as a cold, inhuman science of wealth. Adams assured Seligman that he had "deprecated the ways in which the Association was given birth," but he too counseled some delay before the platform was dropped. James proposed that criticisms of the unrepresentative character of the AEA could be met by making sure that every major institution had a representative on the council. All three seemed to be hoping for a diplomatic way to eliminate the association's ethical overtones and expand its membership without seeming too eager to placate laissez-faire.[14]

At the Boston meeting of the AEA in May 1887, negotiations proceeded. The possibility of change brought all sorts of interests into play. Columbia's economists kept the initiative, however, and the alignments they sought showed where real power in the profession lay. First Seligman and Mayo-Smith neutralized the elder statesmen, Walker and Wright. Later, over "beer and tobacco," a group that included Clark, Adams, James, and "Hodges of 'Science' besides the Cambridge and Boston people," met to consider a strategy for reunion. "We are getting up a conspiracy to oust R. T. E. and draw in the Harvard and Yale men," Mayo-Smith confessed to his wife. "I am taking no active part in it for I don't propose to help kick any man out of office,

14. Clark to Seligman, 25 April 1887, Seligman MSS, published in Dorfman, ed., "The Seligman Correspondence, Part 1," pp. 110-11; Clark to Adams, 4 May 1887, Adams MSS; Adams to Seligman, 27 April 1887, Seligman MSS, published in "The Seligman Correspondence, Part 2," p. 271; James to Ely, 27 April 1887, copy in Seligman MSS.

but a good many men desire a change and the way the gentle-
man has used the Association to advertise John[s] Hopkins
Univ. has aroused some criticism."[15]

Mayo-Smith was hardly as innocent as he claimed. Negotiations with the Harvard contingent—specifically Dunbar—progressed to the point where Adams, James, and Mayo-Smith,
ostensibly Ely's supporters, put a formal agreement in writing.
"I have sent your letter to Dunbar to James and told him to
choose between it and mine and I will sign either," Mayo-Smith
later told Adams. "The only difference between the two is that
I stretch out the hand a little further. My principle is when I am
doing a thing to do it so as to accomplish the desired end."
When the AEA Council voted in June to offer Dunbar a special
invitation to membership, he accepted. "I am brought to this
conclusion in an unexpected way by the letters and conversations of yourself and Professors Smith and James," Dunbar told
Adams. "Your own purpose to let nothing stand in the way of
making the Association broad enough to include all schools and
to save it from being the propaganda of any is so clear to me as
to enlist all my sympathies, and if you are of [the] opinion that
I can be of any service in advancing that which we all have at
heart in economics, I cannot properly refuse." Five years later
Dunbar was elected president of the American Economic Association and Ely was ousted.[16]

The new school platform that had symbolized Ely's influence
was eliminated before Ely was. In December 1887 an AEA
council composed of practically the same members who had
adopted the controversial principles only two years earlier approved dropping them, and the full association ratified the

15. Richmond Mayo-Smith to "My Dearest Wife," 22 May 1887, Richmond
Mayo-Smith MSS.

16. Mayo-Smith to Adams, 10 June 1887; Dunbar to Adams, 1 July 1887, Adams
MSS. Dunbar confirmed the involvement of all three when he told Adams that he
would try to "send a line each to Professor Smith and Professor James." Ely
eventually learned of the alliance between Harvard, Yale, and Columbia, but he
apparently remained ignorant of Adams's cooperation. He wrote to Adams offering
him the important secretaryship of the association in 1888 and explained, "I may tell
you in confidence about a combination of Yale, Harvard and Columbia to capture
the thing and run it." Ely to Adams, 7 December 1888, Adams MSS.

decision a year later. Members denied that the platform was dropped in response to pressure or "in deference to any coterie," but it was clearly a step designed to broaden the association's appeal and lessen the role of controversial issues in its proceedings.[17] For all Clark's emphasis on diplomacy, he still refused to make "undue overtures" to Sumner after the platform was gone. "He is a prominent man," Clark jibed, "but if he is a great man I have never done him justice. He seems to be chiefly what Prest. Walker once called him, a cantankerous man." Actually the architects of compromise were no more interested in attaching importance to Sumner than they had been in leaving Ely in charge of their image. Both men were extremists caught in a trend toward compromise. The change in the structure of the association represented a renunciation of extremes and a merging of interests from both conservative and revisionist sides, not a conservative victory.

The emerging professional standards that led to the dropping of the platform continued to undermine Ely's remaining influence. As economic issues became more controversial, his emotional advocacy was a professional liability to other professors. Between 1887 and 1892 he strengthened his religious connections by teaching at the Chautauqua summer school and writing popular tracts for Chautauqua readers. While ethical leaders continued to praise his work, economists were increasingly critical of his scholarship. Even a man of such humanitarian convictions as John Bates Clark concluded in 1888 that Ely's "only chance for attaining a high scientific standing lies in silence . . . followed by the publication of some work of a character that all will recognize as scientific." Clark was especially distressed by the political content of Ely's work. "What I wish you might manage to do," Clark wrote Adams, "is to make him more cautious as to uncertain meanings, and expressions that lead the average reader to discover a drift or tendency in a socialistic direction. . . . On most points he is really sound," Clark thought, "and it is a pity to sink himself under the odium

17. Seligman to Ely, 29 January 1888; Clark to Ely, 30 March 1889, Ely MSS.

of semi-socialism." When Ely sought reassurance, other friends agreed that he could influence "practical men" only by adopting a more conservative tone.[18]

Once more Dunbar helped to weaken Ely's ground. Shortly before his election to the presidency of the AEA in 1892, Dunbar offered a statement on the meaning of professionalism which was clearly aimed at Ely's style of advocacy. He argued that proper conduct for professional economists, especially regarding advocacy, had to be vastly more restrained than the partisan behavior of the amateurs who had once served as house protectionists or hard-money apologists in various colleges. In Dunbar's view the professional economist simply had to forgo any activity, no matter how constructive, which might interfere with his main function of reasoned, impartial, disinterested inquiry. A university teacher's business was generating raw knowledge and training unformed minds to think, not deciding controverted issues or putting on intellectual exhibition matches for cheering partisans. "On the mixed questions of legislative policy and expediency," Dunbar concluded, "it is not the province of the university to pronounce."[19]

As a spokesman for moderate conservatives, Dunbar had developed an answer for economists who based their right to advocacy on expert knowledge. Dunbar merely denied that economists had any such special ability in solving practical economic problems. He insisted that the truths that economics generated were only applicable to ideal situations set up for abstract reasoning. In the hurly-burly of actual affairs, however, history, tradition, national goals, social needs, and a dozen other factors might dictate a course that pure economics would forbid, or absolutely prohibit the remedies which economic theory demanded. Historical economists would have answered

18. Josiah Strong to Ely, 17 November 1888; George E. Vincent to Ely, 19 October 1888, Ely MSS; Clark to Adams, 13, 14 January 1888, Clark MSS; Clark to Ely, 24 January, 7 February 1888; Alexander Johnston to Ely, 28 January 1888, Ely MSS.
19. Charles F. Dunbar, "The Academic Study of Political Economy," *Quarterly Journal of Economics* 5 (July 1891):397-411.

that reliance on empirical, inductive techniques prepared them to deal with real life. But Dunbar reasoned that politicians were as well qualified for applied economics as academic economists. A politician could afford passionate commitment to particular policies, but that was too great a risk for an economist who wanted to live for the search for truth.[20]

Dunbar granted that the economist, as a citizen, had as much right as anyone else to form opinions and try to get others to agree. "In the university," he added, "he is under other obligations; and there it is for him to decide, how far, with his habit of mind and his temperament, he can give expression to judgments lying beyond his proper sphere, and yet related to it, without injury to the severe neutrality of science which he is bound to preserve within that sphere."[21] What to say—how much to say—became matters of professional judgment. Whether Ely's or Dunbar's view was closer to the opinion of majority, Ely's fate would show.

Plans that dated from 1887 to drop Ely from the AEA secretaryship were frequently reaffirmed by the small circle of academic economists involved in the arrangements. "I quite agree with you," Taussig told Seligman in 1890, "that the Association should be the common center of interest for all of us, and shall be glad to help every step toward making it so. The first step seems to me a change in the officers, which you say is in contemplation." To rid the association of the "peculiar innuendoes"—no longer the forward-looking principles of its beginning—it would be necessary to get rid of Ely. When Ely was accused of using political rather than scholarly standards to select papers for publication by the association, a publications committee including Taussig, Seligman, Giddings, Adams, and Clark was given responsibility for judging articles, despite Ely's angry objections.[22]

20. Ibid., pp. 411-14.
21. Ibid., pp. 414-16.
22. Taussig to Seligman, 14 October 1890, Seligman MSS; Ely to Giddings, 26 January, 7 February 1891; Taussig to Giddings, 5 March 1891, Franklin Henry Giddings MSS, Columbia University Special Collections.

Suspecting a plot, Ely tried to save some of his power in the association. But the excuse that made his scheduled ejection from office easy was the prominent symbol of popularization in the Gilded Age: Chautauqua. Either to disarm his opponents, as Taussig suspected, or simply to suit his own convenience, Ely announced without consulting anyone that the annual meeting of the AEA for 1892 would be held at Chautauqua, where he ordinarily spent summers teaching in William Rainey Harper's Methodist summer school.[23]

An outcry against the Chautauqua location swelled immediately, mainly from the younger, professionally trained economists who were most anxious to project a scholarly image. With his own reputation secure, President Francis Amasa Walker was willing enough "to go there and see the great intellectual Camp Meeting of the Country," but Giddings, Taussig, Seligman, and Adams—all privy to the conspiracy to oust Ely—objected both to the tainted location and to Ely's arrogance in making a unilateral decision.[24] Ely interpreted Walker's suggestion that the Executive Committee should meet to reconsider the site as an attempt to insult and humiliate him; he threatened to resign if plans were changed. When Ely sent a circular letter to members of the AEA Council seeking their support, the Chautauqua location became a litmus test of the image each respondent wanted the AEA—and therefore economists—to project.

Leading academics had the strongest motivation for avoiding Chautauqua but they also hesitated to have Ely resign in a huff. Thus Adams, Giddings, Mayo-Smith, Hadley, Taussig, and Seligman simply indicated that they would not attend the meeting, while the maverick George Gunton insisted that the location be changed, no matter what Ely threatened. A mixed group of

23. Ely to Adams, 7, 17 December 1888, Adams MSS; Amos G. Warner to Ely, 24 November 1891, Ely MSS; Francis A. Walker to Seligman, 10, 19 December 1891, Seligman MSS. Ironically, Ely tried to get first Adams and then Warner to split the secretaryship with him so that he could keep charge of the correspondence. This account of the Chautauqua affair differs somewhat in factual content and interpretation from that offered in Rader, *Academic Mind*, pp. 118-20.

24. Walker to Seligman, 10 December 1891, Seligman MSS; Walker to Ely, 18, 26 December 1891, Ely MSS.

nonacademics, Ely students, and academics from small colleges either approved the location or had no strong preference. Five economists from western universities placed geography ahead of religious symbolism when they praised the choice of Chautauqua as a small step in the westward direction of nationalizing the organization. Two industrialists considered the Chautauqua location favorable precisely because of its religious overtones. And the secretary of the American Statistical Association, also an economist, tried to convince Ely that objections arose not through "any desire to defeat you for the sake of inflicting a defeat," but rather "on the ground that Chautauqua is not associated with the highest academic scholarship."[25]

Ely won the battle over Chautauqua, but he lost his last hold on the leadership of the AEA. Cautious compromisers like Walker and John Bates Clark were convinced that Ely's angry resignation would bring down fire and brimstone from "the socialists & semi-Socialist papers" and rally "the whole Chautauqua influence" behind Ely, while unfriendly newspapers would play up the incident as "another row among the pol. economists." Seligman and other vocal protesters were persuaded to withdraw their objections in return for a guarantee that Ely would "resign peacefully" from the secretaryship. At Chautauqua in August 1892 both Walker and Ely stepped down. An Ely student, Edward Alsworth Ross of Cornell, replaced Ely, while Charles Dunbar of Harvard was elected president, bringing to fruition a five-year-old project of the academic professionals in leading universities to end the one-sided ethical and ideological commitment of the AEA.[26]

25. There are letters in the Ely MSS from Seligman, Taussig, Giddings, Gunton, Clark, Carroll D. Wright, Lester Ward, Albion Small, Henry Ferguson, Katherine Coman, W. W. Folwell of the University of Minnesota, F. W. Blackmar of the University of Kansas, James Canfield of the University of Nebraska, George Garrison of the University of Texas, George W. Knight of Ohio State University (Folwell, Blackmar, Canfield, Garrison, and Knight were the western academics in agreement), Joseph D. Weeks, R. R. Bowker, and Davis R. Dewey. All are dated between 22 December 1891 and 10 January 1892.
26. Walker to Seligman, 23 December 1891; Clark to Seligman, 30 December 1891, 18 June 1892; Taussig to Seligman, 17, 30 May, 11 July, 10 August 1892, Seligman MSS. Walker, Seligman, Clark, and Taussig were involved in selecting Ross;

Between 1884 and 1892, the course of Ely's career brought some refinement in the way economists defined their social role. Particularly as other economists retreated from their insistence that economists possessed a special moral authority, Ely became the symbol of the dubious tie between ethics and economics. New school colleagues gradually came to agree that their former spokesman might be seriously misplaced as head of their professionalization movement. They sought a level of authority which some of his activities undermined. Ely was not toppled by outside pressure. Professionals with training and inclinations similar to his own stripped him of his power in the profession.

When Ely resigned from his influential position as AEA secretary after the Chautauqua incident, his humiliation was only the culmination of an agreement between traditionalists and revisionists reached much earlier. Their decision had been the product of a growing careerist resolution to concentrate on developing recognition of the economist as an academic specialist whose judgment on economic though not on ethical questions was authoritative because of the expert knowledge that informed the economist's views. The campaign against Ely was an example to others. Nevertheless, when the trend to compromise between the schools focused on Ely, it permitted professional economists to avoid settling the larger question of the relationship between advocacy and scientific objectivity.

---

for another account, see A. W. Coats, "The First Two Decades of the American Economic Association," *American Economic Review* 50 (September 1960):564-66. Clark had pressed for Walker's replacement in a letter to Ely, 24 December 1891, Ely MSS. Seligman changed his mind and decided he could attend the 1892 meeting "at some inconvenience" after Ely moved to Wisconsin. Seligman to Ely, 24 June 1892, Ely MSS.

6   *Compliance*

For a decade or so, defining the role that a new breed of professionally trained social scientists would play in American life had been largely a matter for debate within their infant guild. Among economists, discussions of method, content, and competence first sharpened and then gradually began to resolve the most significant generational and ideological differences. By the mid-1880s, however, an alarming new factor intruded upon the professionalization process. As trained observers who were among the first to understand the emerging urban-industrial society and as potentially influential agents in the rationalization of its unfamiliar processes, the new professionals had made themselves important enough to attract invidious attention. Especially at moments when the social order seemed threatened by alien ideas and dissident classes, the interaction between economists and educational, political, or industrial leaders became the single most important force in determining what economists did and what they avoided. Clashes with formidable opponents were stylized in the rhetoric of the emerging profession as academic freedom cases. Thus the concept of academic freedom which each economist held became a decisive factor in determining both that individual's role and the eventual shape of the entire profession.[1]

Not everyone became aware of the special importance of academic freedom at the same time or in the same way.[2] Before the revolution in American higher education that began at the Johns Hopkins in 1876, economics teachers—frequently doubling as moral philosophers—had been expected to express the economic views of the college's benefactors. If opinion was divided, two economists were hired and the students were left to be their own arbiters. The new professional economists were not content to be mere debators. Rather, these research-orien-

ted creatures claimed that scientific economics supported conclusions which could be advocated with a degree of certainty
that overrode the preferences of interest groups. Instead of
deriving their teachings from the accumulated moral and intellectual heritage of the community, these new economists discovered them in the course of their own original investigations.
They claimed a hearing on the grounds of a special competence
which laymen were not qualified to judge. A successful challenge to their teachings was a challenge to the competence that
gave them an important role.

The frequency of academic freedom cases in the 1880s and
1890s reflected the fluidity of academic roles and the uncertainty of professors' rights and responsibilities.[3] That ambiguity
was nearly as persistent among academics as in other circles.
Sometimes academics united solidly behind a claim to academic
freedom as a way of differentiating themselves from amateurs,
whom they hoped to deny equal status. But occasionally an
academic social scientist might support a more limited interpretation of academic freedom if he opposed the position taken by
another academic. When irate trustees disciplined an extreme
leftist, conservatives applauded. Even leaders in the profession-

1. For a general treatment of academic freedom in the Gilded Age and after, see
Walter P. Metzger, *Academic Freedom in the Age of the University* (New York,
1961), especially chapt. 4, or the same material as originally published in Richard
Hofstadter and Walter P. Metzger, *The Development of Academic Freedom in the
United States* (New York, 1955). Howard K. Beale, *A History of Freedom of
Teaching in American Schools* (New York, 1941), was largely superceded by
Hofstadter and Metzger. On contemporary recognition of the importance of academ-
ic social scientists in rationalizing major social issues, see Albert Shaw, "Political and
Economic Literature from the Universities," *Dial* 8 (July 1887):61.

2. Even as late as the end of the century, prominent economists could still
disagree totally on whether wealthy business interests posed a threat to academic
freedom at all. See Albion Small, "Academic Freedom," *Arena* 22 (October
1899):463; Thomas Elmer Will, "A Menace to Freedom: The College Trust," *Arena*
26 (September 1901):249.

3. An excellent discussion of "Rival Conceptions of the Higher Learning,
1865-1910" appears in Laurence R. Veysey, *The Emergence of the American
University* (Chicago, 1965). Veysey describes the conflicts and complementarities
among discipline and piety, utility, research, and liberal culture as goals of higher
education. Similar themes appear with different emphases in Hofstadter and Metzger,
The Development of Academic Freedom, and also in Wilson Smith, *Professors and
Public Ethics: Studies on Northern Moral Philosophers before the Civil War* (Ithaca,
N.Y., 1956).

alization movement occasionally appeared pleased when sanctions were imposed against behavior they considered partisan or
unscholarly. Only prolonged experimentation with the concept
of academic freedom finally yielded a definition of legitimate
advocacy which, willingly or unwillingly, most economists accepted. In turn, that consensus clarified the limits of academic
freedom and further defined the professional role.

Economists were involved in a string of celebrated academic
freedom cases in the 1890s. One after another, Richard T. Ely,
John R. Commons, Edward W. Bemis, Elisha Benjamin Andrews, and Edward Alsworth Ross faced critics who wanted to
put them out of the colleges. Whether these victims emerged as
fallen martyrs or triumphant victors—indeed whether their
colleagues really supported them—their cases provided both
myth and precedent for twentieth-century social scientists in
battles with new opponents.

Yet the case that may have affected the professionalization
of economics more than any other was virtually unknown at the
time. In the early 1880s Henry Carter Adams was a convinced
revisionist who fully supported the ethos of ethical economics.
Though no other economist realized how endangered Adams
was at the time, his academic freedom case formed the background for the vital coordinating role he played in the AEA
settlement of 1886-1888. His personal ordeal brought him into
the Columbia-Pennsylvania-Michigan axis formed to mediate
between the Hopkins-Wisconsin left and the Harvard-Yale right.
As Adams became a member of the professional elite, his
attitudes toward advocacy undergirded decisions that continued
to influence the development of the profession.

Of all the social scientists in the first professional generation,
Adams may provide the best example of the tortuous transition
from professionalism of the style familiar before the modernization period to a new kind of professionalism which fit the
conditions of a more specialized society. At least until the
middle of the nineteenth century, ministers, lawyers, and college presidents possessed the moral authority and traditional

community standing to pronounce their views almost indiscriminately on public issues of every kind. New-style professionalism confined economists, engineers, social workers, city planners, teachers, and assorted other occupants of the specialized roles required in urban, industrial society to a far more restricted exercise of advocacy. From roots in the old-style professionalism as a minister's son who started to prepare himself for the ministry, Adams took with him to economics the same humanitarian earnestness and the same inclination, given the view that all issues were moral at bottom, toward developing and communicating an ethical appraisal of society as an organic whole.[4]

But Adams also developed early the careerism which came more and more to characterize Americans, and especially people who followed occupations that required long training and intense commitment, as traditional identifying marks such as religion and party lost force. Success in his profession was intensely important to Adams. He realized that the direction and quality of his scholarly work would determine not only his influence on society, which would satisfy his ethical obligation, but his professional advancement as well. In Germany, besides socialism and the labor movement, Adams was careful to study the tough financial subjects that he thought mattered to influential people. The early years of his academic career were dogged by the uncertainty of part-time employment without tenure. Returning to America in 1879, he was given a temporary position at Hopkins for half a year until he found a job at Cornell University for the second semester. From 1881 to 1887 he divided his time, teaching half of each year at Cornell and the other half at the University of Michigan. To that precariousness, the social uneasiness of the 1880s added further reason for insecurity.

Facing such uncertainties, Adams wrestled with the tension between his strong desire to be a reformer and his ambition to

4. An illuminating discussion of the character of the new middle class, which included the new-style professional, appears in Robert Wiebe, *The Search for Order, 1877-1920* (New York, 1967), esp. chapt. 5.

be a scholar with good credentials and a secure position. In 1882 he experienced his first brush with disapproving university authorities. President James Burrill Angell of the University of Michigan asked the regents to make Adams's appointment permanent. According to Adams, the president was surprised to learn "that every one of the Regents had received [the] complaint that I was a free-trader. They happened to be all protectionists." With understandable trepidation Adams recalled how John Stuart "Mill feared his *Polit. Economy* would raise up the thinking people of Eng. against him, because of his advanced social ideas." Adams voiced similar apprehension about the possible results of his own work. Aware that universities which trained excellent researchers would soon dominate higher education, he moved quickly to establish the Hopkins system of seminars at Michigan and incidentally to impress Charles Kendall Adams, head of the Michigan department and first seminar master of American historians.[5]

Permanency was no more certain at Cornell. President Andrew Dickson White, a strong partisan of German scholarship, took a kindly interest in Adams and encouraged him to expect a full-time appointment. In 1883 Adams was promoted to associate professor, but the trustees challenged the professional integrity of his position by making a rival appointment in economics. White thought Adams would be "possibly amused to know that the Hon. Ellis H. Roberts, a graduate of Yale in very high standing, and for a considerable time member of the Committee of Ways and Means in the House of Representatives, had been made a special lecturer on the subject of free trade, being expected to present the tariff side." Adams was not amused. The appointment put him on an equal plane with an amateur who had learned his basic economics from Sumner, and it reduced economics to a squabble over protection. New school economists were trying to shift the emphasis in economics toward questions of human welfare. Yet for the second time

5. Adams to "Dear Mother," 14, 23 January 1882; Adams to C. K. Adams, 2, 28 April 1882, Adams MSS.

university trustees belittled Adams's scientific competence because he had not come out in favor of the tariff, a measure that
hardly interested him. Irritated and uneasy, he protested "the
'Duplex Professorship,' as the *Nation* calls it," and vowed to
teach his students "that there is more in Polit. Economy than
the mere discussion of Free Trade and Protection."[6]

Political economy was a great deal more than an academic
subject to Adams. At one point Adams considered economics
a direct avenue to social reform. The intricate relationship
between reform and scholarship which he presented in the
Science "Economic Discussion" of 1886 was the product of a
painful interaction between the religious values he inherited and
the scientific credo of his profession. In the early 1880s his
dedication to the ideal of dispassionate scholarship increased,
but so, as he witnessed the hardships caused by recurring
economic depressions, did his passion for change. He grew more
eager to relieve the suffering of the working classes, more
willing to defend labor and criticize industrial capitalism, more
inclined to expect social science, not religion, to provide an
ethical basis for reforming industrial relations. "If the churches
only would take up the social questions and . . . apply what
they must learn if they study them, a mighty revolution might
be effected," he wrote. Unfortunately the institutional churches
were too busy serving their affluent members to respond to the
needs of the laboring masses. Though religion was still the
"greatest romance" of Adams's personal life, he despaired of
social reform ever coming from the churches. Instead he began
looking to organized labor and—despite the negative reactions
he had formed in Germany—to socialism.[7]

It was Adams's compassion for the working class, not scientific investigation, that aroused his interest in socialism. Main-

6. White to Adams, 12 May, 23 June 1881; Adams to "My Dear Mother," 2 July
1883, Adams MSS. Actually Cornell seems to have been following common practice
in employing professors to present opposing sides of an issue and leave the students
to make their own decisions. See Charles F. Dunbar, "The Academic Study of
Political Economy," *Quarterly Journal of Economics* 1 (October 1886):405-8.

7. Adams to "Dear Mother," 8 June 1882, 7 April 1884; William Salter to Adams,
24 October, 10 November 1882; Calvin Thomas to Adams, 9 May 1886, Adams MSS.

ly he was drawn to the idealism of socialist social criticism. "These socialists are the earnest men of today," he wrote. "The trades unions are I think the great movers of the present, or rather through their organizations it appears to me that the next step toward a nearer realization of Liberty and Brotherhood is taken." For the moment socialist leaders took on the special aura of his boyhood hero. He began to liken Karl Marx to Jesus Christ. Though Adams identified himself privately as "a socialist of the general philosophy of Karl Marx," he never accepted the Marxist "method of work and agitation" or joined a socialist organization. His scholarly writings never advocated Marxian socialism; in fact, he restricted the state's activity to the regulation of natural monopoly, a concept he invented to distinguish essential services from other enterprises, and to the supervision of standards for competition. His discussions of socialism retained the style typical of the historical school; narrative accounts rather than theoretical analyses, they communicated no sense of inevitable class conflict. Except for a brief period when the industrial violence of the mid-1880s was most acute, Adams remained essentially a moderate reformer. Yet for some critics even a tentative academic interest in socialism as a source of ideas for gradual reform was enough to make an inexperienced, untenured academic suspect.[8]

With such ill-matched interests—industrial reform and professional advancement—Adams faced an uncertain future. Particularly in the new social sciences, the roles of academics were changing, and there were no clear guidelines for behavior. Public expectations for the conduct of professors changed abruptly in precisely the years when the first class of professionally trained economists was starting to teach and publish. In 1882 reappointment to the University of Michigan delighted Adams because "a man who has anything to say on social questions can

8. Adams to "Dear Mother," 8 June 1882, 7 November 1884, Adams MSS; Adams, "Relation of the State to Industrial Action" in *Two Essays by Henry Carter Adams*, ed. Joseph Dorfman (New York, 1969), pp. 57-133; Adams, "The Position of Socialism in the Historical Development of Political Economy," *Penn Monthly* 10 (April 1879):285-94.

exert a wider influence there." Just two years later Adams's prolabor views aroused concern for his welfare in academic circles. "The general attitude you take on labor reform is new, not so much absolutely," a friend cautioned, "as for a Professor openly to take."[9] In the past, scholars usually had spoken out to uphold community values, not to challenge them.

The increasing vigilance of university authorities was an ominous sign for a young professor who was likely to ruffle conservative feathers. In 1885 neither White at Cornell nor Angell of Michigan was sure that Adams should be kept. "He has such merits and such limitations," Angell confessed, that "I hardly know whether we want him permanently or not." Adams's fine teaching and creative energy were his merits; his radical opinions were his limitations. In a young university with ambition to expand, the president's standing with the regents rested partly on the reputations of scholars he appointed. Such managerial concerns could erode liberalism. Adams's "peculiar notions" worried Angell increasingly. To a conservative colleague, Judge Thomas McIntyre Cooley of the Michigan law faculty, the president disclosed that Adams had "thus far had only temporary appointments, the fear that he might do or say foolish things preventing more." In March 1886, when Adams raised the tenure question again, Angell requested a formal statement of Adams's views on private property, inheritance, and socialism.[10]

Initially Adams made no pretense to sound economics. By that time his sympathies were largely with labor, and he deliberately professed convictions that diverged decisively from English economics. His views on private property reflected basic acceptance of a fundamental principle of historical economics: that social utility, not logic or tradition, justified economic

9. Adams to James B. Angell, 6 April 1882, James Burrill Angell MSS, Michigan Historical Collections, University of Michigan; William Salter to Adams, 30 December 1884, Adams MSS.

10. Angell to White, 17 July 1884, 10 June 1885; E. J. James to W. H. Payne, 2 June 1884; Adams to Angell, 16 March 1886, Angell MSS; Angell to Adams, 19 March 1886, Adams MSS; Thomas M. Cooley Diary, 30 March 1886, T. M. Cooley MSS, Michigan Historical Collections, University of Michigan.

institutions. The only defense of private property he recognized
was its convenience to society. Leaving farm lands in private
hands probably benefited everyone, but letting avaricious individuals control valuable city real estate bordered on exploitation. Capital was as much a social product as land; theoretically
it could be left in private control or taken over by society,
whichever would produce greater welfare.[11]

On state socialism Adams was far less radical. No doubt
individualism was more difficult than private property for a
devout Congregationalist to give up. Socialist proposals for
outright government ownership of the means of production had
never appealed to Adams. While he believed in government
regulation of obvious natural monopolies, he secretly feared
that socialism—even a welfare state on the German model—
would subvert the working class. Only by relying on their own
exertions could working people remain individualistic, strong,
hard working, and—though the problem seldom bothered economists of the period—free.

What Adams hoped for in place of state socialism or private
capitalism was a gradual transition to a voluntary system of
"diffused" ownership. In the meantime, if he rejected government ownership and a comprehensive welfare program, he was
forced to rely at least temporarily on competition as the organizing principle of the industrial system. Yet he gravely mistrusted the supposed beneficence of competition. Finally Adams
settled his difficulty by devising an ingenious compromise: the
best interim role for the state was to preserve the competitive
system in most industries but to intervene by using a regulatory
arm to raise the level of competition. On that rationale, one
could eliminate vice and keep virtue. To give all competitors an
equal start, Adams favored a high inheritance tax and an income
tax designed to redistribute wealth. Finally, with no apparent
consciousness of inconsistency, he had put together a system
that allowed him to advocate voluntary communalism and yet

11. Adams to Angell, 25 March 1886, Angell MSS, copy in Adams MSS, published
in Adams, *Two Essays*, pp. 205-8.

denounce socialism as an industrial blunder, a practical impossibility, and a political absurdity.[12]

The real test of dangerous radicalism in 1886 was a scholar's position on labor activism. The labor program Adams proposed at that critical time went far beyond negotiations with unions on bread-and-butter issues. He was drawn to the model that the Knights of Labor were developing in their dramatic struggle against the Gould railroad system. The Knights' demands included tenure of employment, no reduction in wages without arbitration, no discharge without cause, promotions only from the ranks, and arbitration of disputed issues. Whether they realized it or not, Adams suggested, the Knights were proposing an extension of proprietary rights which struck a just and reasonable balance between the opposing terrors of Spencerian anarchism and German socialism. "The workmen have at last gotten hold of the right end of the problem," he wrote. Wise men would certainly "recognize the claims of Knights of Labor in the spirit of fairness and assist them in working out their ideas."[13]

In the uneasy spring of 1886, advocating proprietary rights for labor amounted to a radical program. Few industrialists were close to admitting that labor had any rights at all in their companies. Apparently Angell preferred not to risk alienating the Michigan regents, for he decided against nominating Adams for permanent appointment that year. There is no evidence that Angell explicitly told Adams his opinions were the cause for delay. Had he been warned, Adams might have avoided expressing radical views at Cornell, where he was also in his fifth year of successful teaching and eligible for tenure. Cornell's new president was Charles Kendall Adams, the former chairman of the Michigan department and a strong champion of scientific economics who knew H. C. Adams's work well. But the violent summer of 1886—the menacing year when labor's "great up-

12. Adams to Angell, 25 March 1886, Angell MSS; Adams, "Relation of the State to Industrial Action," passim.
13. Adams, "What Do These Strikes Mean?" typescript copy enclosed in Adams to Angell, 25 March 1886, Angell MSS.

rising" produced twice as many strikes as in any previous twelve
months of the nation's history—was hardly the opportune time
for testing a university president's liberalism. As hard times and
repressive police tactics drove more and more workers into
unions, Adams was daring, even reckless, in his support of labor.
Finally his opinions precipitated a crisis at Cornell.[14]

When the eight-hour movement culminated in the Haymarket
bombing of May 4, 1886, panic spread. Conservative businessmen, industrialists, and civic leaders banded together to save
Chicago from the carnage they fancied the anarchists plotted.
Sympathizers with the labor movement renounced their liberalism and demanded swift retribution for trouble-makers. The
trial of the Chicago anarchists was a travesty, but at the time it
added currency to wild rumors of the awful plans being laid by
men who believed in dynamite as the instrument of social
change. Thomas Cooley, Adams's distinguished Michigan colleague, declared that the country was engulfed in "a species of
civil war." Remembering the Paris Commune, knowledgeable
people actually feared revolution.[15]

In the midst of that retrenchment of opinion, well before
sympathy began to mount for the victims of Judge Joseph
Gary's peculiar version of justice, Adams spoke out against the
narrowing range of dissent. Freedom of speech was all the more
vital in dangerous times, he reminded Americans. Anarchists
were low, vile people, mostly immigrants who misunderstood
the democratic system for reform. Yet, to safeguard the search
for truth, even their mad utterances must be protected, so long
as they did not actually incite their hearers to crime. A bombing
was no excuse to stifle debate on the "social question." Adams
denounced scare talk and condemned every resort to force; he
guaranteed that repression of opinion would leave even the
most peaceful dissenters no alternative but violence. In future

14. Ray Ginger, *Altgeld's America* (New York, 1958), chapt. 2, and Henry David,
The History of the Haymarket Affair (New York, 1936), passim, provide accounts of
the rising tide of tension in industrial cities in 1886.
15. Thomas M. Cooley, "Arbitration in Labor Disputes," *Forum* 1 (June
1886):307-13; J. L. Spalding, "Are We in Danger of Revolution?" ibid. (July
1886):405-15.

years academics would make the same argument again and
again, but to many frightened Americans in 1886 the language
of the First Amendment sounded dangerously radical.[16]

A whisper in explanation of anarchists was followed by a
shout in defense of labor. On short notice, Adams agreed to
speak in a forum where he was certain to get publicity: at the
annual Sibley Lecture Series designed to acquaint engineering
students at Cornell University with social issues. Idealism
ablaze, Adams expressed views on the labor question that were
certain to provoke the wrath of Henry Sage, the university's
powerful benefactor, whom Adams failed to recognize in the
audience. The chronic strikes of Chicago lumber shovers could
enrage an upstate New York lumber king. When Adams argued
that labor received an ever smaller share of the wealth as
industrialism increased production, he seemed to justify such
strikes. Worse, Adams charged that the industrialists who profited from exploitation were stirring up a panic about a few
anarchists to divert attention from the legitimate grievances of
workingmen. To revolutionize industrial relations against such
opposition, labor would have to do more than organize, more
than tinker with wages and hours. Like the Knights of Labor, all
workers would have to demand a share of the proprietary rights
held solely by capitalists. For the second time Adams portrayed
the Knights as a bulwark between socialism and anarchy, while
he hinted that the industrialists might be the ones who were
stirring up class hatred.[17]

Reaction was swift. As Adams summarized events, "The New
York papers reported what I said and, three days after, Mr.
Henry Sage, than whom I know no more honest hypocrite or
un-Christian a Christian, came into the President's office, and
. . . said, 'This man must go, he is sapping the foundations of
our society.' "[18] Other trustees agreed with Sage that Adam's

16. Henry C. Adams, "Shall We Muzzle the Anarchists?" ibid., pp. 445-54.

17. Henry C. Adams, "The Labor Problem," *Scientific American*, Supplement, 22
(21 August 1886):8861-63.

18. Quoted in Marvin B. Rosenberry, "Henry Carter Adams," in *Michigan and the
Cleveland Era*, ed. Earl D. Babst and Lewis G. Vander Velde (Ann Arbor, Mich.,
1948), p. 28.

social philosophy was subversive. Cornell had established a reputation for liberalism in the years before Sage dominated the board, but the risk of defending free expression for an outspoken economic leftist must have appeared too great for a new president. Charles Kendall Adams did nothing to oppose Sage's iron conviction that "no socialist was fit to be a professor in a university." At a closed meeting the trustees decided to terminate H. C. Adams quietly upon the scheduled expiration of his current two-year contract in 1887. Though no announcement was made, not even to Adams, a disgruntled alumnus with private sources leaked the secret to the press.[19]

At least three alternatives were open to Adams. He could appeal to fellow economists. He could accept an offer of assistance from a powerful alumni group. Or he could make a loud, principled protest in his own behalf, invoking academic freedom as a defense. Adams did none of those things. Instead, he did his best to suppress the story. When a lawyer representing the Cornell alumni of New York City inquired whether Adams was indeed being dismissed for his economic views and promised that "the alumni will resent this attack upon University liberty of teaching," Adams's cautious response prevented potential defenders from acting. His replies to questions from fellow economists were equally evasive. Though he finally asked Seligman to publish an outline of his lectures on the social question in the *Political Science Quarterly,* Adams admitted only that there was "just enough truth in the delicacy of my relations at Cornell, to lead me to desire the expression of approbation, at least of scholarly attitude, on the part of influential writers." Adams wanted no public defense from laymen or professionals; he shunned defending himself.[20]

19. [R. T.] H[ill], "Cornell University," *Index* [of the Free Religious Association], 29 July 1886, pp. 51-52. Hill was "a disappointed candidate for a degree." His authorship is established in Charles Henry Hull to Adams, 19 September 1886, Adams MSS, which also contains a detailed account of the reactions of various trustees to Adams's Sibley Lecture. Hull's investigation may have been Adams's first sure source for corroboration of his intended dismissal.

20. Adams to C. K. Adams, 29 September 1886; John Frankenheimer to Adams, 6 September, 26 November 1886, 9 July 1887; Adams to "My Dear Mother," 27 March 1887, Adams MSS. Adams to Seligman, 9, 17 November 1886, in Joseph

The precariousness of Adams's professional circumstances was changing him. His conflicting ambitions in scholarship and reform had brought him to a turning point. Considerations of status and protocol contradicted his professional ideals. To preserve the chance that Cornell might reappoint him when emotions subsided, he remained silent on the academic freedom issue. His pride required that he reject President Adams's niggardly tentative offer of temporary employment at reduced rank and pay, but the insecurity of his position at Michigan still kept him impotent.

Gradually Adams's conception of the role of the economist responded to the realities of his situation. In the summer of 1886 he reversed the commitment to ethical economics that had characterized his entire career as a scholar. No longer did he defend the economist's right to act as the conscience of society, speaking out against even the most firmly established customs if they impeded social justice. Instead Adams told his professional colleagues in the *Science* debate that an economist probably ought to realize that tampering with institutions deeply imbedded in the historic life of the community was a risky business which might do more harm than good. The increasing use of government regulation was creating new opportunities. Academic economists might better limit their public statements to less controversial subjects and confine their attempts to influence policy to behind-the-scenes work as technical experts advising legislators or operating government regulatory commissions. On the spectrum that ran from Ely to Taussig, Adams had moved toward Taussig's end.[21]

The tragic events of 1886 changed Adams's social philosophy too. In an effort to convince President Angell of Michigan that his views were sounder than they had been a year earlier, Adams explained how his thinking on labor, capitalism, and socialism

---

Dorfman, ed., "The Seligman Correspondence, Part 2," *Political Science Quarterly* 56 (1941):270-71.

21. Adams to "My Dear Mother," 8, 13, 21 March, 21, 25 April, 29 May 1887, Adams MSS; Adams, "Economics and Jurisprudence," *Science* 8 (2 July 1886): 14-19.

had evolved. Though he had started his career as a convinced individualist, a growing awareness of the evils of extreme individualism and his sympathy for impoverished workers had raised doubts in his mind. For a while, Adams confessed, he had been deeply influenced by socialist theories, but gradually he had seen the inconsistency of his position. Socialist criticism of industrial society was often valid; yet any form of socialism, even a voluntary one, would subvert labor's commitment to individualism as it had his own.[22]

In an effort to combine the best of both systems, Adams invented what he called "the principle of personal responsibility in the administration of all social power." American political institutions had been reformed by extending both power and responsibility to an ever widening electorate. Industrial relations could be improved the same way—by extending jurisdiction over labor policies to labor—without destroying the integrity of the individual workingman. For a while Adams had believed that the Knights of Labor had discovered the same principle, but they had deceived him. He admitted that his prolabor remarks in 1886 had been premature, and he disavowed all that he had written in support of the Knights. Angell, of course, was delighted. He immediately recommended Adams for a permanent professorship, and the repentant economist was appointed without objection.[23]

Out of the unpleasantness that radical advocacy caused him at Cornell and Michigan, Adams learned a lesson that could hardly have failed to affect his future behavior as a social scientist. It altered the direction of his scholarship. To get away from the labor question, he turned to an investigation of public debts and eventually made a major contribution in the area of public finance. As technical questions absorbed more of his energy, he never returned to the kind of basic, cosmic inquiry

22. Adams to Angell, 7, 15 March 1887, Angell MSS; Angell to Adams, 12 March 1887, Adams MSS.
23. Adams to Angell, 15 March, 26 May 1887, Angell MSS; Angell to Adams, 26 March, 4 July 1887; Adams to "My Dear Mother," 29 June, 17 July 1887, Adams MSS.

that had produced his balanced, pioneering analysis of the role of the state in industrial action. Instead he functioned more and more within the framework of existing economic institutions. In 1888 Thomas McIntyre Cooley, apparently convinced that the Cornell experience had chastened Adams, had him appointed chief statistician of the Interstate Commerce Commission. The job was a plum which took Adams to Washington several times a year, provided valuable contacts, and gave him a means of influencing the development of industrial policy without making inflammatory statements in public and jeopardizing his career. It also limited his public impact, monopolized his time for years, and inevitably affected the position he took on the regulatory role of the state, a vital social question throughout his career.

The same critical incidents permanently affected Adams's position on professional prerogatives, including academic freedom. Sooner than many economists, he recognized the awesome power of conservative regents in determining academic policy, including curriculum. It made little difference, his experience proved, whether the university was privately endowed or tax-supported. Professors who dealt with sensitive areas of public policy could expect their social opinions to be monitored diligently. If a professor was attacked, he could anticipate little help from the new, managerial type of university president. However the president might feel personally, his imperatives were institutional; a conservative image and good public relations were worth more to a university than an unorthodox professor, no matter how brilliant.[24]

After his private ordeal, academic freedom seemed unreal to Adams—a poor, tardy substitute for prudence. Principled pleas

24. Veysey, *The Emergence of the American University*, pp. 302-17, describes the appearance of strong university presidents (first Andrew Dickson White, Charles W. Eliot, and James Burrill Angell; then a second group including William Rainey Harper, Nicholas Murray Butler, G. Stanley Hall, David Starr Jordan, Charles Kendall Adams, and others) who took on more and more of the characteristics of professional administrators in any large enterprise and insulated themselves from their faculties with a layer of bureaucratic assistants. Smith, *Professors and Public Ethics*, describes the characteristics of antebellum college presidents.

had not impressed Angell, but soundness had. A public crusade against the prejudice and bigotry of Cornell's trustees would have failed in 1886, and the notoriety would have made it impossible for Angell to reconsider. Years later Adams remained cynical about protesting in defense of academic freedom. He never answered criticism of his views and refused to let his friends do so.[25] When the Ross case broke at Stanford he was cool toward proposals for united action. "Having been unceremoniously dismissed from one institution because of the expression of opinion, the matter does not seem to me so awfully serious as it does to others," he told Seligman from the safe distance of more than fourteen years. "In the case of Ithaca, you may perhaps know that the New York alumni wanted to make a case of it, but the whole matter appeared so ludicrous that I preferred to shake hands with Cornell and take up my work somewhere else. The moral of which is that the intense person ought to be balanced up by a keen sense of the ludicrous."[26] In fact, Adams had developed a keen sense of the secret and the cautious.

Because Adams made such a secret of his dismissal at Cornell, it is impossible to tell how important it was in determining the academic economist's role. Obviously it motivated Adams, first in 1886 when he helped define a new consensus on the relation of economics to policy and again in subsequent years when he plotted with others to remove Ely—as quietly as Cornell had removed him. His own case convinced him that the emerging values which controlled his advancement would not let him practice moral indignation and claim scientific objectivity at the same time. He accepted the reasoning of his enemies and admitted that his passion had outrun his reason. Then he rationalized his own behavior into a professional standard that guided his later actions and shaped his judgments of others.

25. John Bates Clark to Adams, 21 May 1889; Seligman to Adams, 25 May 1889; Jesse Macy to Adams, 6 June 1889, Adams MSS; Adams to Seligman, 27 May 1889, in Dorfman, ed., "Seligman Correspondence, Part 2," p. 271.

26. Adams to Seligman, 27 February 1901 (Letterbook 1900-1902, p. 139), Adams MSS.

How much the Adams case affected others is moot, but Adams himself was influential. When he consciously rejected socialism, he reinforced industrial capitalism. When he stopped pressing for reform and accepted a rule of nonadvocacy, he called the professionalism of other advocates into question. When he defined professionalism in terms of highly specialized knowledge and technical competence, he advanced the quality of scholarship but limited its scope. As time passed he became an effective innovator—a pioneer in search of ways for scholars in a technological, interest-oriented society to influence traditional values and policies without arousing resistance.

7

From Advocacy to Acceptability

In the 1890s the issue of academic advocacy left the scholar's den and the university president's study to claim front-page attention. Social scientists advocated measures that threatened powerful interests. In return they found themselves facing efforts at retaliation which ranged from subtle suggestions that they curb their more radical teachings to heavy-handed measures aimed at purging them from the academic profession. Economists were especially hard hit. An Ely student explained their dilemma by noting the relevance of their investigations to hotly contested political issues. "Nobody cared what we taught so long as we dealt in abstractions and investigated only hypothetical cases concerning such mythical characters as Ricardo's savage," he declared. "But when we talk about railways, sugar trusts, labor unions, strikes & municipal monopolies, the conversation grows personal. It would be contrary to all past experience if we did not arouse opposition and find our Lehrfreiheit sharply challenged."[1] As they clashed with irate trustees and confronted ambitious presidents, economists quickly realized that the level of academic freedom which they were able to establish would influence the character of their advocacy and thus shape their professional mission.

The academic freedom cases of the 1890s were testimony to the importance of the role professional economists were creating, not to their weakness. At the same time, by repeatedly raising questions of competence, those noisy clashes endangered the authority that professional social scientists needed if they were to establish priority in social analysis. Advances in the state of social science endowed the criticisms and recommendations offered by professionals with more importance than the opinions of mid-century amateurs had enjoyed. But scientific progress also spurred opponents of outspoken academic social scientists to find ways of restricting the range and extent of their advocacy. As social scientists rested their claim to authority more and more exclusively on the special competence that the scholarly life conferred, both the substance and the manner of their advocacy became more critical in enforcing their claims. Anything that impugned objectivity endangered the rationale that scholars offered for their special mission. Thus objectivity and advocacy were often in conflict, even in the minds of leading professional social scientists. Through the issues raised by confrontations with critics outside the profession and the discussions each case provoked within, the limits of acceptable advocacy were gradually defined.

In some respects academic economists were poorly equipped to meet attacks. Though they were organized, they were far from unified. Even after the dropping of the AEA platform eliminated overt ideological tests of fitness for the profession, ideological differences continued to provide a basis for factions. Contradictory views on questions as general as the nature of society and as specific as whether labor should organize or cities own streetcar lines hindered concerted activities. Historical and ethical economists faced the ambiguities that often plague people who give up the certainty of an absolute standard. Believers in competition and individualism found traditional values hard to defend in a world where technological change made short work of traditional systems. As long as the source of their authority remained in doubt, social scientists occasionally lacked the confidence they needed for a vehement defense of prerogatives.

As the professionalization process continued, however, certain themes tended to promote unity. A professional culture was developing. Similar experiences in training and practice fostered a feeling of professional kinship that somewhat mitiga-

1. H. H. Powers to Ely, 4 October 1894, Ely MSS.

ted differences in social origins and individual values. Economists used the same journals and attended the same meetings to
keep up with advances in the science. Increasingly they used a
technical language that laymen could not easily comprehend.
They relied on similar conventions in research and reporting.
Most important, they ordinarily worked in college or university
settings where they pursued their investigations while teaching
to earn a living. Though amateurs like Wells or Atkinson had
seemed respectable enough in the 1870s, academics neglected
them in the 1890s, mainly because the self-taught preacademics
had never shared the experiences that united men and women
trained and employed in the universities.

Using higher education as a base for their activities placed
professional social scientists in an anomalous position. As professors, they depended for livelihood on sources of financial
support which they did not control. As scholars, they conducted investigations and developed critical theories which
could adversely affect the very interests that supported them.
Thus they were caught in a situation that inevitably produced
conflict. As professionals, they wanted to defend colleagues
against community pressure. Yet they needed to place reasonable restraints on restless reformers who persisted in under-
mining community support.[2]

The economists most likely to get themselves and their colleagues into trouble were the popularizers. The professionalization of social science coincided with a dramatic increase in
the number and circulation of journals devoted to social topics
as well as an enormous upsurge of public interest in economics.
People were trying to understand the forces of modernization.
Academics engaged in developing the needed rationalizations
often seemed better equipped than anyone else to put difficult

2. For a transition in professional reaction to amateurs, see Simon Patten,
"[David A.] Wells' Recent Economic Changes," *Political Science Quarterly* 5 (March
1890):102; Worthington C. Ford to Richmond Mayo-Smith, 17 March 1890, *Political
Science Quarterly* MSS; W. J. Ashley to Ely, n.d. [ca. 1890], Ely MSS. On the
development of a professional culture, see Ernest Greenwood, "Attributes of a
Profession," *Social Work* 2 (July 1957):45-55.

technical explanations into language that laymen could understand. Editors sought the talents of professional social scientists to write articles and books explaining economic and social conditions. As one example, the *Forum,* a journal devoted to the discussion of public issues, drew from one-third to one-half of its articles from social scientists, more academics than amateurs, throughout the 1890s.

Economics professors also wrote extensively in popular magazines and newspapers and published in journals sponsored by labor organizations, businesses, reform societies, and religious groups. Those who sought notoriety could find it. Substantial citizens found hasty diatribes or serious radical proposals most offensive when they were reaching thousands of readers. Even carefully researched and meticulously documented reports were more likely to bring repercussions if they appeared in journals which nonspecialists were likely to see. And to make the popularizers even more vulnerable, they were often on dubious scholarly ground because their work did nothing to advance the frontiers of knowledge.

Yet professional social scientists often risked the consequences of popularization willingly. A number of the revisionists in economics—men like James, Adams, Ely, and most of his students—had been attracted to the field because they hoped to improve the quality of people's lives. Exposing the evils of industrial society before the widest possible audience was precisely their goal. Such people had no intention of confining their social criticisms to the classroom, where an audience of youngsters could do little with the message they received. Forsaking that protected preserve, these professorial activists wrote enthusiastically for the new journals, offered extension classes for society women and union leaders, followed lyceum and Chautauqua circuits, opened their own summer schools to give courses on the ethical implications of social problems, and generally created a stir. In so doing, reform-minded economists believed they were carrying out their professional mission. Their conservative colleagues were not so sure. At a time when a great deal depended on what economists thought of each other, this was a vital difference.

In microcosm, the celebrated trial of Richard T. Ely by the University of Wisconsin Board of Regents captured the essence of a much larger struggle between two conflicting values of late nineteenth-century social scientists: scholarship versus popularization. Ely was in the vanguard of the professionalization movement. At the same time he was more active than anyone else in taking his findings directly to the people and advocating specific reforms. Some believed that the two activities, scholarship and popularization, were not only a complementary but an essential combination if academic social scientists were to fulfill their potential for putting knowledge at the service of society. Others doubted that a scholar could become a public advocate and still maintain a nonpartisan, objective attitude in research.[3] Ely was for some the most prominent success, for others the most obvious failure of the attempt to combine economics and ethics. Among professional economists no one better illustrated the potential conflict between advocacy and objectivity.

Scholars who placed a premium on scholarly appearances found Ely a constant source of worry and embarrassment. Conservatives among his friends and former students tried to encourage him to distinguish between professional and amateurish behavior. No professional economist precisely defined the difference between professionalism and amateurism, but an operational distinction was evolving to prescribe a standard for noncontroversial academic conduct. When Ely published his *Introduction to Political Economy* (1889), an elementary text that many laymen would see, some professional economists objected to its uneven scholarship and tone. John Bates Clark applauded the work for its excellent combination of a sociolog-

3. Charles F. Dunbar, "The Academic Study of Political Economy," *Quarterly Journal of Economics* 5 (July 1891):397-416. The importance of scientific detachment as an attribute of the professional economist was also stressed by J. Laurence Laughlin, "The Study of Political Economy in the United States," *Journal of Political Economy* 1 (December 1892):1-19, and by Simon Newcomb, "The Problem of Economic Education," *Quarterly Journal of Economics* 7 (July 1893):375-99.

ical perspective with historical method, but the increasingly conservative Clark also complained that "a work of strength" was marred by puerile and sentimental opening pages which Ely must have written with his Chautauqua audience too much in mind. Franklin Henry Giddings praised the broad scope of the volume but suggested that its use would have to be followed by "a severe drill in pure economics."[4] Ely's critics believed that a higher standard of scholarship would curb the dangerous leanings of his work.

In their zeal for objective scholarly values, Ely's professional critics undermined the very features of economic analysis that members of other groups found most useful. People who sympathized with Ely's ethical stance applauded him for providing a popular basis for social reform. "The Christian sense of duty which you bring to bear will make your work far more effectual than the old political economy," wrote one admirer of the *Introduction to Political Economy*. A teacher was grateful for a book that would "destroy the influence of that old Manchester school" and inculcate moral values. Labor leaders and industrialists alike begged Ely for his opinion on economic questions, hoping "to submit their crude work to the criticism, revision and strengthening of a political economist" and incidentally to acquire whatever authority his support might lend to their positions.[5]

Some observers implied that popularization was the most important function an economist could perform. Praising Ely, an admirer commented on the deplorable fact "that the political economists of to-day in their ambition to be scholarly should be afraid of being popular" and was thankful "that one of that number had the courage to give such important information to the general public . . . in such form that the average

4. Clark to Ely, 19 April 1889; Albion Small to Ely, 3 November 1889; Giddings to Ely, 16, 22 March 1889; Jane M. Slocum to Ely, 25 August 1890, Ely MSS. The book was published by the Chautauqua Literary and Scientific Circle, a major outlet for popularizations.

5. W. H. Fremantle to Ely, 9 January 1890; James Riley Weaver to Ely, 1 January 1891; Samuel Gompers to Ely, 21 August 1889; W. C. Warner to Ely, 1 April 1889, Ely MSS.

mind can appreciate it." Another assured Ely that the country would "largely turn for safe and friendly guidance" to him and his new Wisconsin department. When Ely tried to remain aloof from radical ties, the pressure increased. A member of the Nationalist Club taunted him for refusing to "dissipate [his] influence" by joining the Bellamyites and inquired satirically how the public ownership of natural monopolies which Ely advocated was as different as Ely claimed from ordinary socialism. Ely's very popularity tempted partisans to claim him.[6]

For moderates in the profession, Ely's popularity with reformers made him seem even more dangerous, especially as he identified himself with radical causes. Between 1883, when his *French and German Socialism* was published, and the heresy trial, Ely's interest in the socialization of certain important services matured. By 1894 he had published two book-length studies of socialism, a record no other American economist had equaled. Ely took over and popularized Adams's distinction between artificial and natural monopolies. He argued that government ownership of public service industries such as the railroads, utilities, and telegraph was the most practical compromise, "the golden mean" between ruthless competition down to the level of the least principled competitor and complete government ownership of property. Inequities in welfare offended Ely's sense of justice; in turn, he offended business leaders and industrialists by recommending a graduated income tax, another "socialistic" measure, to pay for government services. Though Ely continued to deny that he was himself a socialist, he taught that the only hope of avoiding class revolution and advancing social justice lay in the peaceful adoption of many socialist reforms. No more was needed to provide ammunition for critics.[7]

6. W. L. Phelan to Ely, 27 January 1889 [?]; E. W. Bagby to Ely, 20 September 1892; Charles Lee Smith to Ely, 13 October 1891; Cyrus Field Willard to Ely, 28 February 1889; Fred W. Speirs to Ely, 2 January 1893, Ely MSS.

7. For a more detailed analysis of Ely's developing views on socialism, see Rader, *Academic Mind*, pp. 88-105; Ely, *Problems of Today* (New York, 1888); Ely and John Finley, *Taxation in American States and Cities* (New York, 1888); Ely, *An Introduction to Political Economy* (New York, 1889); and Ely, *Socialism: An*

Socialism was in such a fluid state of definition and Ely's writings were so prolix and unsystematic that criticism was not necessarily ideological disagreement in disguise. For conservative economists surely, and for many moderates, even a hint of socialism was almost certain proof of unfitness for scholarship. Ely repeatedly insisted that he looked to socialism only for the means to preserve what was good of the past and to prevent bloody class revolution in the near future. Yet even one of his friendliest critics, his student David Kinley, believed that well-intentioned people could read his mentor's works and conclude without malicious purpose that he was a socialist. Kinley encouraged Ely to soften his denials of socialism in order to avoid seeming to admit the truth of the charge. Instead of denouncing his critics as "liars and slanderers," Kinley urged Ely to allow sympathetic economists to help him manage his image by emphasizing the essential conservatism of his work. As Kinley recognized, Ely's standing depended not merely on his attitude toward socialism but also on what the literate public and his professional colleagues thought of his scholarship.[8]

Some of Ely's associates were more tinged with socialism than he was. Ely's interest in the prolabor Episcopal Christian Social Union occasioned no alarm among colleagues; amateur and professional social scientists had traditionally belonged to various types of uplift societies. But in 1893 Ely joined with John Commons and the Reverend George D. Herron, a Congregationalist minister whom Ely had helped to place in a professorship at Iowa College, to establish the American Institute of Christian Sociology, a society devoted to applying a distinctly socialist version of Christian teaching to relations between labor and capital.[9]

Examination of Its Nature, Its Strength and Its Weakness, with Suggestions for Social Reform (New York, 1894).

8. The best example of an academic who was deeply suspicious of Ely because of his interest in socialism was Arthur Hadley. See Hadley, "Ely's 'Socialism and Social Reform,' " *Forum* 18 (October 1894):184-91. For Hadley's great antipathy for socialism, see his "Jay Gould and Socialism," *Forum* 14 (January 1893):686-93. Gould was not a greater, only an equal, evil. Ely, *Socialism*, pp. vi-ix; Kinley to Ely, 15 April 1894, Ely MSS.

9. Rader, *Academic Mind*, p. 121, argues that this organization was an abortive

The severe depression of 1893 and the abrupt violence of the Homestead and Pullman strikes heightened class feeling, shortening tolerance among leading conservative interests; yet Herron's public statements grew increasingly radical. Conservative critics retaliated against the tenets of Christian sociology, angrily contending that Jesus had taught a universal ethic that supported no specific political system and sanctioned no particular economic philosophy. Even Commons was alarmed by Herron's extremism. "On one night of his [lecture] series [at Chicago in 1894] our lecturer identified Christianity with pure Anarchism," Commons recalled; "on the next night he identified it with Communism. He identified each with the love of God."[10]

Social scientists began begging Ely to have more regard for his own image and for theirs. Albion Small's reaction indicated the trend. Small was trying hard to establish sociology as a respectable discipline at the University of Chicago. He considered Herron a visionary dogmatist whose total disregard for facts that conflicted with his predetermined conclusions made a mockery of science. Yet Herron was a professor of sorts, and his claim to be a sociologist was a threat to academic sociology. Small objected to Ely's close ties with Herron. Pointing to the danger of amateurism, Small warned that the Institute was "likely to do incalculable harm if it is to turn loose on innocent searchers for social truth a raft of untrained social physicians with a sociological faith cure." Small cautioned Ely of the consequences awaiting a professional social scientist foolish enough to forsake the dry ground of scientific investigation for

---

attempt to establish a society of western social scientists, pointing out that its officers, Ely, Herron, and John Commons, were all Westerners. It should be noted that other prominent Westerners such as Albion Small and Henry Carter Adams were not members. For the Herron program of Social Christianity and a list of members claimed by the Institute which included many social scientists, see Herron to Ely, 15 February 1894; L. T. Chamberlain to the Council of the American Institute of Christian Sociology, 15 February 1895; Chamberlain to Ely, 9 December 1895, Ely MSS.

10. For an example of the academic protest against Christian sociology, see Shailer Mathews, "Christian Sociology: Part 4: The State," *American Journal of Sociology* 1 (March 1896): 604-17; John R. Commons, *Myself: The Autobiography of John R. Commons* (Madison, Wis., 1963), p. 51.

"an attempt at aerial navigation." He begged Ely to renounce Herron and his inflammatory teachings. "In so far as you encourage and tacitly endorse that unscholarly and illiberal course," Small warned, "you must necessarily forfeit a measure of confidence."[11] Events seemed to vindicate Small a short time later when the opposition of the Iowa College trustees to Herron's teachings led to his resignation.

Ely severed his formal connection with Christian sociology, but he continued to use his academic position as a platform for criticizing traditional beliefs and institutions. Instead of expressing his reform ideas in the technical language that less radical intellectuals expected, Ely kept appealing to ordinary people in the simple, evangelical language of mass movements. Actually Ely's efforts were a small part of the popular unrest that called farmers, workers, and other dissidents into the reform movements of the 1890s, but the general instability of the times made his actions seem all the more threatening to conservatives. A frightened editor blamed what he perceived as "menacing socialism"—actually populism—at least partly on the well-meaning but misguided paternalism of visionaries like Ely, the only academic he named, who falsely equated the Populist program and socialist doctrine with the teachings of Jesus, thus radicalizing credulous, God-fearing people.[12] Then, shortly after the Pullman hysteria, a maverick Democrat on the University of Wisconsin Board of Regents, Oliver E. Wells, charged in a letter to the editor of Ely's old foe, the *Nation,* that economics at Wisconsin was being taught by a "college anarchist" who consorted with strikers and, by implication, taught socialism and anarchism to impressionable youngsters.[13]

Basically Wells made four charges: two that were specific and factual in nature, and two that applied to the whole substance and impact of Ely's teaching and writing over his entire profes-

11. Small to Ely, 24 May, 5, 15 June 1894, Ely MSS.
12. Frank Basil Tracy, "Menacing Socialism in the Western States," *Forum* 15 (May 1893):332-42. Tracy referred specifically to Ely's book on the *Social Aspects of Christianity* (New York, 1889).
13. Oliver E. Wells, "The College Anarchist," *Nation* 59 (12 July 1894):27; Rader, *Academic Mind,* pp. 138-39.

sional life. Wells said that Ely had entertained a walking delegate from Kansas City during a Madison printers' strike and that
Ely had removed the printing contract of the Christian Social
Union from the office of a nonunion printer. He also charged
that Ely believed in strikes and boycotts and that his books
justified attacks on life and property, thus tending to promote
the dissolution of the social order. Unable to ignore such
accusations, the Regents appointed a committee to investigate.
For the first time an economist faced something like a public
trial to determine the propriety of his conduct and his views.
Ely confronted the crucial decision of whether to try to confine
the investigation to the specific charges or to let it range over
the opinions expressed in all his books, articles, and teaching.[14]
The significance of the case was recognized immediately by the
press and proceedings were widely publicized. Obviously vital
issues were at stake and important precedents were to be set for
social scientists.

Actually there were a number of things in Ely's favor. His
attackers had enemies and he had powerful friends. Regent
Wells had made himself unpopular with his fellow regents, and
his tenure as state superintendent of public instruction, the
result of a fluke Democratic landslide in the state, was expected
to be short. The *Nation* and its owner, the *New York Evening
Post,* had followed so steadily archconservative a line that their
denunciation often enhanced a writer's reputation in the eyes of
his friends rather than diminishing it. Henry Demarest Lloyd,
for example, called the *Post* "more than any other journal in
the United States the organ, narrow, malignant, false, of the
New York consolidators of the people's wealth." Furthermore,
Wisconsin was already a fairly liberal university with a growing
tradition of respect for individuality in research and opinions.
Ely had the support of influential politicians and journalists. His
very prominence as an economist made it essential for friends of

14. For more detailed accounts of the Ely trial, see Rader, *Academic Mind,* pp.
136-51; Merle Curti and Vernon Carstensen, *The University of Wisconsin: A History,
1848-1925,* 2 vols. (Madison, Wis., 1949), 1:508-27; Metzger, *Academic Freedom,*
pp. 151-53; Veysey, *Emergence of the American University,* pp. 385, 410-11.

the university and particularly for other economists to do what they could to help him defend himself.[15]

Yet the profession made no united effort to help Ely. No meeting of the AEA was called; no association position was taken. Nothing indicates that the Executive Council even met or that there was any official correspondence regarding the danger to Ely, though the matter dragged on for more than a month before the Board of Regents issued a statement clearing him. A united defense might have developed if Ely had actually been dismissed. Lacking that, the risk of being associated with Elyism, radicalism, or socialism was enough to deter most academic social scientists from involving themselves voluntarily. No one publicly defended an economist's right to hold socialist sympathies. Those who supported Ely openly were already associated with him as students, colleagues, or long-time friends and fellow reformers. Beyond that group, as long as it was possible to interpret the disagreeable business as an attack on Ely individually and not on the perquisites of the profession as a whole, social scientists who were not already involved preferred to avoid connection.[16]

The sources of Ely's support illustrated his peculiar position in the professionalization movement. His most vigorous defenders were nonacademic economists who had become prominent outside the universities. While Ely's trial went on, Carroll D. Wright was in Chicago serving as chairman of a federal commission appointed to investigate the Pullman Strike. Wright was horrified at the evidences of industrial exploitation he uncovered, and he interpreted Ely's plight as one more effort to silence

15. Lloyd to Ely, 3 March 1894; Amos P. Wilder to Ely, 19 July 1894, Ely MSS. H. C. Adams remarked: "The New York Nation is a decided Bourbon. Its editors have learned nothing during the last twenty-five years and I doubt if they are capable of learning anything. Perhaps in the general shifting of social forces it is necessary to have a classical expression of incompetent ideas but I must say I weary of the reiteration of major premises which are found in the columns of this paper." Adams thought "that this fuss about Ely is not only a pity but it is a great mistake." Adams to Seligman, 28 August 1894 (Letterbook, 1893-96, pp. 280-81), Adams MSS.

16. Kinley to Ely, 7 August 1894; William Watts Folwell to Ely, 19 September 1894, Ely MSS. See also the letters of Albert Bushnell Hart to Ely, 4, 7 September 1894, ibid., apologizing for criticisms Hart made of Ely when he heard of the *Nation*'s charges while traveling in Europe.

those who insisted on applying an ethical standard to relations between capital and labor. "If your teachings . . . have produced discontent among working men and are in any degree responsible for strikes and violence, the whole pulpit of the country and of civilization can be held responsible," Wright told Ely. "You have taught equity, love, and justice as the guiding features not only in the social but in the industrial order." Wright's whole career had been a sophisticated exercise in popularization, and he shared Ely's ethical views. In defending Ely, he was merely upholding a lifelong commitment to the proposition that a democratic people could govern itself with decency and justice, given the information required to reach enlightened conclusions. Wright's concern was for Ely's views, not for his rights as an academic economist. A critic who defined the professional economist's role as Dunbar did, restricting advocacy, would have thought Wright's favorable testimony convicted Ely.[17]

Social scientists who defended Ely avoided basing their support on academic freedom. Three of his oldest and most trusted friends—Albion Small; Albert Shaw of the *Review of Reviews;* and Charles Kendall Adams, since 1892 the president of the University of Wisconsin—actually urged Ely to ignore his professorial status and respond to the charges as a private citizen, suing both Wells and the *Nation* for libel. Fortunately for Ely, friends who knew the climate of opinion in Madison persuaded him that allowing hostile lawyers and opposition newspapers to engage in an "entire overhauling" of his writings would be a terrible mistake. "In such a tribunal it would be impossible for you to get a fair judgment concerning your work at any time, and least of all now when the public mind is agitated over the strike," one colleague insisted. Professor Frederick Jackson Turner was sure that the *Nation* hoped for nothing more than a chance to make additional "exposures." As coordinator of affairs in Madison, David Kinley insisted that Ely confine his

17. Wright to Ely, 11 August 1894, Ely MSS. Wright's statement was entered in testimony before the investigating committee, along with those of C. K. Adams, E. Benjamin Andrews, Albert Shaw, and Albion Small. See Curti and Carstensen, *University of Wisconsin,* 1:523.

defense exclusively to Wells's factual charges, entirely avoiding the larger questions of academic freedom, ideology, advocacy, and scholarly competence. Partly that counsel was based on principle. The Madison advisers doubted the wisdom of supporting "the notion that the Board of Regents has any right to determine what a Professor should or should not teach in the University or through his writings." But it was also clear that Ely's supporters expected public opinion to turn against him if his views on labor and socialism were thoroughly aired.[18]

Ultimately Ely had to decide how to conduct his own defense. He had enunciated the principles that should logically have guided his choice when he declared in 1886 that a professional economist established his authority on economic questions and earned the right to communicate his opinions freely simply by dedicating his life to the scientific study of economics. If Ely could have convinced other professional economists that an investigation of his teachings impugned the motives and questioned the competence of all, if he could have won the open support of a prestigious group of academic specialists who held varying opinions on economic questions but unanimously defended the right of advocacy, his wisest course would have been to generalize the charges, no matter what Wisconsin colleagues advised. At its fullest, the academic freedom argument would have answered the specific charges of prolabor activity by denying that a professor's actions as a private citizen were subject to administrative supervision. To the general charges that Ely's ideas incited people to violence, socialism, or anarchism, the academic freedom position would have insisted on the scholar's right to seek the truth and publish it freely, without personal responsibility for what others made of the findings. Finally, a defense based on professionalism would have denied to anyone but other economists the right to judge the competence of an academic economist.

18. Small to Ely, 28 July 1894; Shaw to Ely, 19, 26 July 1894; C. K. Adams to Ely, 23 July, 2, 14, 17 August 1894; William Scott to Ely, 21 July, 6 August 1894; Turner to Ely, 4 August 1894; Kinley to Ely, 2, 7 August 1894, Ely MSS.

Ely's actions were in fact a curious denial of his earlier convictions. He never asserted the economist's professional competence in economic questions. He never defended the economist's right to advocate. Ely sat silent on the platform at Chautauqua while Methodist Bishop John Vincent read a public statement for him. Astonishingly, Ely admitted that the grave accusations against him, if true, "unquestionably unfit me to occupy a responsible position as an instructor of youth in a great university." At the trial his defense was organized around proving him innocent of the specific charges. In a courtroomlike procedure, Ely's lawyer introduced evidence to show that a former student of Ely's who was teaching at a local business school, not Ely himself, had been seen with the walking delegate, and that Ely had never removed a printing contract from a nonunion shop but had only explained that the organization he represented might wish him to do so. Proving that Wells's charges were full of factual errors helped to establish Ely's personal character and credibility. Indirectly that strategy enhanced the image of a scientist skilled in dealing precisely with unimpeachable facts. But it did nothing to establish a principle regarding advocacy.[19]

Ely not only avoided the issue of academic freedom; he also recanted his radicalism. Instead of defending his interest in the reform potential of socialist theories and reaffirming his sympathy with American labor, Ely denied both causes. In 1886 he had dedicated his *Labor Movement* to the workingmen of America. Now he claimed that he had written his books "primarily for men of wealth and culture—for those called the upper classes." Earlier Ely had called the Knights of Labor the most constructive and Christian agents working for the preservation of American society. Now he listed wealthy friends by name. He denied, as though it were a crime, that he had more than twice in his life spoken before a labor audience. After the

19. Ely to Kinley, 7 August 1894; Ely to Amos Wilder, 22 July 1894; Ely statement in the Chautauqua Amphitheater, 14 August 1894, Ely MSS; summary of the trial transcript in Curti and Carstensen, *University of Wisconsin*, 1:518-22.

specific charges had been proved false and the investigating committee had decided not to examine his writings, Ely had his lawyer read selected excerpts from his books to demonstrate the moderation of his views on strikes, socialism, boycotts, and other controversial topics. The academics who testified for him stressed the conservative tendency of his thought and denied that he had ever taught socialism. Later in the fall, Ely again appealed to the reading public in a *Forum* article expressing his conservative views on social questions. Of his social philosophy, Ely wrote, "I am a conservative rather than a radical, and in the strict sense of the term an aristocrat rather than a democrat."[20]

When Ely claimed that his views had altered in the direction of conservatism, he was almost certainly telling the truth. The personal anxiety and distress to his family which the "heresy" trial caused undoubtedly made the harassed professor wonder whether expressing sentiments that others considered radical was worth the price. Also, the reaction of prominent fellow economists left little doubt that Ely was no longer in the mainstream of economic thinking, if he had ever been. Some academics hinted publicly that excessive popularization and weak scholarship were at least partly to blame for Ely's straits. With the ink of the trial transcript still hardly dry, Hadley of Yale dismissed Ely's new book, *Socialism and Social Reform* (1894), as an exercise in emotionalism. From Harvard W. J. Ashley assured Ely, if things went badly, "that any real risk to academic freedom would call forth a protest even from the most 'conservative' & 'individualist' of economists"; he even claimed that Dunbar was outraged by Ely's predicament. But an ominous theme recurred in the comments of several leading economists: though you ought to be allowed to express yourself, our views are very different from yours. It was the precedent of suppression in any form, not the possible suppression of Ely's views, that caused concern. In frightened moments Ely

---

20. Ely to Messrs. Chynoweth, Johnston, and Dale, August 1894, Ely MSS; Ely, "Fundamental Beliefs in My Social Philosophy," *Forum* 18 (October 1894):173-83; Curti and Carstensen, *University of Wisconsin*, 1:523.

must have sensed that he was on the fringe rather than in the vanguard of professional economic thought in the 1890s.[21]

After a decade of professional debate, a number of prominent economists simply considered two of Ely's major interests, popularization and reform, inappropriate for an academic economist. Popularization, they thought, was somehow beneath the dignity of the professional. Active participation in reform undermined the economist's impartiality and objectivity. Both endangered the prestige of the entire profession.

To a degree, these views cut across ideological lines. Ely's critics were not all conservatives, and economists who defended public advocacy were not all liberal or radical in their economic opinions. William Graham Sumner had repeatedly advocated extreme, unpopular measures to deal with economic problems. J. Laurence Laughlin was as much identified with his intransigent stand on the money question as Ely was with labor, so much so that William Hope Harvey's tactic of sending Laughlin to "Coin's Financial School" was an effective device in the crusade for free silver. Laughlin and Ely had something in common, in fact; Laughlin believed that the notoriety of his debate with "Coin" made it impossible for him ever to get a serious hearing for his views on money.[22]

But Laughlin and Ely were both extremists by comparison with the new type of academic social scientist which emerged out of the conflict of the 1880s and the quiet scholarly advance of the early 1890s to take over the leadership of the profession. Either because partisanship violated their principles or because it was not compatible with security and advancement in the profession, academic economists of this new type avoided letting themselves become too closely identified with any controversial program. Thus Seligman and Clark at Columbia, Hadley

21. Taussig to Ely, 23 August 1894; Seligman to Ely, 13 August 1894; Fred H. Wines to Ely, 27 October 1894; Ashley to Ely, 23 August 1894; Edward W. Bemis to Ely, 2 December 1894, 15 January 1895; Ely to Bemis, 12 January 1895, Ely MSS; H. C. Adams to Seligman, 28 August 1894, Adams MSS; Hadley, "Ely's 'Socialism and Social Reform,' " pp. 184-91.

22. Laughlin to Ely, 8 December 1899, Ely MSS; Dorfman, *Economic Mind,* 3:226, 273.

and Farnam at Yale, Taussig at Harvard, perhaps E. R. L. Gould at Hopkins, Small at the University of Chicago, and Adams of Michigan comprised a new interest group within economics which defined itself primarily in neither ideological nor methodological, but rather in careerist terms.

This new professional economist was a hybrid combining qualities of both the amateur social scientist and the so-called pure scientist. Though he knew his subject had profound implications for the reconstruction of society, the model new professional was a cautious gradualist who was willing to let men who wanted to be identified as reformers take leadership in applying social science to society. At best, the new professional economist preferred to take an assignment as an expert with a government commission or a private foundation and give advice to be carried out by someone else, after the political decisions had been made. Even then he wanted it clear that he was providing specialist services in his professional capacity as a social scientist, not as a volunteer partisan prompted by reforming zeal.[23]

Such a man Richard T. Ely had never been. As his connection with radical reform increased in the 1880s and early 1890s, Ely was increasingly viewed as a liability by professional economists who had adapted themselves to the new careerist values. Whether conservative or liberal in opinions, the most self-conscious professionals were appalled by the prospect that the whole profession might be identified with such obvious partisanship. Some who shunned the Ely image valued independent scholarship so highly that they believed it was compromised by almost any form of advocacy. Some despised the particular views that Ely advocated. Others simply feared and disliked anyone rash enough to challenge the views of officials who controlled the open positions and donors who held the purse strings of higher education.

By the mid-1890s Ely realized that his evangelistic style made

23. Examples abound, but the best is Henry Carter Adams's transition from a vocal defender of railroad strikers, as he was in the Sibley Lecture which led to his dismissal at Cornell, to a bureaucrat employed as a technical expert devising the means of regulating railroad rates for the Interstate Commerce Commission.

him look like an extremist. After his trial he tried uneasily to demonstrate that he too could practice the scholarly detachment and single-mindedness which the new image required. He tried to show that his reform interests were always subsidiary to sound scholarship, and he tried to redeem the past by insisting that his legitimate claims to priority in several theoretical innovations were unjustly denied by his detractors. He grew cautious about allowing his name to be used by reform societies.[24] He became more sensitive to charges of popularization, denying them with all his might. He bombarded legislators and private foundations with insistent requests for appointments as a technical expert. He seized every chance to advertise his conservatism.[25] In other words, Ely took the new ethos of the professional social scientist into account and deliberately managed his own image to bring it into accord with the model.

Ely's scholarship changed too. He published less, invited former students to collaborate with him on revisions of earlier works, and made a concerted effort to upgrade the scholarly quality of his writings. He stopped publishing with houses like Chautauqua. His old fields of interest, labor and government intervention, were unsuitable for the new image. For a time he floundered in search of something safely scientific to replace them. Unable to push as far as more able theoreticians into the

24. Ely to Kinley, 4 September 1899; W. D. P. Bliss to Ely, 15 September 1899; Ely to Bliss, 25 October 1899, Ely MSS. In the latter exchange, Bliss pressed Ely, who had refused to accept office in "our Union Reform League," to become vice president in the Social Reform Union. Ely declined, explaining: "It seems to me that I can work more effectively apart from your organization. I have held aloof from nearly all organizations, even when their aims have strongly appealed to me." He even remained aloof from the American Economic Association, attending no meeting from 1892 to 1899.

25. Ely to Senator John C. Spooner, 27 December 1897, 12 May 1899, n.d. 1899, Ely MSS. First Ely called Spooner's attention to the appointment of Professor Jeremiah Jenks of Cornell as "Expert Agent of the Treasury Department." Then Ely requested: "Could I not be appointed Expert Agent of the Treasury Department for the investigation of governmental revenues and expenditures?" Later he increased his pressure on Spooner by reciting a list of the social science professors at the University of Michigan (Worcester on the Philippine Commission, Adams as statistician for the ICC and Special Agent for the Census Bureau, and the elder and younger Cooleys) who held government positions as experts. "No University of Wisconsin man has had such opportunities," Ely complained, pointing out that Wisconsin men were as able and should have the chance for public service and recognition. See also Ely to Taussig, 29 November 1899, Ely MSS.

tangled thicket of mathematics and utility theory underlying the new economics, Ely finally hit upon a specialty that called for no esoteric knowledge or skills and had an automatic appeal to a wide audience: the economic problems of rural America. Despite the agrarian radicalism of the Populist movement, the farm somehow seemed farther from socialism than the factory. Ely exalted rural economics to the status of a specialty within the discipline and made it his own preserve for the rest of his life.[26] His subsequent contributions as an administrator, teacher, and catalyst for the more original work of others were great. And finally, when time and change had dulled the hurt of past events, Ely returned to the American Economic Association he had started, eventually becoming its president. But in the events of the 1890s and in the changing expectations of academic social scientists were forces that actually restructured Ely's perceptions of his own role. Never again did he style himself as a reform leader. When Ely relinquished his claim to activism, he exchanged advocacy for acceptability.

26. Ely consulted C. K. Adams about "an intention not to publish very much during the next two or three years." Adams to Ely, 19 September 1894, Ely MSS. Ely's retreat from reform and his struggle to make a distinctive contribution to scholarship in economics are discussed in Rader, *Academic Mind*, pp. 151-64.

8   *The Perils of Radicalism*

"Why should an institution pay a professor to teach social doctrines which are contrary to the consensus of opinions of the faculty, the supporters of the institution, and of the general community?" George Gunton demanded to know in 1895.[1] Why should the University of Chicago harbor Edward W. Bemis, an economist whose views on labor organization, industrial consolidation, government regulation, and private property directly contradicted opinions held by the founder and administrators of the school? Shaped by the stress of a severe depression, the question struck to the heart of the matter. Did academic freedom mean that a social scientist had the right to speak out on current issues, criticize the basic institutions of society, point to conditions he thought were unjust, and propose alternatives? Or did unsettled times demand restraint?

Neither Henry Carter Adams's dismissal, which had unfolded behind a veil of secrecy in the 1880s, nor Ely's deceptive victory, where the issue of academic freedom was deliberately slighted, had resolved the uncertainties surrounding the social scientist's role in American society. Bold on its face, the Wisconsin regents' eloquent defense of the abstract principle of academic freedom fell short of establishing guidelines for behavior in concrete situations. Yet the experience gained in a series of academic freedom cases was more important than any other single factor in setting the pattern for relations between social scientists and society. In the crisis of the mid-1890s, when farmers, laborers, and reformers made a kind of last-ditch stand against industrialism, Bemis and another Ely student, John Rogers Commons, faced the personal and professional crises that provided the next opportunities for clarifying the professional social scientist's role.[2]

If late nineteenth-century economists were ranged along a

spectrum, with those who strove to practice objective, normless science at one side and those who believed in using the results of their scientific inquiries to improve the human condition on the other, Bemis and Commons would fall among the staunchest advocates for relevance and involvement. Trained in the ethical tradition of historical economics, both men considered government action a potent remedy for the ills of industrial society. Both called for reforms in political and economic institutions to deal with the social inequities of a class-stratified society. Both believed in public advocacy as a right and a responsibility of professional social scientists. But professional discourse took on an increasing settled, conservative tone in the 1890s. As the institutions of corporate capitalism hardened, critics suffered. Neither Bemis nor Commons was securely enough established to withstand the growing pressure for conformity or resist the call for sanctions against radical economists who claimed protection under the doctrine of academic freedom.

Historians have usually looked upon an academic freedom case as a contest between the professor and the enemy, with the outcome decided on the academic's merits and the enemy's clout. Following hard on Ely's trial, the Bemis model showed how much a professor's influence and security depended on factors internal to the profession: location, ideological position or "school," and scholarly reputation. By the mid-1890s scholarly professions recognized themselves and were recognized by others as interest groups in which one person's achievements or misfortunes affected all. The individual's situation was never static, for centers of power and influence kept shifting as people moved about and knowledge developed. An important

1. Quoted in "Professor Bemis and the University of Chicago," *Public Opinion* 19 (11 November 1895):582. For Gunton's economic views, see Dorfman, *Economic Mind*, 3:127-28, 218.

2. The statement of the Wisconsin regents is published in Richard Hofstadter and Wilson Smith, eds., *American Higher Education: A Documentary History*, 2 vols. (Chicago, 1961), 2:859-60, and in Richard T. Ely, *Ground under Our Feet* (New York, 1938), p. 232. For a comparative account of the issues involved in the Bemis and Ely cases, see Walter P. Metzger, *Academic Freedom in the Age of the University* (New York, 1961), pp. 153-62.

contribution might give the whole profession higher status; a scare or scandal might make them all seem dangerous. Yet in the moment when a single academic faced a crisis, the outcome was very much affected by his individual place in the scholarly demography of the day.

When a case became public, every interested member of the profession was forced to evaluate the situation and decide what action, if any, to take. In a specific instance the decision might depend as much on whether the two professors—victim and potential supporter—had attended the same graduate school, studied under the same professor, belonged to the same sub-specialty, read and wrote for the same journals, reviewed each other favorably, and took compatible stands on substantive issues in the discipline, as on some abstract definition of academic freedom. An older professor who was in or close to the professional elite and well established in a department that ranked high in the status hierarchy of the profession was more important to every member than a relative unknown or a maverick. All these formal and informal considerations combined to determine support, the extent to which "safe" professional colleagues were willing to aid the endangered professor by attaching their reputations to his.

On all the important counts—location, ideological position, and professional standing, Bemis turned out to be poorly situated. His academic interests included two of the most explosive issues of the period: public ownership of basic utilities and the right of laborers to organize for collective action, including strikes. The fortunes of his employer, the University of Chicago, were tied up with those of the city, and Chicago, in the mid-1890s, was a crucible for class conflict and a proving ground for antiradical measures devised by industrial leaders, the judiciary, and the national executive itself. Sympathy with the labor movement was tantamount to subversion; support for public ownership of gasworks or streetcar lines attacked the interests of the private capitalists who owned them and the politicians who dispensed the franchises.

On ideological grounds, Bemis was caught in a rightward relocation of American political discussion that began in the 1890s and progressed through the first generation of the twentieth century. Economic programs which had been regarded as acceptable if somewhat novel alternatives in the more fluid 1880s sounded, by the standards of a decade that knew even worse economic hardship and greater fear, quite dangerously radical. Almost inexorably, alternatives to capitalism—revisionist schemes that had been celebrated by populists, socialists, anarchists, antimonopolists, and reformers of other stripes—were gradually drying up. A process was already under way which would reinterpret serious right- or left-wing critics of corporate capitalism as lunatics, agitators, or agents of foreign powers. Major industrialists and financiers, officials of conservative unions and farmers' organizations, editors of liberal newspapers and journals, and leaders of both major political parties moved toward accepting a government-regulated market economy combined with welfare measures as the most mutually desirable settlement of the era's troubling economic questions.[3] Economists who persisted in advancing theories that conflicted with the emerging consensus faced increasing danger.

To defend himself, Bemis needed the support of leaders in the profession who both knew and respected his work and commanded respect themselves. His mentor, Ely, was neither as effective nor as willing a champion as he might have been a few years earlier. Yet something—perhaps their own ambitions as well as the increasing distance between their economic assumptions and Bemis's—led other potentially effective supporters to conclude that Bemis was expendable. The people who defended him were not the powerful professional leaders who could have done the most to safeguard his academic future.

3. For various approaches to the emergence of interest group liberalism and its consensual agreement on progressive welfare capitalism, see Robert Wiebe, *The Search for Order, 1877-1920* (New York, 1967), esp. chapts. 5-7; James Weinstein, *The Corporate Ideal in the Liberal State, 1900-1918* (Boston, 1968), passim; Samuel P. Hays, *The Response to Industrialism, 1885-1914* (Chicago, 1957), esp. chapts. 3, 7.

Bemis's crisis coincided with a quiet revolution in economics, a change far subtler than the redirection of the 1880s but nonetheless significant. After two decades of neglect, marginal utility theory was finding American advocates. With its emphasis on demand as the determinant of value, this new theory provided a timely alternative for more socially disruptive explanations that traced value to cost of production or labor cost. Contrary to the arguments of reformers, marginalism seemed to prove that a market economy did indeed contain impartial regulators not unlike the natural laws that classical economists had once insisted upon. As leading marginalists described it, the free market guaranteed that all parties in the productive process—labor as well as capitalists and entrepreneurs—would receive their fair share of the wealth created by industry.[4] If that was the case, then there was less reason for ethical economists to demand sweeping changes. The improvements they sought in the general welfare could be achieved safely, without risking the unknown dangers of socialism, by a process of constant, expert regulation designed to keep economic friction from disrupting the natural distribution of wealth.

It was in these volatile circumstances that the Bemis case was played out. Consciously or unconsciously, Bemis and the others who influenced his fate made their decisions against a background that included not only Bemis's place in the profession but also the profession's place in the society and times. The context made the Bemis affair a classic case.

At first Bemis's career had looked unusually promising. Born in Springfield, Massachusetts, he was educated at Amherst College and the Johns Hopkins University. He taught briefly at Amherst in the 1880s, joined with Ely and other historical economists in forming the AEA, found opportunities to present his research findings before the AEA and the ASSA, published

4. On the content of marginal economics and the reception of marginalism in America, see Dorfman, *Economic Mind*, 3:190-205, 237-52; Craufurd D. W. Goodwin, "Marginalism Moves to the New World," in *The Marginal Revolution in Economics*, ed. R. D. Collison Black, A. W. Coats, and Craufurd D. W. Goodwin (Durham, N. C., 1973), pp. 285-304.

articles in the *Johns Hopkins University Studies* and the *Publications of the AEA,* and shortly moved to Vanderbilt University as a lecturer in history and political economy. When the young professor was called to the new University of Chicago in 1892, it was testimony to his rapid professional advancement. Yet only three years later Bemis resigned under extreme pressure and accused the university of dismissing him because his economic views displeased its major benefactors.[5] To understand this dramatic reversal, it is necessary to analyze in more detail how Bemis's location, ideology, and professional standing affected his ability to defend himself.

The academic setting for the Bemis case was the imposing and prestigious University of Chicago, the joint creation of a determined builder, former Chautauqua executive William Rainey Harper, and another well-meaning Baptist, the incredibly wealthy architect of the Standard Oil Trust, John D. Rockefeller. When the upstart university opened its doors in 1892, its ambitious president had already pirated an excellent faculty away from schools all over the country. The Rockefeller endowment eventually amounted to $34 million. To some contemporaries that made the school a corrupt symbol of the evil genius behind industrialism, a "gas trust" university in which there could be no hope of freedom to inquire, let alone to criticize the actions of the founder or the system that enriched him. In others, a grudging admiration for President Harper's bold rush to greatness was mixed with anticipation to see what might be

---

5. When I was researching the Bemis case, I benefited from reading an unpublished paper, "The Edward W. Bemis Controversy," which Harold E. Bergquist, Jr., had deposited in the Bemis File, William Rainey Harper MSS, President's Collection, University of Chicago. Somewhat shortened, that paper has recently been published as "The Edward W. Bemis Controversy at the University of Chicago," *AAUP Bulletin* 58 (December 1972):384-93. Bergquist's judicious account is almost entirely internal to the University of Chicago. He weighs the evidence to support Bemis's claim that he was fired for his radical views against the counterclaims of Harper and others at the university that Bemis was fired for incompetence. Bergquist concludes that "Harper decided to sacrifice Bemis on behalf of creating a private university sufficiently endowed to rank among the greatest in the country and the world" (p. 393). My effort is to place the Bemis case among other cases in the wider context of social science professionalization and to show, by drawing on widely scattered academic collections, how social scientists all over the United States responded to Bemis's plight.

accomplished when higher education forsook the protection of its usual pastoral isolation and settled, along with most Americans, in the big city.

The city in question has just finished raising a white fairyland on the lakeshore to house the Columbian Exposition. Most observers agreed that the effort failed to conceal Chicago's problems: almost breakneck population growth, a huge immigrant population, incredible corruption in city government, militant labor, determined capitalists, a rough and ready police force, and a volatile political situation.[6] Into this confused and dangerous milieu broke the able, idealistic, aggressive, outspoken, occasionally abrasive reform economist, Edward W. Bemis.

The distinguishing feature of Bemis's economic philosophy was his interest in socializing essential public services. Bemis was one of the first economists to realize how dramatically the mushrooming growth of cities and the specialization of labor in modern industries had increased people's dependence on businesses that provided vital utilities such as gas, water, transportation, and communications. The possibility of monopoly pricing and graft in the letting of franchises convinced Bemis that utilities should be closely regulated, if not actually owned by the public. For his own special emphasis Bemis had chosen the municipal ownership of utilities, especially gas works. In Nashville, where Vanderbilt was located, he had projected himself dramatically into a local civic reform group's crusade for municipal control of the gas supply and received credit for the victory without loss to his academic standing.[7]

In Chicago Bemis's situation deteriorated rapidly. The head

6. For the most evocative account of Chicago in the 1890s, see Ray Ginger, *Altgeld's America, 1890-1905* (Chicago, 1965), esp. chapt. 1. The standard history of the early University of Chicago is Richard J. Storr, *Harper's University: The Beginnings* (Chicago, 1966).

7. Edward W. Bemis, "Socialism and State Action," *Journal of Social Science* 21 (September 1886):33-68; Bemis, "Municipal Ownership of Gas in the United States," *Publications of the AEA* 6 (1891):287-472; Fine, *Laissez Faire*, pp. 211, 217, 227. Natural monopolies that required either government ownership or stringent regulation were routinely recognized by Henry Carter Adams, Ely, and James as well as by more moderate economists such as John Bates Clark.

of the economics department was J. Laurence Laughlin, one of the most resolute conservatives in academic economics. Disillusioned with academic life in the Dunbar regime, Laughlin had left Harvard and returned to business. When he decided to resume his teaching career, first briefly in Adams's vacated chair at Cornell and then as head professor at Chicago, it was with the avowed intention of combating "financial heresy." Harper may have expected that Bemis and Laughlin would balance each other, for the president worked hard to get both men. Predictably, Laughlin had no use for Bemis. To keep his unwanted junior colleague out of the economics department, Laughlin had Bemis assigned to the extension division for most of his teaching load. Extension courses, especially those offered to workingmen's groups in the city, gave Bemis opportunities for public exposure and put him in touch with the Chicago reform community.[8]

In the early 1890s John Peter Altgeld led a disjointed but vigorous attack on privilege in Illinois politics. Bemis joined the fight for reasonable limits on Chicago street railway franchises and launched a crusade for municipal control of the city's gas supply. The Chicago gas trust retaliated, it was later charged, by denying the university its usual reduction in rates as long as Bemis remained on the faculty. Bemis joined with other reformers in the newly organized Chicago Civic Federation to step up the pressure for municipal reform. Soon the trustees began to hear complaints. In the fall of 1893 Bemis's extension teaching was unsuccessful, but Laughlin's continued opposition made it impossible for him to be assigned "inside" teaching. Finally, in January 1894, a frustrated Harper notified Bemis that he was not acceptable as a permanent member of the social science faculty. Unable to fire a tenured professor summarily, Harper

8. Laughlin to Seligman, 11 July 1890, Seligman MSS; Laughlin to Simon Newcomb, 11 May, 6 June 1890, Newcomb MSS; Bemis to Ely, 9 February 1892, Ely MSS; Harper to Bemis, 15 January 1894, William Rainey Harper MSS, President's Collection, University of Chicago; Laughlin to Harper, 31 August 1893, Laughlin File, Harper MSS; Bemis to Herbert Baxter Adams, 12 April 1893, Herbert Baxter Adams MSS, Milton S. Eisenhower Library, Johns Hopkins University.

hoped to ease him out. "I am persuaded," the president wrote, "that in the long run you can do in another institution because of the peculiar circumstances here, a better and more satisfactory work to yourself than you can do here." Harper's explanation was vague—he obviously wanted to avoid a scene— but he assured Bemis that his reputation should make it possible for him to secure a place "in which you will be above all things else independent."[9]

Bemis had no intention of resigning quietly. Instead he attracted more attention. When the city was distracted by the Pullman strike, he mounted the pulpit at the First Presbyterian Church and chastized the railroads. So long as railroad leaders violated laws against discriminatory practices and corrupted legislatures with bribes, Bemis argued, they were hardly justified in accusing strikers of lawlessness. Though Bemis criticized the strikers too, his remarks were widely interpreted as a defense of Debs and the American Railway Union. President Marvin Hughitt of the Chicago and Northwestern Railroad heard the speech and took his outraged denial of Bemis's allegations to the university trustees, whose pressure on Harper apparently increased. "It is hardly safe for me to venture into any of the Chicago clubs," Harper told Bemis. Though Bemis protested that he had done his best to prevent the strike, Harper ordered him to make no more public statements on controversial questions while he remained with the university.[10]

For some time neither Bemis nor Harper revealed the tense situation publicly. Harper kept urging Bemis to resign on the grounds that his "lines of special work in labor, monopoly, and city problems were most valuable but this is not the Uvsty [sic]

9. Ginger, *Altgeld's America,* pp. 168-79; Bergquist, "Bemis Controversy," p. 384; "Prof. Bemis' Secret Out," *Voice,* 17 August 1895, p. 1, in Bemis File, Harper MSS; Harper to Bemis, 14 January 1894, ibid.

10. Bemis Statement, 9 October 1895, published in the *Boston Herald,* 9 October 1895, and many other newspapers. See also the Bemis File, or Book 1, University Scrapbooks, pp. 122-51, University of Chicago Archives. On Harper's position, see Bemis to Ely, 13 August 1894, Ely MSS; Bemis to Harper, 23 July 1894, Bemis File, Harper MSS; Bergquist, "Bemis Controversy," p. 387; Metzger, *Academic Freedom,* p. 152, n. 46.

for them or for forming a connection with the labor movement." Privately Harper was preparing influential friends to
accept the explanation that Bemis was being discharged for
incompetence. In at least one instance Harper claimed that
"where he [Bemis] has lectured once in a place, no one will
hear him a second time," a wild exaggeration of Bemis's difficulties as an extension teacher. Harper also hinted that Bemis's
colleagues doubted his scientific ability for regular university
teaching and research. If a scandal broke, Harper hoped to show
that the university was simply unable to use Bemis because his
talents had proved to be too limited.[11]

Meanwhile Bemis was trying to leave the University of Chicago. When he was unable to locate another position, Harper
agreed to an arrangement that would have permitted him to
continue a somewhat restricted teaching schedule through the
1895-1896 academic year. But Bemis was not inclined to follow
a cautious policy too far. In the summer of 1895, when
Thorstein Veblen was denied permission to offer a course on
socialism, Bemis concluded that the university was "a tool of
monopoly and fraud upon the public." When the confrontation
came, he knew that control of the press would be vital. Bemis
decided, after long deliberation, to announce that he was leaving the university at the request of the administration. Making
no charges, he would simply let himself appear as the innocent
victim of a persecuting monopoly. The newspapers, he hoped,
would do the rest.[12]

11. Bemis to Ely, 15 March, 24 April 1895, Ely MSS; Bemis to H. C. Adams, 3
May 1895, Adams MSS; Lyman Abbott, editor of the *Outlook,* to Harper, 26
February, 15 March 1895; Harper to the Reverend Arthur T. Edwards, 1 August, 22
November 1895, Bemis File, Harper MSS. Abbott started by thinking that Bemis was
"a man of singularly judicial temper, and was doing very valuable work as a
painstaking and fair-minded investigator," but Harper's answer disabused him. Later
Abbott seems to have grown skeptical of Harper's motives. See Bemis to Ely, 16
August, 11 September 1895, Ely MSS. See also "The Statement of the President of
the University for the Quarter Ending June 30, 1895," *University Calendar,* 4, no. 1
(University of Chicago, August 1895):17, for another statement on Bemis's extension
record and competence.

12. "Prof. Bemis' Secret Out," *Voice,* 17 August 1895, p. 1. The first report
actually appeared in the *New York World* of 14 August 1895, ostensibly from
someone close to the president and authorized to speak for him. On Bemis's

For a time the plan worked. All the residual power of midwestern, populist hatred for corporate bigness combined to bring formidable allies to Bemis's column. Early reactions were almost universally sympathetic to Bemis as the independent searcher for truth. His scalp, one newspaper said, "now dangles at the belt of monopoly." The sharpest critics blamed Rockefeller, the Standard Oil Company, the traction magnate Charles T. Yerkes, the Chicago and Northwestern Railroad, and the entire Chicago gas trust for pressuring the university trustees to purge Bemis.[13] The lack of a university position was interpreted as an admission of guilt. Finally, at Laughlin's urging, Harper decided to remain silent no longer. In a restrained statement which cited no particulars about Bemis, Harper resolutely denied that any benefactor had ever made the slightest effort to influence teaching in the social sciences. His speech left the strong implication that the trouble was not with the donors but with the professor.[14]

The inevitable escalation ensued. Still sure that he could vindicate himself, Bemis quoted letters and conversations in which Harper had expressed approval of his teaching. The president knew he was no radical, Bemis insisted, but contributions from wealthy capitalists meant more to Harper than truth. To document corporation pressure on the university, Bemis pointed to the railroad president's angry reaction to his Pullman strike address and quoted the president of a gas consolidation

---

admission of his weakness in extension teaching, especially in 1893, see Bemis to Ely, 5, 18 August 1895, Ely MSS.

13. Book 1, University Scrapbooks, pp. 122-51, contains a complete file of clippings on the Bemis affair. Not all the criticism came from Western papers. The *Philadelphia Inquirer*, 26 August 1895, for example, considered it "just as well after all that the Standard Oil money made in Pennsylvania went to no Pennsylvania College." A few papers, predictably the *New York Sun* and *Evening Post*, opposed Bemis as a crank, anarchist, or socialist from the beginning of the dispute.

14. Laughlin to Harper, 8 September 1895, Laughlin File, Harper MSS; "The Statement of the President of the University for the Quarter Ending 31 September 1895," *Quarterly Calendar*, 4, no. 2 (University of Chicago, November 1895):13, contains Harper's statement to the trustees. The statement was substantially repeated by Harper at the University Convocation of October 11 and described in the *Kingdom*, 11 October 1895; *New York Evening Post*, 5 October 1895; *Dial*, 16 October 1895.

who had read his views on municipal ownership and warned, "If we can't convert you, we are going to down you. We can't stand your writing. It means millions to us." Bemis was unable to demonstrate direct pressure from Rockefeller, but his counter-charges restored a strong presumption that he had been fired because of his quite obvious unpopularity with corporate interests.[15]

When the struggle between Bemis and Harper reached the public as a full-blown academic freedom case, Bemis's fate hung precariously on the support he received from other social scientists. Quickly the factors of location, ideology, and professional standing began to have their telling effect. Though Bemis was well known among economists all over the country, the reactions of his own Chicago colleagues were extremely significant. Here Bemis was unlucky. He had come to the university as an associate professor of political economy in the Lecture Study Department of the Extension Division, but Harper had promised him "inside work," presumably in the economics department, where he belonged by training and experience. From the first, Laughlin had blocked Bemis's progress toward that goal. Unable to dissuade Harper from hiring an Ely protégé, Laughlin at least tried to keep his own students away from the corrupting influence of one who seemed, in his view, to have inherited all of his mentor's unsoundness and misguided passion for reform. Bemis taught some courses in the regular program, but Laughlin consistently refused to accept him as a member of the economics department. When Harper tried to insist, Laughlin pointed out that Bemis really wanted to "lecture on Labor &c rather than on Trades Unions &c," and proposed that "the

15. Bemis Statement, 9 October 1895, Bemis File, Harper MSS; Bemis to Ely, 15 March 1895, Ely MSS. The railroad president was Marvin Hughitt of the Chicago and Northwestern. Bemis twice identified the gas executive as Walton Clark of the United Gas Improvement Co. of Philadelphia. See Bemis to Herbert Baxter Adams, 14 May 1894, H. B. Adams MSS. Bemis never said anything specific about Standard Oil and apparently did not believe "Rockefeller had so much to do with the matter as local corporations." He had no absolute proof of monopoly control, he admitted, but considered the circumstantial evidence of plutocratic influence "almost conclusive." Bemis to Ely, 18, 16 August 1895, Ely MSS.

Labor course might go under Soc. Sci.—if Small does not object." Except in the extension division, Laughlin had no intention of letting Bemis teach anything that he considered economics.

Like Harper, Laughlin must have been influenced by his ambitions for the university. His early work had established him as a prominent student of railroad problems and he hoped, with the good will and financial support of railroad executives in Chicago, to make his new department a center for railroad economics. Yet the whole project seemed to hang on the antics of a man whom he considered so "wholly one-sided on the railway problem" that the only hope of changing him was "throwing out all his railway lectures." Throwing out Bemis himself was a highly desirable alternative, especially if it could be accomplished in a manner that helped to restore public confidence in the university. When Harper hung back from making a statement that might harm Bemis's reputation irreparably, Laughlin insisted that the president's duty to the university transcended "any softheartedness to an individual." "I do not see how we can escape saving ourselves," Laughlin added, "except by letting the public know that he goes because we do not regard him as up to the standard of the University in ability and scientific methods."[16]

When the news of Bemis's forced resignation broke, Laughlin was in Vienna. For the crucial scholarly appraisal of Bemis's competence, people naturally turned to the head professor of social science, Albion Woodbury Small. Even close contemporaries might have expected Small to defend Bemis, for their backgrounds were strikingly alike. A product of the evangelical tradition that influenced so many reform economists, Small had been a typical Ely student. Born in 1854 the son of a Baptist

16. Laughlin to Harper, 6, 31 August, 8 September 1895, Laughlin File, Harper MSS. To deflect possible charges of bias against Ely students, Laughlin suggested bringing in David Kinley, whose work he judged to be "of a radically different kind from Bemis' and yet he was one of Ely's men." See Bergquist, "Bemis Controversy," pp. 386-87, on the Harper-Laughlin dispute over Bemis. Bemis's version is in Bemis to Herbert Baxter Adams, 4 April 1893, 6 April 1894, H. B. Adams MSS.

minister, he was educated at Colby College and Newton Theological Seminary. Like other aspiring ministers in the 1870s, he
gradually became disillusioned with the possibility of changing
society through the institutional churches of his day. Instead he
turned to the new social sciences in search of a comprehensive
explanation for social change. Small studied at the German
universities of Leipzig and Berlin and later at Hopkins. When
history and economics failed to provide the perspective he
desired, he helped to pioneer the new field of sociology.[17]

As a professional social scientist Small was a complicated
mixture of the old-style moral philosopher and the modern
rationalist with administrative inclinations. During the 1880s he
taught history and political economy at Colby College, where
he became president. In 1892 he accepted Harper's invitation to
establish at Chicago the first academic department in the United
States devoted exclusively to sociology. Urbane, erudite, and
dignified, Small was an academic entrepreneur who wrote one
of the first textbooks in sociology, started the new discipline's
first journal, and became fourth president of the American
Sociological Society he helped to found. His ethical inclinations
were always balanced internally by ambition and externally by
a habit of handling situations in the most diplomatic way.[18]

As Bemis's immediate superior, Small took a position that
can only be described as equivocal. Given the difficulty of
coexisting with Laughlin—especially for one who had deserted
economics to work in a discipline that was frequently confused
with social work, socialism, or both—Small was still far too
cautious in taking a stand on Bemis's ability. The record indicates that Small weighed Bemis's worth and welfare against
three other factors: the unfavorable impression that Bemis's
occasionally flamboyant actions might make on the public; the

17. For a general background on Small's contribution to sociology and higher
education, see Charles Hunt Page, *Class and American Sociology: From Ward to Ross*
(New York, 1940), pp. 113-42, and Jurgen Herbst, *The German Historical School in
American Scholarship: A Study in the Transfer of Culture* (Ithaca, N.Y., 1965); Fine,
Laissez Faire, pp. 264-66.
18. Page, *Class and American Sociology*, pp. 113-16.

long-term implications of a messy dispute for the development of social science, particularly sociology in his own university; and his own not-yet-resolved confusion about the proper level of involvement for a scholar in reform.

As long as the controversy remained intramural, Small often threw his weight to Bemis's side. When Harper excused his own failure to provide the promised "inside work" by claiming that Small refused to have Bemis in his department, Small tactfully denied it. Small "said frankly that he had heard no unfriendly criticism of my class work & knew of no weakness in it," Bemis reported. "In fact he considered me altogether competent & my courses suitable to his department, but I was injuring the department & the Uvsty [sic] because of my participation in so many phases of public questions such as in the work of the Civic Federation." Apparently at least partly with the hope of protecting Bemis, Small warned him repeatedly that the university would be a ruthless adversary if the matter became public.[19]

If Bemis's reports were accurate, Small simply believed that a scholar in a vulnerable position should avoid taking a stand on hot issues. As a matter of economic theory, Small agreed with Bemis on municipal ownership. Yet he earnestly cautioned Bemis against working for reform. "I do not say that your conclusions are wrong," Bemis quoted Small, "but in these days a man is not considered scientific, who claims to speak on more than one small corner of a subject. Then, too, there is so much misapprehension of Sociology as a science of reform that, although I hope to take up reform movements years hence, I am now going off in my lectures into transcendental philosophy so as to be as far as possible from these reform movements and thus establish the scientific character of my department." Bemis quickly realized the import of Small's posture. "Isn't that rich?" he complained. "With Prof. Small jealous and afraid of the trustees & the feelings of Laughlin, Harper is left free under

19. Bemis to Ely, 12 January, 11 March, 16 August 1895, Ely MSS; Bemis Statement, 9 October 1895, Bemis File, Harper MSS.

the pressure of the trustees & moneyed men & of Laughlin to go back on all his pledges to 'stand by' me."[20]

Small's private reaction to the Bemis case conflicted with his public position on advocacy and objectivity. In an issue of his own *American Journal of Sociology* that appeared less than a year after Bemis was fired, Small made a statement on the reform obligations of social scientists that came down flatly in favor of advocacy. "I would have American scholars, especially in the social sciences, declare their independence of do-nothing traditions," he counseled. "I would have them repeal the law of custom which bars a marriage of thought and action." Evolutionary theories implied not only the imperfection of things but also their perfectibility. Yet modern philosophy and changing technology had combined to break down the old certainties that might have guided a plan for social development. As traditional values slipped into the past a new social ethic was desperately needed, and scholars must help to supply it.[21]

On every hand, Small noted, men plagued by doubt and anguish still tried to solve their problems by referring to "the desiccated stalks of yesterday's conceptions." A legion of untrained charlatans stood ready, armed with untried panaceas, to prey upon their vulnerability. "Scholars are shirkers unless they grapple with these problems," Small declared. Sociologists ought to continue their theoretical work, but they should also seek solutions for society's moral and physical problems. For their own improvement as well as society's, scholars should involve themselves in the "concrete work" of "perfecting and applying plans and devices for social improvement"; otherwise

20. Albion W. Small, "The State and Semi-Public Corporations," *American Journal of Sociology* 1 (January 1896):398-410; Bemis to Ely, 12 January 1895, Ely MSS. Bemis claimed that he took notes on this and other conversations immediately. Small later insisted that he had used the phrase "transcendental philosophy" figuratively, but he did not deny the substance of the remarks. See Bemis to Ely, 23 October 1895, Ely MSS. In a corroborating account, Bemis reported to Herbert Baxter Adams that Small approved his work but "acknowledges that because of the attempt to separate sociology here from economics he must bend his greatest energy to developing biological & other not strictly or even indirectly economic phases of social science." Bemis to Adams, 6 April 1894, 31 July 1895, H. B. Adams MSS.
21. Albion W. Small, "Scholarship and Social Agitation," *American Journal of Sociology* 1 (March 1896):564-82.

higher education was pointless and universities parasitic.[22] What Small recommended seemed exactly like what Bemis was doing. Thus Bemis's social agitation became a test of Small's conviction.

Publicity brought Small to the defense of the university. His first statement to the press repudiated charges of monopoly interference and blamed Bemis's dismissal bluntly on his own incompetence. "Prof. Bemis was not a success in his university extension work, and was not transferred to a position within the university. The reasons for this were in no way connected with his economic doctrines, no one of which has ever been called to question by any university authority," Small maintained. "It is simply grotesque exaggeration to represent his case as in any way raising the question of freedom of thought, of investigation, or of instruction." In an attempt to acquaint professional economists with the university's position, Small assured Ely that Bemis's views had never been discussed "in any way, shape, or manner, as a reason for his unfitness, by anybody having any influence with the administration of the Univ." As Small saw it, Bemis's "mythical martyrdom" was pure fiction.[23]

Finally, when criticism of the university reached unbearable proportions, Small and Nathaniel Butler, the head of the extension division, released the statement that destroyed Bemis. Both men had supervised his work directly and now, with cold precision, they reviewed his record. Following Harper's lead, they claimed that Bemis had been hired for extension work, but he had not been successful. Far from persecuting Bemis, the university had given him ample notice and even continued his salary while attempting to help him find a new position, a venture frustrated by the foolish professor's increasing rashness of expression. At some cost to the university's reputation, every effort had been made to avoid revealing the true reasons for his

22. Ibid., pp. 581-82.
23. "Prof. Bemis' Dismissal," *Washington Post,* 27 August 1895, in Book 1, University Scrapbooks; Small to Ely, 9 August 1895, Ely MSS. Coincidentally, Small invited Ely to become an advisory editor on the new *American Journal of Sociology.*

dismissal. But finally, Small and Butler concluded, "Mr. Bemis had compelled us to advertise both his incompetence as a University Extension lecturer, and also the opinion of those most closely associated with him that he is not qualified to fill a University position."[24]

The Small-Butler statement effectively shifted public attention from Rockefeller to Bemis, but it did so at the expense of accuracy and fairness. The evidence fails to support Small's version of the extension record or justify his insinuations about Bemis's competence as a teacher. First, Bemis had not been hired to remain indefinitely in extension work. Harper wooed him away from Vanderbilt, where he was considered an excellent teacher, by promising him inside teaching. As all universities learn in hard times, extension teaching has its ups and downs. Bemis attributed his low enrollments in 1893 to the depression, his effort to maintain university standards, and the fact that the bulk of the students in some centers were women who found other courses more attractive than economics. Though his enrollments were generally good in 1894, he explained, the apparent decline at one series of lectures was caused by an excess of complimentary tickets for the first meeting and a mixup on location at the last. Bemis admitted some defects as a popular lecturer, but he was also able to point to letters from six extension secretaries who praised both the interest he aroused and the factual, nonpartisan quality of his presentations. One noted that attendance kept increasing and another credited Bemis's successful course with establishing extension work in his otherwise benighted city. There was never any stipulation by the university that Bemis's extension work was expected to pay for itself, but he was able to show that the fees he brought in had more than equaled the portion of his salary assigned to extension until the university removed him from the extension lists.[25]

24. "A Statement by Professors Small and [Nathaniel] Butler," Bemis File, Harper MSS.
25. Bemis's refutation was printed in full in "Prof. Bemis' Defense," *Chicago*

Another concern Small had about Bemis's work was probably more telling, but Small failed to articulate it fully and it was never treated as an issue. Though he was much more sympathetic to Bemis's opinions, Small seemed to share Laughlin's view that the courses Bemis liked to give were somehow suitable for extension but unsuited for proper university instruction. In Small's public statement this sense was only inference: "if the trustees could appropriate money without limit . . . , work might be assigned to Mr. Bemis which would be important and valuable in itself, but . . . the money which would be available for some time to come was much more needed for kinds of instruction which he was not competent to give." In a letter describing a stormy meeting with Small and Harper, Bemis revealed much more. "Small held that the fundamental courses had been provided for & such courses as I mentioned, viz., trades unions, cooperation, building and loan assns., profit sharing, life insurance, population, factory legislation, immigration were too special to be fitted for University instruction." To Bemis, Small's fine distinctions were mere twaddle. To Small there was a real difference between courses designed to inform special groups of laborers, teachers, ministers, or businessmen on a topic of current interest and courses designed to introduce students systematically to the content and methods of a discipline.[26] It was a vital emerging distinction between theoretical and applied social science that was to have all sorts of important ramifications over the next decade. In the Bemis matter, however, Small was unable or unwilling to identify the distinction and deal with it directly. Instead he characterized as bad teaching extension teaching that was probably perfectly appropriate for its purpose, and thus skewed the issue altogether.

Bemis's extension record alone neither justified nor caused his dismissal; it only facilitated it. A bad semester in 1893 was

---

Record, 19 October 1895, and a number of other papers in Book 1, University Scrapbooks. See also E. M. Nealley to Ely, 19 September 1895, Ely MSS. Bergquist analyzes this part of the controversy judiciously.

26. Small-Butler statement; Bemis to Ely, 8 March 1895, Ely MSS.

followed by two good semesters. The charge of incompetence was almost certainly a strategy adopted by Harper and finally accepted by Small to draw attention away from the issue of academic freedom. Bemis was probably costing the university donations, and Harper was expanding the university in advance of his funds. Given the wave of sympathy that Bemis's accusations had evoked and the president's responsibility for maintaining an acceptable image, Harper's actions were understandable if not admirable.[27] But he stumbled on an effective tactic that others would use in eliminating undesirable professors: never challenge a professor's opinions if some other weakness can be found or fabricated.

Bemis's chief sins were two: he not only theorized about radical alternatives to existing economic arrangements but actually became involved in the dangerous business of organizing resistance to the status quo, and he strayed from the emerging consensus of the 1890s in social science, particularly economics. With no support at his own institution, Bemis had to depend on the efforts of social scientists at other schools to save him. Yet his first mistake, visible radicalism, cost him the support of like-minded ethical economists who wanted to keep their own jobs. His second error deprived him of real assistance from leading economists and sociologists who were constructing new definitions of their disciplines that drastically reduced the former emphasis on finding solutions for practical problems and defined the most important concerns of social scientists around theoretical questions. Specifically, Bemis's antimonopoly activism did more than make Laughlin despise him; it cost him meaningful support from Ely. His devotion to applied social science not only took Small from his column; it deprived him of the even bigger guns of John Bates Clark.

Of the top professional economists in major universities, only Ely supported Bemis with any vigor, and he not publicly. Without question Ely believed that Bemis was being dismissed

27. See "The Statement of the President," no. 1, p. 17; Veysey, *The Emergence of the American University*, pp. 306-8.

unfairly for his views. He was convinced that there were more radical men than Bemis in the Chicago department—Charles Zeublin and Thorstein Veblen, surely—who avoided persecution simply because their work was theoretical and did not bring them into conflict with corporations. Ely recognized Bemis's limitations as a platform orator but maintained that he was as able a classroom teacher or researcher as anyone at either Chicago or Wisconsin. There was no real difference in their approach to the discipline.[28]

In the course of the controversy, Ely very nearly became a principal. It was a point of pride with Ely that he had once turned down Laughlin's chair. Bemis tried to capitalize on that fact by hinting that Ely had refused the Chicago offer because he feared he would not be free in his teaching. Soon an unidentified spokesman for Harper informed a New York newspaper that the University of Chicago had never actually invited Ely to come. Ely was positively furious, but his first reaction was a telegram that ordered Bemis to make no further public statement regarding him. In a letter to Harper demanding a retraction, Ely insisted that copies of his correspondence with Harper had convinced influential friends that a positive offer had been made. When Harper coolly evaded the issue, Ely expressed his growing frustration by telling liberal journalists and former students who were already sympathetic what was really going on at Chicago. His only move toward direct intervention was the pressure he brought on Small to consider the adverse effects that bad publicity could have on his department. Bemis obviously bent every conceivable effort to incite or embarrass Ely into dramatic public action, but beyond recommending Bemis for other jobs Ely refused to let his name be used at all. In this contest between advocacy and objectivity, Ely chose security.[29]

28. Bemis to Ely, 8 March, 13 August 1895; Ely to Hamilton Mabie, 24 August 1895, Ely MSS; Ely to Harper, 7 September 1895, Ely File, Harper MSS.

29. E. M. Nealley to Ely, 19 September 1895; Ely to Hamilton Mabie, 24 August 1895; Harper to Ely, 20 August 1895; Bemis to Ely, 9 January 1896, Ely MSS; Ely to Harper, 17 August, 7 September, Ely File, Harper MSS. Small referred several

John Bates Clark was in a better position than Ely to help Bemis fight the University of Chicago, and his support would have been more valuable. Clark's failure to defend his former colleague was a symptom of the transition that Clark had made as an economist by the mid-1890s—a fundamental shift in opinions and emphases that Bemis never made. Clark began his career as a moderate Christian Socialist who nearly went into the ministry. When he and Bemis taught at Amherst together in the 1880s, they differed more over means than ends. Clark was classicist enough to believe that actual or potential competition was essential to keep the economic system working, while Bemis hoped to do away entirely with competition. Bemis advocated municipal ownership of natural monopolies and a greatly expanded role for the state, but Clark rejected state socialism because he feared that government action would subvert the self-reliance of the individual. Even so, Clark looked forward to the time when voluntary cooperatives and profit sharing would diffuse ownership enough to eliminate the distinction between labor and capital. The special form of socialism that Clark favored in the 1880s was really a sort of ethical voluntarism that placed him only slightly left of center, among the moderate revisionists. Yet he did believe, with Bemis, that fundamental changes would be needed to guarantee a just division of the wealth that modern industry created. As a scholar there was much that pulled Clark toward the symmetry and precision of laissez-faire, but as a compassionate Christian he was equally drawn, especially in the 1880s, by his sympathy for the laboring masses.[30]

Unfortunately for Bemis, Clark grew more conservative in the 1890s. The same events that radicalized Bemis tended to moder-

---

times to a professor who had threatened a publicity campaign against the university. Bemis's letter to Ely, 13 August 1895, Ely MSS, suggests that Small attributed the threat to Ely.

30. Dorfman, Economic Mind, 3:188-95; Adams to Clark, 16 December 1886; Giddings to Clark, 24 October 1886; Andrews to Clark, 22 October 1886, Clark MSS. Clark's reform leanings were most evident in The Philosophy of Wealth (Boston, 1886), esp. pp. 174-202, 221-36.

ate Clark's interest in reform. In the face of Henry George's radical teachings, the terrorist tactics of anarchists, and increasing violence from laborers who believed that capital was robbing them of a just reward, Clark felt impelled to search for evidence of the validity of a system based on private property and contract. He accepted conservative trade unionism, but he opposed socialism more and more vigorously as radical demands for government intervention showed signs of upsetting the delicate economic and political balance that he believed held the country together. In the aftermath of the Pullman strike, when Bemis demanded far-reaching reforms, Clark argued that social scientists must exert a stabilizing influence.[31]

Clark's role in stabilizing the capitalist system was a major theoretical contribution to the development of marginalism in economics. In the last quarter of the nineteenth century a revolution in economic theory was in progress, with contributions coming from several different places in the West. In the early 1870s William Stanley Jevons in England, Carl Menger in Austria, and Léon Walras in France had independently discovered the principle of diminishing marginal utility. Clark began to work along marginal lines in the late 1870s.

For a number of reasons, marginal utility theory was slow to take root. The international community of economists was imperfectly developed and communication was poor. Since marginalism was a deductive theory that had little application in practical situations, it had limited appeal where economists had adopted a historical approach, particularly in Germany, the United States, and to a large extent in England. Also, a lack of training in mathematics made the work of Jevons and Walras difficult for many economists to comprehend. But the growing threat of Marxism, Fabianism, and the single-tax argument of Henry George made nonradical economists increasingly receptive to a theory of value that deflected criticisms of the prevail-

31. Dorfman, *Economic Mind*, 3:196-205; Clark to Ely, 3 November 1890, Ely MSS; Clark, "The Scholar's Political Opportunity," *Political Science Quarterly* 12 (December 1897):589-602.

ing system of capital and wages. In 1891 the eminent English economist Alfred Marshall wrote a treatise that showed how marginal utility economics could be reconciled with classical theories. In the United States a short time later John Bates Clark extended the marginal concept to the field of productivity and showed how it influenced the distribution of wealth among and within the various classes of producers.[32]

Clark was acutely aware how important it was to discover whether a fair mechanism determined the wages of labor. "The welfare of the laboring classes depends on whether they get much or little," he wrote, "but their attitude toward other classes—and, therefore, the stability of the social state—depends chiefly on the question whether the amount that they get, be it large or small, is what they produce. If they create a small amount of wealth and get the whole of it, they may not seek to revolutionize society; but if it were to appear that they produce an ample amount and get only a part of it, many of them would become revolutionists, and all would have the right to do so." Critics of capitalism charged that workmen were regularly robbed of what they produced, "within the forms of law, and by the natural workings of competition. If this charge were proved, every right-minded man should become a socialist; and his zeal in transforming the industrial system would then measure and express his sense of justice." Nothing less was at stake, Clark recognized, than the right of society to exist in its present form and the probability that it would continue to exist. He then set out to prove that where natural laws operated freely every contribution to the productive process received back in rent, wages, and profit exactly what it produced.[33]

In marginal economics, the value of one commodity over another always depended on which would provide the greater utility or satisfaction to the person contemplating buying them, not on labor cost or cost of production. According to marginal

32. Mark Blaug, "Was There a Marginal Revolution?" in *The Marginal Revolution*, ed. Black, Coats, and Goodwin, pp. 3-14.

33. John Bates Clark, *The Distribution of Wealth: A Theory of Wages, Interest and Profits* (1899; reprint ed., New York, 1956), pp. 3-5.

productivity theory, value was determined by the amount that a consumer would pay for the final unit of a particular good or service that he would add to his supply before switching his consumption to some other item. In any series of increments there was constantly diminishing return. Thus the value (or wages) of labor was determined by the final increment added to the total output of an enterprise such as a farm or factory by the last laborer who could profitably be added to the force. That was what an employer would pay for the last laborer he would hire, and what the last laborer would take before he would offer his services somewhere else. The value (rent or interest) of capital was determined by the amount added to the product of the industry by the last unit of capital (land, tools, machines, buildings) that could be profitably invested in a given industry. That was the amount of interest or rent that an entrepreneur would pay on the last land or other instrument of production he acquired, and the lowest amount that the capitalist would accept before he switched his investment to some other enterprise.

As Clark explained it, the whole income of society was divided between rewards for labor and rewards for capital. Capital deserved reward as much as labor did, for it represented the important social service of delaying gratification in order to develop wealth-producing capacity that all society could use. If the market was perfectly free, both capital and labor would constantly follow the highest possible return. Therefore, each would constantly tend to receive exactly what it deserved— about the share of wealth that each had contributed to the process of production.[34]

Since competition was the mechanism that constantly set the

34. Ibid., pp. 3, 6-9, 21, 29, 41-42, 47-49, 77-156, 173-87; Dorfman, *Economic Mind,* 3:196-201. Note Clark's view that profit, or gains above the amount that went to the entrepreneur for bringing capital and labor together in productive use, tended to be a reward for technical or administrative innovation that was quickly eliminated by competition and so hardly counted. Clark was willing to concede that there might be inequities in individual reward within economic classes even though marginal productivity guaranteed equitable functional shares. For a penetrating criticism of Clark's views on the role of the entrepreneur, see Thorstein Veblen, "Industrial and Pecuniary Employments," *Publications of the AEA,* 3d ser., 2 (1901):190-235.

margin and determined value, marginal theory functioned as a new way of legitimizing the old classical doctrine of the necessity of competition as a motive force in the economy. Marginalism provided a new rationale for a natural law system, but with a flexible law whose workings were not so vulnerable to the criticisms of the historical school nor quite so offensive to opponents of competitive capitalism. Instead of placing the motivating power for economic actions in a sort of hedonistic, self-interest guided set of choices between pleasure and pain, it redefined pain and pleasure in terms of utility. People made their choices according to final degrees of utility. In other words, they selected this or that product or service for consumption according to which was the more useful to them. Economists in a society of Puritan origins could accept this version of motivation without having to spell out the elaborate rationalizations that they had needed to reconcile classical economics with Christian ethics.

The early marginalists tended to have certain characteristics in common, and those characteristics influenced their social effect, whether their conscious social views were affected or not. They thought less of the socioeconomic relations between classes of people as producers and more of the psychological relations between people and goods. They emphasized demand over supply. They tended to turn away from macroeconomic to microeconomic theory. They valued precise definitions and techniques and they often expressed relationships in mathematical terms, thus hindering the comprehension of nonspecialists. They narrowed the scope of economics by concentrating on analysis rather than on the application of theory to practical problems. Most important, they extended the principle of economic rationality and the spirit of maximization beyond the marketplace into every household. More than any previous system, marginal economics expected the individual to drop the restraints of tradition and custom and to operate on the same principles of economic rationality that guided business firms, thus extending the field of capitalism. Undoubtedly the marginal emphasis on maximizing production provided strong support for competitive capitalism, but the emphasis in marginalism on maximizing utility pointed in another direction as well. Marginalism eventually provided the programming capability and much of the inspiration for welfare economics and supplied the means to welfare capitalism. Potentially, when marginal economics was applied to the problems involved in planning economic development for the welfare of a whole society, it also offered much to socialism.[35]

In Clark's hands, however, marginalism was used primarily to explain and defend what happened under competitive capitalism. Though the flow of events and the influence of his research fell a good deal short of throwing him back on laissez-faire, time did tend to dilute the sympathetic humanism that had been so evident in *The Philosophy of Wealth*. Social concerns now fell outside the realm of economics. On the major issues of the day, labor and monopoly, Clark's views in the 1890s were relatively conservative. Though he believed the unimpeded flow of capital and labor would ordinarily safeguard competition, he recognized some danger of monopoly and approved of limited state action to prevent it. He saw nothing wrong with pools or trusts per se, however, and considered corporate bigness the product of efficient management of resources, a healthy species of economic growth that was still regulated by potential competition even after actual competition had disappeared. Honest trusts helped the United States to compete with other countries in foreign trade and lowered domestic prices to consumers. Only dishonest practices such as rebates and boycotts needed to be controlled by legislation. Clark was willing to accept municipal ownership of utilities if it came about naturally, as a result of experiment, but not if it was deliberately devised by agitators to promote the spread of socialism.

Perhaps the greatest shift was in Clark's views on labor. He still believed that laborers should unionize to equalize their

35. Ronald L. Meek, "Marginalism and Marxism," in *The Marginal Revolution*, ed. Black, Coats, and Goodwin, pp. 240-45.

competition with big business, especially in specific situations where the flow of labor was not absolutely free or excessive numbers drove the unit value down. But it was folly, he believed, to expect a real increase in wages without a corresponding increase in the efficiency of labor, which would naturally be passed on to the laborer in increased wages anyway according to the law of marginal productivity. No strike, no boycott, no union small or large would alter the natural law that distributed wealth according to each party's contribution.[36]

Not all marginalists agreed with Clark on labor. Taussig accepted marginalism as an important addition to theory, but he continued well into the twentieth century to espouse a mildly updated version of the wages fund. Commons disputed Clark's theory that every worker's wage necessarily fell to the level of the marginal worker. According to Commons, the equalizing tendency actually functioned only part of the time—with "unorganized, unskilled, incapable" laborers who were accustomed to a low standard of living and unable to control their own numbers. A quite different rule applied with skilled workers, whose superior talents, trade secrets, and experience set them above the mass and enabled them to organize in disciplined unions and restrict access to the trade by limiting apprenticeships and keeping out nonunion workers. This aristocracy of labor was able to make its desired standard of living a factor in setting the wage rate by interrupting the flow of marginal workers from other trades into their own. Commons favored unions, but he also believed that unorganized workers should be guaranteed a fair share of the social product through tenure in their jobs during prosperous times and work relief in depressions.

On a more basic level, Charles August Tuttle denied Clark's view that the wage rates set by marginal productivity were fair to labor. Workers hired farther up the line contributed more to

36. Dorfman, *Economic Mind,* 3:196-203.

production than the last one hired, Tuttle insisted, and the surplus value they created was regularly carried off as excess profits by the very entrepreneurs whom Clark had said were almost never overpaid. Labor could reclaim its rightful product by striking for a wage based on the average, not the final increment. Along similar lines, Thomas Nixon Carver conceded that capital, management, and labor received about what they contributed, but he was never sure by what ethic or logic the various classes became entitled to the income that their contribution earned. As Thorstein Veblen slowly elaborated his fundamental distinction between industry and business, he was even more profoundly at odds with his former teacher than other critics, but Veblen's work was not yet widely known.[37]

Despite these differences, Clark was fairly representative of the economic synthesis that emerged in the 1890s. To the extent that other economists accepted marginalism and/or feared revolution and/or believed in the superiority of a mature industrial capitalism, as demonstrated by the enormous productivity of the American economy, they tended to agree with Clark that radical solutions were no longer necessary. There is no intention here to imply a conspiracy among marginalists to maintain the status quo. If marginal economists tended to ignore such important economic problems as monopoly and poverty, it can be argued that they simply started using the new theory

37. On Taussig, see Dorfman, *Economic Mind,* 3:266-67; xxxvii, n. 13, 14; on Commons, see ibid., pp. 280-84; Commons, *The Distribution of Wealth* (1893; reprint ed., New York, 1965), pp. 174-82; on Tuttle and Carver, see Dorfman, *Economic Mind,* 3:303-5, 354-55. By the early twentieth century a modified marginal productivity school including Carver, Allyn A. Young, Roswell McCrea, Henry L. Moore, and Henry R. Seager had further qualified Clark's theory of wages. Veblen believed that constructive industrial employments were overlaid in modern times by an exploitive veneer of pecuniary employments that were facilitated by modern credit, organized solely for profit, and in no way essential—indeed often detrimental—to human welfare. It was this business civilization, which Veblen conceived as an artificial and harmful growth, that Clark considered a beneficial system in which rewards were regulated by natural mechanisms. Veblen's critique of Clark was largely implicit until Veblen published "Professor Clark's Economics," *Quarterly Journal of Economics* 22 (February 1908):147-95. See also Veblen, "Industrial and Pecuniary Employments," pp. 190-235; Veblen, "The Instinct of Workmanship and the Irksomeness of Labor," *American Journal of Sociology* 4 (September 1898):187-201; Veblen, *The Theory of the Leisure Class* (New York, 1899).

where it seemed most applicable, on the problems of scarcity and exchange. Some did use their work specifically to combat Marxism and radicalism, but some did not.[38] It is Clark's explicit refutation of socialism that makes it necessary to look for a change in his attitude toward Bemis.

Over the years, Clark's attitude toward Bemis showed the same initial sympathy, ambivalence, and gradual hardening. Quizzed by Henry Carter Adams in 1887, Clark reported that Bemis was "a good fellow, and a tireless worker" whose "attainments as a writer seem to me to be considerable." Though he admitted that Bemis was "very liable to make blunders and to put himself into absurd positions," Clark considered his teaching entirely adequate and his professional judgment good. On balance, Clark concluded at the time, Bemis deserved "a pretty good position as a teacher of Political Economy."

In 1895, when Bemis desperately needed the offer of a good position to redeem his academic reputation, Clark was sympathetic but not enthusiastic. Before the situation at Chicago was generally known, Clark recommended Bemis for a job in sociology, not economics, at the Meadville Unitarian Theological Seminary and probably at Oberlin College, where radical expression had often been tolerated. Clark's own decision to move to Columbia University created an economics vacancy at Amherst, where Bemis had once established a creditable record, but Clark told Bemis that he was "prevented from active canvassing by his personal friendship for some of the other 20 applicants." That fall, when news of the forced resignation was public, Clark included Bemis's name in a huge list of candidates for a sudden, one-year vacancy at Smith College. In a frank response to Bemis's appeal for advice on how to handle his fight, Clark warned Bemis that winning his case before the public might actually harm his chances for a good appointment; a president

38. For a balanced analysis of this issue, see Meek, "Marginalism and Marxism," pp. 236-39. Meek quotes Jevons as follows: "Given, a certain population, with various needs and powers of production, in possession of certain lands and other sources of material: required, the mode of employing their labour which will maximise the utility of the produce."

with a large list "instinctively takes a man who had gotten on without friction in former positions." Clark agreed to help Ely in "passing the hat" to finance a lecture series for Bemis, but rather than rely on charity he thought it might be wiser for Bemis to "take a place in a secondary school."[39]

What Bemis needed most, of course, was an economist of impeccable reputation who was willing to step forward and affirm in the most decisive public terms the truth of Bemis's own oft-repeated cry: "I am no radical." Other than Ely, who was disqualified by his own reputation, Clark's knowledge of Bemis as a person and a scholar placed him in the best position to act. If testimonials were not enough, the university's position left a clear course to follow. In alleging incompetence, Harper, Small, and Butler had cited particulars that an impartial investigation could have proved one way or the other. When Bemis asked for such an inquiry, Harper simply refused, and no pressure was exerted by Clark or anyone else to force the issue. Before the public disclosure Bemis apparently expected Clark to help him; by the end of the year he realized how far they were apart.[40]

The cooling between them—the sense of expectation followed by disappointment on Bemis's part, the half-embarrassed desire to avoid involvement without directly saying why on Clark's—was unmistakable. At the darkest moment of a troubled decade, before progressivism put a moderate face on reform, Clark must have decided that Bemis really was dangerously radical on monopoly and labor. In the tight job market of the depression years, there were simply people safer than Bemis whom Clark preferred to see hired. The two men moved in opposite directions on the currents of the times.

However one judges Clark's motives and actions, he was not

39. Clark to Adams, 17 February 1887, H. C. Adams MSS; Bemis to Ely, 24 March, 2 April 1895; Clark to Bemis, 18 September 1895; Clark to Ely, 26 February, 2 March 1896, Ely MSS; Bemis statement, 9 October 1895, Bemis File, Harper MSS.

40. Bemis to Ely, 27 December 1895, Ely MSS. In this letter Bemis was sharply critical of what he considered to be the unwarranted optimism and hopeless conservatism of Clark's AEA presidential address. See John Bates Clark, "The Theory of Economic Progress," *Publications of the AEA*, Economic Studies, 1 (1896): 5-22.

alone. Other prominent social scientists showed even less inclination to be involved with Bemis. Franklin Henry Giddings,
another New England associate, reacted defensively to the
charge that social scientists were the pawns of large corporations and seemed at first to doubt reports that Bemis actually
was being dismissed for his views. When Bemis hinted for an
offer from Ann Arbor, Henry Carter Adams responded sympathetically but offered no encouragement. For some time Adams
had privately doubted Bemis's suitability for university teaching; instead he suggested that the jobless economist might try to
find "a good place as editor of a semi-trade paper." Lump
Bemis with Patten as representative economists, Adams told his
wife, "and I do not wonder you have a low opinion of the
whole tribe."[41] Though Taussig and Seligman were out of the
country when Bemis resigned, both men later inquired to see
whether his rights had been violated. Taussig's Harvard ties with
Laughlin may have prevented him from acting. There is ex parte
evidence that the general danger to the emerging social science
professions which the Bemis precedent represented was realized
most clearly at this stage by Seligman of Columbia. But his
sense of the structural weakness and the potential for organizational action—or perhaps his capacity for risk—was not clearly
enough formed to produce an effective response. Seligman
followed Bemis's career in subsequent years and occasionally
helped him find work. There is no evidence that either Taussig
or Seligman ever lodged any protest at Chicago in Bemis's
behalf.[42]

41. "More on the Bemis Case," *Buffalo Enquirer,* 25 October 1895, Book 1,
University Scrapbooks, p. 141, University of Chicago Archives; Giddings to H. C.
Adams, 3 March 1896; Adams to Bemis, 10 May 1895; 1 March, 6 August 1894
(Letterbook, 1893-1896), H. C. Adams MSS; Adams to C. K. Adams, 30 November
1886; Adams to Bertha Adams, n.d. [1893]; Bemis to H. C. Adams, 3 May 1895, 10
December 1897, H. C. Adams MSS.
42. Taussig to Bemis, 18 September 1895, Ely MSS; Seligman to Bemis, 11
October, 25 December 1896, Seligman MSS. Later Seligman referred to Bemis as a
professor expelled from Chicago university "for advocating an increase of governmental functions." Seligman to the trustees of Brown University, 23 July 1897, File
259, J. Franklin Jameson MSS, Library of Congress. Ely seems to have collected a file
of copies of letters Bemis received. If Ely's file was complete, there was no communication at all from Hadley.

Nonacademic economists sensed no general problem either. Speaking, no doubt, for most amateurs, George Gunton derided the notion that a university was obligated "to lend its influence and wealth to the support of a person who propagates the idea of destruction of what it regards as the sacred institutions of civilized society."[43]

Not everyone deserted Bemis. Ely students other than Small were almost universally outraged. No doubt they feared that the near removal of their mentor from a major state university and the almost simultaneous dismissal of a fellow Ely student from a powerful private university indicated trouble ahead for everyone who had studied with Ely. Two friends who would shortly have that fear confirmed reacted with special bitterness. John Commons considered Chicago's treatment of Bemis "utterly abominable." The mixed reactions of other economists mystified him. "How strangely people take his case," he noted; "some with whom I have talked are enraged, others say how foolish in him to incur the enmity of a great institution." Edward Alsworth Ross, scheduled for an Armageddon of his own with Stanford University in 1900, tried to persuade President David Starr Jordan to hire Bemis and vowed never to send another student to the University of Chicago. David Kinley respected Bemis's scholarship so much that he attributed Small's betrayal to jealousy. Kinley believed that united action would eventually be necessary to defend "independence of thought and speech within the limits of reasonable discretion," and he was willing to stake his own position on the principle. In October 1895, when the newspaper controversy was hottest, he brought Bemis to the University of Illinois for a series of public lectures on the labor movement and municipal monopoly, the subjects that had caused all the trouble.[44]

The complex and delicate influences that determined how

43. George Gunton, "Liberty in Economic Teaching," *Gunton's Magazine* 18 (March 1900):231-32.

44. Commons to Ely, 13 November 1895; Bemis to Ely, 13 September 1895; Kinley to Ely, 27 February, 13, 22 August, 15, 29 October 1895, Ely MSS; Ross to Bemis, 5 September 1895; Charles Spahr to Bemis, 3 May 1895, copies in Ely MSS.

people reacted to Bemis's plight were probably best analyzed by an Ely student who had moved from Smith College to Stanford University in 1895. H. H. Powers grasped the underlying personal and ideological animosities that shaped decisions. He told a story that captured Laughlin's stereotype among economists who favored government regulation in the economy. Seeking someone to write a dissertation on Australian railroads, Laughlin reportedly questioned all his students on their attitudes toward government ownership. When he found that every one of them favored the practice, he refused to let anyone write on the topic. "It would be well that all should know that investigations emanating from Chicago University are not undertaken till the proper bias is first assured in the investigator," Powers quipped.

But Powers also recognized the institutional problems that created conflicting loyalties for academics. "While almost everyone sympathizes with him," Powers remarked of Bemis, "no college . . . could appoint him without seeming to take an aggressive attitude in matters of reform." Most people believed that universities existed to promote impartial inquiry, not to advocate reform. It was Bemis's misfortune, Powers added, "that by virtue of this incident he stands more for certain conclusions than he does for inquiry. He is as impartial as any of us, but the dismissal had laid undue emphasis on his conclusions. For all these reasons I doubt his ability to secure a worthy position for some years."[45]

Colleges and universities did close their doors to Bemis. Friends attempted to place him, but at Iowa College, Oberlin, Amherst, Smith, Northwestern University, and the state universities of Illinois, Nebraska, and Colorado, either trustees or presidents balked. For a time Bemis was almost entirely dependent on the charity of Chicago friends and Ely students. When

45. Powers to Ely, 23 January, 14, 20 November 1895, Ely MSS. The study which Laughlin supposedly wanted to commission was actually done by a Chicago student. See William Hill, "State Railways in Australia," *Journal of Political Economy* 3 (December 1894):1-23.

supporters were able to arrange paid lectures at a university, Bemis was usually "much ignored by the faculty & president." In letters he wrote inquiring about openings, a growing sense of despair was veiled only thinly by strained good cheer.[46]

Meanwhile Bemis threw himself wholeheartedly into the urban Progressive movement, working as a free-lance social science expert for various commissions, testifying on specialized topics, and drafting legislation on municipal ownership and regulation of utilities. Wealthy reformers and liberal politicians tried to keep him employed. Henry Demarest Lloyd, Mayor Samuel Jones of Toledo, and Carroll D. Wright were constant friends. Governor Hazen Pingree of Michigan tried to make Bemis his labor commissioner, but "the hostility of the corporations and the ignorance and blind local jealousies of Michigan laborers" combined to prevent the appointment. Failing that, Bemis added, Pingree intended to consult President Angell and Henry Carter Adams, "offering even to nominate as labor commissioner one of their men, if they will make a place for me." In desperation, Bemis was not above wondering whether "the liberal governor of some of the far western states might be induced to urge the same program on their own universities."[47]

At last a Populist victory in Kansas opened the way. Social science professorships at the Kansas State Agricultural College were frankly political. In 1897 a Populist majority of the regents fired all Republican appointees and allowed the new

46. See Bemis to Seligman, 11 October, 25 December 1896; 11 August 1897, Seligman MSS, for Bemis's account of his interim activities. He taught briefly the year after his dismissal at Wisconsin, Illinois, and Syracuse, while editing the *Biblioteca Sacra,* writing labor bulletins for Carroll D. Wright, working for the Illinois Bureau of Labor Statistics and the Chicago Civic Federation, and serving legislative commissions in Michigan, New York, and Ohio. See also Bemis to Ely, 7 January, 3 March 1896, Ely MSS.

47. Lloyd apparently tried to place Bemis at Northwestern, offering a donation. See Bemis to Ely, 13 January 1896, Ely MSS. Ely tried to raise a fund to endow a position for Bemis at Syracuse University. A steady flow of letters from Bemis to Ely details the dozens of leads Bemis followed in 1896 and 1897 and outlines his role in the development of municipal ownership and state regulation movements. See especially Bemis to Ely, 24 January, 2 March 1896; 2 February 1897, Ely MSS. In the entire exchange, Ely was unfailingly solicitous and scrupulously private in supporting Bemis.

president, economist-Populist-Christian Socialist Thomas Elmer
Will, to bring in radical refugees from other schools. Will named
Bemis to a chair in economics and Frank Parsons, another
advocate of public ownership, in history.[48] All the Populist
appointees expected their tenure to be brief, but Bemis avoided
the silver question and gained a reputation for impartial treatment of issues in his teaching. Even so, the Republicans re-
gained control of the board in two years and fired every social
scientist the Populists had chosen. Bemis was not entirely disappointed. There were numerous demands for his investigative
skills in Eastern cities, he explained, and "my work here absorbs
so much of my time and strength among rather immature
students that I cannot get the time I want for influencing the
thought of the country." By the developing standard that
emphasized mainly teaching and research, Bemis was no longer
a professor. Never again did he hold a position as an academic
social scientist.[49]

Another economist shared the stigma of radicalism that made
Bemis an academic pariah. Only minor variations in the pattern
spared John Rogers Commons the near total exclusion from
academic influence that haunted Bemis. Because Commons was
willing to leave quietly when his services were no longer wanted,
he never made an enemy as powerful as the University of
Chicago. Still his controversial views and radical activism caused

48. Will, an Illinois native, had been trained at Harvard and taught in the early
1890s at Lawrence University, where he claimed he was dismissed for political
reasons. Will to Ely, 24 June 1897, Ely MSS. After 1899 he served as president of W.
D. P. Bliss's correspondence school, the College of Social Science; as dean and
professor of social sciences at Ruskin College in Trenton, Missouri (1900-1903); and
as president of the American Socialist College at Wichita, Kansas (1903-1905), before
obtaining a position with the Census Bureau. See Dorfman, *Economic Mind,*
3:299-303, for a summary of his work. Parsons had been a professor of law at Boston
University and a prominent advocate of public ownership of natural monopolies.
Arthur Mann, *Yankee Reformers in the Urban Age* (Cambridge, Mass., 1954), devotes
a chapter to his thought.

49. Bemis to Ely, 23 April, 23 June, 1 July 1897; n.d. [1898]; 19 January, 29
February, 10 May, 12 June 1897; Bemis statement on dismissal, attached to Bemis to
Ely, 12 June 1897, Ely MSS. From 1901-1909 Bemis was superintendent of water
works in the administration of Cleveland's progressive Mayor Tom Johnson. From
1913 to 1923 he worked for the Valuation Bureau of the Interstate Commerce
Commission. Metzger, *Academic Freedom,* p. 161.

him to lose two academic positions and spend five years in a limbo of temporary free-lance jobs before Ely could take him to the University of Wisconsin to start the work on labor history for which Commons became famous. Without Ely's help, Commons might have spent his life doing reports for the United States Industrial Commission, the National Civic Federation, or some similar body.[50]

Commons clearly considered advocacy a part of the economist's professional responsibility. His background included experiences similar to those that shaped the ethical perspectives of other new school economists who achieved prominence earlier. His mother's Presbyterian forebears made the ritual trek from Vermont to the Western Reserve, while his father's Quaker ancestors left North Carolina as a protest against slavery. Born in 1862 in Hollandsburg, Ohio, John Commons grew up on stories of the exciting experiences his mother and father had shared as they helped runaway slaves move along the underground railroad to freedom. Commons's father was a mildly indolent fellow who never made a good living for his family, but his interest in Darwin and Spencer, newspaper publishing, and Republican politics whetted Commons's awareness of social issues. His mother was an Oberlin graduate whose abolitionist, feminist, temperance-crusading example toughened her son and made him an activist.[51]

When economics lured Commons away from the ministry, he later recalled, it was Newcomb's *Nation* diatribe that attracted

50. There is no major collection of Commons papers dating before his Wisconsin years, although letters are scattered through the collections of other social scientists and public figures. The major primary source is Commons's autobiographical memoir, *Myself* (Madison, Wis., 1963), but it was written when Commons was past eighty and offers more impression than precision on some factual matters. This account relies on Dorfman, *Economic Mind*, 3:276-94, for analysis of Commons's economic thought. Fine, *Laissez Faire*, contains scattered references to his thought, esp. pp. 210, 327-28, 338. His sudden dismissals at Indiana University and Syracuse University are mentioned in the standard academic freedom sources: Metzger, *Academic Freedom*, pp. 147-49; Veysey, *Emergence of the American University*, p. 410.

51. Commons, *Myself*, pp. 7-15; Frank A. Fetter, "John Rogers Commons, 1862-1945," reprinted from *Yearbook of the American Philosophical Society* (1945), pp. 361-63, in Commons MSS, Wisconsin Historical Society; Dorfman, *Economic Mind*, 3:276.

him to Ely. The meeting was fateful, for Ely encouraged Commons to retain his faith in religion as a reforming agent while he developed economic theories to guide the technical restructuring that was needed in society. Commons cooperated with Ely in founding the Institute of Christian Sociology in 1893, and his *Social Reform and the Church* (1894) outlined the responsibility of organized religion for the promotion of social justice. Like Ely and Bemis, Commons retained in the 1890s perspectives that other ethical economists had abandoned in the 1880s. Thoroughly prolabor, he hoped that a moral reawakening would prompt Americans to provide voluntarily for an equitable distribution of wealth and avoid the stifling effects of state socialism. Commons saw no point in breaking up big business, but he did believe that government should own or regulate necessary monopolies. To make government responsive to the needs of all classes, Commons favored a number of progressive reforms, including initiative, referendum, and proportional representation of economic interest groups. He believed in municipal ownership, compulsory arbitration, progressive taxation, and a managed currency. The most radical reform he advocated was proprietary rights for labor, including an ironclad guarantee of the right to work.[52]

Commons's faith that moral exhortation could inspire people to voluntary reform was exactly the commitment that had led Ely, Bemis, and others to appeal directly to the public. If only economists could be persuaded to abandon abstract theorizing and focus all their intelligence on making plans for social action, Commons believed that they could improve society infinitely. He became involved. To study the Baltimore poor, Ely had sent him to join the city's charity organizations. Commons trained his own students at Indiana University the same way, taking them to prisons and asylums, having them compare the actual value of real estate with politically motivated property tax

52. Commons, *The Distribution of Wealth*, pp. i-xiv, 79-85; Commons, *Myself*, p. 21; Dorfman, *Economic Mind*, 3:277-83; Selig Perlman, "John Rogers Commons, 1862-1945," *American Economic Review* 35 (September 1945):782-86.

assessments, and steering them into all sorts of social service projects. Criticism of selfish industrial and political interests prickled from Commons's own utterances.[53]

Before long professional economists grew wary of Commons's advocacy. Some of the bitterest criticism followed the appearance of his *Distribution of Wealth* in 1893. Taussig dismissed it as an "unbaked performance." Hadley criticized the book's assumption that "men, as a rule, make money by hurting society" and concluded, in a thinly disguised slur at Ely, that Commons's "lack of familiarity with facts is due to his training in the so-called historical school, and will wear off." Besides sloppy scholarship, Columbia's Mayo-Smith thought Commons's work suffered from a lack of impartiality and was controlled by a "hidden purpose" to discredit capitalism and glorify socialism. Naturally Laughlin could find no redeeming social value in the book.[54]

Even economists who respected Commons feared the impression he made. Thoughtful colleagues could see that Commons believed too much in individual regeneration to be a socialist, but such refinements escaped popular observers. As Commons repeatedly spoke against capitalists, Ely begged him to restrain his zeal. When Indiana University consulted Henry Carter Adams for a professional appraisal of Commons's work, Adams pointedly advised the president that "an attempt to investigate a professor of political economy for doctrines held would not only be detrimental to general education but would do more than anything else to check the conservative influence which writings of economists are exerting upon the general social and industrial question." Even the indulgent David Kinley found Commons's behavior too reckless to defend. "I cannot sympathize with the position of men like Commons, nor assent to

53. Commons, *Myself,* pp. 54-56.
54. Taussig to Seligman, 3 December 1893, Seligman MSS; Arthur T. Hadley, "Review of Commons's The Distribution of Wealth," *Yale Review* 2 (February 1894):439-40; Richmond Mayo-Smith, "Review of Commons's The Distribution of Wealth," *Political Science Quarterly* 9 (September 1894):568-72; Dorfman, *Economic Mind,* 3:284-85.

such radical opinions as he expresses," Kinley fumed. "He is doing himself, his university, and his fellow economists in the country a great wrong in laying himself so vulnerably open to criticism. It is the action of hot-heads like him that makes the position of the more conservative of us so difficult."[55] Thus conservatives and moderates often disapproved of Commons's views, while liberals considered his conduct dangerous for a scholar.

It was not idle to fear that Commons was courting trouble. "There have been several parties urging my removal by the Trustees on the ground of Socialism, Free Trade, Single Tax, Populism, Etc. etc.," he told Adams. "The Indianapolis papers especially have been making considerable noise, but the matter did not take definite shape until our university lobby met with some difficulty before the Legislature on the ground of attacks against me." Still certain that Indiana University would defend his freedom, Commons decided to bargain for a higher salary by using an offer he had just received from Syracuse University as leverage. The nervous Indiana president, Joseph Swain, immediately recommended that Commons take the Syracuse offer, and the surprised economist had no choice but to accept.[56]

Syracuse officials seemed liberal at first, but circumstances changed four years later when Commons began making speeches that praised Henry George and Karl Marx as prophets of a rising radical movement to secure the rights of labor. According to Commons, Chancellor James Roscoe Day simply informed him one day that his chair of sociology was being abolished. Day explained that potentially important donors refused to grant funds while Commons remained on the faculty, and he warned

55. Commons to Ely, 30 January 1894, 6 May 1895; Kinley to Ely, 27 February 1895, Ely MSS; Adams to Seligman, 28 August 1894 (Letterbook, 1893-1896), pp. 280-91, H. C. Adams MSS; Dorfman, *Economic Mind*, 3:285. See Adams to "My dear Mother," 3 August 1894, H. C. Adams MSS, for his private view of Commons's rashness of expression.
56. Commons to H. C. Adams, 6 April 1895, H. C. Adams MSS; Commons to Ely, 17 September 1894, 6 May 1895, Ely MSS; Commons, *Myself*, p. 52; Dorfman, *Economic Mind*, 3:285, xl, n. 14. Commons's chair at Syracuse was established by a candy manufacturer who was a trustee and also happened to favor municipal ownership.

Commons of a recent agreement among college presidents to hire no radicals. Disillusioned, Commons simply retired from academic life without a murmur. When reporters questioned him about his sudden separation, Commons refused to comment. Day rewarded him with a "rousing send-off," amidst a flood of compliments. "So I learned the virtue of silence," Commons explained. "It makes eulogists instead of avengers. You keep their secrets." He was right. It was probably Commons's restraint—compared with Bemis's spectacular protest— that enabled Commons to return to academic life five years later armed with flattering testimonials from influential economists.[5][7]

In late 1895 the wave of academic repression that followed in the wake of the Pullman strike abated briefly. An assessment showed that the victims followed a pattern. Ely and his students had admitted from the start that they valued economics for the impact their investigations could have on institutions more than for any intrinsic value that the discipline possessed. As social science professionalized and the tone of discourse changed, they clung assertively to the popular mode. When most economists withdrew from activism, they stayed on the stump. While other social scientists associated primarily with businessmen and professionals in polite society, they openly mixed with reformers, labor leaders, and radicals. They claimed that they were not socialists; yet it seemed that they constantly agitated against capitalism and impugned the motives of anyone who defended it. At a time when the paramount concern of conservatives was holding the strife-ridden country together, they found justice in labor's complaints and incited demands. In short, though they valued the authority that scientific status lent to their sugges-

57. Commons, *Myself,* pp. 58-62; Dorfman, *Economic Mind,* 3:288, xl, n. 18. Metzger, *Academic Mind,* p. 149, n. 34, points out that the evidence in the Syracuse case is entirely "ex parte." To one attempt to investigate, the Syracuse librarian replied that the material was not available. W. F. Galpin, writing a history of Syracuse University, told Metzger that he had been unable to discover grounds for assuming Commons was dismissed. At the time Commons told Ely that "matters were shaping up so that I could not stay," and asked him to say nothing about it. Commons to Ely, 2 March 1895, Ely MSS.

tions, they refused, their critics thought, to conduct themselves as scientists should.

Circumstances chastened Ely but spared him, eventually reprieved Commons, and ruined Bemis as an academic. Yet the differences between them were largely superficial and the outcome depended on how the game was played. For other social scientists a clear lesson emerged: Avoid radicalism. Avoid socialism. Avoid excessive publicity and refrain from public advocacy. When trouble strikes, unless there is certain assurance of massive support, accept your fate in austere and dignified silence. Above all, maintain a reputation for scientific objectivity.

So far the crisis of the 1890s had done little to resolve the conflict between advocacy and objectivity. Even after extensive debate, academic social scientists still found themselves in a quandary regarding policy. As scholars, they possessed expert knowledge that qualified them better than many others to make recommendations for reform. Yet their fear of losing the aura of impartiality that their station in the new universities demanded disqualified them again. In judging colleagues who acquired radical reputations academics were not very different from the rest of educated society. They went by appearances. A person who became too involved with radical causes soon found his scholarship as suspect in the academic community as it was in the wider society. More orthodox scholars doubted his competence and distrusted his commitment to truth. The best defense to offer nonspecialists was the positive recommendation of respected colleagues; yet individual action required the defender to risk the drastic consequences that followed from association with a trouble maker. Until some formal procedure for collective defense emerged, the profession remained in jeopardy. The development of standard procedures awaited agreement on what deserved defending.

Permissible Dissent

A cartoon on the cover of *Life* showed the dignified figure of a university president and former economist leaving the college gate with his suitcase, while a plump trustee nailed a want ad to the ivy-covered pillar. The message read: "WANTED: By the Corporation of Brown University, a young man of submissive disposition as president. A reasonable amount of scholarship will not be a disqualification, but the chief requisite will be an obsequious and ingratiating behavior toward millionaires and an ability to RAKE IN THE DOLLARS. Opinions and first-class board furnished by the Corporation. No gentlemen encumbered with a back-bone need apply."[1]

If the near dismissal of Elisha Benjamin Andrews from Brown University could generate humor when earlier academic freedom cases involving social scientists could not, it was because the Andrews case was actually a good deal less serious. Between 1897 and the end of the century, three more professional social scientists—Andrews, J. Allen Smith, and Edward A. Ross—were endangered or actually removed for their views. Though the personal consequences were temporarily rending, in each case the victim emerged stronger than before. In addition, academic social scientists further clarified the level of advocacy that they believed their professional authority should permit. The techniques they devised for united action enhanced their image and broadened their opportunities.

The difference in the outcome of these cases that occurred in the late 1890s lay partly in the experience that economists had gained in defending their interests and partly in a change in the nature of the issues. From Haymarket through Pullman, the possibility that organized labor might precipitate social upheaval seemed real enough to unite conservative trustees and administrators against academics who encouraged the spread of

frightening foreign ideologies like socialism and anarchism, and
to cool the ardor of defending social scientists as well. The hard
economic demands of insurgent western and southern farmers
and their startling success at the polls in 1894 had added
populism to the list of dangerous beliefs. Through 1895 the
menace of mass radicalism fueled repression, but the fears that
coalesced in the Bryan campaign of 1896 were dispelled by his
crushing defeat. There would be no class party, no radical union
of producers against the propertied classes. The academic freedom cases of the late 1890s grew out of unresolved ambiguities
in the academic power structure and domestic disagreements
over conventional American political issues such as money and
the tariff.

Both elements were present in the Andrews case. Some of the
Brown trustees wanted to fire E. Benjamin Andrews because he
favored international bimetallism and free trade. Both policies
were detrimental to certain economic interests, but they fell
well within the institutional borders of industrial capitalism and
found support in conservative quarters. Other trustees approved
of disciplining Andrews merely because they believed that his
public advocacy of views that were unpopular with wealthy
industrialists drove huge gifts away from the university's embarrassingly empty coffers. They pointed to John D. Rockefeller,
who had showered millions on the University of Chicago but
allowed his son to graduate from Brown in 1897 without
donating a cent of the grand bequest expected. When the
trustees met in June, the specter of Bryanism could still be
conjured to cover more pecuniary motives. The board agreed to
a proposal made by Massachusetts Republican Congressman
Joseph H. Walker, a trustee long at odds with Andrews over the
money question, that a committee meet with Andrews to
discuss the impact of his political activities on the welfare of the
university.[2]

1. "How to Build Up a University," *Life* 30 (26 August 1897), File 259, Jameson
MSS.
2. "Pres. Andrews's Views," *Providence Journal,* 19 June 1897. Newspaper articles

Probably because of the nature of the issue, no question of scientific competence was ever raised. The controversy focused on Andrews as president, not economist. No one denied that Andrews was an excellent president with a distinguished reputation for expanding and modernizing the university.[3] Nevertheless, Congressman Walker questioned whether the university should "be conspicuously advertised as a basis of operations for an active propaganda through the country of principles and views antagonistic to the purposes of its friends, and all its present supporters and patrons as well." As Andrews's most vigorous opponents stated the issue, it was not so much that the views the president advocated were shocking as it was a question whether a university president's qualifications as an economist entitled him to oppose the economic doctrines favored by most influential residents of his section.[4]

Andrews was less vulnerable than the ordinary economist. Service with important monetary commissions named by both Democratic and Republican presidents had rescued him from the obscurity that surrounded many social scientists. He was a Civil War hero and a Brown graduate. In conformity with the Brown charter, he was a Baptist minister, as his father and

here are from the large collection of clippings and letters on the Andrews case preserved by J. Franklin Jameson, File 259, Jameson MSS. Much of the same material formed the basis for the standard account of the Andrews case by Elizabeth Donnan, "A Nineteenth-Century Academic Cause Celebre," New England Quarterly 25 (March 1952):23-46. Her account of the course of events at Brown is both perceptive and accurate in light of additional information, with the exception that she ignores the role of economists Henry Gardner of the Brown faculty and Seligman of Columbia in Andrews's defense. Here the emphasis is on the reactions of academic social scientists, a problem that Donnan treats only peripherally.

3. The record indicates that during Andrews tenure from 1889 to 1897 the number of students had increased from 265 to 798, including the 157 newly admitted women. The number of graduate students had grown from 3 to 110, and the faculty had increased from 26 to 90, counting temporaries. See the faculty open letter to the corporation, Jameson MSS.

4. "Prof. Andrews's Views," Providence Journal, 22 June 1897; Donnan, "Academic Cause," pp. 25-26. Walker was chairman of the House Committee on Currency and Banking. He had earlier requested an investigation of the textbooks used in economics classes and wanted the corporation (trustees and fellows combined) to question economist Henry Gardner on his views. Andrews refused to permit either step and protected Gardner from being dismissed after a hostile exchange of letters with Walker. All along Walker and Andrews differed on both money and trade.

grandfather had been, and his personal integrity was above
question. After teaching homiletics until 1882 at Newton Theological Seminary and then following the classic shift from theology to economics, he studied for a year in Germany and taught
history and political economy at Brown. In 1888 he was called
to Cornell University, where the scrupulous Henry Sage considered him sound enough to fill Henry Carter Adams's vacant
position. When Brown named Andrews president the following
year, he was already the author of a popular economics textbook and numerous articles on economic and social questions.[5]
His views on money and trade were well known.

Though Andrews was an ethical economist, his advocacy was
more progressive than radical. He helped to organize the American Economic Association because he believed economics was
an evolutionary science which could lead to social reform. He
denied the notion that laissez-faire was in any special way
natural or moral and he insisted that it was ridiculous to
conceive of the state as "a mere policeman." Like others in the
evangelical tradition, he argued that monopoly endangered the
individual by stifling competition and limiting opportunity.
Andrews conceded that consolidation in industry yielded some
of the advantages of socialism by promoting efficient planning,
conservation, and controlled production without the evils of
government ownership. In practice he approved some limitations on competition, provided the state had power to regulate
the conditions of production and control monopoly prices. Yet
he frequently favored self-help over social welfare proposals and
never advocated socialism. Andrews's greatest impact in the
1880s and 1890s was as a leading exponent of bimetallism,

5. E. L. Hinman, "E. Benjamin Andrews," *The University of Nebraska, 1869-1919*
(Lincoln, 1919), pp. 130-33, in University of Nebraska Archives; Dorfman, *Economic
Mind,* 3:179-82; E. Benjamin Andrews, *Institutes of Economics* (Boston, 1889);
Andrews to Adams, 14 May 1888, H. C. Adams MSS. In going to Cornell Andrews
felt, he told Adams, "somewhat as if about to enjoy a stolen heritage." To his credit,
he submitted a statement of his money views to the Cornell trustees before accepting.
For an unsigned biographical article on Andrews by Jameson, see *Review of Reviews*
16 (September 1897):261. For Jameson's authorship, see several letters from him to
Albert Shaw instigating and arranging publicity, Jameson MSS. Andrews's brother,
Charles B. Andrews, was governor of Connecticut, 1879-1881.

eventually to the point of advocating free silver and precipitating the dispute at Brown.[6]

Andrews's prominence and the timeliness of the issue assured notoriety. When the news of an investigation leaked, a furor arose instantaneously. There was no need for professors to raise the issue of academic freedom; it was the central question from the start. Newspapers all over the country took sides, and sentiment outside Providence strongly favored Andrews. The Rhode Island air was blue with vituperation before the president, who was still on a European sabbatical, even knew of his trouble. When he returned to Providence, after a private session with his key faculty supporters, J. Franklin Jameson and Henry Gardner, he met with the trustees' committee. The meeting was civil, one member reported, and the committee left thinking that Andrews agreed with them on the advisability of restricting his public statements on silver. Instead Andrews had decided that he had backing enough to fight. On July 17 the president suddenly submitted his resignation, explaining that he could not surrender "that reasonable liberty of utterance which my predecessors, my faculty colleagues and myself have hitherto enjoyed, and in the absence of which the most ample endowment for an educational institution would have but little worth."[7]

Immediately pressure on the trustees began mounting. Ironically, one of the first prominent figures to defend Andrews publicly was William Rainey Harper. "In free and fair New England," Harper wrote, "the very ground on which freedom of

6. Andrews, *Institutes,* pp. 19-30; Andrews, "Individualism as a Sociological Principle," *Yale Review,* o.s. 2 (May 1893):13-27; Dorfman, *Economic Mind,* 3:179-81. In Andrews, "Political Economy, Old and New," *Andover Review* 6 (August 1886):139, he stated: "It is now on all hands silently taken for granted that the actual subject-matter of our science is *weal,* whereas in its classical days *wealth,* a very different notion, held that post of honor." Actually Andrews never advocated free silver until his trip to Europe in 1897 convinced him that other nations would follow if the United States adopted bimetallism unilaterally. That was, of course, after the trustees decided to discuss his utterances with him. See "Dr. Andrews's Views," *Providence Journal,* 4 July 1897.

7. George G. Wilson to Jameson, 10 July 1897, Jameson MSS; "President Andrews' Resignation," *Boston Herald,* 24 July 1897; "His Ultimatum," *Providence Journal,* 23 July 1897; "Brown's Presidency," ibid., 24 July 1897. Donnan, "Academic Cause," analyzes the newspaper controversy at various stages in some detail.

opinion was fought out, an old and established institution only yesterday censured its head because, forsooth, he had the courage to think for himself and to speak what he thought."[8] A Baptist himself, Harper was also obviously still smarting with embarrassment from the Bemis case.

Members of the Brown faculty provided the effective leadership. The trustees had erected an ideal point of attack when they protested Andrews's advocacy on strictly mercenary grounds. In the absence of any evidence of indoctrination in the classroom, it appeared that the university's guardians were willing to sell both free speech and free inquiry for a mess of pottage. Exactly that charge was made in an open letter to the Brown corporation signed by two-thirds of the Brown faculty. They asked that the president's resignation be refused and his liberty restored.[9]

The academic community began to mobilize itself in defense of Andrews. Circumstances were fortuitous, for plenty of time remained before the next scheduled meeting of the Brown Corporation on September 1. Strong individual remonstrances from influential academics set the tone that others would follow. For the first time a prominent economist defended advocacy in terms of the obligation of a profession to the community. The day after the president's resignation, Seligman addressed a protest to the Brown trustees. Though he did not agree with Andrews's views on silver, Seligman considered any attempt to muzzle pro-silver views a "severe blow" not only to Brown but "to the very basis of all true University life and of all true scientific progress." He admitted that he did not approve of

8. "Universities and Freedom of Opinion," *Baltimore News,* 27 June 1897; Veysey, *The Emergence of the American University,* p. 368, n. 95. Veysey explains that Harper did his best to improve the image of the university after the Bemis case made its connection with Standard Oil suspect.

9. For an example of such defense, see "President Andrews's Resignation," *New York Evening Post,* 23 July 1897. Stories attacking the board's position appeared on July 23 and 24 in the *Providence Telegram,* the *Boston Traveler, Journal,* and *Globe,* and many others. On the faculty protest see Donnan, "Academic Cause," pp. 33-35. The text is printed in the *Chicago Record,* 3 August 1897. A few gold monometallists and a few professors (mostly pro-Andrews) who considered a faculty protest impertinent refused to sign.

political activity on the part of professors. Yet, he asked, "if the politics of the country chance to turn upon a question that is at once practical and scientific, ought a scientific investigator to be therefore debarred from expressing his conception of the truth in a scientific way?"

Finally Seligman articulated clearly the conflict between expert knowledge and advocacy which had worried economists since 1886. "To say that the University teacher should express no opinion upon controverted questions unless that opinion happens to be shared by the Powers that be is to strike a death blow to all intellectual progress," he added. If eastern professors had to preach gold and western scholars had to swear by silver, if Northerners were fired for teaching free trade and Southerners for favoring the tariff, if every college did what the University of Chicago had done to Bemis, it was the beginning of hypocrisy and the end of science.[10]

Other economists defended Andrews on more conventional grounds. Henry B. Gardner of the Brown department supported his president by analyzing the content of his economic views. In a letter to the hostile *Providence Journal,* Gardner tried to lay the ghost of "free silver at 16 to 1" by insisting that Andrews had never advocated free coinage or repudiation in any form. Recently, Gardner admitted, Andrews had reached the conclusion that the United States could safely adopt bimetallism with the certainty that other nations would quickly follow, but even that opinion was public knowledge only because his private correspondence had been published without Andrews's consent. Gardner submitted that Andrews was an international bimetallist pure and simple, the same as the patron saint of American economics, Francis Amasa Walker.[11] Although Gardner's approach was intended as a liberal defense of free inquiry, it actually reinforced the notion that economists could advocate safely only within a range of accepted doctrines.

10. Seligman to the Trustees of Brown University, 23 July 1897, Jameson MSS.
11. Gardner, "A Correction," *Providence Journal,* 27 July 1897; "Resignation of Dr. Andrews," *Boston Herald,* 30 July 1897.

In another sphere, the courts were engaged in elaborating a contingent, tenuous "rule of reason" to evaluate the competitive practices of large corporations. The distinguished Harvard philosopher Josiah Royce entered the Andrews debate to explore the general question of "reasonable liberty" of utterance. Professors were not entitled to unlimited expression, Royce concluded. The scholar's special commitment to knowledge carried with it an ethical obligation to be cautious and deliberate in all utterances and especially to avoid "mischievous agitation." If Andrews had so conducted himself as to lose the confidence of his colleagues and the trustees, there would be no defense for him in academic freedom. But Andrews was in fact admitted to be an excellent president whose sole error, by the stipulation of the board, was having an opinion on a single policy issue that could "do harm to the cash box of the university." Because the Brown trustees had judged Andrews by an improper standard, Royce considered their action pernicious and hoped they would rescind it. Like Gardner, Royce stopped far short of endorsing entirely unrestrained expression, even within a scholar's own discipline.[12]

The organized academic protest eventually divided itself into two statements: a general pronouncement signed by college presidents along with a sprinkling of prominent academics from various fields, and a special petition from social scientists. For the presidents the case was obviously important not only as an academic freedom case but also as a test of presidential tenure. The proposition that a board could discipline or dismiss a president because an opinion he held might drive away gifts had never appeared in a form so blatant and at the same time so ripe for attack. Presidents Charles W. Eliot of Harvard, Daniel Coit Gilman of Hopkins, and Seth Low of Columbia were summering in Maine; in daily consultation with Jameson and encouraged by Royce, that eminent trio decided to make an aggressive move. They drafted a cooly worded memorial designed to appeal to as

12. Royce to the Editor of the *Boston Transcript,* 18 August 1897, Jameson MSS.

many presidents as possible and planned to submit it privately, just before the meeting of the Brown corporation, requesting that Andrews's resignation be declined.[13]

For professional economists the Andrews case provided an almost ideal opportunity to test their right to public advocacy. None of the earlier cases had focused so sharply on an instance in which an economist had challenged the prevailing orthodoxy on a single, specific theoretical question. Some other issue had always altered the meaning of supporting each victim. In the Adams case there had been the unusual social tension of 1886 and Adams's own desire for secrecy. Ely was charged with indoctrination, and other professionals resented his popularization. In the Bemis case socialism and the suggestion of incompetence became issues, while with Commons rashness, interpreted as a character fault, and again socialism complicated the little-known proceedings.

Extraneous issues might have entered the Andrews case, but the candor or ineptness of the trustees prevented that. There was no hint of shame, no charge of any affiliation outside the expected uniformities: the two party system, Christianity, and "common decency." Here was an upright man, a respected teacher whose sole fault, stated at its inaccurate worst, was that he favored free silver and said so. Here, ostensibly, was a trained professional who was to lose his position as an educational leader because inquiry led him to believe in international bimetallism—exactly, Seligman and others observed, the teaching of every reigning don in every distinguished university in England.[14] Surely reasonable people could differ on money or the tariff, questions that had been the steady political fare of Americans for as long as anyone could remember.

Suddenly leading professional economists began to come together. When Henry Gardner begged economists at nearby institutions to help organize support for a special petition from

13. Eliot to Jameson, 13 August 1897; Low to Jameson, 15 August 1897, Jameson MSS.
14. Seligman to the Trustees of Brown University, 23 July 1897, ibid.

professors, Taussig swiftly drafted a memorial designed to establish the principle of immunity for professional opinions. Taussig's statement condemned the idea "that the opinions of university teachers and administrators are in any way subject to review by governing boards or that tenure of office is dependent on anything but ability and faithfulness" in assigned duties and responsibilities.[15]

At that point Seligman emerged as a leader in defining the case more specifically in terms of the discipline. In Seligman's view, the crucial point was not simply that Andrews was a professor. He was an economist speaking on an economist's question, and a challenge to him was an affront to the entire profession. That was enough to make the case a matter for action by the American Economic Association. With the current AEA president, Henry Carter Adams, out of the country, Seligman contacted Charles Henry Hull, the secretary, and Walter F. Willcox, the treasurer, to propose that the association take an official position in the Andrews case.

United professional intervention in an academic freedom case had never been attempted before. Now Seligman moved cautiously to strengthen Andrews's position and to establish serviceable precedents for a professional role in such matters without risking a damaging controversy within the association. Initially he proposed that the AEA "act corporately" through its executive committee, with that small, manageable body taking a position in the name of the entire association of economists, whatever the views of individual members might be. The suggestion was a complete reversal of Seligman's earlier rather limited conception of the prerogatives of the AEA.[16]

Undoubtedly Seligman favored decisive action because the Andrews case was such an excellent risk. An economist who believed in the right of advocacy on controversial issues would almost certainly dare to say so in the Andrews case. In most

15. Quoted in Gardner to Seligman, 13 July 1897, Seligman MSS.
16. Hull to Seligman, 5 August 1897, Seligman MSS. By coincidence, Hull and Willcox were both at Cornell, where Andrews had earlier taught.

places little harm was likely to come of a temperate pro-Andrews position. At many eastern schools a board of regents that wished to punish an economist for petitioning in favor of Andrews would first have to reprimand the president, who had also signed. Public opinion rallied to Andrews as an underdog. For possessing the courage to advocate an unpopular opinion, he faced a penalty that everyone could understand—financial loss and empty pockets. Here was a classic juxtaposition of the pecuniary motive against the right of free expression that called forth all the latent guilt which money-making evoked in most Americans. Powerful critics still sided with Andrews's detractors, but support for the president was growing. Even close friends of Brown University began to suggest that the trustees looked foolish.[17]

Even in such propitious circumstances, the Seligman proposal split the executive committee of the AEA. An official statement from the economics profession would dramatize the significance of the case for the role of economists. It would also go a long way toward committing professional economists to the defense of a fairly extensive right of public advocacy on policy questions. Undoubtedly Walter Willcox represented a sizable number of his fellow economists when he protested—speaking rather cautiously in opposition to a colleague as important as Seligman—against so radical a step. Willcox failed to see the issues involved in the Andrews case as a blow to professionalism that fell with special weight upon economists. Apparently he operated within a somewhat more traditional frame of reference, for

17. Some of the trustees denied that a majority of the board had ever had any intention of removing Andrews or accepting his resignation and declared that they had never intended to allow the appointment of the committee or its conference with Andrews to be made public. See Gardner to Jameson, 17 August 1897, Jameson MSS. When Congressman Walker claimed that the board unanimously agreed "that the question upon which Dr. Andrews was at variance with it is far more vital to the well-being of the country than were the questions upon which the Civil War was fought," another board member, Judge F. A. Gaskill of the Massachusetts superior court, announced that Walker spoke neither for him nor for the whole board. Gaskill to the *Boston Evening Transcript,* 7 August 1897. On the other hand, the *Chicago Tribune,* for example, was calling the Brown faculty members who had petitioned for Andrews "deluded professors" backing up a "knavish chief." "Andrews' Fool Friends," *Chicago Tribune,* 7 August 1897.

he seemed to look upon the Andrews problem as a fairly routine abridgment of the general right to freedom of teaching and as such a matter that fell largely within the purview of local agents. Willcox conceded that "some form" of protest should probably be made at the proper time; but while the controversy remained hot, further criticism from professors would only stiffen the resistance of the Brown trustees. Action should await the corporation's decision and then come from "all sorts of teachers and not especially from teachers of economics." Willcox doubted that "outsiders" should do more than suggest that allowing Andrews to resign would tend "to hamper university teachers and to shake the public confidence in the sincerity and candor of their treatment of mixed questions." He had no desire to use the case to make professional policy.[18]

The differences between Willcox and his Cornell colleague Hull showed how varied contemporary perceptions of professionalism were. Hull's analysis of the difficulties was a prototype of all later deliberations on the proper role of professional associations in matters that had policy implications. Hull doubted that the officers of the AEA had the authority to speak for the entire membership. He even conceded that an association position on Andrews's rights could be construed with some justice as an endorsement of a particular set of economic views, something the association had long since decided to avoid. In response to such an unauthorized and unprecedented action by the executive committee, Hull feared that blocks of disgruntled members might secede from the AEA and thus destroy the organization. Yet he was prepared to risk all that if Seligman's plan for official action appeared likely to have the desired effect.

In Hull's mind the fundamental issue in the Andrews case was a moral question that required a radical solution. AEA members were not merely economists but also citizens and educators. As economists they might be primarily concerned with economic

18. Willcox to Seligman, 5 August 1897, Seligman MSS; Willcox to Jameson, 6 August 1897, Jameson MSS.

theories, but as citizens and teachers, Hull insisted, they must believe "that the unfettered search for truth is the noblest discipline for the human mind, the truest incentive to right living." No matter what the outcome, an academic had not only the right but the obligation to defend free inquiry with every possible weapon, including his professional association. The AEA might better "go to pieces, if need be, in an attempt to purify the intellectual atmosphere, than to continue in an atmosphere which must make its continuance a useless impertinence."[19]

Though Hull was prepared to make a total commitment, he was restrained by a sense that executive committee action, however justified, was practically ill advised. Probably the committee would divide on its right to act for the association. Even if the committee was united, it did not include the most prominent economists whose support would have the greatest influence. Except for Adams and Giddings, who was technically a sociologist, the members of the executive committee were junior professors who were little known outside their own institutions. Even if the entire AEA Council were marshaled in Andrews's support, the names of major figures would still be buried among a long list of unknowns. As a "more weighty" alternative, Hull proposed that Seligman, Taussig, and perhaps James draw up a list of distinguished economists who might offer a public statement on the Andrews case, presenting themselves simply as a group of interested members of the AEA Council.[20] Hull's proposal was actually an ingenious compromise, for it skirted the issue of official action while it preserved an authoritative appearance.

19. Hull to Seligman, 6 August 1897, Seligman MSS.
20. Ibid. Hull's list included Davis R. Dewey, W. W. Folwell, George Gunton, Jeremiah Jenks, Small, H. C. Adams, W. J. Ashley, James, Richmond Mayo-Smith, Albert Shaw, Taussig, and about a dozen younger, less familiar figures. The junior members of the Executive Committee were Gould of Hopkins, Roland Falkner of Pennsylvania, Willcox, and Hull. On the Publications Committee, which may have been consulted, were Taussig, free-lance economist John Graham Brooks, H. H. Powers of Stanford, Davis R. Dewey of MIT, William A. Scott of Wisconsin, and Sidney Sherwood of the University of Pennsylvania.

As Hull had predicted, the executive committee was not unanimous. Roland Falkner of the University of Pennsylvania was enthusiastically in favor of committee action. There is no record of the position Giddings took, but he was Seligman's colleague at Columbia and probably supported him. Gould of Hopkins tended to be more conservative. Gardner and Jameson pressed for an official stand, but Davis R. Dewey agreed with Willcox that Andrews's plight was mainly a question of freedom of teaching, not a special concern of economists, and opposed any executive committee action. Finally Seligman decided to give up the plan for an official AEA protest. For a time it appeared that economists would simply sign the general petition that the eastern presidents were backing, but Seligman and Gardner persisted in keeping academic social scientists separate. They shifted to Hull's plan and sent an unofficial petition drafted by Taussig to a selected list of well-known social scientists, mostly economists of professorial rank.[21]

Though the economists' petition was not an official professional action, it remained a strong plea for scientific autonomy. The prominent petitioners asked the Brown Corporation to take no action "that could be construed as limiting the freedom of speech in the teaching body of our universities." In an attempt to define an area where the technical expert was immune from the judgment of laymen, Taussig designated aspects of an economist's activity which nonspecialists were incompetent to judge. "We believe that no questions should enter except as to capacity, faithfulness, and general efficiency in the performance of appointed duty," the statement read. "To undertake inquiry as to the soundness of opinions expressed on any question, or set of questions, must inevitably limit freedom of expression, tend to destroy intellectual independence, and to diminish public respect for the conclusions of all investigators." Appended to the petition was a copy of the statement of the University of Wisconsin Board of Regents in defense of academic free-dom.[22]

Social scientists responded with enthusiasm. A list of thirty-three "good names" was presented to the Brown Corporation on September 1, and twenty more social scientists signed peti-tions later or indicated they would have signed had the request arrived before they left for summer vacation. Almost all the prominent first-generation professionals supported the protest. In addition to Taussig, Seligman, Dewey, Hull, and Willcox, the names of Adams, James, Clark, Commons, Giddings, Ely, and a dozen Ely students were also there. Besides James there was one other signer from the University of Chicago. Neither Small nor Laughlin was listed, but a letter from Gardner to Jameson indicated: "J. Laurence Laughlin—signature enclosed, came too late to print." Yale professors were under special strain because Francis Wayland, the dean of the Yale law school and the son of a prominent former Brown president, had been one of the trustees appointed to confer with Andrews on his views. Never-theless, Hadley implied that only his absence from the country, not disagreement, had prevented him from cooperating with Taussig and Seligman. There was a younger Yale signer, Irving Fisher, but a senior Yale economist, Henry Farnam, refused in disgust when the newspapers announced that Andrews had agreed to serve as president of a "correspondence university" to be operated by the *Cosmopolitan*. Both Sumner of Yale and Dunbar of Harvard signed the general petition, though each refused to allow his name to be shifted to the economists' list.[23]

Observers interpreted the significance of the economists'

22. Petition to the Corporation of Brown University, 24 August 1897, Jameson MSS.

23. Petition to the Corporation of Brown University, 24 August 1897, with additions; Hadley to Seligman, 16 September 1897; Patten to Seligman, 30 August 1897; Farnam to Seligman, 24 August 1897; and numerous other letters and telegrams; Gardner to Jameson, 28 August 1897, Jameson MSS. Laughlin had opposed Harper's desire to bring Andrews to Chicago in 1894, mainly because he objected to Harper's secretive methods. Laughlin to Harper, 8 January 1894, Laughlin File, Harper MSS.

defense of Andrews variously, according to their professional economic perspectives. A unique interpretation occurred to William James Ashley, an Englishman who taught economic history at Harvard from 1892 to 1901 and considerably liberalized both the content and philosophy of Dunbar's department. For some time Ashley had been critical of the homogenizing tendencies he observed at work in the American Economic Association of the 1890s. He believed that "it *was* the office of the A. E. A., and its duty, to protest, *indirectly* as well as *directly* against the teaching that was dominant in certain circles when the association was founded." Ashley realized that the decline of controversy in the AEA and the "rapprochement between the younger men" indicated at least a partial victory of the historical perspective and support for state action over the iron laws of laissez-faire. Even so, he regretted that economists had been brought into the AEA "against whose teaching it was once the business of the association to protest." When the economists rallied to defend Andrews, Ashley thought he saw a revival of the combative spirit whose loss he had mourned. "Ultimately I hope the Economists' address will obtain publicity, with the signatures attached," he told Seligman, suggesting announcements in the Harvard and Columbia journals. "Unless we make a stand, and let it be generally known, too, we shall all remain under a stigma."[24]

There were also social scientists who viewed the protest negatively. Some of the refusals to sign were predictable, some surprising. Simon Newcomb, who received the request too late, indicated he would probably not have participated in what he thought would be a futile effort. In his usual surly manner, George Gunton announced that the managers of universities had some rights as well as professors. James Burrill Angell sided with

24. Ashley to Seligman, 21 August 1897, in Joseph Dorfman, ed., "Seligman Correspondence, Part 4," *Political Science Quarterly* 56 (1941):586; Ashley to Ely, 12 March 1893, Ely MSS. For Ashley's influence on the development of social science at Harvard, see Robert Church, "The Economists Study Society: Sociology at Harvard, 1891-1902," in *Social Sciences at Harvard*, ed. Paul Buck (Cambridge, Mass., 1965), pp. 61-78.

the trustees instead of a fellow university president because he had a number of friends on the Brown board. Alone among former close associates of Jameson and Gardner, Woodrow Wilson declined to add his name, arguing that an impasse would result at Brown if the board was forced to yield to criticism and Andrews stayed on.[25]

Finally all the signatures of presidents, economists, and alumni were put together into a bundle more than a foot high and delivered to the meeting of the corporation. On the next day the trustees asked Andrews to withdraw his resignation. The matter had been complicated badly by Andrews's flirtation with the Cosmopolitan University, but Seligman was still jubilant. "It doesn't now matter whether Andrews withdraws his resignation or not," he wrote; "the principle is saved."[26]

If the principle was saved, it was saved in a very small corner of the country for a very short time. At Kansas State Agricultural College, a Populist Board of Regents fired practically their whole faculty the same summer, and in other western state universities and colleges professors of social science played musical chairs to a political tune.[27] Actually established and moderate members of the economics profession had mobilized themselves to defend Andrews precisely because his threatened position was in the civilized East, where church and college were expected to stand serenely above politics, not in the raw and undisciplined West where political appointments and dis-

25. Newcomb to Seligman, 2 September 1897; Gunton to Seligman, 19 August 1897; Angell to Jameson, 31 August 1897; Gardner to Jameson, 28 August 1897, Jameson MSS. Donnan, "Academic Cause," p. 42, quoted the Wilson letter of refusal. Gardner wrote to Jameson that Wilson had refused when asked by Taussig and signed when asked by Seligman; Gardner suggested that Jameson use his judgment. Wilson had moved from Wesleyan University to Princeton in 1890.

26. See Statement of Trustees in *The Andrews Controversy* (Providence, R.I., 1897), p. 37; Seligman to Dunning, 3 September 1897, *Political Science Quarterly* MSS. Andrews resigned the next year to serve as superintendent of the Chicago public schools. In 1900 he became chancellor of the University of Nebraska.

27. Board of Regents, *The Reorganization of the Kansas State Agricultural College,* (Manhattan, Kans., 1897), copy in Jameson MSS. Frederick C. Hicks was investigated, though eventually exonerated, at the University of Missouri. Hicks to Ely, 13 October 1897, Ely MSS; "Objection to Gold Teachings," *New York Post,* 27 August 1897.

missals seemed rather like the fortunes of war. An action that might be tolerated if not approved in a public university like Wisconsin or even in a private but new and money-lustered place like Chicago was entirely out of acceptable dimension in Brown of Providence.[28]

How much Andrews's status had to do with the reaction of professional social scientists is measured by the startlingly opposite treatment accorded an academic beginner who ran afoul of the money question at the same time. When J. Allen Smith was fired for obviously political reasons his plight was virtually ignored. Beyond a small circle of friends who had experienced similar difficulties in the aftermath of the election of 1896, no official notice was taken, no help arrived. Yet the two cases, at least in terms of the economic questions at issue, were strikingly similar.[29]

In background, Smith resembled Taussig or Laughlin more than he did Andrews or any of the ethical economists whose reform inclinations kept irritating trustees. "Allen's early training & education—family background was all conservative," his widow recalled. He was born on a Missouri farm in 1860. When the Civil War came Smith's family freed its slaves, but their sympathies remained with the Confederacy and everything but their land was confiscated. Smith was forced to finance his own education.

During the middle 1880s the campus of the University of Missouri seethed with the social questions of the times. Prompt-

28. The sectional aspect of the economists' response irritated a Westerner such as H. C. Adams of Michigan, though he did not disagree with the protest. Adams hoped that "this episode in connection with Andrews will show the people of the East that Kansas and Washington have not the monopoly of bigotry and shortsightedness." Adams to Seligman, 21 August 1897; Adams to Andrews, 21 August 1897, Adams MSS. Adams played a small role in the case. He had already turned his responsibilities over to the Executive Committee. He would have left for Europe in July but an accident to one of his children forced him to return from New York to Ann Arbor and delay departure.

29. The Smith case is mentioned briefly in Metzger, *Academic Freedom*, pp. 149-50. More extensive biographical treatments of Smith are in Eric Goldman, "J. Allen Smith: The Reformer and His Dilemma," *Pacific Northwest Quarterly* 35 (July 1944):195-214; Thomas S. Barclay, "J. Allen Smith: An American Scholar," *Missouri Alumnus* (April 1931):234, 239, 241.

ed by a professor's advice to avoid the works of Henry George, Smith read many books of social and economic criticism, though at the time he remained "a strong gold standard man." After college he followed his boyhood plan to become a lawyer, "but in real practice found it a hide-bound career ruled by precedent" and grew restive. Meanwhile disputes over monopolies and money swirled around him, serious and fascinating. When Smith decided to study the social sciences, the growing reputation of Henry Carter Adams attracted him to the University of Michigan.[30]

Graduate study opened a new vista for Smith. His first strong sympathy with labor emerged from an experience as a Missouri militiaman called out to "quell a mining strike and riots." A close investigation of conditions left him on the miners' side. Further reflection convinced him that industrialization had changed dozens of old relationships. In a penetrating study of the supply and value of money in industrial economies, Smith challenged established economic orthodoxy. His doctoral thesis argued that a dollar based on a single commodity (gold) caused frequent fluctuations in prices, which produced unnecessary hardships both for rising entrepreneurs and for debtors. Those ups and downs could be avoided by the adoption of a multiple money standard and government control of the supply of money through devices that would contract or expand the circulation as prices rose or fell, thus stabilizing price levels. Smith's study aroused the stiff disapproval of gold standard men in the Michigan department, but Adams defended him. Actually what Smith proposed was far more complex than free silver. His work anticipated the stabilized dollar theory worked out by Irving Fisher, and it favored labor in its contention that wages in industrial societies must claim an ever larger share of the product in order to maintain "efficient demand." The study

30. Notes in the margins of a clipping, "Missouri Gave Us Our J. Allen Smith," *University of Washington Daily*, 19 November 1914, J. Allen Smith MSS, University of Washington Archives, probably by Mrs. James Falconer, to whom, through interviews, Eric Goldman attributes similar information; Barclay, "J. Allen Smith," p. 234; Goldman, "J. Allen Smith," p. 196.

was published in 1896, just in time to make Smith's thought a factor in the silver crusade.[31]

In 1895 Smith had accepted a position at Marietta College in Ohio where Christian ethics, economics, and sociology were still being taught in the old tradition by the president. Smith's lectures must have presented a conspicuous contrast. His syllabus showed that he used Mill as a basis for a detailed criticism of laissez-faire, explored the defects of monopoly and the gold standard, and then stressed the waste, immorality, and easy avoidability of economic depressions. Critics thought Smith interested students in topics too advanced for their years. A student who knew Smith two years later considered him "a handsome man, an excellent lecturer and an outstanding teacher," who was able to demonstrate unbreakable ties between economics, political science, and sociology. Smith would have his students read a conservative text and recite. Then "he'd pound on the table with his fists and tear the conclusions to shreds. He was what you'd call an iconoclast. He didn't have a constructive program." But, the student added, "I worked with J. Allen Smith for two years and at the end of that time I not only understood monopolies but I hated them. I hated the injustice that occurred in the industrial field; the exploitation of common resources by the few and the exploitation of the workers, many of whom were ignorant foreigners too helpless to remedy their lot." In 1896 Smith joined the Bryan campaign and voted Democratic. The next spring he received notice of dismissal.[32]

Marietta College authorities claimed that financial exigency,

31. Falconer notes, Smith MSS; Dorfman, *Economic Mind,* 3:294-96; Goldman, "Smith," pp. 197-98; Barclay, "Smith," p. 234; Fisher to Smith, 5 November 1914; Smith to Fisher, 25 November 1914, Smith MSS.

32. John W. Simpson to Smith, 10, 27 August 1895, Smith MSS; notes on Junior Exhibition and outline of the lectures in political economy, in "The Case of Professor James Allen Smith," *Industrialist* 23 (2 September 1897): 180; Theresa Schmid McMahon, "My Story," unpublished memoir in the University of Washington Archives, pp. 8-9, T. McMahon MSS. Smith's treatment of natural and artificial monopoly was pure Adams. McMahon was a student of Smith when he arrived at the University of Washington in 1897. She later studied under Commons at Wisconsin, worked with Jane Addams, and returned as a professor of economics and radical labor reformer at the University of Washington.

not any dissatisfaction with Smith's teaching, made it necessary to abolish his professorship of economics and sociology, but several other professors were fired at the same time, "all of whom happened to have voted against McKinley." Smith privately blamed "Chas. G. Dawes, next comptroller of currency, his father, father-in-law, uncle, and several other relatives of the Dawes family," a clan of "partisan Republicans" with interests in gas and other monopolies who controlled both the college board and the new president and desired to suppress Smith's economic teachings. Students apparently agreed; at a mass "indignation meeting" a number of them threatened to leave when Smith did unless the board reconsidered. It did not, and the next semester another professor of economics and sociology was appointed.[33]

Jobless, Smith suddenly found himself in nearly the same straits as Bemis—with one major difference. In the Smith case there was no extended controversy. Indeed there was very little publicity of any kind, for Smith had foreseen the impossibility of coexisting, except by "intellectual prostitution," with a board that favored the "gold standard, McKinley protectionism, and non-interference with monopolies." When the ax fell, he accepted his fate and asked friends to help him find a position where his views would be more congenial. Though Smith's record was good in both teaching and scholarship, no state university where the silver question was a major issue could afford to ignore his opinions. There was talk of a vacancy at the University of Missouri, where Fred C. Hicks was under fire for his support of the gold standard, but Smith declined to consider a vacancy created as his had been. In spite of his scruples the next two offers he received were equally political. Thomas Elmer Will, Populist president of Kansas State, held a vacancy for Smith—he wanted to hire Bemis and Frank Parsons as well,

33. W. W. Mills to Smith, 25 March 1897; Smith to Frank Doster, 3 May 1897; Washington Gladden to Smith, 10, 27 April 1897, Smith MSS. Gladden corroborated Smith's suspicion after a discussion with President Mills. On Smith's replacement, see Goldman, "Smith," p. 198. A student petition is printed in "The Case of Professor James Allen Smith," p. 180.

but had only two positions—until the Populist president of the University of Washington acted on Will's recommendation and offered Smith a professorship in history and political science.[34] All these negotiations with western schools were characterized by the frankest admission that the candidate and the position must be right for each other on the critical economic issues of the 1890s.

The knife of political preference cut two ways. As Smith was coming to Washington, Professor Edmond Meany began to fear that he would soon be leaving. A Republican political appointee, Meany was a lecturer in forestry who doubled as registrar. For a year after the Populist victory friends were able to protect him. In fact he received what was obviously a political promotion to the professorship of history and announced, overwhelmed with relief, that he hoped "to make this my life work and to keep from out of the whirl of politics." Meany had no great interest in scholarship, but he busied himself preparing lectures, collecting stamps and seeds, and organizing a debating club. One by one his friends were removed and the Populists kept "howling" for his position. A Tacoma senator reportedly wanted to replace him with "a philosopher like George Howard" of Stanford. In 1898, Meany reported, the regents "combined the chairs of history and political economy, thus legislating me out of my place in the University." To occupy himself, Meany ran for the state senate. With the next Republican victory he returned to his old job as registrar.[35] Even though Meany was an obvious hack, the impact of politics on his tenure demeaned the profession of social science as much as the dismissal of Smith did.

The economics establishment failed to defend Smith's right

34. Smith to Frank Doster, 3 May 1897; Will to John Wiley, 13 May 1897; John Wiley to Charles G. Slack, 3 June 1897; Will to Smith, 11 June 1897; Clark Davis to Smith, 3 June 1897, Smith MSS; Smith to Henry Carter Adams, 27 June 1896, 15 June 1897, Adams MSS. See also Metzger, *Academic Freedom,* p. 150; Dorfman, *Economic Mind,* 3:296.

35. Meany to Hon. Edmund P. Dole, 19 February 1898; Meany to Hon. A. A. Lindsley, 25 February 1898; Meany to E. C. Hughes, 7 September 1898; Meany to Prof. Charles V. Piper, 14 April 1898, Edmond Meany MSS, University of Washington Archives.

of advocacy. The same scholars who were outraged that Andrews's silver views could affect his tenure tended to overlook political dismissals and gold or silver professorships in small colleges and western state universities. Smith's only defender was the *Industrialist,* the organ of the Populist professors at Kansas State. In that paper a former president of Marietta College (a Republican who had hired Smith "upon the recommendation of Dr. Herbert [*sic*] Adams of the University of Michigan, and other eminent political scientists") defended Smith's scholarship and his exceptional talent for teaching, while he condemned the "Narrow, Conservative Political Views" of the trustees who had eliminated both men. The only published protest that might have come from a social scientist was anonymous: "A university professor in another state" recommended Smith for a position in "the great, liberal state of Kansas," where a man's progressive views would not disqualify him as a teacher. Smith's most logical defender was his major professor, but Henry Carter Adams took no public stand. Though Adams knew that Smith's dismissal was politically motivated, his letters of recommendation to President Will and the Kansas Regents accepted the budgetary rationalization. Apparently Adams was no more willing to confront the issue of advocacy in Smith's interest than he had been in his own case at Cornell a decade earlier.[36]

There was some irony in the fact that economists defended Andrews and not Smith. Eventually Smith made a far greater contribution to scholarship. In addition to his work in monetary theory, his *Spirit of American Government* (1907) was a classic in the development of an economic interpretation of the American constitution. Andrews, on the other hand, turned out a passable economics textbook in the 1880s and spent the rest of his career as a university administrator. Even in 1897 Smith had established his capacity for brilliant scholarship, though

36. John W. Simpson to Regent C. B. Hoffman, 31 May 1897; "A University Professor in Another State" to Hoffman, 19 May 1897, in "Case of Professor Smith," p. 180; Adams to Hon. C. B. Hoffman, 18 May 1897; Adams to Prof. T. E. Will, 18 May 1897, Adams MSS.

those who knew him made no effort to advertise the fact. Smith was young, relatively unknown, and still a potential liability. No one knew, as his career developed, what he might do to vindicate or to embarrass those who might support him. Furthermore, if scholarly opinion in colleges and universities all over the country had been polled in 1897, as many social scientists as not would probably still have thought of their own positions as political sinecures where advocacy that conformed to local expectations was properly expected. Social scientists who were professionalized beyond that stage considered themselves an academic elite.

Professionalization had not progressed so far in 1897 that a principled defense of the economist's right of advocacy had become an aspect of professional identity. Yet the leading professionals had tentatively established a policy of defending established scholars under certain conditions: when the subject at issue was clearly a conventional concern of economics; when the controversial doctrines fell into an area where the accuracy of calculation and reasoning—one test of objectivity—could be easily demonstrated; where there was no violation of ethical procedure, excessive popularization, or indoctrination; and where the support of influential scholars and citizens somewhere, if not in the immediate area, located the controversial teaching within the range of permissible dissent.

10 *Collective Security*

The distinctions of scholarly reputation, personal status, and professional influence that accounted for the dramatically different fates of Andrews and Smith in 1897 were tested among the social scientists of a single institution a short time later. At Leland Stanford Junior University a little-known sociologist named Harry Huntington Powers was quietly and unceremoniously dumped in 1898 at the whim of the university's powerful benefactor and sole trustee, Mrs. Leland Stanford. Hardly anyone noticed. Two years later Stanford fired its most prominent economist and pioneer sociologist, Edward Alsworth Ross, and blew the academic world wide open.[1]

The difference was simple. As a former officer of the AEA, Ross was an established scholar who had performed effectively on several university faculties and earned respect in the profession. Though he conceived the social scientist's political role more broadly than most economists, his public expressions were confined to topics within his scholarly competence and his advocacy fell within the range of permissible dissent. The Ross case was revolutionary because it attracted so much attention. Yet for social scientists the case was only the final resolution of a question of professional propriety that economists had raised in the *Science* discussion of 1886 and an obvious extension of the principles enunciated in the Andrews case of 1897.

By subsequent generations of historians, Ross has been remembered primarily for the extreme racial views that placed him in the vanguard of those ardent proclaimers of Aryan supremacy who rationalized imperialism as a racial mission and encouraged immigration restriction to prevent the further mongrelization of Anglo-Saxon America. Actually Ross's racial views were not unusual at the turn of the century. Other scholars such as the popular historian John Fiske and important

public figures such as Theodore Roosevelt were equally committed to racist principles, and Ross only made his opinions more
widely known than most. Through his rather pessimistic but
determined evolutionism, his solid commitment to science as a
social solvent, his acceptance of an expanded state function,
and his pronounced careerism, Ross was typical of the social
scientists of his day.

Ross was a member of the second generation of professional
social scientists. The major attractions of academic life for him
were upward social mobility and intellectual challenge. His early
experience shaped a reckless, expansive nature. Ross was born
in 1866 in rural Illinois to restless parents—an independent,
determined mother who had taught high school in Iowa and an
adventurous, erratic father who campaigned ardently against
slavery, dug gold with the forty-niners, homesteaded on the
Kansas sod-house frontier, and finally retreated ailing to a farm
in Iowa. Both parents died before the boy was ten, leaving him
to be passed from aunt to aunt for care. Finally he landed near
Marion, Iowa, in the family of the local justice of the peace,
"Squire" Beach and his young wife, Mary, the foster mother
who built his self-confidence and shaped his character.

A Presbyterian of serious but not spiritual conviction, Ross
developed abounding faith in his ability to sway people with
charm and good looks. As a country school teacher he established his "moral ascendancy" with the help of well over six

1. Of all the cases involving social scientists, the Ross case achieved more notoriety at the time it occurred and has enjoyed more attention from scholars since than
any other. The standard accounts of Stanford University during the period and of the
Ross case are in Orrin L. Elliott, *Stanford University, the First Twenty-Five Years*
(Stanford, Calif., 1937). Elliott was the university registrar and a partisan of David
Starr Jordan, but the book is fair on the Ross case, analyzing Jordan's motives in
particular as well as any source. Metzger, *Academic Freedom*, pp. 162-71, discusses
both the Powers and Ross cases. Veysey, *Emergence of the American University*, esp.
pp. 384-418, interprets the Ross case as an event in the development of faculty
prerogatives (one of them academic freedom) and administrative powers in the new
university. More recently, in James C. Mohr, "Academic Turmoil and Public Opinion:
The Ross Case at Stanford," *Pacific Historical Review* 39 (February 1970):39-61,
there is an analysis of how the principals in the case attempted to mold public
opinion and how the outcome was affected. My treatment emphasizes the role of
professional social scientists in the case.

feet of brawn. Both at home and as an undergraduate at Coe College in Cedar Rapids, Iowa, he moved in a "tight little intellectual world" where the tenets of Republicanism, protectionism, and capitalism were only slightly offset by smuggled volumes of Henry George. After graduation Ross taught at a Presbyterian preparatory school in Fort Dodge, Kansas, simultaneously reveling in the delights of local society and navigating cautiously through the intellectual passage that characteristically resulted from an intelligent young man's first reading of Spencer and Darwin. Finally his fascination with ideas outweighed the joys of courting, and in 1888 he left the security of village America for the serious discipline of graduate study at the University of Berlin and rough confirmation of the toll that large cities and an industrial routine exacted from individual freedom. From that point on his progress was almost programmed: from philology, "through the spell of philosophy," back in 1890 to America, the Johns Hopkins, and Richard T. Ely.[2]

Convinced that it was possible to combine scholarship and service, Ross completed his degree in economics, jurisprudence, and ethics, married the niece of Lester Frank Ward, and in 1891 accepted an offer from President David Starr Jordan to teach social science at Indiana University. Ross's thesis on the sinking fund was published by the AEA and his teaching was unusually successful. Though he attracted local attention for making speeches against the gold standard, in 1892 he received offers of associate professorships at Northwestern, Stanford (where Jordan was opening the new university endowed by Senator Leland Stanford in memory of his teenage son), and Cornell, plus reappointment at Indiana. Ross chose Cornell, where he joined Hull and Willcox under the leadership of the political scientist Jeremiah W. Jenks. The following fall Ross inherited Ely's mantle as secretary of the AEA. In his economics classes

2. E. A. Ross, *Seventy Years of It* (New York, 1936), pp. 1-41. A stimulating sketch of Ross's life and social philosophy is in R. Jackson Wilson, *In Quest of Community: Social Philosophy in the United States, 1860-1920* (New York, 1968), chapt. 4.

he had students investigate current problems without arousing community resistance, and according to his testimony his public lectures were considered impartial.[3]

Had Ross remained at Cornell, where rigid supervision of faculty views had given way to a more permissive climate, he might have escaped a confrontation with authority. But the next year Ross accepted Jordan's third offer to become a member of the "Stanford band." Friends who recognized Ross's need for attention wondered immediately what the outcome would be. "Ross is taking quick rank among university economists," a former colleague commented. "He is a bright, brainy man of sure promise, but he needs ballast. He will get it on the coast, about the time he sets his students to working up the expose of the Pacific R. R. dealings *a la Stanford*. Will, then, the 'spirit of reform' continue with him its perfect work?"[4] At Stanford the risk of advocacy increased after the death of Leland Stanford left the university in the maternal care of the imperious, moralistic, possessive, and superstitious Mrs. Jane Lathrop Stanford. The school became a memorial to her son and husband which she intended to keep inviolate.

Ross involved himself in politics, he claimed later, not to achieve "immediate practical results, but in my role of public teacher." Though he avoided any affiliation with socialist organizations, on a narrower range of issues Ross developed a reputation among laborers and political figures somewhat like Ely's had been before his reversal in 1894. One local admirer referred to Ross as "a political economist of the people."[5]

3. Ross, *Seventy Years*, pp. 42-52. Ross's Hopkins classmates were an illustrious group which included David Kinley, James Woodburn, William A. Scott, the Willoughby twins, Charles Homer Haskins, and John Commons.

4. Woodburn to H. B. Adams, 4 March 1893, in W. Stull Holt, ed., *Historical Scholarship in the United States, 1876-1901: As Revealed in the Correspondence of Herbert B. Adams,* Johns Hopkins University Studies in History and Political Science, Series 56, no. 4 (Baltimore, Md., 1938), pp. 192-94. Henry Carter Adams had refused the Stanford position, though Jordan had promised he would have complete academic freedom despite the divergence of views between him and Senator Stanford on railroad matters. Jordan to Adams, 7 August 1891, H. C. Adams MSS.

5. Ross, *Seventy Years,* p. 63; J. E. Scott to Ross, 29 March 1897; R. Morrison to Ross, 3 September 1898; Dick Miller to Ross, 10 September 1896, Ross MSS.

Ross's trouble with Mrs. Stanford started over the same issue that involved Andrews and Smith in controversy. Ross was the first academic economist to come out openly for free silver instead of international bimetallism. Naturally he quickly attracted the attention of silverites and Democrats, including William Jennings Bryan himself. In 1896 Ross produced a popular campaign pamphlet, "Honest Dollars," and made a few speeches for Bryan. Professors all over the country were commenting on the issues in the McKinley-Bryan contest, but even the fact that thirty-two other Stanford professors declared publicly for McKinley and the gold standard made Ross's advocacy on the other side no less offensive to Mrs. Stanford. Reacting with sudden rage, she demanded his dismissal.[6]

Only President Jordan's expression of faith in Ross's fundamental soundness and ability spared him in 1896. Hoping that the tension would ease with time, Jordan persuaded Mrs. Stanford to give Ross a sabbatical leave in 1898-1899 so that he could look for another position. In return Ross agreed to resign in 1899 if he was still considered unsuitable. Even more significantly, his retention was based on a transfer from economics to social science, exactly the switch that Laughlin had forced on Bemis at Chicago. The change was designed to underline Jordan's stern warning that the university should never again be made to look responsible for Ross's economic opinions. To remove any doubt, Mrs. Stanford placed a total ban on any further political activity by Stanford professors.[7]

6. Charles B. Spahr to Ross, 11 February 1896; Bryan to Ross, 24 February 1896; Dick Miller to Ross, 10 September 1896, Ross MSS; "Stanford University Professors Declare for Bryan," *San Francisco Examiner*, 27 September 1896; "Six out of Seven of Stanford Faculty Are for McKinley and Hobart and Prosperity," *San Francisco Chronicle*, 27 September 1896. These clippings and many others are in "The Ross Affair: Newspaper Clippings and Documents Collected by O. L. Elliott," Orrin L. Elliott MSS, Stanford University Archives. On Mrs. Stanford's view of the patriotic and nonpartisan role of the university see Jane Stanford to Jordan, 23 March 1899, Stanford Family MSS, Stanford Correspondence, Vol. 5, Stanford Univ. Archives.

7. Jordan to Ross, 20 October 1896; 8 April 1897, Ross MSS; Jane Stanford, *Address on the Right of Free Speech* (Stanford, Calif., 1903); "Memorandum in re Ross," Jordan Letterbook, p. 230, David Starr Jordan MSS, Stanford University Archives. Subsequent letters of appointment referred to Ross's position as a chair of sociology, and he was head professor of sociology upon his return from leave in 1899.

A widening circle of professional social scientists viewed Ross's conduct with some disapproval. When he became involved in the Bryan campaign, important economists warned him. Taussig supported the role of an economist as a technical expert on purely economic questions, but he considered flamboyant pronouncements published in popular form equally "undignified & objectionable" whether Ross or Laughlin penned them. Simon Patten was so impressed by Ross's early work in theoretical sociology that he begged him to give up any other diversion. "Have you not been giving a little too much time to politics lately?" Patten gently inquired. "That miserable money problem gets lots more attention than it deserves and I never see an article of yours on it but what I feel that intellectual force has been wasted which might have produced far greater results in other directions."[8]

If Ross failed to heed the warnings of friends in other institutions, the fate of his own colleague, H. H. Powers, should have restrained him. Powers was given to expressions of cynicism which endeared him to neither the founder nor the president. Though he had previously taught at Smith and Oberlin he had no tenure, for all Stanford appointments required annual renewal. An unfortunate accident befell him when he agreed to address a group of students on religion. Failing to recognize Mrs. Stanford in the audience, Powers expressed opinions of sufficient "pessimism and heterodoxy" to injure the founder's orthodox Catholic sensibilities. When he added offense by publicly challenging the gold standard in 1896, Mrs. Stanford demanded his resignation. Jordan managed to give Powers a terminal year, but with no significant scholarly publications Powers expected a good deal of difficulty in finding a position as desirable as Stanford. Accordingly, like Adams and Commons, he wanted to avoid publicity at all costs. Otherwise Powers, not Ross, might have provided the test of academic

---

8. "Wit Sparkles," *Indianapolis Sentinel*, 1 January 1896, copy in Mayo-Smith MSS; Taussig to Ross, 16 November 1896, 7 March 1901; Albert Shaw to Ross, 3 December 1896; Patten to Ross, 2 December 1896, Ross MSS.

freedom that was certain to come at Stanford University.[9]

Briefly it appeared that Ross might weather his probationary period and reinstate himself with Mrs. Stanford. Apparently Ross showed no great sympathy with Powers. He reacted to his colleague's departure with nonchalant relief and helped Jordan out of a difficult administrative problem by taking a large part of Powers's assignment. Though the "rich men and big bugs," including the powerful Southern Pacific Railway president, Collis P. Huntington, had opposed his money views, Ross believed in late 1897 that he was safe as long as he confined his utterances to economic questions "about which it was my business to know." As time passed Jordan's friendliness and the precedent that the Andrews case had established seemed to afford ample protection, and Ross looked forward to his sabbatical leave as nothing more than a well-deserved rest. Matters seemed amicably settled when Jordan notified Ross at the end of his European sojourn that his annual appointment had been continued for 1899-1900.[10]

Professional security and public advocacy were still incompatible at Stanford. On several occasions in 1900 Ross expressed opinions that directly contradicted the Stanford family interests. Leland Stanford had made his name and his enormous fortune by investing in railroads. In a speech on "The Twentieth Century City," Ross predicted the liquidation of that achievement through a gradual transition from private to public ownership of all natural monopolies, including railroads. Stanford had built his railroads with cheap oriental labor. Speaking before a group of San Francisco labor leaders, Ross extolled racial purity and condemned the supporters of coolie immigration. Parts of the speech were recklessly inflammatory. According to some reports Ross advised that "should the worst come to the worst it would be better for us if we were to turn our guns upon every

9. Powers to Ross, 9 November 1897, Ross MSS; Powers to Ely, 12 December 1897, 14 January, 21 February 1898, Ely MSS.
10. Ross to "Dear Mamma," 28 November 1897; Jordan to Ross, 1 May 1899, Ross MSS. Ross referred to his foster mother, Mrs. Beach, as Mamma.

vessel bringing [Asiatics] to our shores rather than to permit them to land."[11]

Recalling the devotion of oriental workers who had defended her household during the "sand-lot riots" of 1877, Mrs. Stanford would have been disturbed enough by Ross's position. Her husband's former business associates added to the pressure, urging her to rid herself of an irresponsible agitator. Angry and humiliated, she denounced Ross's disconcerting tendency "to associate himself with the political demagogues of this city, exciting their evil passions" and bringing dishonor to the university. When Jordan begged her to consider Ross's loyalty and scholarly ability, she replied that it was precisely the outspoken professor's growing scholarly reputation that made his support so desirable to "the socialistic element" and so dangerous to the minds and souls of students. Mrs. Stanford was "weary of Prof. Ross."[12]

Within the limits of his total dependence on the founder's good will, Jordan continued his efforts to prevent disastrous consequences. He not only defended Ross's personal qualities vigorously, but he supported his right to express opinions on controversial public issues. A social scientist had to study social movements, Jordan explained; sooner or later, if he was honest, he was sure to come in conflict with vested interests. Probably Jordan went far beyond his real convictions when he insisted that even in endorsing Bryan and free silver Ross had "never stepped outside of the recognized rights of a professor," and when he pronounced Ross's views on immigration and municipal

11. Jordan, "Memorandum in re Ross," pp. 226-28; Jane Stanford to Jordan, 9, 17 May 1900, Jordan MSS; Stanford, *Address on the Right of Free Speech.* On Ross's commitment to Anglo-Saxon superiority, see Ross, *Seventy Years of It,* p. 273; Ross's statement in "Dr. Edward A. Ross Forced out of Stanford University," *San Francisco Chronicle,* 14 November 1896; Wilson, *In Quest of Community,* pp. 108-13. For part of the text of the Coolie Immigration Speech, see "The Address That Caused the Trouble," *San Francisco Chronicle,* 15 November 1900. For the influence of Ross's opposition to San Francisco street railway interests that Mrs. Stanford largely owned, see Edward W. Bemis to Herbert Baxter Adams, 19 November, 3 December 1900, H. B. Adams MSS.

12. Jane Stanford to Jordan, 9, 17 May 1900, Jordan MSS. Jordan's appeals to Mrs. Stanford are summarized in her *Address on the Right of Free Speech.*

ownership entirely scholarly. Such extravagant praise of Ross would haunt Jordan later, but it did nothing to alter Mrs. Stanford's determination. On May 17, exercising the enormous power of her position as sole trustee, she finally ordered Jordan to fire Ross. At Jordan's suggestion Ross appealed to Mrs. Stanford, reminding her of his loyalty, protesting his devotion to her as "the mother of the university," and tempting her ambition for the university's prestige by enclosing articles from the "great journals" of Harvard, Chicago, and Columbia which praised his work. Unimpressed, Mrs. Stanford granted a final six-months extension to give Ross time to find a new position but still insisted that he leave.[13]

Clearly Jordan would never have fired Ross. Before the controversy embittered relations between them, Jordan thought highly, even fondly of his boisterous junior colleague. "He is one of the ablest, most virile and clear classroom lecturers I have ever known, and I do not see how he can be replaced in his department," Jordan commented. "His discussions in the classroom are scientific and fair and have not to my knowledge been of such a nature as would tend to indoctrinate the students working with him. In his line of social science I consider him the most effective worker in the country. His character has always been unblemished and his reputation without a cloud." But the decision was not Jordan's. When the die was cast, the president was forced to follow institutional imperatives, while Ross looked to his own professional survival.[14]

By 1900 Ross was wise to the ways of the emerging professional culture. He arranged his separation from the university in the manner most advantageous to his future career in academic social science. In order to stifle any claims that his scholarship

13. Jordan to Mrs. Stanford, 21 May 1900, Jordan MSS, copy in Ely MSS. This letter probably provides the best indication of Jordan's actual opinion of Ross, before the conflict embittered the two against each other. Ross to Mrs. Stanford, 19 May 1900, copy in Jordan MSS; Jordan to Mrs. Stanford, 26 May 1900, and Mrs. Stanford to Jordan, 28 May 1900, reprinted in her *Free Speech;* Jordan to Ross, 15 June 1900, Ross MSS.

14. Jordan's comment appeared in an interview in the *San Francisco Chronicle,* 14 November 1900.

was less than able, he timed the public announcement to coincide with the completion of his major scientific work, *Social Control.* At a carefully managed press conference on November 13, 1900, he revealed his forced resignation, presenting himself to the scholarly world as the victim of a benighted woman's prejudices and, by implication, of a president's cowardly failure to defend academic freedom against a new application of the ubiquitous pressure of corporate wealth. After outlining the professional credentials that entitled him to comment publicly on economic issues, Ross defined the grounds on which he would base his defense: "I cannot with self-respect decline to speak on topics to which I have given years of investigation. It is my duty as an economist to impart, on occasion, to sober people, and in a scientific spirit, my conclusions on subjects with which I am expert. . . . The scientist's business is to know some things clear to the bottom, and if he hides what he knows he loses his virtue."[15] Ross defended advocacy as a duty. Anyone who condoned the university's action must deny that the economist had a proper function as a public teacher.

Within a day Ross had lost the support of David Starr Jordan. With some justification, the president believed that he had done everything possible short of resigning himself to keep Ross in the university. Presidents of Jordan's style remained humane and liberal toward erring academics until a professor's actions brought the university into imminent danger of losing the conservative image that was essential to its continued prosperity. In such circumstances, as Laurence Veysey has noted, private friendships and strong moral commitments were sacrificed to the exigencies of the institution which determined the president's image of himself and provided the ultimate measure of his success or failure. When Ross blamed his dismissal on corporation executives who influenced Mrs. Stanford and

15. Ross to Ely, 24 July 1900; Ross to "My Dear Mamma," 9 September 1900, Ross MSS; "Dr. Edward A. Ross Forced out of Stanford University," *San Francisco Chronicle,* 14 November 1900. The extensive press coverage of the Ross affair is preserved in the Elliott and John M. Stillman clipping files in the Stanford University Archives.

praised Jordan publicly for resisting until the founder overruled him, he forced Jordan to choose between an expendable social scientist and an absolutely essential patron. Jordan went to Canossa. In subsequent days, following the precedent set by Harper in the Bemis case, Jordan tried to shift the ground of controversy first by impugning Ross's character privately and then by attacking him publicly.[16]

Jordan's change of heart converted a deadlock between a professor and an eccentric old woman into a confrontation between a prominent academic and a major university. Once more social scientists were forced to assess their convictions on proper professional behavior. A dramatic gesture set the tone. The day after Ross's announcement George Howard, head of the Stanford history department, released a statement condemning an obvious violation of academic freedom and blaming "the sinister spirit of social bigotry and commercial intolerance." The next day, standing "pale and nervous" before his French Revolution class, Howard eloquently compared the university's action to the excesses of European absolute monarchs. He feared that Ross's dismissal would convince his students that their professors dared not speak the truth when it conflicted with accepted dogma. As if to reassure the students by risking everything himself, Howard swore his own allegiance to a "negative creed": "I do not worship St. Market Street. I do not reverence Holy Standard Oil, nor do I doff my cap to the Celestial Six Companies."[17]

16. Jordan had done his utmost to place Ross in institutions where he had friends and influence, but neither President Schurman at Cornell nor Eliot at Harvard would cooperate. See Jordan to J. W. Jenks, 2 June 1900; Jordan to Eliot, 1 October 1900, Jordan MSS. On Jordan's pattern, Veysey, *Emergence of the American University,* pp. 304, 309-10, suggests he was constitutionally more authoritarian and paternalistic than other new-style university presidents. Jordan's extensive correspondence shows his gradual hardening toward Ross as Jordan attempted to defend the school. For example, see Jordan to Charles Lummis, 16 November 1900; Jordan to Albert Shaw, 5 December 1900; Jordan to Frank Fetter, 4 December 1900; and a letter sent to university presidents at Yale, Hopkins, Indiana, and Washington, 19 November 1900, Jordan MSS.

17. "Professors and Public Denounce the Action," *San Francisco Chronicle,* 15 November 1900. Howard was a seasoned professional. Educated at the University of Nebraska, A.B. 1876, A.M. 1879, Ph.D. 1894, he had also studied history and

Howard based his defense of Ross on the social scientist's right of advocacy. "The economist, the sociologist, and to some extent the historian deal with questions that are near the battle-line," he argued. Yet especially in the work of sociologists there was some hope of finding solutions for the growing problems of an urbanizing world. The sociologist, in Howard's view, "must be the savior of his generation,—the scout whom humanity sends out to seek a safe pathway out of her difficulties." Like any scout he might occasionally blunder off the trail, but he was indispensable in the search for true direction. If his young colleague was indiscreet, Howard added, so were Luther, Abelard, James Otis, Patrick Henry, Cromwell, Washington, even Jesus Christ. The test of intellectual endeavor was not discretion but courage in the pursuit of truth.[18]

Howard's dramatic action deepened the crisis at Stanford. To maintain a consistent public posture Jordan was forced to deny that Ross was in any respect a martyr to free speech; yet to control his faculty he added somewhat menacingly that the right of academic freedom was no more vital than the duty of governing boards to release professors in whose integrity they had lost confidence. Mrs. Stanford was beginning to believe that Jordan's authority could only be preserved by teaching rebellious professors how to conduct themselves with proper decorum. But Howard had based his accusations of corporate influence on admissions that Jordan had made to him privately, and he had no intention of abandoning a stand he considered not only just but obligatory in such circumstances. When Howard

jurisprudence in the universities of Munich and Paris, 1876-1878. He taught at Nebraska (1879-1891) and went to Stanford when it opened. He had served as secretary of the Nebraska Historical Society and helped to form the Pacific Coast Historical Society. That his views were liberal, not radical, is plain in George E. Howard, "The American University and the American Man," Stanford Commencement Address, 31 May 1893, George Howard MSS, University of Nebraska Archives.

18. Two versions of Howard's lecture exist. One was pieced together some months later by a student, Mary E. Hyde, and published in the *Baltimore News,* 29 April 1901. Another in the Jordan Letterbook, pp. 119-23, seems to be a verbatim transcript of the lecture taken by someone in attendance. Because the Jordan version seems closer to accounts in various Howard letters, that account has been followed when there are discrepancies. For newspaper accounts of the address see the San Francisco papers of 16 November 1900.

refused to apologize, his resignation was requested. Even more than before, other members of the Stanford faculty were pressured to declare themselves.[19]

Unbelievably, the social scientists rallied. Even before Howard's dismissal Morton A. Aldrich, an assistant professor of economics who had recently been brought to Stanford from Harvard, resigned in defense of Ross's right of advocacy. Howard's thunderbolt induced the resignation of David E. Spencer, an associate professor of history. From the sole remaining historian, a young assistant professor who must have been under incredible pressure to complete the cancellation of that department, came a helpless statement insisting that a self-respecting social scientist could stay in the university if he continued to exercise free speech. Away on leave, Frank Fetter, the new head of economics and sociology who had come from Cornell in 1898, tried to obtain a written, public guarantee of free inquiry and expression for all professors in the future. When Jordan refused, Fetter announced that the university's treatment of Ross and Howard would prevent his resumption of his duties.[20]

The impact of the Ross case on academics was determined by more than simple academic status. As Seligman had anticipated a few years earlier, identification with a particular discipline was critical. While thirty-seven out of the forty-eight senior faculty members at Stanford finally pledged their loyalty to Jordan, every professor in the social sciences who could afford the gesture resigned. The departments of economics and history were virtually expunged. A sociologist named Mary Roberts

19. Hyde and Jordan Letterbook accounts of Howard lecture. "Professor Jordan Issues Another Statement," *San Francisco Chronicle*, 16 November 1900; "Dr. Howard Forced out of Stanford," ibid., 14 January 1901; Jane Stanford to Jordan, 14 December 1900, Stanford MSS; Jordan to Howard, 10, 13 January 1901; Howard to Jordan, 12 January 1901, Jordan MSS. For Howard's later summary of events, see Howard to Seligman, 15 February 1901, Seligman MSS, copy in Ross MSS; Howard to J. Franklin Jameson, 30 November 1900, File 781, Jameson MSS.

20. Jordan to Morton Aldrich, 19 November 1900, Jordan MSS; Ross to "Dear Mamma," 18 December 1900, Ross MSS. Accounts of Spencer's resignation and Duniway's statement appeared in the San Francisco papers of 17 and 18 January 1901; Fetter's on 20 March 1901. All these clippings are preserved in the John M. Stillman Scrapbook, Stillman MSS, Stanford University Archives. See also Fetter to Ross, 24 April 1901, Ross MSS; Fetter to Jordan, 7 June 1900, Jordan MSS.

Smith, the wife of another professor who refused to resign, told friends remorsefully that she would have left "were she a single woman." From the related field of philosophy, Arthur O. Lovejoy was so appalled by the docility of most of his colleagues that he felt compelled to express his disapproval by resigning too. Sociology, the dangerous field that had produced the trouble, was eliminated by Jordan's administrative decision. In all, Stanford's booming social science program was almost totally destroyed by Ross's dismissal.[21]

Of course the reaction of the national community of social scientists was ultimately of far more consequence than the response of Stanford colleagues. Ross fully realized how important professional opinion would be. Certain professional matters that would affect the outcome had come full circle. Ely, the disreputable mentor whom Ross had replaced as AEA secretary in 1892, had returned to the fold and occupied the presidency. Albion Small, in some respects Bemis's worst nemesis in 1895, had committed himself totally to sociology, the new center of Ross's intellectual attention, and the University of Chicago's *American Journal of Sociology* was publishing Ross's *Social Control*. Both Ely and Small responded warmly. "It is simply professional insurance [for sociologists] to stand together as loyally as possible," Small told Ross, as he tried at first to persuade Jordan to protect Ross and then began canvassing the country for other positions.[22]

As the chain reaction of events at Stanford claimed increasing attention, Ross managed professional opinion with consummate skill. Jordan was frantically trying to persuade influential university presidents and conservative social scientists that ac-

21. On Mrs. Smith see Aldrich to Ross, 4 February 1901; C. N. Little to Ross, 23 February 1901, Ross MSS. The San Francisco papers of 2 and 3 May 1901 covered Lovejoy's emphatic statement in defense of academic freedom against whimsical lay interference and administrative abdication. Lovejoy analyzed the principles involved in the case in a letter to O. L. Elliott, 15 April 1901, Elliott MSS.

22. Small to Ross, 17, 28 June, 16 November 1900, Ross MSS; Small to Lester Ward, 22 August 1900, in Bernhard J. Stern, ed., "The Letters of Albion W. Small to Lester Ward, Part 3," *Social Forces* 15 (December 1936):184; Ross to Ely, 10 June 1900; Ely to Small, 21 June 1900; Small to Ely, 5 July 1900, Ely MSS; Bemis to Ross, 19 November 1900, Ross MSS.

ademic freedom was not involved. To make the story stick, he continued to imply that character faults made Ross unacceptable. Ross simply sent copies to leading economists of the famous "Gaelic letter" in which Jordan had admitted that Mrs. Stanford opposed Ross because of his views on economic issues. Carefully chosen supporters were allowed to see copies of Jordan's most fervent testimonial to Ross's scholarly ability and personal integrity. In consultation with Ross, George Howard enlisted the support of J. Franklin Jameson to spread the word among historians of Jordan's damaging admission that Nob Hill industrialists had influenced Mrs. Stanford to overrule him.[23]

Throughout the proceedings Ross showed that he was determined to avoid the mistakes made by earlier advocates, especially Bemis. After his well-timed resignation, Ross planned future actions to avoid providing any excuse for charges that he was either a popularizer or a radical. "I am going to continue working in pure sociology and shall refuse to be drawn into any practical work or discussion of burning issues," he wrote. "Macmillans will publish my work on Social Control this spring and I have in contemplation two or three other books on sociology. I am going to fight it out on strictly scientific lines; since I am in no wise a 'reformer.' "[24] Ross would have preferred actual privation to accepting work as a government functionary or free-lance expert without a university base. No amount of publicity would help if his scholarship was doubted.

Individual responses from economists representing varied ideological positions indicated that Ross had wide potential support. "The Dowager of Palo Alto has captured the booby prize, with no competition in sight," scoffed Small. Taussig was ashamed to be an economist in a country where such things were possible; he urged Ross to put leading economists in a

23. Jordan's letters to Presidents Hadley of Yale, Gilman of Hopkins, Swain of Indiana, and Eliot of Harvard, as well as to Albert Bushnell Hart, Charles Haskins, Small, and others are in the Jordan Letterbook, 19 November 1900 to 6 February 1901, Jordan MSS. Of the lengthy Howard-Jameson correspondence, the most typical are Howard to Jameson, 30 November 1900, 31 January, 6, 27 February 1901, Jameson MSS.
24. Ross to Seligman, 1 December 1900, Seligman MSS.

position to defend him by sending them all the facts. E. Dana
Durand, a young Stanford economist on leave for work with the
United States Industrial Commission, reported that Jenks and
Willcox of Cornell, Commons, and Carroll D. Wright agreed that
Ross had been wronged. Durand expected a general rallying of
support among economists to find Ross "a high place as a
vindication of the right of free speech" and he hoped "the
American Economic Association might see its way to pass some
resolutions on the subject." As newly appointed chancellor of
the University of Nebraska, Andrews began making arrangements to hire Ross for sociology. The old Populist savior of
fired radicals, Thomas Elmer Will, started preparing a place at
Ruskin Hall. Seligman, powerful proponent of the economist's
right of advocacy in the Andrews case and perhaps the most
influential economist in the country, called Ross's removal an
outrage from which Stanford would not recover "during the
lifetime of its present dictatress" and offered to publish anything Ross cared to send in Columbia's *Political Science
Quarterly*.[25]

The only truly effective defense of advocacy depended on
establishing the principle that specialists in a discipline were the
only ones qualified to judge each other's work and ability. Ross
logically turned for assistance to those professional colleagues
who had succeeded in defending a similar cause. Shortly after
Christmas he made a dramatic appearance at the annual meeting
of the AEA in Detroit, where he immediately showed all relevant documents to Seligman. The next day Seligman called an
informal meeting of the economists present and quoted enough
from Jordan's letters, while Ross sat silently by, to demonstrate
a strong presumption that a social scientist was being persecuted
for his views. Though some had hesitated to consider action the
day before, Seligman's avowed faith in Ross's "completely
scientific" attitude was extremely influential. "Without a dis-

25. Taussig to Ross, 20 November 1900; Durand to Ross, 21 November 1900;
Seligman to Ross, 25 November 1900; Andrews to Ross, 13 September 1900; Will to
Ross, 28 December 1900, Ross MSS.

sentient voice," a committee was authorized to "look into the matter," presumably with the intention of giving both Ross and the Stanford authorities a chance to present their versions of the case so that both the profession and the public could make a fair judgment.[26]

Ostensibly the committee represented no one but the economists present at the informal meeting in Detroit. According to Metzger, the economists made a serious mistake in failing to make the investigation an official association venture. Actually they were probably wise in following a model that had proved effective in the Andrews case without introducing a potentially divisive procedural issue. Apparently Seligman and a few others considered the alternatives and rejected official action at least partly because Ely was the president of the AEA. "Any official action would have had to go out with Ely at the head of the list, &—much as I respect Ely—I recognize that his name would not carry so much weight with the 'solid business men' as some others," Ashley told Seligman. "You are just the man to take the lead—for you are persona grata to conservatives and radicals." Seligman admitted that he had proposed the unofficial action "for the very same reason that you suggest." From Ross's standpoint the committee could hardly have been more desirable, for it united the experience and prestige that Seligman and Gardner had gained in the Andrews defense with the symbolic importance of a man from the most conservative segment of the profession, Henry Farnam of Yale.[27]

Whether the economists actually intended to conduct an impartial investigation can never be ascertained, for President Jordan refused to cooperate with an inquiry that he obviously

26. Accounts of the meeting are in Ely to Sidney Sherwood, 8 January 1901, Ely MSS; Seligman to Ross, 27 February 1901; Seligman to Taussig, 13 January 1901; Ely to Seligman, 7 June 1901, Seligman MSS.

27. Metzger, *Academic Freedom*, p. 169; Ashley to Seligman, 18 January 1901; Seligman to Ashley, 21 January 1901, Seligman MSS. Metzger attributed the mistake to "either their lack of long-run objectives, or to their inexperience in those matters." In light of the Andrews case, it seems unlikely that the economists who became involved in the Ross case suffered from either disability. Lists of signatures on Detroit Hotel Cadillac stationery in the Ross folders in the Seligman MSS probably indicate who attended the informal meeting.

considered both impertinent and embarrassing. Suffering from a nervous condition, he delegated the task of dealing with the economists to a faculty committee. The economists persisted in pressing Jordan to account for the vast difference in his attitude toward Ross before and after the announcement of his forced resignation. If Ross's views on silver, coolie immigration, and municipal socialism had not caused his dismissal, the economists queried, then what were the actual grounds? Jordan only continued to insist that Ross had simply not proved to be the proper man for the place.[28]

Lacking any cooperation from Stanford, the committee faced a difficult tactical situation. Above all, a report that sought to vindicate advocacy based on scientific competence must appear objective. Seligman had two purposes in view: to do what was necessary to prove that Ross had indeed been dismissed for his views and at the same time, recognizing the nearly insoluble problems that Jordan had faced and the danger that Mrs. Stanford might cut off her support for the university entirely, to make the charges against Stanford no more severe than was necessary to the defense of Ross, the colleagues who had resigned to support him, and the principle of responsible advocacy for social scientists. For a while the committee considered a full disclosure of all the documents in the newspapers. Gardner inclined to favor such publicity in order to protect the committee, but Farnam counseled restraint. In the end Seligman established the professional procedure—a spare, terse report addressed directly to the profession which summarized events at Stanford, described the committee's activities, and presented textual evidence that Ross had been fired for his opinions. As insurance, the committee indicated its willingness to publish all the documents if the reported facts were challenged. Then, following the Andrews precedent precisely, Selig-

28. All official correspondence between the committee and the university was published in *Report of the Committee of Economists on the Dismissal of Professor Ross from Leland Stanford Junior University* (n.p., 1901). There are copies of this pamphlet in the archives at Stanford, Nebraska, Columbia, and the Wisconsin Historical Society. The report was published in "The Case of Professor Ross," *Science*, n.s. 13 (8 March 1901):362-70.

man sent the report to fifteen carefully selected social scientists, mostly prominent economists, for permission to publish their signatures in support of the report.[29]

Among leading professional social scientists, support for the economists' report on the Ross case was almost universal. The fifteen signers included the most prominent professors in the most important institutions: Clark, Giddings, and Mayo-Smith at Columbia; Taussig and Ashley at Harvard; John C. Schwab and Henry C. Emery (but not Hadley or Sumner) at Yale; Patten and Henry Seager at Pennsylvania; Ely at Wisconsin; Adams at Michigan; Davis R. Dewey at MIT; Sidney Sherwood at Hopkins; and Charles Henry Hull at Cornell. The only non-academic signer was Horace White of the *New York Evening Post*. Reactions indicated that Seligman's influence was of critical importance to those who were asked to sign, especially in convincing them that it was necessary to print excerpts from Jordan's confidential letters. Seligman had simply come to occupy such a respected position in the adjudication of such matters that those who wondered were willing to take his word that such a course was necessary.[30]

The strongest objections to the report came from social scientists who knew Ross more intimately than others, especially his former colleagues at Cornell. Jeremiah W. Jenks, the head of the Cornell department, flatly refused to sign the economists' report. Jenks's reaction was especially significant for two reasons. As an administrator, he had worked in a capacity with Ross which was similar to the supervisory relationship occupied by Jordan. Furthermore, Jenks himself had recently begun to play a very active role in civic affairs, but in a much less public and flamboyant manner than Ross. In 1898-1899, when Ralph

29. Farnam to Seligman, 16, 25 January 1901; Seligman to Farnam, 16, 20 January 1901; Seligman to Farnam and Gardner, 23 January 1901, Seligman MSS; *Report on the Dismissal of Professor Ross.*

30. Dewey to Seligman, 19 February 1901; Taussig to Seligman, 19 February 1901, Seligman MSS. Letters from most of the other signers are also in the Seligman MSS at about the same date. See also Seligman to Ross, 24 February 1901, Seligman MSS. The most detailed refutation of the economists' report is a statement prepared by a member of the Stanford faculty committee and enclosed in G. A. Clark to Hon. Whitelaw Reid, 30 March 1901, Jordan MSS.

248 ADVOCACY & OBJECTIVITY

Easley began building the National Civic Federation (NCF) as a structure for discussions between major industrialists and labor leaders and an agency for the promotion of conservative reform, Jenks became and for many years remained his primary academic adviser. Jenks was also more active than any other academic economist in conducting hearings and preparing reports for the United States Industrial Commission. Chartered by Congress in 1898, the Industrial Commission was midway in its massive investigation of industrial combinations, transportation, manufacturing, agriculture, marketing, labor organization, and strikes when the Ross case broke, and Jenks was frequently engaged in interrogating industrialists who had ample reason to object to some of Ross's activities. As an expert serving a government agency, Jenks undoubtedly wished to maintain an objective appearance. Whether his own activities prejudiced his reaction to Ross's situation or not, Jenks explained his rejection of Seligman's strategy in professional terms, complaining that the report might be taken for an official AEA venture. He also indicated that his intimate acquaintance with both Jordan and Ross gave him reason to doubt that Jordan was being fairly treated.[31]

Charles Henry Hull, another of Ross's former Cornell colleagues, was equally dubious about the case. Though Jenks must have influenced Hull, he claimed that his negative estimate of Ross stemmed largely from association. Hull considered Ross a man of a "good deal of ability and absolutely no judgment" whose kindness of heart and keenness of mind often failed to restrain him from rudely offensive and unscholarly behavior.

31. On Jenks's role, see Marguerite Green, *The National Civic Federation and the American Labor Movement, 1900-1925* (Washington, D.C., 1956), pp. 8, 26, 29-31, 446-58; James Weinstein, *The Corporate Idea in the Liberal State, 1900-1918* (Boston, 1968), pp. 73, 77; United States Industrial Commission, *Reports*, 19 vols. (Washington, D.C., 1900-1902), especially Jenks's report on the effect of industrial combination on prices, *Preliminary Report on Trusts and Industrial Combinations*, 1:39-57; report on statutes and decisions of federal, state, and territorial law, *Trusts and Corporation Laws*, 2:3-264; report on prices of industrial securities, *Trusts and Industrial Combinations*, 13:913-45; Jenks to Seligman, 19 February 1901; Seligman to Patten, 25 February 1901, Seligman MSS. Jenks's general skepticism about the academic freedom cases is confirmed in Jenks, *Great Fortunes: The Winning, The Using* (New York, 1906), pp. 68-69.

Other economists tried to assuage Hull's doubts. After working with Ross at three different schools, Fetter thought his rambunctious colleague had matured. "I believe that Mr. Ross is just now ripening for his best work, that his scholarship is broader than it was five years ago, that his critical sense is keener, that he has grown steadily in dignity of manner and wisdom of expression," Fetter commented. "I found that I had been much deceived as to the radicalism of his social views by statements of those who either knew him years ago, or judged by superficial evidence." Ely also testified to Ross's increasing conservatism, but Hull was adamant. "I can easily believe that it might have been both desirable and proper to dismiss him from his position in Stanford University," he concluded, objecting, finally, only to the unusual manner in which the deed was done.[32]

Hull's opinion can hardly be ignored, for it was a complete reversal of the attitude he had displayed in other cases. As a student at Cornell in the 1880s he had supported Henry Carter Adams vehemently when the Cornell trustees evicted him. To defend Andrews, also a former Cornell colleague, Hull had been willing to destroy the AEA if necessary. In Ross's case Hull finally signed the economists' report as an individual but refused to approve it in his official capacity as acting secretary of the AEA. He remained in touch with friends at Stanford throughout the proceedings and made it clear that he sympathized more with Jordan than with Ross. More than a year later, he was still denying that the AEA had taken any official action.[33]

32. Hull to Seligman, 19, 22 February 1901; Seligman to Hull, 20 February 1901, Charles Henry Hull MSS, Cornell University; Hull to Ely, 5, 13 March 1901, Ely MSS, copies in Hull and Elliott MSS; Ely to Hull, 9 March 1901, Ely MSS; Hull to O. L. Elliott, 13 March 1901, Elliott to Hull, 6 March 1901, Hull and Elliott MSS; Fetter to Hull, 9 February 1901, Hull MSS; Henry Seager to Seligman, 19 February 1901; Sidney Sherwood to Seligman, 19 February 1901, Seligman MSS. The Cornell historian George Lincoln Burr believed that most Cornell professors doubted Ross's innocence. See Burr to Elliott, 9 April 1901, Elliott MSS.

33. Hull to Seligman, 14 April 1902, Seligman MSS. The Cornell department was in some turmoil from 1899 to 1901, due partly to Jenks's heavy commitment to the United States Industrial Commission and partly to the two-year absence of Walter F. Willcox for statistical work with the Census Bureau. Willcox and Hull were close

At one level, Hull's dilemma was simply the product of human relations. He liked and respected Adams and Andrews, while he found Ross's occasional cocksure bravado too offensive to overlook. From another perspective, Hull faced a professional crisis that would become typical in such situations as emerging professions developed more regular patterns of authority. In retrospect, it appears that Hull was pulled in one direction by his relationship with his own chairman, Jenks, who was at odds with Ross both ideologically and politically. Yet Hull's chance position as an AEA officer when the elite in economics wanted to defend Ross created counterpressure on Hull to act in the opposite direction. Hull's solution was apparently a compromise. He performed his minimal duty to the organized profession by signing the petition as an individual, but he made no secret of his negative feelings about Ross. More self-conscious professionals—or individuals with less to lose—were ready to sacrifice their personal doubts for the policy that best served the profession.

Some, such as Seligman, realized that providing for Ross's future was as important as upholding the ideal of academic freedom. There was no point in defending a scholar's right to reasonable advocacy if the victim was still to be driven out of academic life. Even a reduction in circumstances was unacceptable if the faith of prominent social scientists was to be demonstrated. Seligman turned to Harvard, where there was a vacancy in sociology in 1901, for help in placing Ross, and he also insisted that clearing Ross was futile if new positions were not found for all the other historians and economists who had left Stanford in the name of academic freedom. In effect he was

---

friends, and Hull assumed much of Willcox's AEA responsibility. Hull's letters to Willcox show that Hull neither trusted nor fully respected Jenks; pressure on Hull increased when President Schurman and Jenks initiated a reallocation of teaching fields and titles. Then Fetter, Jenks's former student, was hired. Shortly thereafter, Hull's insecurity as an assistant professor, together with an earlier interest in history and family obligations that required him to remain in Ithaca, prompted him to transfer to the Cornell department of history, where advancement seemed more certain. See the many letters between Hull and Willcox in the Walter F. Willcox MSS, LC.

trying to establish the principle that professional responsibility for the protection of advocacy extended to include a guarantee of employment.[34]

Strong sympathy for that view developed among the social science faculty at Harvard. Taussig and Ashley were acutely embarrassed to discover that President Jordan had been able to fill both of his history vacancies less than a week after George Howard and David Spencer resigned by the simple expedient of hiring two young Ph.D.'s from Harvard who accepted Jordan's offer with the encouragement of some of Harvard's historians, including Albert Bushnell Hart. Taussig and Ashley were obviously horrified, for they promised to support Aldrich, their own student, when he resigned in protest against the treatment of Ross and Howard.[35]

Harvard's embarrassment exposed a fundamental strain in the new social science professions. Uniform training and experiences fostered common role definitions and cooperative approaches to opposing interests. Yet loyalty to different universities and competition for available positions in choice locations promoted disunity. Ashley instantly perceived that the quick filling of Stanford's vacancies would disastrously weaken the economists' effort to establish a broader sphere of competence and greater immunity from pressure. Though Ashley thought less of Ross's scholarship than Seligman did, he considered Ross's opinions on money and immigration "well within the limits of sanity (and that is the only limit I should draw)." Consequently Ross's dismissal was "a blow at the position of all professional economists" and "an apparent justification of what our socialist friends say of us." Collective action could repair the damage. "The only way in which governing boards or

34. Seligman to Taussig, 13 January 1901; Seligman to Ashley, 21 January 1901; Taussig to Seligman, 14 January 1901, Seligman MSS.

35. Jordan wrote to Hart several times in December 1900 and early 1901. In February he thanked Hart for "helping us in our educational crisis" and reported that Mssrs. Lapsley and Warren had been well received by the students. Jordan to Hart, 6 February 1901, Jordan MSS. Hart's action was consistent with his opposition to Ely in 1894 until Ely was cleared by the Wisconsin Regents, when Hart quickly apologized.

universities and the 'constituencies' that support them can be made to take a more fitting view of the functions of a professor," Ashley concluded, "is by encountering unwillingness on the part of young men to accept office when such scandals have occurred."[36]

The numerous dismissals and resignations at Stanford generated a crisis in professional discipline. Ashley viewed this "second phase" of the Ross case as a problem of the generations. In his indignation and mortification, he condemned the younger scholars. "It looks as if our young Ph.D.'s were, like the graduates of technological schools, ready to take a 'job' anywhere," he mused. If Ross's merits had been debatable, the resignation of three department heads and other professors should have brought home "to all men of sensitive honour the need for very careful scrutiny before entering upon the vacant places." Lacking a natural inclination in younger men from great universities to exercise restraint, Ashley believed, "it is the duty of the older men to influence them in that direction."[37]

The Harvard economists were not the only ones to feel responsibility for Ross's employment. Chancellor Andrews of the University of Nebraska acted so swiftly in behalf of a fellow sufferer that by January 7, 1901, Ross was under contract for sociology lectures in Lincoln during the second semester. Ely immediately began investigating the possibilities of bringing Ross to Wisconsin, but the administration there had taken a conservative turn. When the testimonials forwarded by Seligman, Fetter, and Taussig failed to persuade the regents, Ely was finally forced to inform Ross that he could expect nothing at the moment from Wisconsin. Actually Ely had pursued the position none too aggressively. Harking back to his own similar experience, he counseled patience and forbearance in living down the inevitable residue of doubt that lingered after vindication.[38]

36. Ashley to Seligman, 18 January 1901, Seligman MSS.
37. Ashley to Seligman, 22, 18 January 1901, Seligman MSS.
38. Ely to Seligman, 16 January 1901; Ely to Ross, 24 January, 19 March 1901, Ross MSS; Ross to Ely, 30 January 1901; Seligman to Ely, 6 February 1901; Fetter

The prominent professional economists began to develop techniques for redeeming a colleague's reputation. To neutralize the action of their own defecting historians and to demonstrate their faith in Ross's scholarship, the Harvard social scientists invited him to deliver a series of lectures on the development of sociology in the spring of 1902. They listed Ross as the Harvard University Lecturer in Sociology and published his lectures in the *Quarterly Journal of Economics*. Five years later, after *Social Control* and subsequent publications had rehabilitated his reputation, Ross was appointed to a chair of sociology at Wisconsin which he held for thirty years. His five-year detention at the University of Nebraska, a less prestigious institution than Stanford, had proved the truth of Ely's fear that it would be "extremely difficult for Ross to get back into any desirable academic position."[39]

With one exception, the other Stanford casualties fared no better than Ross. Fetter was quickly reappointed at Cornell, but George Howard, Ross's most outspoken defender, suffered deepening anguish in a fruitless quest for appointment. Finally he was called back to his alma mater, Nebraska. To some academics, Howard's transgression seemed more serious than anything Ross had done, for it included what many viewed as an uncontrolled outburst before a captive audience of students. The economists' defense of Ross had deliberately been kept spare, and it failed to show sufficient provocation for Howard's action. Though Seligman and Gardner were deeply sympathetic and J. Franklin Jameson remained interested, historians did nothing to approximate the efforts of the economists in defending and providing for Ross.[40] Taussig immediately offered

to Ely, 8 February 1901; Ely to Ross, 27 February, 9, 19 March 1901, Ely MSS. Both the Ely and Ross collections contain abundant correspondence pertaining to the job hunt. Small tried unsuccessfully to bring Ross to Chicago for at least a summer, but Harper refused to consider it. Small to Ross, 19 April 1901; George Kriehn to Ross, 9 May 1901, Ross MSS.

39. Taussig to Ross, 30 March 1901, Ross MSS; Ely to Fetter, 25 March 1901, Ely MSS. For Ross's account of the Stanford affair and its influence on his career, see Ross, *Seventy Years*, pp. 64-100.

40. Seligman urged Gardner to convince Jameson that "the historians in the country ought to do something to see that Howard secures a good position";

Morton Aldrich temporary employment at Harvard, but Aldrich was able to obtain a professorship at Tulane University, where he remained for the rest of his career outside the mainstream of economics, developing interests in university extension and business administration which appealed to the New Orleans mercantile community.[41]

A few leading professional economists flirted briefly with the intriguing notion of boycotting Stanford. Ashley and Ely both tried to prevent their students from accepting offers there. For a time Jordan thought that Paul Samuel Reinsch, a Wisconsin product, would come to Stanford and show "that competent young men are not badly scared by the noise," but Reinsch withdrew, either too principled or simply cautious. Ely's advice to Balthasar Henry Meyer, the next economist Stanford approached, captured in microcosm several of the contradictory pressures that the Ross case unleashed. "There is a great deal of feeling in the country," Ely explained, "and I should greatly fear for your future if you should seem to fly in the face of what many regard as righteous indignation. You cannot afford to put yourself out of touch with men in Yale, Harvard, etc., and lose their sympathy and esteem. The intellectual center of the country is still in the East, and that must not be overlooked." Meyer received identical advice from Seligman. Despite the great temptation of a position in which a young man would have had unusual opportunity and responsibility immediately, Meyer decided to reject the Stanford offer. The pressure was effective. By June Ashley was able to report that the young Harvard historians who had so rashly decided to go

Seligman to Gardner, 17 March 1901, Seligman MSS. Howard's extensive correspondence with Jameson in the Jameson MSS portrays the growing disappointment of a proud and courageous, if occasionally unrealistic and embittered, unemployed historian. Howard eventually switched to sociology.

41. Aldrich's search for a job is outlined in Aldrich to Ross, 14 January, 30 May 1901, Ross MSS. His gradual diversion from the intellectual development in theoretical economics which he seemed to have started at Stanford is obvious in "Tulane Topics: The Department of Economics," *New Orleans Picayune,* 20 December 1902, in "Tulane Scraps," 6 (1902-1913):136-37; "Tulane to Have a College of Commerce," *Picayune,* 7 January 1902, in "Tulane Scraps," 5 (1900-1902):166-67, Tulane University Archives.

to Stanford at midyear had declined to accept reappointments.[42]

Fortunately for Stanford, the academic economists were neither disciplined nor doctrinaire enough to continue a boycott long. Social scientists at Cornell and Michigan were the first to condemn the action. In April 1902 Ely reported rumors emanating from Stanford that two signers of the Ross report had subsequently applied for positions at Stanford. Ely was furious, but others were ready to relent. Henry Carter Adams rejected Ely's assumption that accepting a position at Stanford would weaken the economists' defense of Ross. "I did not sign that report in the Ross case because I wished to boycott Stanford University, or to try to teach President Jordan a lesson," Adams insisted. "I did so simply and solely as a means of stating to the working people of the United States that the economists of the country had not been bought." Adams saw absolutely no reason why any professor, even an economist who signed the report, could not teach with dignity at Stanford so long as it was clear that liberty of discussion would be honored.[43]

At Cornell both Hull and Fetter were equally antagonistic toward a boycott. Hull insisted that he had signed the report to protest an absurd situation in which one donor had absolute power in the institution. Time would terminate that arrangement. For the recovery and future influence of the university, Hull had fond hopes; he would recommend his own students and answer inquiries about positions there exactly as if they pertained to any other place. Jenks was already performing that service for Jordan; after a time Hull took over the role of the main social science adviser to Stanford.[44] When consensus

42. Jordan to S. F. Leib, 5 March 1901, Jordan MSS; Ely to B. H. Meyer, 1 April 1901; Meyer to Ely, 14 April 1901, Ely MSS; Ashley to Seligman, 2 June 1901, Seligman MSS.
43. Ely to Seligman, 1 April 1902, Seligman MSS; Adams to Seligman, 14 April 1902, copy in Hull MSS.
44. Hull to Adams, 16, 18, 24 April 1902; Hull to Seligman, 16 April 1902; Hull to Jordan, 13, 27 April 1905, 4 January 1906; Jordan to Hull, 19 April, 9 December 1905, Hull MSS; Jordan to Jenks, 2 April 1901, Jordan MSS. Jordan several times

among the leading economists of major universities failed to develop, the movement to punish Stanford collapsed. Eventually the social science vacancies at Stanford were filled by able products of the better schools.

Even though the attempt to boycott Stanford's social science departments failed, the economists won the Ross case. Ross was without an academic position for only two months, while the Stanford authorities suffered such humiliation that they, along with academic administrators all over the country, learned to deal far more circumspectly with economists.[45] Actually, however, the effort to establish at least a limited right of advocacy for professional economists had needed only a final consummation. Earlier cases had tested the limits of advocacy that an economist could risk and still muster professional support. After watching while several encounters between economists and opposing interests proved ruinous for the economists, leading professionals such as Seligman and Taussig had decided to act in defense of the profession. They had chosen the Andrews case because it was an easy one to defend, and it had provided an excellent laboratory for experimentation with strategies of united action that proved effective in the next emergency.

To a degree, the Ross case was a freak. Given the fact that Stanford was the only institution of higher learning in the United States where a sole trustee had the authority to fire professors at will, the economists might have ignored the Ross case. Such a course could have been disastrous for Ross, for the charges against his character needed answering. But the motives that led Seligman and other established economists to make Ross's cause theirs went far beyond his individual welfare. His case contained so many elements which were important to the

---

tried to get Hull to move to Stanford. Walter F. Willcox turned down a firm offer in economics at Stanford, but he assured Jordan that he did not "share in the judgment of many Eastern teachers of political economy regarding Professor Ross's departure from Stanford." In fact, after working with Ross at Cornell, Willcox was "surprised that [Ross] remained so long at Stanford University." See Willcox to Jordan, 27 April 1901; Jordan to Willcox, 2 May 1901, Willcox MSS.

45. Jordan's realization that his reputation had suffered far more than Ross's is apparent in Jordan to Andrew Dickson White, 25 July 1901, Jordan MSS.

economist's professional mission that it could not be over-looked. In defending Ross, the professional leaders were demon-strating that no character faults could be magnified enough by a desperate university president to divert his colleagues from the substantive issues. Ross's opinions had clearly started the trouble; yet those opinions were based on scholarship, entirely compatible with objective inquiry as it existed at the time, and well within the range of permissible dissent. Neither a mere popularizer nor a radical, Ross occasionally advocated specific policies on questions within his competence, but he never seriously questioned fundamental American values. By assuming his defense, the economic leadership seized another ideal oppor-tunity to strengthen the principle of professional responsibility for attacks on individuals, if the charges questioned prerogatives claimed by the profession.[46]

From Adams to Ross, the academic freedom cases helped to establish the dominance of a small, highly professionalized elite which determined a model for younger, less self-conscious academics to follow. In perilous times it was imperative to be able to count on the support of one's colleagues. Comparing the disastrous fates of Bemis and Powers with the comfortable circumstances that awaited Andrews and Ross was enough to provide an instructive deterrent to rebellious action. Out of all the cases emerged a rudimentary discipline which identified the degree and type of advocacy that was entitled to collective security. Within the limits where agreement could be reached on goals and tactics, the economists had exchanged the capricious discipline provided by powerful external opponents for the more steady influence of national professional control.

The academic freedom cases contributed to the gradual narrowing of the range of dissent that seemed safe for profes-

46. It should be noted here that Seligman's role as "manager" in earlier academic freedom cases provides the context that explains his failure to defend James McKeen Cattell and Charles A. Beard in the Columbia University crisis of 1917-1918. For an able account of the compliance of prominent faculty members (led by Seligman) with policies that restricted freedom of expression and penalized eccentricity, see Carol Signer Gruber, "Academic Freedom at Columbia University, 1917-18: The Case of James McKeen Cattell," *AAUP Bulletin* 58 (September 1972): 297-305.

sional social scientists. Too much involvement, too much taking of sides where the public remained divided, undermined the scholarly authority of all social scientists and threatened their freedom to continue working. In social science the distinction between basic and applied research is not as clear as in physical science. Even the researcher is not always sure when he leaves the one and begins the other. The academic freedom cases cut two ways. They established more autonomy than professional social scientists had enjoyed before. They also demonstrated the negative results of partisanship. For better or worse, these troubles taught many academics to conserve their image and preserve their institutions, to prepare to defend themselves but avoid the necessity, to exert influence quietly as experts rather than noisily as partisans.

By the end of the 1890s it was clear that economists had established a strong sense of professional identity. Even more important, the profession had developed the will, the influence, and the machinery to defend its own. Along with advances in scholarship and an increasing homogeneity of experiences, a real need for collective security had made it possible—even essential—for unity and discipline to grow. The profession was national, hierarchically organized, and dominated by senior, mostly eastern economists in major universities. Standardized professionalization procedures gave the leading professors a large measure of control over the mobility and advancement of junior scholars. A maturing network of communications through organizations and journals that were accepted both within the profession and outside it as authentic forums for professional economists gave even more authority to the top academics in important schools who selected editors and officers. Managed by a powerful professional elite, the academic freedom cases had isolated unacceptable practices and underscored areas of consensus on doctrine, method, mission, and protocol which economists had reached in the 1890s.

The outcome—captured in the Ross case—was a progressive, liberal profession that supported a positive role for the state while it barely tolerated either radicalism or philosophical conservatism. Ideological differences persisted, but they were no longer couched in terms of the relatively simple dichotomies of the 1880s. The change reflected more than the increased complexity that prolonged analysis of social questions yields. It portrayed an actual narrowing of the range of social views, an actual contraction of the debate among economists on a desirable political economy for industrial America. Professional economists were neither so hard-rock conservative on the one hand nor so radical-reformist on the other as they had been in the 1880s.

By the end of the 1890s professional status and security competed with ideological and methodological considerations as values for economists. Direct appeal to the public on controversial social questions was retained as a theoretical right, but economists were expected to channel most of their reform efforts through government agencies or private organizations where scholars could serve inconspicuously as technical experts, after the political decisions had been made, rather than as reformers with a new vision of society. By 1900 economists spent their time and energy mostly on internal questions, working out principles and processes for managing money, trade, industry, labor, rent, credit, or taxation within the existing framework of American institutions. The quality of their scholarship was higher, but its focus was narrower than a generation earlier. Outspoken critics were clearly rebels. Rarely did academic economists deal publicly with the controversial normative questions that had preoccupied the emerging profession in the 1880s.

11 *Patterns of Authority*

Beneath the growing homogeneity and centrism of economics in the 1890s, ideological and methodological diversity in social science survived. Between 1895 and 1905 conflicting views and ambitions sought a variety of outlets as social scientists experimented in an effort to find safe and effective ways of expressing their differences. One such strategy involved attempting to conceal ideological interest groups behind a geographical facade, as dissidents tried to undermine the powerful American Economic Association by forming regional societies. Ultimately a second, more substantive pattern prevailed which recognized differences in academic interests, political and social theories, and professional goals by creating discrete, formal divisions within social science. By 1905 political science and sociology were established as separate disciplines and controlled by autonomous professional societies. Thus a greater degree of diversity in social science was institutionalized while the outward appearances of academic unity were preserved.

Regional loyalties had habitually challenged the influence of emerging national organizations in the United States, and that pattern continued in the 1890s. As graduate education rooted firmly in Wisconsin, Michigan, and Illinois, men like Ely, Henry Carter Adams, and Albion Small became proud and occasionally chauvinistic Westerners. Yet they could never quite forget their distance from older centers of learning in the East, nor overcome their resentment at always being treated like provincials. To attend professional meetings, western social scientists usually had to travel great distances; when meetings were held in the West, prominent Easterners seldom took the trouble to attend. Despite such irritations Ely, for one, nursed a longing to return to a prestigious eastern school.[1]

To some extent a regional distribution of the members of

economic "schools" actually existed. Traditional hiring policies had encouraged the selection of professors according to their views, and "old-boy" networks operated best within proximate limits. In the mid-1890s students or close associates of Ely held professorships in almost every western institution, while Harvard, Columbia, and Hopkins tended to supply the East. Genuine interest in truly regional problems of teaching and research combined with these latent sectional jealousies to promote several schemes for regional associations of professional social scientists.

For a time the academic freedom cases strengthened feelings of regionalism. Until 1897 all the celebrated cases occurred in the West, while Easterners seemed smugly certain that they were in no danger of catching the infection. Ely was usually the focal point of proposals for a regional defense system. In the mid-1890s both Commons and Thomas Elmer Will urged Ely to organize a group of progressive Westerners in opposition to conservative critics. After the Wisconsin trial, Ely was far too cautious to involve himself with a league of leftists, but Will became a clearinghouse for information on attempts to curb radical inquiry and teaching.[2]

Throughout the 1890s Ely's cautious posture was crucial in the failure of proposals for a rival organization of left economists. Without a leader at least as respectable as Ely, the movement could attract only casualties of academic freedom cases, and before the turning point in 1897 these men were often radicals who were suspect even among liberal professors. In 1900, when the professional elite in economics committed itself wholeheartedly to the defense of Ross, a Westerner, the

1. Ely was even willing to recant his earlier "heresies" in exchange for eastern respectability. Hoping to be called to Harvard to balance Taussig, he confessed, "I have done a great deal of popular work—some features of which I say frankly I now regret as a mistake—but I have at the same time been engaged in the preparation of my serious scientific work, the publication of which I am just beginning." Ely to Professor John H. Wright, 10 October 1900, Ely MSS. See also Kinley to Ely, 24 May, 22 June 1900, Letterbooks Vol. 2, David Kinley MSS, University of Illinois.

2. Commons to Ely, 17 September 1894, Ely MSS; Commons to H. C. Adams, 9 January 1895, Adams MSS; Will to Ely, 15 October 1895; Bemis to Ely, 16 November 1896, Ely MSS.

radical movement for collective defense was totally eclipsed by a comprehensive national policy that at least implied potent guarantees to all deserving scholars. Until well into the twentieth century, only exiles from academic positions remained much interested in separate action to promote free inquiry, and they concentrated on plans for establishing independent colleges for radical teaching and research. The American College of Social Science founded in 1899 by ousted Professors Bemis, Commons, Parsons, and Will was such a venture.[3]

Eventually, however, a regional association with a broader constituency did briefly threaten the national professional societies. While leading economists were attending the annual AEA meeting in New York, a group of Westerners met in Chicago in 1894 to form the Political Science Association (PSA) of the Central States, ostensibly as nothing more than a convenient, nonideological association to deal with local problems ignored by the AEA.[4]

Though the initiative was geographical at first, ideological factors quickly emerged. The central states contained the two symbolic ideological opposites in economics—Laughlin, who had never joined the AEA and continued to keep his students out, and Ely, who had refused to attend any meetings since his expulsion from high office in 1892. Both the conservative Chicago cadre that revolved around Laughlin (including the historian Hermann von Holst) and a reform-oriented group led by Ely's close friend Jesse Macy hoped to capture the new association and use it to orient at least part of academic social science toward a more conservative or, conversely, a more progressive political economy than the moderate liberalism that dominated the AEA.[5]

3. Frank Parsons to Ely, 26 July 1899, enclosing a clipping from the *Topeka State Journal* announcing the American College of Social Science, Ely MSS.

4. J. W. Jenks to Adams, 1, 9 January 1895; George W. Knight to Adams, 8 January 1895, including a copy of the constitution of the Political Science Association of the Central States; Adams to Jenks, 7 January 1895, Adams MSS.

5. Ely refused to attend this meeting. For an account of the persistent separateness of Chicago economists, see A. W. Coats, "The Origins of the 'Chicago School(s)?'"

To expose the intentions of conservatives and reformers alike, moderates who had no desire to compete with the AEA proposed a regulation that meetings of the regional association never be held in conflict with a national meeting. The subsequent debate erupted into a confrontation between two Chicago professors, Laughlin and Bemis, which was so noisy and embarrassing that it succeeded in thwarting ideological ambitions on both sides and permanently diluted Chicago's influence in the meeting. Any possibility that the new association might adopt a platform endorsing a specific ideology was eliminated by the election of officers who represented varied opinions, including some whose first concern was to preserve the dominance of the national professional organizations in economics and history. Jesse Macy, a reform political scientist at Grinnell College, was made president of the PSA, but he was obviously chosen mainly to avoid the troublesome task of singling out someone from a major university. The more important post of secretary went to George Knight of Ohio State, a vice president of the AEA.[6]

The new association recognized diversity by dividing social science into four distinct fields: history, political science, economics, and sociology. A vice president was chosen from each of the four disciplines. The men selected were established and noncontroversial scholars from major universities. The sociologist was Small of Chicago, the historian Charles Haskins of Wisconsin, and the political scientist James A. Woodburn of Indiana University. An even clearer signal that AEA supporters had outmaneuvered dissidents came when Henry Carter Adams, not Ely, was elected PSA vice president for economics. "I was a member of the Committee on Permanent Organization, and of the Committee on Nominations," one of the moderates told

Journal of Political Economy 71 (October 1963): 487-93. See also Coats, "First Two Decades of the American Economic Association," *American Economic Review* 50 (September 1960): 567-70.

6. J. W. Jenks to Adams, 8 January 1895, Adams MSS; David Kinley to Small, 10 February 1902, Kinley MSS.

Adams, "and can assure you most positively that the new organization will in no way interfere with the others."[7]

As AEA leaders watched developments in the new western association with nervous interest, Adams seized the opportunity to consolidate his influence in the national association. He would do his best to keep the PSA from encroaching, he assured AEA President John Bates Clark and Secretary Jeremiah Jenks, if the national association would hold western meetings that Easterners would actually attend. Predictably, the AEA scheduled a joint meeting with the PSA in Indianapolis the following year.[8]

PSA president Jesse Macy rightly feared that progressive economists were again about to be "swallowed." In a final effort to revive the thrust toward ethical reform, which the early AEA had supported, Macy begged Ely to lead his supporters into the new society. But Ely was no more willing to identify himself with an ideological movement in 1895 than with an academic freedom crusade. Any real possibility of using the PSA as a focal point for left economists perished a year later when Adams became the first Westerner to be elected president of the AEA.[9]

The AEA victory reflected more than mere geographical compromise. For the time being, there would be no recognized professional association of social scientists who were openly committed to a political economy consciously left or right of the moderate liberalism espoused by the prominent economists

7. Jenks to Adams, 8 January 1895; Frederick C. Hicks to Adams, 13 January 1895, Adams MSS.

8. Adams to Clark, 7, 14 January 1895; Clark to Adams, 4, 10 January 1895; Adams to Jenks, 7 January 1895; Jenks to Adams, 8 January 1895, Adams MSS. For Adams's attempts to assess and influence the character of the PSA, see Commons to Adams, 9 January 1895; James Woodburn to Adams, 19 January 1895; Adams to Frederick C. Hicks, 16 January 1895; Adams to Albion Small, 18 January 1895; George Knight to Adams, 19 February, 12 October 1895; Macy to Adams, 29 February 1895, Adams MSS. Adams had raised some alarm earlier by starting a Michigan Political Science Association, but its purpose was largely to raise money for his department. The entire Adams Letterbook 1895-1900, Adams MSS, contains MPSA correspondence. See also *Publications of the Michigan Political Science Association* 1-4 (1893-1905) for their local emphasis.

9. Macy to Ely, 19 April 1895, Ely MSS.

who controlled the AEA. With regional outlets for ideological differences closed, many disgruntled economists simply stayed in the AEA and complained of the lack of honest debate under what David Kinley derisively termed its new, "caste-ridden" management. Periodically Ely's supporters pressed their mentor to return to the association, assuring him—"if you count out Hadley and his satellites and Walker and his"—that he would be cordially received and that his presence would make the association more truly representative of the diversity in American economics.[10] In 1900, when Ely rejoined the AEA and was rewarded with the presidency, the nostalgic pressure for a western economic association of Elyites eased. By that time the radicalism had gone out of Ely's economics. His presence in the AEA was not evidence of greater diversity, but of even greater homogeneity.

As the AEA grew more neutral politically, practical social scientists learned to participate in reform movements cautiously, without endangering their jobs or weakening their professional credentials. A difficult feat in the years between Haymarket and Pullman, it became easier as public acceptance of social scientists increased and the nature and goals of reform changed. In the late 1890s large numbers of business and professional people became involved in various kinds of civic betterment movements. Concentrated first at the urban and community level but spreading rapidly to include problems that could only be handled by state or federal action, this progressive impulse gradually obliterated the harshest memories of nineteenth-century radicalism and rendered reformism respectable. Unlike earlier movements that called upon masses of Americans to resist modernization, many of these new reform programs were oriented toward developing agencies and techniques for continuous and efficient regulation of the complex processes involved in urban, industrial life.

10. W. W. Folwell to Ely, 12 January 1895; David Kinley to Ely, 28 November 1896, 1 August 1897; H. H. Powers to Ely, 31 December 1899, Ely MSS; Kinley to Walter F. Willcox, 26 December 1899, Kinley MSS.

Progressivism was a complex, broad-gauged, and inclusive movement. Businessmen became progressives to involve the government in regulating competitive practices and economic cycles they could not control themselves. Politicians became progressives to forge new political alliances. Members of new professions such as social work, public health, and city planning became progressives to advance their causes and enhance their status. Ordinary citizens followed to secure needed services. Humanitarians became progressives as they had always urged reform to aid the downtrodden. Whatever motivated the individuals involved, progressivism was preeminently a movement of specialists. With all their expert knowledge and the prestige conferred by their advanced degrees, academic social scientists had no difficulty gaining influence.[11]

In the late 1890s and the early twentieth century, as the functions of government enlarged, the attention of social scientists turned increasingly to the practical problems of planning, financing, and delivering city, state, and national services. Their orientation was increasingly bureaucratic, and their impact was felt through regulatory agencies or from behind the scenes in organized pressure groups. Beyond their purely academic functions as creators of new knowledge, their services fell increasingly into the areas of fact gathering and administration.

Even as the progressive temper and its political corollary, the administrative state, helped social scientists to define their role more precisely, subtle differences between the mainstream liber-

11. The outlines of debate on the nature of progressivism are familiar. Progressives were identified as urban, middle class, business and professional people by George Mowry, *The California Progressives* (Berkeley, Calif., 1951). Richard Hofstadter, *The Age of Reform: From Bryan to F.D.R.* (New York, 1955), emphasized the difference in reform type between Populists and progressives and ascribed the motivation of middle-class progressives to a status revolution. Robert Wiebe, *The Search for Order, 1877-1920* (New York, 1967), explained the role of a new middle class of managerial and professional people who identified strongly with their occupations and endeavored to develop flexible mechanisms for the efficient management of a complex urban society in which their specialties were important. Gabriel Kolko, *The Triumph of Conservatism: A Reinterpretation of American History, 1900-1916* (Glencoe, Ill., 1963), showed how big business used regulatory measures that have been considered "progressive" to consolidate political capitalism. For a good brief resumé, see David M. Kennedy, ed., *Progressivism: The Critical Issues* (Boston, 1971).

als and the old radicals persisted. A process of careful observation and experimentation showed which groups were safe and which were not, or, conversely, which agencies would make it possible for a social scientist to accomplish some concrete, if limited goal, and which would leave him flailing ineffectually against basic economic and social conditions which were by that time essentially fixed.

The events that led to the rise and decline of the Social Reform Union were a good example of this selection process. In 1896 a seed group of left social scientists that included Commons, Bemis, David Kinley, and Frank Parsons met quietly at Lake George with several Social Gospel ministers to discuss effective ways of organizing for "moral, social, and economic reforms." A year later their invitation list was expanded to include more prominent and moderate social scientists such as Adams, Seligman, Ely, Jenks, Ross, and Andrews, along with such well-known social reformers as Jane Addams, Clarence Darrow, Henry George, Edward Bellamy, Carroll D. Wright, Washington Gladden, and Eugene Debs. With Bemis and Commons in the lead, Adams, Seligman, Ely, and Andrews agreed to appear publicly as sponsors of a National Social and Political Conference to be held in Buffalo in 1899.

Ostensibly the conference was designed to promote public discussion of important issues, but the leaders hoped that a successful convention with widespread public support might pressure both major parties to incorporate significant reforms in their platforms for the election of 1900. The Buffalo program read like a catalog of progressive reforms: direct legislation and taxation, proportional representation, anti-imperialism, and public ownership of natural monopolies. Even so, the radical tone of a few sessions frightened most of the more moderate professors. When the Social Reform Union was established to lobby for the Buffalo platform, only Bemis and Frank Parsons remained with the movement. By that time Kinley, a weathervane for the liberal economists, was scoffing at the Buffalo group as "dilettantes and superficial reformers," while Ely once more refused to allow an organization with a radical tinge to use his name. After one last conference the Social Reform Union died, while liberal economists turned to less conspicuous allies and less politically oriented activities.[12]

Economists in the liberal elite were more comfortable in socially conservative organizations like the National Civic Federation. The idea of bringing together the nation's most prominent industrialists and its most powerful trade union leaders particularly appealed to Jeremiah Jenks, the Cornell economist. A lawyer and a close student of the national political economy of Henry Carey as well as a German-trained economist, Jenks was always more interested in practical questions than in theory. Rather like Sumner, Jenks believed that great fortunes were often just rewards for the superior service that talented capitalists performed in organizing resources and labor so that society might benefit. Not surprisingly, Jenks's major economic interest was the "trust problem," especially during the great wave of industrial consolidations from 1897 to 1904. As a consultant for the Chicago Civic Federation, he helped organize the Chicago Trust Conference of 1899 and believed, according to Ralph Easley, that it "had resulted in mollifying the radical sentiment prevailing at that time." With the National Civic Federation, Jenks continued to support efforts to wean public opinion away from the trustbusting advocated by insurgent progressives and to promote a climate of acceptance for large corporations under government regulation.[13]

12. The connections between these meetings and groups are difficult to piece together. For a representative sample of social scientists who were interested in meeting and working with prominent social reformers, see H. D. Lloyd, Ernest H. Crosby, and George A. Gates to E. A. Ross, 5 May 1897, Ross MSS; copy to H. C. Adams, Adams MSS. For a list of those invited to the 1897 conference, see Lloyd, Crosby, and Gates to H. C. Adams, 16 May 1897, Adams MSS. On plans for the Buffalo Conference and the Social Reform Union, see Eltweed Pomeroy to Ely, 8 February 1899; Kinley to Ely, 7 July 1899; W. D. P. Bliss to Ely, 15 September 1899; Ely to Bliss, 25 October 1899, Ely MSS. In a similar flirtation, Taussig, James, Ely, Jenks, Hull, and Walter F. Willcox endorsed George Shibley's short-lived scheme for "a sort of Social-Science Chautauqua." Yet when the Civic Union was actually formed, only Ross, Bemis, and Commons accepted official connection. See Frederick W. Sanders to Ross, 2, 21 June, 13 July 1897; George Shibley to Ross, 27 October, 16, 31 December 1897, 6 June 1899, 20 July 1900, Ross MSS; Fine, *Laissez Faire*, pp. 349-51.

A number of other economists worked with the National Civic Federation. With the understanding that they would provide expert knowledge, not partisan enthusiasm, Seligman, Ely, Adams, and Taussig agreed to plan an ambitious national conference on taxation for the NCF in 1901.[14] In succeeding years respectable progressives took up the old Populist cry for public ownership and operation of public utilities, while private owners of utilities began to wonder whether state or federal regulation might not stabilize conditions in their industries and give them some protection against constant pressure from reformers. The NCF formed a Commission on Public Ownership and Operation of Public Utilities to study the problem and recommend legislation. Jenks appeared on the executive committee of the commission, while John Commons, then at the University of Wisconsin, Frank Goodnow, a Columbia University expert on municipal government, Frank Parsons, who was president of the Public Ownership League, and Bemis, the superintendent of waterworks in Cleveland, were named, along with a number of utility magnates, union leaders, and city utility commissioners, to the investigating committee.

The investigation was a classic example of progressive legislative research. With an ample budget and opportunity for extensive field comparisons of public and private gas, water, electricity, and street railway operations in the United States, England, and Ireland, the committee exhaustively sifted the evidence to determine the pros and cons of public and private ownership. Hundreds of witnesses were questioned. The pres-

---

13. The best analysis of National Civic Federation conservatism is James Weinstein, *The Corporate Ideal in the Liberal State, 1900-1918* (Boston, 1968), esp. chapt. 3 on trust regulation. On Jenks's views on wealth, see his *Great Fortunes: The Winning, The Using* (New York, 1906), pp. 15-22 and passim. The quote is from Weinstein, *Corporate Ideal*, p. 73. In 1908 Jenks and Nicholas Murray Butler were the academic representatives appointed by NCF president Seth Low to a National Civic Federation Committee that President Theodore Roosevelt had requested to draw up new legislation to replace the Sherman Act. Preparation of the Hepburn bill involved Jenks in frequent contacts with the White House and congressional leaders. Weinstein, *Corporate Ideal*, pp. 77-79.

14. Ralph M. Easley to Ely, 22 January, 3 May 1901; Ely to Easley, 24 January 1901; Seligman to Ely, 4 May 1901, Ely MSS; National Civic Federation, *National Conference on Taxation* (New York, 1901).

ence of three economists with expert knowledge in the utilities field and strong leanings toward municipal socialism probably upgraded the scientific quality of the investigation and neutralized pressures from powerful business representatives such as Samuel Insull, head of the Edison Electric Company. A deliberate effort was made to balance "pros" and "antis" in all commission endeavors. Eventually the Public Ownership Commission published a voluminous narrative and statistical report that unequivocally demonstrated the ineffectiveness of competition to regulate utilities and endorsed monopoly. The choice between a public monopoly or private ownership under government regulation was left to a decision according to local circumstances, but the commission recommended that franchises be awarded for fixed terms and reserved the right of the municipality to take over a utility with fair compensation at any time. The commission report provided a model for legislation such as the Wisconsin public utilities law that Commons later wrote for Charles McCarthy's Legislative Reference Bureau in Wisconsin, and it also further demonstrated the usefulness of social science experts.[15]

Government officials were quick to see that usefulness. In 1898 public anxiety over the explosive growth of big business exerted pressure in Congress that led to the creation of a United States Industrial Commission with instructions to make an official study of the problem as a basis for legislative action. In recognition of his expert knowledge on the subject of trusts, Jenks was given important staff responsibility for conducting hearings and preparing reports. Like President Roosevelt, Jenks accepted large corporations as a natural outgrowth of industrial

15. National Civic Federation, *Municipal and Private Ownership of Public Utilities,* Report of the Commission on Public Ownership and Operation, 3 vols. (New York, 1907), esp. 1:12-19, 88-112, 122-85. The report was so moderate that only Walton Clark, the Philadelphia gas trust owner who had threatened Bemis in 1894, felt obliged to dissent. In Bemis's individual section of the report, he had concluded that "in both water, gas and electricity the municipal plants have done far better for the taxpayer and consumer than the private plants in anything like a similar situation" (1:184). Clark, of course, concluded the opposite (1:29-32). See also Weinstein, *Corporate Ideal,* pp. 24-26; Bemis et al., *Municipal Monopolies* (Boston, 1899), for earlier contributions on the subject by Bemis, Commons, and Parsons.

development, a desirable business form that should be regulated in the public interest, not destroyed. This was exactly the position taken in the NCF by prominent businessmen and politicians—and for that matter by union leaders, if they could get certain guarantees. In part because of Jenks's influence, witnesses and data that supported a strict, trustbusting view of the Sherman Act had little influence in the Industrial Commission's proceedings. Besides Jenks, the other economists who were involved in the proceedings also tended to approve of corporate enterprise and welcome proposals that called for expert supervision. Discriminatory practices such as price fixing and rebates were sharply criticized, but consolidation to achieve economies was frequently defended. Ultimately the Industrial Commission called for federal licensing and regulation, not destruction of large corporations. The report was an affirmation of bigness. Its recommendations were partly achieved in the Bureau of Corporations and fully realized in the Federal Trade Commission. One of the most influential drafts of the Federal Trade Commission Act was written, under NCF auspices, by Jenks and John Bates Clark.[16]

In an individual career, perhaps the tie between progressive reform and liberal social science was best exemplified by Seligman. The Columbia economist not only defended advocacy for others within the range of permissible dissent; he continually practiced involvement himself. He did much of the theoretical work that made it technically possible to finance the expanded role that progressives envisioned for government. As the son of a prominent New York financier, he had the confidence of

16. For Jenks's authorship of Industrial Commission reports, see above, chapt. 10, n. 31. Economists who testified included Henry Carter Adams, Seligman, Commons, Bemis, Emory R. Johnson and Walter E. Weyl of the University of Pennsylvania, William Z. Ripley of the Massachusetts Institute of Technology, and George Gunton. On the role of the commission, see Weinstein, *Corporate Ideal,* p. 69; Dorfman, *Economic Mind,* 3:216-18. Adams had called for public disclosure and federal supervision of corporations in "Statistics as a Means of Correcting Corporate Abuses," *Publications of the AEA* 6 (1891):73-78. As ICC economist, he consistently favored federal rate regulation powers. See Adams, "Difficulties in Adjusting Rates," ibid., 3d ser., 1 (1900): 245-49. For Seligman's middle-of-the-road position, see United States Industrial Commission, *Reports,* 4:598-617.

businessmen even when he was defending a living wage for laborers or advocating progressive taxation. The federal income tax amendment was based on his work, and he wrote the New York State income tax law and worked as a consultant on taxation for several investigating commissions. He served as president of the National Tax Association and supported federal regulation of commerce and industry and federal control of banking through the federal reserve system. Eventually he helped to coordinate the economy during World War I and served as financial expert to the League of Nations.

But Seligman also devoted himself to the more mundane business of breaking ties between the New York police and organized prostitution. A prominent feature of the progressive mentality was its passion for clean government and its hatred of city bosses. In the mid-1890s Seligman backed an early anti-Tammany candidate. Thereafter he worked diligently with the City Vigilance League, the Bureau of Municipal Research, and the City Club of New York, until finally he was instrumental in getting Columbia University president Seth Low elected reform mayor of the city. With his private fortune, Seligman supported a tailors' cooperative, financed a model tenement, endowed an educational foundation for Russian Jews, and promoted a civil rights organization that eventually became the Urban League.[17]

As progressivism fostered a new kind of reform temper and created enormous opportunities for practical research, the American Economic Association took on some of the characteristics of an investigative agency. Prominent economists rather self-consciously narrowed the range of their investigations to exclude philosophical questions. They confidently predicted a time when statistical methods would make it impossible for "two distinguished senators, discussing an economic question, to make distinctly opposite statements in regard to the same state of facts." An expert-witness mentality flourished in the

17. Joseph Dorfman, "Edwin Robert Anderson Seligman," *DAB*, 22 (Supplement 2): 606-9; R. Gordon Hoxie et al., *A History of the Faculty of Political Science, Columbia University* (New York, 1955), pp. 70-71.

AEA, and a growing percentage of the papers read at meetings had to do with what one officer proudly identified as "public economy."[18]

In 1898 the change was sanctified in an incredible presidential address by Arthur T. Hadley. The posture of economists vis-à-vis American society was so dramatically altered that the leading academic purist of the 1880s, who had insisted in the *Science* "Economic Discussion" that dabbling in matters of public policy would leave an economist too partisan for impartial investigation, now called upon his professional colleagues to come out of their ivory tower and play a more active part in practical politics. It was an amazing reversal. More than any other young economist in the 1880s, Hadley had insisted on the primacy of intellectual work. By the end of the 1890s his fear of reprisals and concern for the corrupting influence of involvement were apparently gone, and his priorities were reordered. As Hadley explained it, two forces impelled him—the failure of competition as an efficient regulator of business, and the degeneration of legislatures from forums for enlightened debate to arenas where representatives of vested interests made selfish compromises that robbed the general public. These forces had enhanced the importance of the executive and increased the power of administrative agencies where, in Hadley's view, economists could influence policy without being politicized. The nuisance question of bias might still be raised, but professionalism answered it. Trained economists could rise above class and party. They could transcend even the backward pull of their own class origins and the stirrings of their present sympathies in order to provide expert counsel on issues of universal importance. As objective students, they were better qualified than any other group to identify the general interest. They should recognize their highest duty: to promote the welfare of society as a whole.

Hadley's program must have come as some surprise, especial-

18. William Watts Folwell, "The New Economics," *Publications of the AEA* 8 (1893): 19-40.

ly to colleagues that he had once branded as reformers. The informal discussion that took place after the meeting provoked Hadley to repeat substantially the same position in his second presidential address the following year. This time the opposition was prepared. In a carefully planned rebuttal, John Commons accused Hadley of deliberately trying to obscure important class issues. Only the dominant classes, and professions that served the interests of dominant classes, had anything to gain from concealing the existence of class conflict, Commons declared. No group was likely to consult an economist unless its leaders believed an expert could help to demonstrate the correctness of their policies or run their program. Economists had historically achieved their greatest influence when they were helping to shape legislation for a new class just acquiring power. In the 1880s, while class conflict was raw and the outcome uncertain, Hadley had preferred academic isolation. The class that came to power in the 1890s was Hadley's class. Now, Commons hinted, out of naive optimism or sheer deception, Hadley equated the interests of economists with those of a closeknit elite in big business and government and then pretended that the interests of the corporate managers were in the best interest of all.

Commons and Hadley were fundamentally opposed on the issue of class. In a mobile and democratic society the only competition that Hadley considered constructive took place between members of the same class as each individual tried to get ahead. Hadley abhorred class conflict and believed that prosperity, the general welfare, indeed the only true patriotism lay in subordinating and eventually eliminating the selfish and potentially destructive opposition between classes. Commons, on the other hand, considered open class competition healthy and constructive, the real source of all progress. His greatest horror was a political system that submerged true class interests and placed the power that should have gone to authentic class leaders such as Gompers or Debs, J. P. Morgan or Andrew Carnegie, in the hands of unscrupulous bosses who were responsible to polyglot coalitions or to no one. If legislatures were impotent, Commons argued, it was not because they had come to represent classes but because they had ceased to represent them. Representation of localities instead of classes obscured the real issues. In place of true class compromise, there could only be logrolling. So Commons favored a resurgence of class opposition, with proportional representation in a strong legislature for every economic interest, instead of further transfer of power to the executive.

Since class was the ultimate reality for Commons, he considered Hadley's proposal for expert economists operating above class interests as little more than a scheme for placing consenting economists in the service of political capitalism and silencing the rest. Commons's counterproposal called upon economists to become representatives of all classes, choosing not out of bias but after careful study and only when they were convinced that the class selected was "the temporary means of bringing about the permanent welfare of all." So bluntly that he alienated some in attendance, Commons challenged Hadley to consider his conviction: that freedom could only survive where the class struggle was recognized and provided for in a manner that gave each class hope of achieving justice, with economists helping to identify class interests and striving to give excluded classes a larger, fairer share in government and industry.[19]

In one of the earliest confrontations between radical and consensus economics, clearly the majority was with Hadley. Americans had chosen a high production, high consumption, corporate economy, and the new AEA was not at odds with America. With the exception of a very few unreconstructed dissenters, professional economists at the turn of the century accepted their nation's dominant institutions pretty much as given. At the annual meeting held in the winter of 1898, the

19. Arthur T. Hadley, "The Relations between Economics and Politics," ibid., Economic Studies 4 (1899): 7-28; Hadley, "Economic Theory and Political Morality," ibid., 3d ser., 1 (1900): 45-61; Commons's remarks in "Discussion," ibid., pp. 62-88, 287-88. Seligman and Bemis tried to cover the rift by citing potential points of agreement. Seligman chastised Commons for bad manners and denied that economists identified themselves as representatives of any one class. Mayo-Smith and H. H. Powers also rejected the implications of Commons's proposal.

AEA ratified the expansion of American capitalism by appoint-
ing a blue ribbon committee under the chairmanship of Jenks,
with the assistance of Seligman and Hull, to work out the best
means of administering colonies. A few years later Jacob
Hollander commented with obvious pleasure on how instructive
the "recent financial experience of Porto Rico" had been in
showing the mutual obligation of the financial theorist and the
financial administrator. Experts had been given a great deal of
responsibility for devising financial instruments in Puerto Rico,
and the problems they encountered putting theory into practice
had stimulated new advances in the science. Henry Carter
Adams considered it "propitious for the future of political
economy" that so many economists with strong academic credentials were willing to take administrative jobs. Reminiscing
about the people who had assembled years before at Saratoga to
form the AEA, he recalled with pride how many of them—"as
directors of public bureaus, or as experts"—had placed their
trained intelligence at the service of the government. The AEA
had come full circle.[20]

And with good reason. It was clear by the turn of the century
that social scientists who favored moderate state action within a
conventional political and economic framework would indeed
be more influential than those who advocated radical change.
Renown as a brilliant and careful scholar, not a reputation for
outspokenness, made the economist's technical competence
desirable. An economist appointed by a government commission to work out tariff schedules or exchange rates, to draft
legislation for railroad regulation or stock sales, exercised more
effective power than a visible reformer with no actual opportunity to affect decision making.

At national, state, and local levels, the cherished appointment
as a technical expert was likely to be influenced by political
considerations, but status in the profession was an equally

20. "Preliminary Report of the Committee on Colonies," *Publications of the AEA*,
3d ser., 1 (1900): 283-86; "Discussion—Thomas S. Adams, 'Porto Rican Finance
under the Spanish and American Governments,' " ibid., 3d ser., 3 (1902): 342-50.

important test. Occasionally the two factors interacted. In 1899 Commons and Bemis were partners in the Bureau of Economic Research. Henry Carter Adams recommended Commons to a senator who was about to conduct an investigation of the postal service. "Should [the senator] ask you to call upon him," Adams cautioned Commons, "it might perhaps be best, in view of certain prejudices existing, not to mention that Professor Bemis is your partner. This is a purely voluntary suggestion on my part. I have never heard the senator speak of Bemis, but it occurred to me that Professor Bemis's known inclination toward government ownership of everything sizeable might tend to discredit a report with which his name was connected."[21]

By 1900 a secure position within academic social science was ordinarily the key to influence outside academic life. The profession had taken on the character of a clearinghouse. A social scientist of low standing in his field could anticipate influencing mainly people who were already inclined to share his views, whereas a person of high scholarly reputation could expect his technical knowledge to be widely respected and his specialized services sought by representatives of varied political and social positions. Even a very able scholar who became too closely identified with one position—Laughlin on gold, for instance—risked being pigeonholed as a representative of special interests and ignored by others. While Laughlin dominated the Chicago school of economists, it remained an enclave, not a serious challenge to the national leadership or the liberal consensus in economics.[22] If there was to be more than one hierarchy in academic social science, it would come from increased academic specialization, not regional or ideological splintering.

21. Adams to Commons, 16 October 1899 (Letterbook 1899-1900, pp. 161-62), Adams MSS.

22. Coats, "Origins of the 'Chicago School(s)?'" pp. 487-93. This professional isolation did not prevent Laughlin from influencing policy where he possessed expert knowledge and inclinations that coincided with the aims of political leaders. He is credited, for example, with primary authorship of the Federal Reserve Act. See Kolko, *Triumph of Conservatism*, pp. 218-24, 228, 242-47, and extensive material on the authorship controversy in the J. Laurence Laughlin MSS, Manuscripts Division, LC.

12 *Specialization*

Some of the pressure for diversity in academic social science found release through the professionalization of political science and sociology as independent disciplines. The most significant factor behind the separation of political science from economics and history was the rise of public administration as an important separate study. In the 1890s, when management emerged as an important function in government and industry, there was a marked increase in social scientists' activity outside the classroom in administrative roles. The intellectual substance of political science evolved in a similar direction.[1]

Very roughly, the intellectual emphasis in political science moved through three phases as professionalization progressed. At mid-century the study of government comprised a major part of moral philosophy. As scholars, political scientists were preoccupied with abstract philosophical questions such as the ideal nature and purpose of government. In their teaching they tried to implant habits of good citizenship and supply guidance on public issues for young men who would take responsible positions in society. In the 1870s and 1880s the emphasis on training for citizenship continued, but the scholarly interests of political scientists turned toward historical examination and description of the various ways in which different types of governments had developed and actually worked in practice. In the 1890s and the early twentieth century, when an expanded government role made administration important, some self-conscious political scientists invented and described processes for administering agencies and providing services, while others trained specialists to do the administering. The pervasive influence of scientific naturalism and the problems encountered in actual practice fueled interest in finding out how and why (not how well or badly) people behaved politically. As the Progressive Era matured, behavioralism and empiricism became the significant substantive and methodological concerns of second-generation professionals.[2] It was their emphasis on good government through expert administration and, less obviously at first, their interest in the sources and manipulation of political behavior, that tied the new political scientists into progressivism.

The changing interests and activities of political scientists clearly demonstrate the importance of the emerging field of administration as a professionalizing agent. Yet that outcome might not have been predicted by the early proponents of political science in higher education. Indeed, the specialized study of administration arose only after the failure of more sweeping programs designed to include a sound political indoctrination as a part of the general education provided for the social elite that would occupy positions of leadership in private and public life. The academics who wanted to build a modern professional discipline found themselves working in the shadow of some rather awe-inspiring progenitors who had been influenced by German educational practices and oriented toward broader civic goals. The most popular mid-century treatises on government were written by Francis Lieber, a transplanted German liberal who taught political science at Columbia Univer-

1. For the backgrounds of political science, see Gladys Bryson, "The Emergence of the Social Sciences from Moral Philosophy," *International Journal of Ethics* 42 (April 1932): 304-23; Anna Haddow, *Political Science in American Colleges, 1636-1900* (New York, 1939); Bernard Crick, *The American Science of Politics: Its Origins and Conditions* (Berkeley, Calif., 1959), pp. 3-15; Albert Somit and Joseph Tanenhaus, *The Development of American Political Science* (Boston, 1967), pp. 7-48; Edward A. Purcell, Jr., *The Crisis of Democratic Theory: Scientific Naturalism and the Problem of Value* (Lexington, Ky., 1973), esp. chapt. 6.

2. Major works that represent these stages of development in the discipline are: for the moral philosophy phase, Francis Lieber, *Civil Liberty and Self Government* (New York, 1853); for the historical approach, Woodrow Wilson, *The State: Elements of Historical and Practical Politics* (1889; rev. ed., Boston, 1898), and much that was published in the early numbers of the *Johns Hopkins University Studies in History and Political Science;* for the administration emphasis, Frank Goodnow, *Municipal Home Rule* (New York, 1895), and Goodnow, *Politics and Administration* (New York, 1900); for emerging behavioralism, Arthur F. Bentley, *The Process of Government: A Study of Social Pressures* (1908; reprint ed., Bloomington, Ind., 1949). The intellectual evolution of political science resembled the growth of economics in its movement from a natural law-deductive emphasis through a historical-inductive stage toward analysis of working institutions and the motivation of behavior.

sity, mostly to law students, as a paean to national unity and strength. Andrew Dickson White, one of the first Americans to study history and government in Germany and later ambassador to Berlin, established a department of "History, Political and Social Science" at Cornell in 1868, when he served as the university's first president. In justifying political science, White stressed the importance of providing appropriate training for young men who aspired "to rise to positions of trust in public service." White was thinking primarily of guided analysis of political issues, not specialized professional training. When the German-trained historian Charles Kendall Adams founded a department of political science at the University of Michigan in 1881, he took the logical next step and proposed that the department do its best to train highly skilled graduates to enter an expert civil service. Finally John William Burgess, Lieber's successor at Columbia, combined the method of inquiry he had learned in German doctoral seminars with the mission he had subsequently observed at the Ecole Libre Sciences Politiques (a newly founded school for high-level civil servants and statesmen in the Third French Republic) to establish the Columbia School of Political Science with the express purpose, in addition to the scholarly development of the discipline, of training professional public servants and equipping students to pass the civil service examinations.[3]

A number of factors contributed to this heavy emphasis on sensitizing members of the genteel, college-educated population to their civic duty. In the years after the Civil War, the class that had traditionally provided civic leaders was very much con-

3. The best sources on Lieber's academic career are Thomas Sergeant Perry, ed., *The Life and Letters of Francis Lieber* (Boston, 1882); Allan Nevins and Milton Halsey, eds., *The Diary of George Templeton Strong,* 4 vols. (New York, 1952), vol. 4; Frank Friedel, *Francis Lieber: Nineteenth Century Liberal* (Baton Rouge, La., 1947); Joseph Dorfman and Rexford Tugwell, "Francis Lieber: German Scholar in America," *Columbia University Quarterly* 30 (1938): 159-90, 267-93. On Burgess, see John William Burgess, *Reminiscences of an American Scholar* (New York, 1934); Charles E. Merriam, "John William Burgess," *DAB,* 21 (Supplement 1):132-34; on both, Bernard E. Brown, *American Conservatives: The Political Thought of Francis Lieber and John W. Burgess* (New York, 1951). On the development of departments of political science, see Crick, *American Science of Politics,* pp. 15-36.

cerned about the impact of new wealth, an unprecedented concentration of power in the national government, and an apparent geometric increase in political corruption. In early efforts to deal with these disruptive forces, they increased the social content of education and extended publicly supported education to more people, for they generally believed that an educated citizenry would clean up its politics and preserve traditional values. Gradually they turned to more specific proposals, such as civil service reform, for stability and a higher political tone.

These early advocates of political science were motivated by a strong class consciousness, which was most pronounced in Burgess. A strict constitutionalist, Burgess had little faith in the good instincts of the people. His abhorrence of mass action was no doubt the product of the disastrous toll that the Civil War had taken on his mid-Tennessee, Whig-Unionist family and the personal anguish that the war had caused him, as his Confederate neighbors turned into hostile enemies and forced him to flee his boyhood home. In manhood, Burgess could hardly imagine social injustice severe enough to justify revolution. In the 1880s he feared the propertyless workers in the growing labor and socialist movements as a potential threat to liberty, while he looked to the middle class as the substantial, conservative element. A professional civil service drawn from the educated middle class would resist leveling tendencies and stabilize society.[4]

In a much less embittered and exaggerated form, class consciousness also motivated men such as White, C. K. Adams, and other influential members of the early ASSA, who were not opposed to gradual social reform but still counted on a professional civil service to place trustworthy people of their own kind in office. In an 1881 address on "The Relations of Political Science to National Prosperity," Adams pointed to the absence in America of any "class, accustomed by tradition to positions

4. Burgess, *Reminiscences,* pp. 3-137; Crick, *American Science of Politics,* pp. 97-99.

of honour and responsibility," who thus had reason to fit themselves for offices of public trust. With office holding open to everyone, Adams feared that preparatory education would be neglected and reliance "based upon the baser arts of political manipulation."[5] Such people favored civic education for its conservative effect. With the emergence of rival interest groups, they had lost their once-firm hold on the electorate. The best alternative was to tie as many government positions as possible to the acquisition of credentials.

In a very real sense, then, the early proponents of political science were advocates of social control. While the development of knowledge was important to them, they were also eager to ensure a perpetual supply of people with wide, general competence in handling affairs and conservative social attitudes. The product they envisioned was an old-style professional.

The tie between political science and public service created certain pressures. At Columbia, for instance, Burgess had to walk a tight line, offering courses that appealed to prospective lawyers without allowing political science to slip into the status of a service department for the law school. Law faculties were in the process of trying to upgrade their professional standards at about the same time, and the two fields had enough joint interest in such areas as constitutional law that they seemed to threaten each other. Burgess's School of Political Science was established as a separate college in 1880 over the opposition of the Columbia Law School, but the political science faculty remained more interested in problems related to public law than political philosophy. Of the five full-time staff members in the School of Political Science before 1889 (Burgess, Munroe Smith, Frank Goodnow, Richmond Mayo-Smith, and Seligman), only the two economists, Mayo-Smith and Seligman, were not lawyers.[6]

In the 1880s and 1890s, when younger people with a higher

5. Quoted in Crick, *American Science of Politics*, pp. 24-25.

6. The best account of the social sciences at Columbia is R. Gordon Hoxie et al., *A History of the Faculty of Political Science, Columbia University* (New York, 1955). See esp. pp. 5-35.

level of academic preparation and an inclination toward research and teaching entered the emerging discipline, tensions of
another kind developed. There were no sharp distinctions between political science and the related disciplines of history and
economics, especially at schools where the older disciplines
were strong. Often dominance was almost accidentally determined. Interest in government was active at Hopkins, but in
Herbert Baxter Adams's time it was widely understood that
political science was nothing more than present history. When
Charles Kendall Adams left Michigan to replace White as president of Cornell, aggressive development in social science at
Michigan shifted to economics, where Henry Carter Adams's
major interests lay. The American Academy of Political and
Social Science was founded at the University of Pennsylvania,
but James and Patten also worked largely in economics and the
Michigan pattern was repeated. Even at Columbia, beyond the
impressive tradition established by Lieber and Burgess, the
fortuitous location in a major city, at an institution where a
flourishing law school provided students, and the understandable desire of an ambitious group of young scholars to make a
niche for themselves between Harvard and Wisconsin, which
were both strong in economics and history, were undoubtedly
factors. So was the sheer growth of American higher education.
In the 1890s Burgess's faculty stopped advertising preparation
for civil service tests and concentrated on meeting the growing
demand for college teachers. By 1900 more than half of all the
students with a primary interest in political science were being
trained at Columbia.[7]

Columbia's prominence helped boost the importance of
administration in political science. For at least a decade academic economists as prominent as Henry Carter Adams had
been doing important statistical work for government bureaus,
but they tended to focus on the impact of government on
economic activities such as transportation and trade rather than

7. For an illustrative account of Columbia's internal development from a disjointed collection of colleges to a modern university in this period, see ibid., pp.
29-49, 53-55, 60-61.

on the governmental process itself. A Columbia political scientist, Frank Goodnow, seized the unclaimed opportunity. He virtually annexed the field of public administration and raised it to the level of a serious academic specialty in political science.

Once more, Columbia's location in the nation's largest city was of overwhelming importance, as were the university's close connections with New York's legal, commercial, and financial communities. All the familiar problems of providing transportation, utilities, housing, and welfare services for a mushrooming urban population plagued New York in the 1880s. Allied with reform elements, members of the infant political science faculty supported Abram S. Hewitt or Theodore Roosevelt in 1886 and remained active in the reform agitation that culminated in the Lexow Committee's exposé of corruption in city government. In 1894 Goodnow supported the reform candidacy of a Columbia benefactor, William L. Strong, and then conducted a number of administrative studies for Strong's administration. As municipal progressives battled the Tammany machine throughout the 1890s, Columbia social scientists not only adorned the cause with academic respectability but contributed mightily to the political work, especially when their president, Seth Low, was an unsuccessful mayoral candidate in 1897 and subsequently won the office in 1901. Between 1895 and 1904 Goodnow brought out four big books on city administration, massively dominating the field. His scholarly work on municipal government was directly related to his reform activity as an urban progressive.[8]

As political scientists helped to shape civic affairs, so they were shaped. The New York State Chamber of Commerce endowed the Waring Municipal Fund to finance research on municipal government. In 1903 Goodnow was appointed to the Dorman B. Eaton Professorship of Public Law and Municipal Government, a chair endowed by a prominent civil service reformer of the 1880s who subsequently channeled his reform energies to finding nonpartisan, administrative solutions for city

8. Ibid., pp. 68-71.

problems. Eaton's purposes for political science investigation—"to provide the best method of municipal administration; to create councils in cities and villages which shall . . . represent their public opinion rather than their party opinion; to greatly reduce the number and frequency of elections in municipalities; to prevent the control of their affairs by parties and factions; and to make good municipal government the ambition and endeavor of the worthiest citizens"—were in line with Hadley's contemporary views of what economists should be doing. Goodnow's appointment to the Eaton professorship was symbolic of the use that conservative reformers could make of political science and the kinds of alliances that political scientists could safely make with reformers.[9]

What Goodnow did in municipal administration, others were doing in different phases of government. John A. Fairlie, a young professor at the University of Michigan, developed the science of local government outside the major cities. Woodrow Wilson and Paul Samuel Reinsch, an Ely student on the Wisconsin faculty, examined the workings of Congress. John H. Finley, another Ely student, specialized in describing the administrative methods of the executive branch. Several scholars investigated various levels of the judiciary, while Jesse Macy concentrated on the workings of political parties.

Specialists soon became experts, and experts became appointees. Under Jenks's leadership, Cornell social scientists were particularly active in the developing national bureaucracy. In addition to Jenks's service with the United States Industrial Commission, Walter F. Willcox of Cornell became chief statistician for the United States Census Bureau and served as a statistical expert for the War Department in conducting censuses of Cuba and Puerto Rico after the Spanish-American War. Working with economists through the AEA, political scientists

9. Quoted in ibid., p. 60. Similarly endowed professorships for prominent social scientists became common at Columbia, as at other important schools. Goodnow subsequently served as legal adviser to the Chinese government, 1913-1914, where he wrote drafts of a constitution for the Chinese Republic. He finished his career as president of the Johns Hopkins University, 1916-1929.

were especially influential in developing the technical know-
how to administer a farflung colonial empire. Jenks's AEA
Committee on Colonies published detailed reports on the ad-
ministrative systems employed by every major colonial power.
Jacob Hollander went out from the Johns Hopkins economics
department to revise the tax laws and to act as treasurer of
Puerto Rico, while Thomas S. Adams, after working under
Willcox in the Census Bureau, went along as Hollander's assistant. William Frank Willoughby of Hopkins succeeded Hollander as treasurer of Puerto Rico. Jenks and E. W. Kemmerer of
Princeton guided the reorganization of Philippine finances.
From the University of California, the conservative political
scientist Bernard Moses went to the Philippines as superintendent of public instruction. Samuel M. Lindsay of the Wharton
School organized and administered the Puerto Rican school
system from 1898 to 1902.

These pioneers in public administration also shaped public
opinion. Reinsch and Willoughby together published the major
works that introduced Americans to the history of European
colonial policy, compared the various patterns of colonial government, and analyzed the problems of colonial administration
that Americans would encounter in the new overseas empire.
Both men looked upon the colonies as an interesting new
administrative problem. Besides providing valuable technical
assistance, political scientists dignified the race for empire by
their interest and presented imperialism as a natural stage in
economic development and a civilizing mission.[10] Like the

10. For the AEA Committee on Colonies Report, see "Essays in Colonial
Finance," *Publications of the AEA,* 3d. ser., 1 (1900): 385-688. See also William
Franklin Willoughby, *Territories and Dependencies of the United States: Their
Government and Administration* (New York, 1905); Paul Samuel Reinsch, *Colonial
Government: An Introduction to the Study of Colonial Institutions* (1902; reprint
ed., Freeport, N.Y., 1970); Reinsch, *Colonial Administration* (New York, 1905).
Willoughby was glad that "the exploitation theory" of colonial government had
"never met with any acceptance in the United States" (*Territories,* p. 12). Reinsch
ascribed the resurgence of interest in colonies to the development of excess investment capital in industrial nations. "It has become a necessity in the present stage of
economic life," he explained, "that all parts of the world where potential wealth
exists should be policed and put under an orderly administration, so as to make the
improvement of their resources a safe and profitable undertaking" (*Colonial Govern-*

economists who worked in bureaucratic roles, they tended to avoid the normative questions that had characterized moral philosophy and to concentrate instead on the structural and procedural problems involved in implementing established policies.

In the early twentieth century social scientists who were attracted to public administration found their field expanding rapidly. Cities offered more services, states increased their regulatory activities, and the national government expanded beyond traditional borders to rule foreign territory. Whether political scientists worked primarily in the universities or in agencies as technical experts, they were quick to realize that there was a great deal to be learned by comparing problems and solutions from city to city, state to state, and colony to colony. They also noticed that certain administrative structures and practices were equally effective whether the problem at hand was supervising factories or assessing taxes, that a workmen's compensation or incorporation law that worked in one state was likely to do equally well in another.

It was this common interest in comparative administration that ultimately led to the creation of a separate national association of political scientists. In December 1902 a group that included Goodnow, Burgess, and Jenks issued invitations for a meeting to consider forming an American Society of Comparative Legislation. Once together, the political scientists apparently resolved their anxieties about seeming to compete with existing professional societies. They decided that an association "whose province should embrace the whole field of Political

---

ment, p. 84). It should also be noted here that Hollander, as financial adviser to the Dominican Republic in 1906, received a finder's fee of $100,000 for arranging the sale of Dominican Republic bonds through Kuhn, Loeb & Company. While not unusual in financial circles, that sizable reward created something of a scandal when it was disclosed in 1911 by the Pujo Committee. Hollander's public service career, including this fascinating affair, is described in David Michael Grossman, "Professors and Public Service, 1885-1925: A Chapter in the Professionalization of the Social Sciences," (Ph.D. diss., Washington University, 1973), esp. chapt. 2. Unfortunately Grossman's thesis was not available when these chapters were written, but it should be consulted for a wealth of information about the work of social scientists in government agencies.

Science" was necessary, and they appointed a committee headed by Jenks to confer with leading members of the AHA and AEA. Almost all of this first committee's members were involved with the new subjects in practical politics, not theory. All the major universities with political science programs and important government agencies such as the Interstate Commerce Commission and the Census Bureau were represented, but Columbia, Cornell, and Hopkins clearly dominated the movement.

Over the next few months the committee conducted polite inquiries and learned, in Goodnow's words, that "many of those whose main interests are centered in distinctly political problems" had indeed concluded that the declared purposes of the AEA and the AHA did not permit those bodies "to devote the necessary attention to political questions, particularly to questions of public law and administration." The committee arranged with the AEA and the AHA to hold an organizational session for political scientists at the joint meeting of historians and economists in New Orleans in 1903.[11]

There was some sentiment in the older organizations for keeping political science contained as a section of the AHA, AEA, or ASSA, but the rising consciousness of the political scientists prevailed. At a meeting controlled by Columbia, Cornell, and Hopkins, Frank Goodnow was elected first president of an independent American Political Science Association (APSA). The new leadership appointed standing committees that dealt primarily with comparative government and practical administrative problems, but a theorist, Westel Woodbury Willoughby, was elected secretary, and a committee on theory was created to attract political scientists with more traditional interests. In fact, the whole proceeding was characterized by an obvious desire to avoid controversy of any sort—internal or

11. "The Organization of the American Political Science Association," *Proceedings of the American Political Science Association* 1 (1904): 5-12; Frank Goodnow to W. W. Willoughby, 5 January 1904; Goodnow to H. C. Adams, 23 March 1904; Goodnow to J. Franklin Jameson, 4 August 1904; Goodnow to J. W. Jenks, 31 January 1905, Frank Goodnow MSS, Johns Hopkins University Library.

public. In his opening remarks Goodnow refused to attempt to define the field. Economists and historians were encouraged to join, and prominent civic and educational leaders such as Andrew Dickson White and the eminent Connecticut jurist and Yale law professor, Simeon E. Baldwin, were honored with places on the executive committee. Early programs were mainly devoted to sessions on practical, nonpartisan, administrative questions in colonial policy or state regulation, but a few sessions appealed to those who were still concerned with constitutional and philosophical topics.[12]

In the 1880s, when economists had organized their discipline, nineteenth-century concepts of truth and knowledge had impelled contending factions to battle it out until one side or the other emerged victorious. By 1903 concepts of truth were more relative and tentative. Higher education had evolved and modernized like other social institutions. Universities were built to tolerate diversity. The college and department structure was flexible enough to adapt to new developments in knowledge and absorb new academic interests by simply adding on sections (or bureaus) to house them. In time, when preferment went to the new and the useful, the old—like moral or natural philosophy—would wither away. Only when one subspecialty partly defined its mission in terms of eradicating another was confrontation inevitable. And that was not the case in political science at the turn of the century.

The dominant spirit of the political science profession in 1904 was captured in the APSA policy statement: that the organization would not "assume a partisan position upon any question of practical politics, nor commit its members to any position thereupon." For years a tiny core of political scientists had hoped that their emerging profession might establish the moral tone and provide the ethical leadership for enlightened public debate on political questions. Ely's old friend Jesse Macy

12. "Organization of the American Political Science Association," pp. 12-17. In common parlance of the day, Goodnow referred to this distinction as static and dynamic political science.

was typical of the small reform group, and there were factors in his background that resembled the evangelical origins of early reform economists. He was a Quaker who grew up on an Indiana farm that served as an Underground Railway stop for fugitive slaves. He served as a medic in the Civil War and then dedicated himself to rebuilding the shattered nation psychologically as well as physically. With neither legal nor formal graduate training, he found in Darwin and Spencer the basis for a lifelong faith in the perfectibility of society. Macy saw the United States as a vast laboratory full of opportunities for advancing human welfare. At every level from school board to statehouse, government could be used to make people's lives easier and fuller. Macy wanted social scientists to guide the reformation of industrial society. In the heat of the labor controversy of 1886 he had proclaimed his activist commitment. "A political science which does not at least honestly seek to give direction to actual politics is an unmitigated nuisance," he told Ely. Again in the nervous mid-1890s he had tried, in the Political Science Association of the Central States, to forge a radical coalition. By 1903, however, the times and the science had changed so much that the political science elite could put Macy on the APSA executive council with no fear that his influence would spread.[13]

Political science existed, according to Goodnow's presidential address, to advance the study of the state and to perfect the machinery for administering the public law. There was no mention of a public policy-making role for political scientists. No early discussion struck the militant interventionist note that Jesse Macy would have preferred; no one suggested, as Commons recently had in economics, that political scientists try to bring government to the aid of the lower classes. Objectivity was a part of the emerging professional identity, but the new leaders defined it in a special way. It restricted open public advocacy of the sort that allied political science with reforms

13. Charles E. Payne, "Jesse Macy," *DAB*, 12:176-77; Macy to Ely, 16 October 1886, Ely MSS.

which threatened the status quo, but it did not preclude administrative work or research that indirectly supported the interest already in power. Goodnow was extremely careful to manage the image of the APSA in a conservative direction. Despite his own interest in municipal reform, he refused a request to affiliate the APSA with the progressive Alliance of Civic Organizations and declined to make a public address at their meeting. The Alliance of Civic Organizations was not very radical, but it was not academic, and the APSA leadership wanted to avoid creating the wrong public impression. More than anything, the young academics who had created the field of public administration wanted to demonstrate that political scientists were not advocates but specialists, not reformers but objective experts who better than any other group could systematize the gathering of information, routinize the execution of administrative decisions, rationalize, and, if called upon, run the complex, modern, bureaucratic government.[14]

With economics oriented toward developing the technical skills required to regulate the economy and political science equally preoccupied with shaping techniques of administration for various government functions, social scientists who still wanted to find solutions for the broader "social questions" had no safe or appropriate niche in academic social science. In quiet desperation, a few serious social reconstructionists turned to a new alternative, sociology. By the turn of the century Commons, Bemis, Ross, and the historian George Howard had all more or less completed the transition, though not necessarily by choice. Because these refugees from other disciplines wound up in sociology, it is tempting to think of the radical remnant as a major force in defining and professionalizing the discipline. In fact, there is some truth in that, but only as part of a more complicated pattern.

In the 1890s and the early twentieth century, the central

14. Frank Goodnow, "The Work of the American Political Science Association," *Proceedings of the American Political Science Association* 1 (1904): 35-46; Clinton Rogers Woodruff to Goodnow, 14, 27 December 1904, 2 January 1905; Goodnow to Woodruff, 16 December 1904, 5, 13 January 1905, Goodnow MSS.

problem for self-conscious professional sociologists was finding
a manageable, unifying research focus for sociology. In a university-based profession, a clearly defined direction for useful
research and teaching was essential, but in the formative period
rivalry for subject matter was keen. American sociologists were
quickly repulsed if they encroached on territory already
claimed by more mature disciplines, particularly economics.
Sociologists were also threatened by competition from the
infant disciplines of anthropology and psychology; though these
fields appeared later in the universities, each was more precisely
and easily structured, as the moment arrived, by developing
concepts and research techniques unique to the field. The
intellectual heritage of nonacademic sociology was sweeping—a
synthesis of all knowledge regarding society in the grand
manner of August Comte and Herbert Spencer. American academic realities were far more limiting. Perhaps the frustration
that sociologists experienced as they threaded their way
through the intellectual jungle of first-generation academic
social science was best captured in 1908 by Albion Small. "The
main business of my life [has been] to show that there is a
definitely definable field for the division of social science to
which we are applying the name Sociology," Small admitted
privately. "The chief obstacle which specialists of my sort
encounter is the inveterate opinion that Sociology is merely a
convenient label for left-overs within the range of human
knowledge that cannot be classified under any other head."[15]
In its first generation as an academic subject, sociology never
really found a center.

Perhaps because of this insecurity, sociology is a discipline

15. The confusion of purposes and terms in early sociology is pervasively apparent
in L. L. Bernard and Jessie Bernard, *Origins of American Sociology: The Social
Science Movement in the United States* (New York, 1943). For a perceptive account
of the factors that forced sociologists to divest themselves of models and analogies
drawn from the evolutionary natural sciences and to develop concepts and methods
that pertained uniquely to an autonomous discipline of sociology, see Hamilton
Cravens, "The Abandonment of Evolutionary Social Theory in America: The Impact
of Academic Professionalization upon American Sociological Theory, 1890-1920,"
American Studies 12 (Fall 1971):5-20. Small to Walter A. Payne, 30 April 1908,
Sociology Folder, President's Collection, University of Chicago.

that, more than most others, has venerated "great thinkers." Before professionalization, American sociology had its indigenous giants. The early boundaries of American sociological debate were marked out by William Graham Sumner and Lester Ward. In 1873 Sumner began using Herbert Spencer's *Study of Sociology* with Yale undergraduates in a course that became a traditional Yale experience. Sumner's early sociology was the social side of his laissez-faire economics. A deceptively progressive conservative philosophy, it received its classic statement in *What Social Classes Owe to Each Other* (1883), a sharp rebuke to humanitarian reformers who tried to mitigate the natural harshness of life and eliminate beneficial inequities with puny legislation. Sumner was a confirmed evolutionist, but he believed that any attempts to alter the course of social development by artificial means could only end in disaster.[16]

In dramatic contrast, Ward argued that artificial measures were the only sure way to guarantee that society evolved in a desirable direction. If legislation accomplished nothing at all, he contended, there would be reason to despair. The fact that laws made by incompetents often got bad results was ample proof that laws made by people who understood sociology could indeed get good results. In his momentous *Dynamic Sociology* (1883), Ward laid out the distinction between two kinds of evolution: the genetic, which unfolded automatically among unthinking animals and plants, preserving the creatures more adapted to a particular environment whether they were in any absolute sense fittest or not; and the telic, which human intelligence could shape to achieve positive social ends. Earlier attempts at legislating a better social environment had largely failed, Ward conceded, but the failure stemmed from the lack of

16. American sociology in the nineteenth century was largely derivative from European sources, particularly August Comte and Herbert Spencer. Don Martindale, *The Nature and Types of Sociological Theory* (Boston, 1960), is a good summary of intellectual developments. For an account of the development of sociology in relation to other disciplines (though not always related correctly), see Albion Small, "Fifty Years of Sociology in the United States," *American Journal of Sociology* 21 (May 1916):721-88. Crick, *American Science of Politics*, pp. 49-70, is a useful account of the similarities and differences between Sumner and Ward that also reveals the progressive side of Sumner's thinking. See also Fine, *Laissez Faire*, pp. 252-75.

sociology in legislative halls, not from any failure in the science itself. "No legislator is qualified to propose or vote on measures designed to affect the destinies of millions of social units," he wrote, "until he masters all that is known of the science of society." Sociologists would find out how social evolution occurred and show the legislators how to harness the social forces to achieve desired social goals.[17]

Despite such glowing portents, sociology failed to catch on. Just as Ely and Newcomb had polarized the discussion in economics in the 1880s, Ward and Sumner raised formidable barriers to fruitful discussion in sociology. For a while younger, less assertive scholars let the intellectual distance between the two giants remain a virtual no-man's land. With the attention of all classes riveted on economic changes, the battle between laissez-faire and intervention seemed to belong primarily in economics. Also, however incredible it might seem later, academics sensed a real danger in the mid-1880s that a person called a sociologist might be taken for a socialist. As a defender of conservative interests, Sumner was safe, and Ward had no academic position. Others refrained.

Gradually, however, the groundwork was laid for a different approach to developing sociology. The comprehensive scope of the old political economy slowly narrowed, and in the emerging, problem-oriented academic economics, new concepts and statistical techniques defined a field that excluded important social questions. Major sociological studies continued to appear in Europe and found a small but appreciative American audience. In the late 1880s some tentative attempts were made to define sociology as a broader social study that could supplement or perhaps eventually incorporate economics. At an AEA

17. As a soldier in the Civil War and a long-time government employee (eventually United States paleontologist), Ward developed a consciousness similar to that of Carroll D. Wright and Francis Amasa Walker (described in chapter 2 above) of the positive contributions the state could make to advancing human welfare. On Ward's background, see Bernhard J. Stern, ed., *Young Ward's Diary* (New York, 1935); Samuel Chuggerman, *Lester F. Ward: The American Aristotle* (Durham, N.C., 1939). For Ward's views on evolution, Social Darwinism, and the role of sociology, see Lester Ward, *Dynamic Sociology*, 2 vols. (New York, 1883), 1: 81-93, 249-52; Fine, *Laissez Faire*, p. 258.

session in 1887 Franklin Henry Giddings tried to encourage a sociological perspective in economics. He proposed that sociological studies might provide useful data on the underlying customs of people in various civilizations and discover the natural and acquired human traits that conditioned economic behavior. Charles Horton Cooley was taking advanced work in economics at the University of Michigan, but in his private reflections he envisioned a science of sociology comparable to the new biology, so comprehensive that it included economics and "all conceivable social phenomena."[18]

No systematic graduate training in sociology was available in the United States until the University of Chicago opened in 1892, with Albion Small as head of the first sociology department in the country. Harper's example encouraged Columbia, where Giddings was appointed in 1894 to the first chair of sociology in the East. A year later Small's *American Journal of Sociology* began to reach the academic community and intelligent laymen with serial versions of two major new American works, Ward's *Outlines of Sociology* and Ross's *Social Control*. Encouraged by this sudden activity, imbued with some urgency by the general crisis of the 1890s, intrigued by the possibility of applying new concepts such as marginalism to the study of society, and emboldened by a decade's progress toward establishing the university's dominance in intellectual affairs, would-be sociologists renewed their efforts to define a field.[19]

For the first time in the social sciences, this mid-1890s phase in sociology amounted to a self-conscious effort to turn an academic discipline into a profession. Unfortunately, except for

18. Franklin H. Giddings, "The Sociological Character of Political Economy," *Publications of the AEA* 3 (1888): 29-47. Charles Horton Cooley to Elsie Jones, 4 December 1888, 2, 5, 29 January 1889; Cooley's notes on "The New Conception of Political Economy," ca. January 1889, Charles Horton Cooley MSS, Michigan Historical Collections.

19. On the rivalry between the University of Chicago and Columbia, see Giddings to Small, n.d. [ca. 1916], quoted in Small, "Fifty Years of Sociology," pp. 762, 765. Giddings offered his first graduate course in sociology at Bryn Mawr in 1890 and then began teaching sociology at Columbia in 1891, first as a sabbatical replacement for Richmond Mayo-Smith, before the establishment in 1894 of a regular chair in sociology. Small first taught sociology in 1890 as a kind of updated moral philosophy to seniors at Colby College.

the biological analogy to progressive stages of social evolution
that almost everyone accepted, and the Sumner-Ward ethical
controversy over state action that everyone hoped to avoid, the
discipline was still very ill defined. In fact, there was so much
imprecision that Small actually had one of his graduate students
conduct a survey of some forty social scientists in the United
States to see whether any consensus existed on the nature and
limits of sociology. The questions revealed the prevailing condition: "Which term do you prefer, Social Science or Sociology? Do you think the study is entitled to be called a science?
In what department does it belong? What is its relation to
Political Economy, History, Political Science, Ethics? Would
you divide the subject into descriptive, statical and dynamic,
and in what sense do you use each of these terms? What relative
importance does the treatment of the dependent, defective and
delinquent classes hold?" The results of the survey fell a good
deal short of clarifying the situation. Nearly everyone agreed
that "Sociology" was preferable to "Social Science" (in one
person's mind because it would be easier to convert to an
adjective). Only three-fourths of the respondents were sure that
sociology was a science, but almost all of them thought it
should form a department by itself. Some thought that all the
other social sciences were branches of the Department of Sociology, while others believed that sociology existed as a separate
department only to coordinate the findings of all the other
social sciences. Perhaps the clearest if not the most helpful
answer came in response to the question "What is its relation to
Political Economy, History, Political Science, Ethics?" An un-
named wit and lover of brevity replied, "The relation of Sociology to Political Economy, History, etc., is *close*."[20]

The problem was, how close, and coming in from what

20. Ira W. Howerth, "Present Condition of Sociology in the United States,"
Annals of the American Academy of Political and Social Science 5 (September
1894): 112-21. Cravens, "Abandonment of Evolutionary Social Theory," pp. 5-10,
depicts the prevalence of biological analogy. Robert Wiebe, *The Search for Order,
1877-1920* (New York, 1967), p. 121, shows how university departments served as
cocoons for emerging professions.

direction? In an exchange of papers and articles that elicited definitions from Ward, Small, Giddings, and Patten, one thing was clear. Leading theoretical sociologists could agree easily enough that they were not philanthropists or social workers, but they could not agree about where they stood in relation to the other academic disciplines. There was particular urgency in this question for, as Giddings realized, "the university cannot afford," and probably would not tolerate, "duplication of work." As things then stood, economics and political science were defined by their identification with the economy and the state, social institutions whose overwhelming importance everyone recognized. Because of its evolutionary content, the new sociology might have conflicted with history, but patrician history had secured a place in the traditional college curriculum, and for many it still belonged to the liberal arts. In the nineteenth century more than the twentieth, history was written for and read by large numbers of people other than academics. Furthermore, the past had objectively happened. Even without the embellishments and promises of the new seminary method, history was instructive, interesting, even exciting, and the study of it seemed to justify itself. Except for popular works like Ross's *Social Control,* however, much of the best sociology was already so laden with highly specialized jargon that its appeal and usefulness seemed sure to be limited to a small portion of the college-educated elite and to advanced students of social process. Circularly, the problem kept coming back to relations with the other disciplines.[21]

By the mid-1890s leading figures in academic sociology had developed two different plans for fitting their new discipline into the larger pattern of American social science. The most popular scheme envisioned sociology as a coordinating science,

21. Franklin H. Giddings, "The Relation of Sociology to Other Scientific Studies," *Journal of Social Science* 32 (1894): 144-50. For academic history in its social context, see John Higham, *History: The Development of Historical Studies in the United States* (Englewood Cliffs, N.J., 1965), pp. 3-86, 132-44. Besides the popular interest in history, Higham stresses the importance of history, in a period of rising nationalism and territorial expansion, as a carrier of national myth.

the queen discipline that Comte, Spencer, Ward, and Small desired. According to their classification system, detailed investigation would be left to the component fields of economics, political science, and jurisprudence. Sociology, the synthetic discipline, would coordinate the findings of all the lower fields and derive from them the general laws of social evolution. Conversely, others took sociology to the very bottom of the hierarchy of sciences and contented themselves with topics that their critics did indeed consider leftovers: marriage, the family, poverty, crime, education, religion, and sex. From this general position, Giddings proposed that sociology function as a fundamental science, organizing the basic data on population, birth and mortality rates, racial and ethnic distribution, and moral and mental traits, and identifying the beginning principles of social organization from which the specialized fields of economics, political science, and jurisprudence developed. According to both plans, sociology cut across all the other disciplines, in one case as the overarching superstructure and in the other as the undergirding floor.[22]

Thus in either case sociology threatened economics. According to the claims of sociologists, their discipline either preceded economics with more fundamental inquiries that would implicitly shape the direction of economic inquiry, or it followed economics, raising the incomplete findings of economists to more significant, synthetic, final conclusions. But economists obviously considered their discipline a science complete in itself. With no help or hindrance from sociologists, economists claimed, they started their own investigations with the most basic data and developed explanations that ultimately acquired the force of scientific laws which were final and complete in themselves. Though economics was well established and sociol-

22. From academic sociologists, good examples of these two proposals are Albion Small, "The Relation of Sociology to Economics," *Journal of Political Economy* 3 (March 1895):169-84; Giddings, "Relation of Sociology to Other Scientific Studies," pp. 144-49. The similarity between the Giddings version of the role of sociology and the ASSA conception of social science should be noted. Also, Giddings had started as a laissez-faire economist and was clearly overshadowed at Columbia by Burgess, Seligman, and Clark.

ogy barely organized, professional economists took the claims of their competitors seriously enough to ask Small to present the sociologists' case before the 1894 meeting of the AEA. Simon Patten considered the pretensions of sociologists "an important crisis in the development of the social sciences." From his influential place as editor of the *Annals of the American Academy of Political and Social Science,* he was prepared to resist any scheme for demoting economics to "a mere subdivision of sociology." Patten was willing to recognize sociology as an equal discipline within the social sciences, but no more. "I am at least one economist," Patten told Ross, "that proposes to die game."[23]

Patten's battle with the sociologists is more instructive as a clash between rival professional groups than it is interesting in itself. Like the *Science* "Economic Discussion" of the 1880s, this fight had a public aspect that consisted of a series of papers in which each side stated its case, and a private side in which partisans coached or cautioned each other in an effort to develop a common, effective strategy. Because the sociologists were divided into two camps, Patten found it necessary to aim his criticisms in two directions.[24]

As the more powerful opponents, the synthesizers were Patten's main concern. Astutely, he realized that a grand scheme for organizing all knowledge might easily survive minor quibbles with the placement of this or that science and yet be exceedingly vulnerable to a sweeping criticism that undermined the intellectual supports of the entire system. Consequently, he turned a review essay on Ward's *Psychic Factors of Civilization* (1893) into a sharp criticism of the nineteenth-century habit, particularly strong among sociologists, of relying on biological analogies to explain nearly everything. In evolutionary fashion,

23. Patten to Ross, 2 March, 25 April, 8 October 1894, Edward Alsworth Ross MSS, University of Wisconsin.

24. The correspondence between Small and Ward regarding Patten's criticisms and Giddings's alternative approach to sociology is especially illuminating. See Bernhard Stern, ed., "The Letters of Albion W. Small to Lester F. Ward: Parts 1-4," *Social Forces* 12 (December 1933): 163-73; 13 (March 1935): 323-40; 15 (December 1936): 174-86; 15 (March 1937): 305-27; see esp. Part 1: 166-70.

Ward had laid out a hierarchy of sciences that dealt with the various forces that influenced life. As they proceeded up the scale from simple to complex, these forces were identified with sciences: physical, chemical, biological, psychical, and, at the pinnacle, social. Each important science summarized the knowledge of each set of forces, and sociology therefore generalized from all the lower sciences. Patten charged that biologic sociology failed on conceptual and methodological grounds. Conceptually, Ward's excessive reliance on biological analogies had caused him to misconceive the origins of social behavior and the structure of social knowledge. At that point in his career, Ward considered all actions, whether bodily or mental, the result of objective desires that were physical in origin. Patten argued that the economic activities of individuals in organized societies had social sources. To support his case, he relied on the theory of utility, familiar to economists, which assumed that a socially conditioned, subjective process of weighing alternatives occurred within the individual engaged in choosing between various ways of satisfying wants. Patten agreed that animal behavior was controlled by urgent physical need. As human society progressed, he argued, individuals learned to control their hostile feelings, to defer gratification, to share, to organize themselves for production, to extend their range and variety of consumption, and to cooperate—against their immediate animal instincts for individual survival—in order to achieve greater satisfaction than any one person could acquire alone. This was an example of social forces that had origins outside the purview of the life studies, and it proved to Patten that the proper way to approach the study of sociology was through economics, not biology.

On methodological grounds, Patten charged the biologic sociologists with equally serious blunders. Instead of working inductively by direct observation of the behavior of people in society, they arrived at conclusions either by facile analogy or deductively, by applying the laws of biology to other realms. In so doing, they constructed generalizations that had no basis in reality. Instead of developing sciences independently, out of their own subject matter, they built pseudosciences of psychology and sociology that were nothing more than "ghost biology." The "laws of social development" that they created by such imperfect methods were easily repealed by specialists in a field such as economics when they merely looked to the facts. Undoubtedly sociologists might benefit from the findings of economists, Patten conceded, and they might even stimulate new economic insights. To make a significant contribution and merit independent status, they would have to develop a line of original inquiry that was entirely their own.[25]

If the synthesizers were misled by biology, Patten charged, the advocates of sociology as a fundamental discipline poached on and perverted psychology. Giddings was Patten's main target. At that stage of his thinking, Giddings was preoccupied with the idea that all human behavior, physical and social, was largely determined by basic psychological traits that were present in all animal life from the earliest stage of evolution to the development of complex human societies. The most important of these forces was fellow-feeling, or consciousness of kind. This same inherent psychological faculty was the basic force behind social organization among all living creatures, Giddings argued, and in studying such basic drives sociology could provide a basis for economics. Unfortunately, Giddings's theory failed either to account for the economic phenomena that Patten had observed or to provide the transition in origins of economic behavior that Patten needed to sustain his distinction between the biological

25. Lester F. Ward, *The Psychic Factors of Civilization* (Boston, 1893). The best summary of his views on the role of sociology is Lester F. Ward, "The Place of Sociology among the Sciences," *American Journal of Sociology* 1 (July 1895): 16-27. See also Albion Small, "The Era of Sociology," ibid., pp. 1-15. Patten's criticism is in Simon N. Patten, "The Failure of Biologic Sociology," *Annals of the American Academy of Political and Social Science* 4 (May 1894): 919-47. For a conservative economist's equally ascerbic review of the first sociology text, Albion W. Small and George E. Vincent, *An Introduction to the Study of Society* (New York, 1894), see Bernard Moses, "The Nature of Sociology," *Journal of Political Economy* 3 (December 1894): 24-38. Moses thought that the zeal of sociologists was noteworthy, "particularly in getting a name." He also charged that their interest in developing means of managing social policy indicated that the discipline remained an art, not a science.

and the social side of humanity. In Patten's system, animals (including primitive humans) were originally driven by physical need and recognized only the initial utility of food and other goods that could satisfy their immediate, urgent desire. Even toward others of their own kind, their actions were generally individualistic and hostile. Gradually, however, probably among the weakest species that were driven out of the choicest areas, certain individuals realized that they must resort to cooperation or perish. Here was the beginning of society, the origin of social bonds, the source of social forces, and the first recognition of marginal utility, which was the basis of economics. By experimentation, imitation, and eventually conscious planning, human beings could maximize utilities and create an economy of abundance. Obviously, Patten believed that the science that would make such economic planning possible was the social science of economics. Psychology was a physical science, not antecedent but parallel. Like biology, psychology should be developed on its own terms by empirical methods, not preempted by deductive sociologists. Once more, Patten suggested, sociologists should get out of biology, psychology, and economics, and plow their own garden.[26]

The synthetic sociologists thought no more of Giddings's proposals than Patten did. In a bitter private comment to Ward, Small remarked, "If *consciousness of kind* is the mouse which his mountain has brought forth perhaps we ought to forgive Giddings on the Scotch girl's plea—'it's such a little one.' " Small actually agreed with Patten that "the individualistic rather than the associational point of view" predominated in Giddings's work and that its direct contribution was to what might be called "the higher psychology rather than to sociology proper." Small was "anxious for the development of a type of sociologists [sic] willing to leave the analysis of subjectivity to

26. Franklin Henry Giddings, "Utility, Economics and Sociology," *Annals of the American Academy of Political and Social Science* 5 (November 1894): 398-404; Simon N. Patten, "The Relations of Economics to Sociology," ibid. (January 1895): 577-83; Giddings, "Sociology and the Abstract Sciences: The Origin of the Social Feelings," ibid. (March 1895): 746-53.

the psychologists, and willing to concentrate their own attention on the social environment."[27]

When the major contenders in the sociological controversy met at the 1894 meeting of the AEA, lines were already clearly drawn. Small appeared more or less on summons to explain to his fellow economists what he and his fellow sociologists were up to. Conscious of his predicament, Small categorically denied any sympathy with people who attempted to "make the term 'Sociology' stand for an effort to supersede or to discredit economic science." He also continued to insist, with no apparent sense of contradiction, on the need for a social science that existed not to discover primary facts but to generalize from the findings of antecedent sciences such as economics and political science, deriving the general laws of social development. In the ensuing discussion Giddings reiterated his much ridiculed scheme for evading the problem of priority by thinking in terms of two intersecting axes in the scheme of knowledge, with sociology at the head of the list of concrete sciences, and economics just below ethics among the abstract disciplines. Patten's patience wore thin. He bluntly asserted that the sociologists had "no right to stake off for themselves a portion of the field of social science without consulting the economists." Economists were willing to have other inquirers go to work in a coordinate field, "providing, of course, they would let economics alone." Sociologists should quit trying to define their discipline horizontally, either above or below the other social sciences, should make their cut vertically, and stop making trouble. Bristling, Ward confessed his willingness to "be read out of the synagogue of economics," but the idea of sociologists seeking consent from economists sounded to him like "the tail wagging the dog." At last a note of sanity returned to the proceedings when W. J. Ashley, Harvard's historical economist, reminded his colleagues that great thoughts that profoundly

27. Small to Ward, 3 March, 29 April 1896, printed in Stern, ed., "Letters of Albion W. Small to Lester F. Ward," 2:325, 334-36; Small to Ross, 19 December 1901, Ross MSS.

affected men's minds had usually come from doers like Darwin who "cared but little about the classification of the sciences."[28]

Compared with the economic controversy of the mid-1880s, the sociological controversy of the mid-1890s revealed important changes in the structure of American social science. It was no longer possible to establish a discipline by proclamation. Only if a sizable group of university-based practitioners could agree on a research focus, a method, and a mission—and then only if that mission did not challenge the prerogatives of another well-organized and viable discipline—could the effort succeed. There was more to the economists' resistance than mere jealousy. Economists had not labored for a generation to escape the constraints of moral philosophy only to have their hard-bought separate identity expunged by a new synthetic philosophy and the continuity of their university status threatened as well. The major issue in the sociological controversy was whether the European pattern, which conceived of sociology as a science of sciences—a unified, coherent, descriptive, historical, explanatory science of society as a whole—was to take root in America, where the claims of other disciplines—among them economics, law, and jurisprudence—to total explanatory power in certain aspects of social life were already established. A small, unorganized group, divided among themselves and headed, in prestige at least, by a government paleontologist, had made the abortive attempt to establish a normative science. Undoubtedly men like Ward and Small were trying to preserve a place for the kind of synthetic, ethical function that moral philosophy had once served. Now that we know all this about society, they questioned, how do we act? By what social laws do we govern ourselves? The little support that they mustered came largely from the men like Ely, the outspoken reformers and ethical economists of the 1880s. Even Patten, who had that back-

28. Albion Small, "The Relation of Sociology to Economics," *Journal of Political Economy* 3 (March 1895): 169-84; "Discussion—Albion Small, 'The Relation of Sociology to Economics,' " *Publications of the AEA* 10 (1895): 106-17.

ground, had blocked sociology's efforts partly to preserve a chance to realize his own unique and special dream of economics as a gateway to the good society.[29]

In the end, then, the synthesizers simply backed down. Through the next decade people engaged in all sorts of work came under the sociological umbrella. The theorizers survived and continued to offer comprehensive explanations of society as they turned out the textbooks that made it possible for newcomers to offer elementary college courses.[30] The radical remnant, Ross, Commons, Bemis, and Howard came in, and their persistent interest in reform tied sociology to the practical grievances of workers, farmers, and city dwellers. Despite the claims of prominent leaders, much of the empirical work being done in sociology was concerned with marriage, poverty, dependency, and deviancy—substantially related to social work. Under aggressive leadership at several universities, however, social work was professionalizing also, and it pressed in on sociology from the practical side as economics did from the scientific.

Finally, in the decade after 1895, a number of American sociologists began to converge on a strand of inquiry that promised to be extremely useful in organizing the field. The most original and productive scholars began to investigate the social group. For different reasons and from varying perspectives, these people wanted to know what the social group was, where it came from, how it functioned, how it lasted, how it

29. Ely's correspondence with Small, his publishing ventures, his hiring policies, and his own interest in Christian sociology attest to his sympathy for the synthetic and normative mission that Small had in mind. See Ely's notes for an address delivered in Milwaukee, "The Study of Social Science and the Christian Minister," 28 September 1892, Ely MSS. See also Ely to M. M. Miller, 4 January 1898, ibid. On the laissez-faire side, Laughlin, for example, made his opinion clear by demanding that Bemis be transferred to sociology, but compare Laughlin to William Rainey Harper, 17 July 1894, Laughlin Folder, President's Collection, University of Chicago. In the formative period there was more sociology in the West, where Ely students and friends were more numerous. Giddings at Columbia stayed close to John Bates Clark and laissez-faire, making no pretense that sociology was superior to economics.

30. The most influential were Small and Vincent, *An Introduction to the Study of Society,* and Franklin H. Giddings, *The Principles of Sociology: An Analysis of the Phenomena of Association and of Social Organization* (New York, 1896).

controlled its individual members, and how it might be destroyed. Out of this interest came theories and concepts with such magnetic simplicity and explanatory power that they quickly found their way into the vernacular of educated people. Cooley's primary group, Giddings's consciousness of kind and socialization, Sumner's folkways and mores, Ross's social control: they all in one way or another helped to define the social group as a phenomenon that could be analyzed on its own terms, without dependence on the jargon and methods of another discipline. Among the most professional elite, this focus on the social group began to provide the center that American sociology had lacked.[31]

When professionalization is studied by following the process of differentiation among ideas, there is some risk of losing sight of the individual human forces and the social context that shaped the disciplines. As was true in the formative stage of professional economics, people were often attracted to their inquiries for highly personal reasons, and not, it should be noted, primarily as part of a coordinated group effort to construct a discipline. This was true of the early students of the social group. One could almost say that Cooley was attracted to sociology because it allowed him to make a profession of being what he already was. Cooley was a shy, self-conscious, idealistic, sickly, introspective youth, the often uncomfortable opposite of his aggressive, worldly, eminent father, Judge Thomas McIntyre Cooley of the Michigan Law School. Contemplative and solitary, he was fascinated with his own thoughts; as he

31. Some of the works where these formulations appeared were Charles Horton Cooley, *Human Nature and the Social Order* (New York, 1902); Cooley, *Social Organization: A Study of the Larger Mind* (New York, 1909); Franklin Henry Giddings, *The Theory of Socialization: A Syllabus of Sociological Principles* (New York, 1897); William Graham Sumner, *Folkways* (Boston, 1906); Edward Alsworth Ross, *Social Control: A Survey of the Foundations of Order* (New York, 1901). Ross's *Social Control* first appeared serially in the *American Journal of Sociology,* beginning with the first issue in 1895. Though I differ somewhat from his account of the origins and timing of this "shift to the group," I am indebted to Hamilton Cravens, "Abandonment of Evolutionary Social Theory in America," esp. pp. 10-17, for the concept and for his explanation of the connection between this intellectual transition and professionalization in sociology.

graduated from engineering school to work as a draftsman in Bay City, Michigan, and a statistician in Washington, D. C., his greatest fear was that he would expend so much nervous energy in "active life" that he would be unable to make the intellectual contribution he felt capable of. He worried constantly about having time to himself, "keeping regular and civilized hours," reading, reflecting, and making notes in the fascinating diary, begun when he was eighteen, that recorded his intellectual and emotional inner life. In 1888, when he started graduate work in social science, he first followed the careerist model of Henry Carter Adams, his economic mentor. Cooley did a thesis on the hard subject of railway transportation "both because of its great intrinsic interest and because it is attracting so much attention that anything good upon it would give its author some reputation." But all the time Cooley knew that his real interest was in sociology, not economics. By rigorous intellectual preparation, he hoped to understand the social questions and help to find the bases for a just society. Yet he feared that any involvement in the "active life" of philanthropy or reform would sap the strength and undermine the objectivity required for true intellectual achievement. For such a man at such a time the academic life and sociology were natural choices.[32]

Though Cooley devoured the European masters, his infatua-

32. Cooley to Elsie Jones, 4 December 1888, 5 January 1889, 11 March 1890, Cooley MSS. For a brief but insightful biographical study of Cooley by his nephew, see Robert Cooley Angell's introductory essay in Albert J. Reiss, Jr., ed., *Cooley and Sociological Analysis* (Ann Arbor, Mich., 1968), pp. 1-12. Cooley's conscious weighing of the merits of the two disciplines is revealed in all its youthful contradiction by his diaries, now available on microfilm. In 1890 he wrote: "In all matters where I work under the stimulus of contact with people I move too fast. I am over-sensitive to the contagion of the world. Where eagerness is I am eager. My 'active life,' that is my life among men, will surely absorb all my energy unless I show remarkable self-control. It looks as if I would have to withdraw from active life, for a time at least. . . . I would not wholly withdraw but would, perhaps, teach. I would seek some activity not too stimulating." Charles Horton Cooley Diaries, Number 6 (2 May 1890-9 July 1890), entry of 2 May 1890, Cooley MSS. In the entry of 6 June 1890, ibid., he weighed the conflicting claims of reform and contemplation and decided, somewhat guiltily: "I need more of the purely intellectual activities than I will get if I devote myself too much to active life. Pure sociology, apart from social reforms, should be looked to." See also his own autobiographical account of early influences in ibid., Number 10 (12 July 1895-26 April 1896), entry of 21 July 1895.

tion with Spencer was over by the mid-1890s. "Spencer perhaps confuses a little success with survival," he noted. In response to the 1894 Chicago survey on the relationship of sociology to other disciplines, Cooley claimed that the distinctive quality of sociology was its peculiar point of view. While Small and Ward were campaigning for a synthetic discipline, Cooley quietly reported his own conclusion that sociology was "a distinct science—not merely a general view of the others." A short time later his diary recorded his shift from biology to society. "In sociology we begin where biology leaves off," he noted, "and study the parallel development of the social man and the institutions in which he lives." The institutions that most fascinated Cooley were those close human associations in which he had always felt most comfortable. He was constantly concerned with relationships. He abhorred confrontation, feared intensity, and retained "an insistent desire to find the order that he felt sure underlay the seeming disorder of the world." In the rich and complicated intellectual life that yielded so much insight into organic group process, Cooley built on the work of masters in the humanities and the social sciences, but he also guarded the integrity and followed the logic of his own individual life.[33]

Ross's contribution to knowledge of the social group was also greatly influenced by his own peculiar sense of society around him. Yet what happened to Ross surely happened, in different degree, to others. In the 1890s especially, an opposition developed between social reform activity designed to liberate the oppressed classes and a new emphasis, sometimes associated with the same people, on finding ways to control the volatile, frightening urban masses. In Ross's case, the expansive Christian humanitarianism that guided his reform activities in the 1880s was diverted somewhat by his growing fear, in the 1890s, that hordes of European and Asiatic immigrants would undermine the virtues of individualistic Anglo-Saxon civilization in North America and eventually amalgamate the Anglo-Saxon people.

33. Ibid., pp. 15-23; Cooley to Ira W. Howerth, 16 February 1894, Charles Horton Cooley MSS; Reiss, *Cooley and Sociological Analysis*, p. 7.

By mid-twentieth century standards, Ross was an inveterate racist, and even for his own day he was inordinately committed to the superiority of Aryan stock. A country boy and a Presbyterian, he believed that the distinctive character of Anglo-Saxon people was their individualism and their consequent ability to come together in the natural group life of the frontier or village community as equals, to govern themselves democratically with little fear of exploitation or crime. Urbane and cosmopolitan he became, but Ross still viewed cities as artificial growths that carried the natural man out of nature and into society, where injustices quickly developed. Urban industrial society destroyed the intimate bonds that kept people in village communities virtuous and set so many atomized individuals on each other with moral restraint. Aryans were especially disadvantaged, for they fared less well in cities and factories than the Latins, Slavs, and Asiatics—normally Catholic or non-Christian—who adapted better to crowded, regimented life. The only hope for survival was a set of new restraints, imposed by society, to control the irresponsible individual. In that context, *Social Control* was more than an empirical study. It was a "program for survival," a catalog of all the influences—public opinion, law, belief, education, custom, religion, ritual, art, and more—that society might use to mold the individual to the necessity of the group.[34]

Others besides Ross were beginning to have mixed feelings about the masses. Patten's keen interest in the nature of sociology stemmed from his own interest in social control. His distinction as an economist was his realization that industrial progress in the Western world had finally reached the point where it was possible to dispense with concepts based on pe-

34. This interpretation of Ross's work on social forces is based on an incisive essay on Ross in R. Jackson Wilson, *In Quest of Community: Social Philosophy in the United States, 1860-1920* (New York, 1968). The most relevant sections of Ross, *Social Control,* are the chapters on "Natural Order" and "The Need of Social Control," pp. 41-61. Ross's fear of race suicide and his enthusiasm for immigration restriction are by now familiar. In contrast to Ross's belief in the necessity of imposed restraints, Sumner and Giddings, both laissez-faire theorists, believed that "natural" social controls were inherent in the group.

rennial scarcity and to contemplate a life of abundance for all. In the 1890s, as he worked out his conception of an economy of abundance, Patten feared that people might simply exhaust all the surplus over what was needed for survival in a mad orgy of hedonistic consumption. In order to prevent people from wallowing in excess, consuming gluttonous quantities at a low level of appreciation, Patten believed it would be necessary to provide a special kind of education to elevate the taste of the masses.

It was here that Patten feared the reformist tendencies he sensed lurking in synthetic sociology. Though he had no great regard for the selfish individualism of competitive scarcity economics, he believed it would be prudent to leave some inequities in wealth undisturbed so that private capitalists in search of a return on investment might channel enough of the product of industry back into new production. In order to prevent people from squandering the resources needed to maintain abundance, people would have to be educated to consume a greater variety of goods and to work voluntarily to spread the benefits of society. Patten's reliance on new educational theories such as associationism and conditioning should not obscure the essential conservatism of his purpose. Patten's conflict with the telic sociologists was not a battle between advocates and an objective scientist but an impasse between advocates of different sorts. As much as his Puritan ancestors, Patten believed in the necessity for shaping attitudes and restraining evil passions. Education for intelligent consumption was also social control.[35]

With all these disparate strands—reform and restraint, optimism and misgiving, analysis and synthesis, philanthropy and theory—sociology lumbered into the twentieth century. Some people were doing empirical studies, but others who called themselves sociologists still worked in charities. An elite had

35. Patten's conception of marginal utility and the need to train people to recognize new forms and degrees of utility in a greater variety of goods and experiences is described in Daniel M. Fox, *The Discovery of Abundance: Simon N. Patten and the Transformation of Social Theory* (Ithaca, N.Y., 1967), esp. pp. 44-59, upon which this account of Patten's motivation relies.

found a research focus in the social group, but many questions of purpose and content were unresolved. Small felt the unformed discipline's tenuous position keenly when he confessed to Ely: "As near as I can discover there are not half a dozen men in our whole outfit who would think the University had lost anything but a lot of fad material if our department were summarily wiped out altogether."[36]

The American Sociological Society (ASS) was formed in 1905 primarily because political science had been organized a year before. On the APSA's proven pattern, a circular went out from the same neutral location—George Washington University—to inquire whether leading sociologists thought the time had come to organize. They did, and a call went out for an organizational meeting at the 1905 annual gathering of the AHA, the AEA, and the APSA in Baltimore. The established leaders, Ward, Small, Sumner, Giddings, and Ross, all signed the invitation. Harvard's Thomas Nixon Carver and the University of Pennsylvania's Samuel M. Lindsay represented younger scholars and new programs. Finally, the signature of Simon Patten indicated that the awesome foe of the mid-1890s was ready, in quieter times, to grant the chastened sociologists separate but no more than equal status.[37]

When the American Sociological Society was founded at the December 1905 meeting of the AHA, AEA, and APSA, it was a kind of mechanical completion in imitation of the older social disciplines rather than a symbol of either maturity or consensus in the field. In fact, a number of ASS supporters hoped that a national organization would break the traditional spell of "great thinkers" on sociology and help to foster some agreement on

36. Small to Ely, 27 May 1901, Ely MSS.
37. "Organization of the American Sociological Society: Official Report," *American Journal of Sociology* 11 (January 1906): 555-69. The timing of the organization movement may also have been influenced by the inability of unorganized sociologists to influence the program of the Congress of ·Arts and Sciences in the Louisiana Purchase Exposition held at Saint Louis in 1894. For an account of the program, which most sociologists considered a disaster, see A. W. Coats, "American Scholarship Comes of Age: The Louisiana Purchase Exposition 1904," *Journal of the History of Ideas* 22 (July 1961): 404-17.

basic questions. The academics stuck together well enough to write a constitution that clearly subordinated practical sociology and concentrated power in the hands of the university elite. To consummate the new spirit of unity, Ward was elected president and Sumner the first vice president, to follow his old enemy in the executive chair. No one offered or permitted a definition of sociology. So this time, with no opposition, the society was simply voted into existence. An official report of the new organization admitted that most academics still failed to see any purpose for sociology, while the founders took comfort in the existence of sociological societies in France, England, and the United States as evidence that "a few men and women, in full possession of their senses" thought otherwise. With academic social science on its way to institutional completion, the creation of an association to foster each new department had become ritualized and, in this case, nearly automatic.[38]

38. [Small], "The American Sociological Society," *American Journal of Sociology* 12 (March 1907): 579-80.

13 *Resolution*

At the beginning of the twentieth century the relationship between amateur and professional social science was exactly the reverse of what it had been at the close of the Civil War. Economists, political scientists, and sociologists had taken over the theoretical analysis of society, while sociology's close cousin, the rapidly professionalizing field of social work, claimed responsibility for the practical, day-to-day necessity of ministering to the needy. Amateur social science, which had shouldered the whole burden at the start of the Industrial Era, finally lost its reason for being and disappeared. Unchallenged, academic social scientists dominated the study of society.

Amateur social science had declined as academic professionalism grew. In the mid-1880s, when academic organizations first began whittling away their territory, forward-looking members of the ASSA responded with aggressive militance. For twenty years they had been working toward a professional standard of investigation and a professional prerogative in interpreting social phenomena. Suddenly, when victory seemed to lie within their grasp, academics with higher educational qualifications began to organize separate professional societies for their disciplines, insinuating that the study of social science belonged in colleges and universities. Partly because a faction within the ASSA had been headed in that direction anyway, and partly as a defensive response to the threat posed by the American Historical Association and the American Economic Association, the ASSA tried to claim a place in higher education for its own comprehensive approach to social science.

ASSA members responded to student eagerness for knowledge about social questions by attempting to create a practical social science curriculum. Their courses typically included a broad range of topics—from straightforward treatments of property, wages, taxes, and rent to a visit to the local asylum. If the approach was unsophisticated by later standards, it won approval from prominent educators at the time. Though Andrew Dickson White could have chosen a German-trained professional economist to establish a model social science course at Cornell, he invited ASSA secretary Frank Sanborn instead. White deliberately instructed Sanborn to steer a middle course between ethics and economics, stressing the welfare and service roles of government, to inform young people who would someday serve as local or state officials about the practical problems of social life. Sanborn lectured on various classes of public dependents: "the insane, the poor, the vicious, and the criminals of an American state." He took his wide-eyed students to see inmates and patients at state institutions, hoping to teach them to use what Ely, at about the same time, was calling the "look and see" method of investigation as a basis for deciding how society was performing its welfare function. Reports from other colleges indicated that similar approaches were catching on; current economic questions and practical welfare problems, not theoretical analyses, were common starting points in undergraduate social science courses in the 1880s, and the mold seemed only to need setting. Sanborn sensed that he was pioneering in a promising and important field.[1]

The change in Sanborn's thinking indicates how the ASSA might have progressed if its development in higher education had not been interrupted by rival academic professionalization movements. In 1874 Sanborn had not been enthusiastic about the reorientation of the ASSA toward more scholarly purposes. A humanist and a reformer at heart, he felt much more affinity for the practical accomplishments of the Conference of Charities and Corrections than he ever did for any scientific society.

1. Frank B. Sanborn, "The Social Sciences: Their Growth and Future," *JSS* 21 (1886): 7-12. For White's view of social science in colleges, see Andrew Dickson White, "Instruction in Social Science," ibid., 28 (1891):1-20. On the proliferation of practical social science courses in the 1870s and 1880s, see L. L. Bernard and Jessie Bernard, *Origins of American Sociology: The Social Science Movement in the United States* (New York, 1943), p. 637.

Commenting in 1875 on the association's interest in education, Sanborn noted that the ASSA hoped to "supply lessons" on social science "not so much to the pupils in our schools and colleges as to the general public." Yet a decade later he was avidly promoting higher education as the best place to pursue and disseminate social science knowledge. "I regard the introduction of definite instruction in the social sciences, as a whole, into so many American universities as both the result and the extension of our work in this Association," he proclaimed. Sanborn was beginning to believe that the humane and empirical social science he favored would be hard-pressed to survive between the aggressive scientism of traditional academics on the one side and the uncompromising militance of radical reformers on the other.[2]

In 1885, when the AEA was formed, the academic contingent of the ASSA moved to extend the association's relationships with colleges and to exert more influence on the still amorphous social science curriculum. Working with Sanborn were two well-established academic social scientists: Francis Wayland, dean of the Yale Law School, and Edmund J. James, economist in the University of Pennsylvania. Together those three combined the diverse perspectives that converged in academic social science in the mid-1880s. Sanborn contributed his comprehensive familiarity with philanthropy and a rudimentary conception of inductive methods for studying social problems. Wayland had grown out of the moral philosophy tradition to establish himself as an influential classical economist. James, the youngest, was a German-trained, academic, ethical, historical economist, a proponent of state planning, and a founder of the AEA. Perhaps it is not surprising that three such different men created a social science curriculum expansive enough to absorb almost every discipline that dealt with human beings. Their syllabus included pedagogy, public health, finance and political economy, social and domestic economy, and the entire field of

2. Frank B. Sanborn, "The Work of Social Science, Past and Present," *JSS* 8 (1876): 32; Sanborn, "The Social Sciences: Their Growth and Future," p. 12.

jurisprudence. In every field topics were arranged to show how knowledge could be applied to social problems.[3]

Sanborn and his committee established an impossible goal. What they hoped for was a problem-oriented social science that kept all of society in view, a comprehensive perspective that never allowed its fascination with definitions and processes to obscure the needs of the human beings who composed society. In encompassing so much of social interaction, the amateurs encroached on the preserves of the medical, legal, and teaching professions at a particularly inopportune time. Doctors and lawyers had just begun to recover from the drastic deprofessionalization both had experienced in the Jacksonian era, while teachers were beginning to show some interest in effective organization to raise standards.[4]

The Sanborn prospectus posed a greater potential threat to professionalizing academic social scientists than to anyone else, but the proposal for increased ASSA emphasis on college-level instruction met its stiffest resistance inside the amateur organization. Opponents of the college curriculum were influential leaders who simply refused to accept any new departure that ignored the association's traditional mission of taking social science directly to the people.

One such objection showed the anti-intellectual side of amateur science. A thinly veiled attack on academics, it came, embarrassingly enough, from a man who spoke with considerable authority both as president of the ASSA in 1885 and as United States Commissioner of Education. General John Eaton despised any emphasis other than a purely practical one in social science. A veteran of the Freedmen's Bureau effort to educate former slaves, he had no patience with scholars who thought it was more scientific to investigate gravitation or the

3. "Methodical Education in the Social Sciences," *JSS* 21 (1886):13-21.

4. This view of social science appears over and over in ASSA literature. See Frank B. Sanborn, "The Commonwealth of Social Science," *JSS* 19 (1885):1-10. On professionalization of medicine, law, and teaching, see Morris Fishbein, *A History of the American Medical Association, 1847-1947* (Philadelphia, 1947); Roscoe Pound, *The Lawyer from Antiquity to Modern Times* (St. Paul, Minn., 1953); Robert Wiebe, *The Search for Order, 1877-1920* (New York, 1967), pp. 111-23.

pottery of dead people and then report their findings in language no one else could understand than it was to study problems of sanitation, education, delinquency, and industry. Eaton thought society needed social scientists who were willing to come down from the clouds of theory and help men use the truths of social science to improve their daily lives. People should not have to hunt social science in the colleges. Social science should come to them where they were, through public lectures, cheap tracts, press, pulpit, popular library, museum, and forum. Eaton's complaint was not only utilitarian; it was a timely reminder of class obligations. If common men sometimes rampaged in angry mobs, it was because they lacked the guidance of science. When the scientific method was popularized, Eaton promised, it would quiet and elevate the masses.[5]

Objections from Eaton might have been ignored, but Carroll D. Wright's criticisms of the Sanborn committee's proposals were more telling. Wright represented the best scientific tradition of the ASSA. As he turned the better bureaus of labor statistics into nonpartisan agencies for gathering, interpreting, and widely disseminating useful information to provide a background for legislation, his own career reflected the traditional tripartite mission of amateur social science. Now Wright refused to allow would-be professors to prevent the ASSA from reaching out to the people. If professionalization meant diligence, perseverance, and uniformity in research, rationality in method, objectivity in judgment, and humane treatment of all classes, Wright favored it. If professionalization meant withdrawing social science to an insulated bastion behind ivy-covered walls, he opposed it.[6]

For the old guard that Wright represented, popularization of social science remained the highest priority. As president in 1886, Wright rededicated the ASSA to communicating directly

5. John Eaton, "Scientific Method in the Common Affairs of Life," *JSS* 21 (1886):ix-xxiii; Eaton, "Scientific Methods and Scientific Knowledge in Common Affairs," *Science* 4 (12 September 1884):246-48.

6. Carroll D. Wright, "Popular Instruction in Social Science," *JSS* 22 (1887):28-30.

with the masses. He rejected Wayland's plea that the common school curriculum was already too overloaded to accomplish much. Instead Wright called for a heavy infusion of practical social science in the upper grades. What the people could not learn in the public schools, he hoped they could acquire in Sunday schools and from attractive popular magazines. Wright still had abundant faith in the ability of the laboring classes to rear their children decently, take care of their homes, manage their money, and exercise common sense at the polls, if only they received appropriate instruction. Even a decade after the association had supposedly given first priority to the cultivation of knowledge, his attitude was probably more typical of ASSA members than the academic inclinations of a Sanborn or a Wayland.[7]

The division in the ASSA in the mid-1880s was based upon a difference between a bureaucratic outlook that prized implementation above theory and an academic spirit that valued theory above practical application. Eaton and Wright were willing to support social science in higher education, but only after the common people were instructed. By later standards they remained essentially amateurs as social scientists, but as civil servants they were professionals. Neither in 1874, when the ASSA adopted some academic values, nor in 1885-1886, when another academic advance was attempted, did such people intend to allow the association that most facilitated and dignified their rationalizing, ordering, network-building work to become another society for professors.

With its leadership divided on goals, the ASSA produced no clearcut program for expanding practical social science in higher education. The syllabus that Sanborn, Wayland, and James had prepared received favorable comment from friendly academics, but little action, at a time when delay was a serious mistake. A survey by the Education Department in 1886 showed 103 institutions teaching at least some of the ten social science

7. Ibid., pp. 30-35. For Wayland's position, see "Discussion of Papers of 1885," *JSS* 21 (1886):xxvi-xxxiii.

topics that the ASSA committee proposed.[8] But the report showed even more clearly the turmoil that undergraduate curriculum was in, especially in the social sciences. There was administrative and financial support for practical courses, and there was student demand for specific knowledge about society and social issues. But no one knew exactly how the product should be delivered at the undergraduate level, where professional objectives were still considered less important than general education. Obviously research-oriented social scientists in the new academic disciplines could use undergraduate programs as vehicles for establishing their claim on social science and recruiting students for graduate school. When the amateurs failed to mount an effective campaign for their problem-oriented approach to social science while conditions were still fluid, the ASSA simply missed the best opportunity to proselytize for its practical, melioristic perspective. In 1886, after a desultory discussion that concealed the disagreement on goals, a rump group at a poorly attended business meeting passed a vague resolution agreeing that the time had come to extend social science instruction and urging the association to circulate information to colleges and universities.[9] That puny statement was lost in the cacaphony of strident voices making proclamations about Haymarket, anarchists, and the menace of the working classes.

Perhaps even among the most sympathetic social scientists, the trauma of 1886 temporarily extinguished faith in the ability of the masses to govern themselves. The bitter confrontations between labor and capital which modernization produced turned a number of academics to investigating mechanisms of social control, and the problems of holding American society together seemed foremost to ASSA leaders as well.[10] After the

8. "Social Science Instruction in the Colleges, 1886," *JSS* 21 (1886):xxxv-xlix.
9. "Business and Debates of 1886," ibid., 22 (1887):xiii.
10. Several articles in *JSS* show the momentary hesitation of ASSA members who had long rejected laissez-faire and defended labor. Even Sanborn was reduced by the anxiety of the times to frantic talk of maintaining order "by soldiers and by executions." See Sanborn, "Address of the Chairman," *JSS* 22 (1887):105; H. L. Wayland, "The State and the Savings of the People," ibid., pp. 159-60.

abortive higher education project of 1885-1886, professionalization in the amateur association progressed no further. As the developing disciplines of economics, sociology, and political science took over the college social science curriculum, less and less was said in the amateur society about disseminating social science knowledge.

For the next several years the ASSA served a useful purpose as a forum where a cross section of amateur and professional social scientists could meet to debate the crucial economic questions that Americans faced in the anxious decade framed by Haymarket and the election of 1896. Major portions of several meetings were devoted to lectures and discussions on profit sharing, savings banks, building and loan associations, cooperatives, the single tax, labor unions, the sweating system, and the silver question. The single tax debate of 1890 was a full-dress occasion that arrayed a coalition of prominent professional economists against a group of Henry George supporters. What began as a civil, though spirited confrontation of ideas quickly degenerated into a name-calling session, with the professionals—especially Seligman—denouncing the amateurs as unschooled but dangerous enthusiasts, and the amateurs—especially George—indicting the professionals for truckling to the wealthy while they offered "goody-goody palliatives" to the masses.[11]

The ASSA continued its efforts to influence policy. Indeed, within conventional assumptions, ASSA members were more constantly concerned than most academic economists with the welfare of the working class. The ASSA remained almost unanimously in favor of private property and sound money, but any measure favorable to labor and short of communism was at least an open question. Members praised the moral and educational functions of labor unions, upheld the right to strike, demanded compulsory arbitration, and opposed Pinkertons. There was variety and controversy, but the overall pattern of the amateur

11. The Single Tax Debate is in *JSS* 27 (1890):1-24. For Seligman's and George's remarks, see ibid., pp. 34-44, 73-98.

organization remained a consistent economic conservatism and an equally persistent social liberalism.[12]

By the mid-1890s, however, the ASSA began to lose the unity of purpose that had once fired its members with shared enthusiasm for the good that social science could do. While the finance and social economy departments still grappled with major questions, the departments of health and jurisprudence devoted increasing attention to encouraging the professionalization of medicine and law. Political scientists and sociologists each used the ASSA as a staging ground for their professional organizations and then moved on. Now and then prominent public figures, often reformers or professional social scientists temporarily estranged from academic connections, used the meetings to reach a cultivated audience and the journal to get a message into print; nearly as frequently the programs offered strange quacks with bizarre suggestions. Around the edges of the association a number of hangers-on dabbled with increasingly trivial topics. Discussions on the nature and method of social science had disappeared.

At last the ASSA succumbed totally to specialization. Lacking a cohesive program and without a clearly defined constituency, its membership began to dwindle. Old-timers motivated largely by nostalgia staged periodic membership drives to revive the organization. As a desperation measure in 1899, the ASSA exchanged affiliate memberships with the National Institute of Arts and Letters, thus adding nearly 1,900 "members" to the rolls, and a rather aesthetic humanism began to replace the scientific spirit. Finally Frank Sanborn retired. George William Curtis, W. T. Harris, and many other former leaders died. Every journal seemed to open with another obituary. At last the surviving amateurs admitted that their concept had died too. The immediate needs of social workers, journalists, city planners, health workers, lawyers, teachers, and

12. Representative samples of prolabor sentiments are H. L. Wayland, "Has the State Abdicated?" *JSS* 30 (1892):v-xviii; Wayland, "Compulsory Arbitration," ibid., 31 (1894):lxii-lxxii; Louis D. Brandeis, "The Incorporation of Trades-Unions," ibid., 41 (1903):16-21; Oscar S. Strauss, "Industrial Peace," ibid., pp. 46-53.

specialists of every sort were better served by their special organizations. With academic social science differentiated into several professions, there was no place for the synthetic, operational view of social science that the amateur organization had tried to articulate. Little was left for the remaining amateurs but what they had started with in 1865, culture and philanthropy. In 1909 the ASSA met for the last time. Appropriately, its last president asked for space on the program of the American Sociological Society to announce that the American Social Science Association had ceased to exist.

The death of the ASSA signified more than the passing of a once powerful organization. It meant that professionalization in academic social science had eliminated the amateur social scientist's reason for being. Unless they were trained to the graduate level in a social science discipline and employed in an academic setting, people working with social phenomena failed to retain a sense of themselves as social scientists. The peculiar blend of attributes and experiences that had made the amateurs value the search for truth and still care passionately about putting their findings to practical use in social life did not survive.

In some respects the professional social scientists who preempted the role by the early twentieth century were not terribly different from the amateurs. Whether the practitioners were academics or not, a constant tension between knowledge and reform was characteristic at every stage. The professionals were not less reform-minded than the amateurs. Frequently academic social scientists were more so, but they wrapped their reform intentions in a mantle of professional prerogative that shielded them from consequences of advocacy which would otherwise have been too severe to risk. In the process the form and even the substance of their advocacy was tempered, and the tension between reform and knowledge reappeared as a conflict between advocacy and objectivity.

With professionalization, objectivity grew more important as a scientific ideal and also as a practical necessity. After a good deal of experimentation with other positions, professional social scientists finally based their claims to competence in social analysis on the authority conferred by scientific methods and attitudes. The value of objectivity was emphasized constantly in both training and professional practice, until it occupied a very special place in the professional ethos. Faith in scientific objectivity spurred many social scientists to make important theoretical advances, while others merely produced work that was methodologically sound. The development of socially useful knowledge remained the recognized goal of research in social science, but in practice investigators were usually guided more by the state of existing knowledge and by their own interests than by social conditions. Ideological considerations were inevitably present, but they were ordinarily unacknowledged. Formally at least, academics judged each other primarily on skill in original investigation for two reasons: because that was the only index which could be kept relatively free of divisive ideological considerations, and because they could best preserve their autonomy by developing public acceptance of the principle that the work of specialists in social science could be judged only by other specialists. On the negative side, at least the appearance of objectivity was essential to survival, for without it there was no assurance of professional support in time of need.

From the standpoint of scholarship, the impact of academic professionalization on social science was eminently positive. It promoted caution, self-scrutiny, care with sources and methods, and a generally heightened rationalism. Dividing the study of society so that a separate compartment was devoted to each of the major social institutions facilitated a high level of technical competence and promoted depth instead of superficiality in research. For a time in the 1890s the component disciplines were really only three self-conscious segments within a still recognizable whole that was academic social science. When the disciplines became institutionalized divisions of knowledge, when the departments became self-perpetuating separate entities in colleges and universities, when the segments viewed themselves as distinct professions, the whole disappeared. The social sciences replaced social science. Specialization increased technical expertise and made professional social scientists valuable members of commissions and bureaus, but it also left a number of important questions outside the range of academic competence.

Finally the tension between advocacy and objectivity which characterized the professionalization process altered the mission of social science. Only rarely did professional social scientists do what no one else was better qualified to do: bring expert skill and knowledge to bear on cosmic questions pertaining to the society as a whole. Instead studies and findings tended to be internal, recommendations hedged with qualifiers, analyses couched in jargon that was unintelligible to the average citizen. A fundamental conservatism developed in the academic social science professionals, though conformity was often to a liberal rather than a conservative consensus. The academic professionals, having retreated to the security of technical expertise, left to journalists and politicians the original mission—the comprehensive assessment of industrial society—that had fostered the professionalization of social science.

Bibliography

The most important sources for this study were the personal papers of social scientists intimately involved in the professionalization of social science in the Gilded Age. Without the letters preserved by history-conscious academics it would have been impossible to recapture their developing sense of mission or to reconstruct the events that shaped their views. The largest and in some ways the most valuable collection, the Richard T. Ely Papers at the Wisconsin Historical Society contain approximately 300,000 items in 254 boxes of letters, notes, speeches, pamphlets, and records. The 100,000 or so items that fell within the period of this study revealed Ely's professional attitudes at the height of his influence, disclosed the pattern of his decline, and showed how other economists reacted to him in both circumstances. Reading through that collection made it impossible to underestimate the importance of careerism as a countermotive to reformism.

There is no compact manuscript source on E. R. A. Seligman's developing consciousness of himself as an economist, for the huge collection of his papers at Columbia University contains mostly incoming correspondence. Seligman served as a clearinghouse for economic opinion in the 1880s and 1890s. His papers are the best single source for a cross section of opinion from the literally dozens of prominent social scientists who were his correspondents. His primary role in the Andrews and Ross cases made his correspondence a major source of information on the reaction among social scientists to challenges to academic freedom. Along with Seligman's, several smaller collections at Columbia University made it possible to trace the growth of professionalism in one department.

Though the Henry Carter Adams Papers at the University of Michigan have been less used by students of social science, the approximately fifty boxes, twenty-five letterbooks, scrapbooks, notes, and lectures are a very valuable collection. For this study the most useful feature was the remarkable correspondence between Adams and his mother. For almost twenty years until his marriage at thirty-nine, Adams wrote to Mrs. Ephraim Adams at least once a week, and she preserved nearly every letter. Adams considered his mother an intellectual equal, and he discussed his ideals, ambitions, and fears very candidly with her. His correspondence with Bertha Wright before their marriage showed another, more intimate side of Adams. Besides providing perhaps the best single model of the way in which professionalization altered a social scientist's character and goals, the Adams papers also helped to straighten out some inaccuracies in previous accounts of the internal politics in the American Economic Association and the economics profession.

Other manuscript collections were of great value for parts of the study. The presidential papers preserved by James Burrill Angell, William Rainey Harper, David Starr Jordan, and Andrew Dickson White helped to illuminate the developing network of relationships in Gilded Age academic life and to place the academic freedom cases in their institutional setting. The Franklin B. Sanborn Collections at the Concord Free Public Library and the Library of Congress disclosed the cosmopolitan interests of an amateur social scientist and the special combination of intellectual and reformist motivations he felt. The following list of papers consulted in this study indicates the richness of manuscript sources available for research on social scientists and the professions in this period:

Adams, Henry Carter, MSS. Michigan Historical Collections, University of Michigan.

Adams, Herbert Baxter, MSS. Johns Hopkins University Archives.

Angell, James B., MSS. Michigan Historical Collections, University of Michigan.

Carey, Henry C., MSS. Pennsylvania Historical Society.

Clark, John Bates, MSS. Columbia University Special Collections.

Commons, John R., MSS. Wisconsin Historical Society.

Cooley, Charles Horton, MSS. Michigan Historical Collections, University of Michigan.

Cooley, Thomas McIntyre, MSS. Michigan Historical Collections, University of Michigan.

Elliott, Orrin L., MSS. Stanford University Archives.

Ely, Richard T., MSS. Wisconsin Historical Society.

Giddings, Franklin Henry, MSS. Columbia University Special Collections.

Goodnow, Frank, MSS. Johns Hopkins University Archives.

Harper, William Rainey, MSS. President's Collection, University of Chicago Archives.

Howard, George Eliot, MSS. University of Nebraska Archives.

Hull, Charles Henry, MSS. Cornell University Archives.

James, Edmund J., MSS. University of Illinois Archives.

Jameson, J. Franklin, MSS. Manuscripts Division, Library of Congress.

Jordan, David Starr, MSS. Stanford University Archives.

Kinley, David, MSS. University of Illinois Archives.

Laughlin, J. Laurence, MSS. Manuscripts Division, Library of Congress.

Mayo-Smith, Richmond, MSS. Department of Special Collections, University of Chicago.

McMahon, Theresa Schmid, MSS. University of Washington Archives.

Meany, Edmond, MSS. University of Washington Archives.

Newcomb, Simon, MSS. Manuscripts Division, Library of Congress.

Political Science Quarterly MSS. Columbia University Special Collections.

Ross, Edward Alsworth, MSS. Wisconsin Historical Society.

Sanborn, Franklin B., MSS. Concord Free Public Library, Concord, Massachusetts.

————, MSS. Manuscripts Division, Library of Congress.

Seligman, Edwin R. A., MSS. Columbia University Special Collections.

Smith, J. Allen, MSS. University of Washington Archives.

Stanford Family MSS. Stanford University Archives.

Stillman, John M., MSS. Stanford University Archives.

"Tulane Scraps." Tulane University Archives.

University Scrapbooks. Department of Special Collections, University of
Chicago.

Wells, David Ames, MSS. Manuscripts Division, Library of Congress.

White, Andrew Dickson, MSS. Cornell University Archives.

————, MSS. Michigan Historical Collections, University of Michigan.

Willcox, Walter F., MSS. Manuscripts Division, Library of Congress.

Though not as valuable as the manuscript sources, a number of published collections of letters, diaries, memoirs, and autobiographies
provided additional insight into the actions and perceptions of important
individuals. These works include:

Adams, Henry. *The Education of Henry Adams.* New York, 1931.

Burgess, John William. *Reminiscences of an American Scholar.* New York,
1934.

Commons, John R. *Myself: The Autobiography of John R. Commons.*
Madison, Wis., 1963.

Donnan, Elizabeth, and Stock, Leo F., eds. *An Historian's World: Selections from the Correspondence of John Franklin Jameson.* Philadelphia, 1956.

Dorfman, Joseph, ed. "The Seligman Correspondence, Parts 1-4." *Political
Science Quarterly* 56 (March-December 1941):107-24, 270-86,
392-419, 573-99.

Ely, Richard T. *Ground under Our Feet: An Autobiography.* New York,
1938.

Holt, W. Stull, ed. *Historical Scholarship in the United States, 1876-1901:
As Revealed in the Correspondence of Herbert B. Adams.* Johns
Hopkins University Studies in History and Political Science, Series
56, No. 4. Baltimore, 1938.

Nevins, Allan, and Thomas, Milton Halsey, eds. *The Diary of George
Templeton Strong.* 4 vols. New York, 1952.

Noyes, Katherine Macy, ed. *Jesse Macy: An Autobiography*. Baltimore, Md., 1933.
Perry, Thomas Sergeant, ed. *The Life and Letters of Francis Lieber*. Boston, 1882.
Ross, Edward Alsworth. *Seventy Years of It*. New York, 1936.
Stern, Bernhard J., ed. "The Letters of Albion W. Small to Lester F. Ward: Parts 1-4." *Social Forces* 12 (December 1933):163-73; 13 (March 1935):323-40; 15 (December 1936):174-86; (March 1937):305-27.
———, ed. *Young Ward's Diary*. New York, 1935.

Other primary material fell into four major categories: textbooks, professional journals, general journals of opinion, and commission reports. The *Journal of Social Science* (1869-1909), published by the American Social Science Association, provided the basis for understanding the con-cerns of amateur social scientists throughout the period and insight into the origins and character of nonacademic professionalization. Academic social scientists published their work in a number of specialized journals that appeared during the period. The most important of these follow, with the date of origin indicated for each: The *Johns Hopkins University Studies in History and Political Science* (1883), the *Publications of the American Economic Association* (1886), Columbia University's *Political Science Quarterly* (1886), Harvard's *Quarterly Journal of Economics* (1886), the *Annals of the American Academy of Political and Social Science* (1891), the University of Chicago's *Journal of Political Economy* (1892), the University of Chicago's *American Journal of Sociology* (1895), and the *Proceedings of the American Political Science Association* (1904). In addition, social scientists wrote frequently in such popular periodicals as *Arena, Dial, Forum, Review of Reviews, Nation,* and *North American Review*. Three other journals, *Science,* the *Scientific American,* and *Popular Science Monthly,* showed the reaction of various segments of the scientific community to the achievements and pretensions of social scientists. The reports of public and private investigating commissions, such as the United States Industrial Commission *Reports* (1900-1902), are a relatively neglected source of information on the social scientists who served with them as members or consultants. The specific books, articles, and reports listed below include those cited in this study and some others of importance:

"Acting Secretary's Report." *Journal of Social Science* 7 (1874):342.
Adams, Henry Carter. "Another View of Economic Laws and Methods." *Science* 8 (30 July 1886):103-5.
———. "Difficulties in Adjusting Rates." *Publications of the AEA*. 3d Ser., 1 (1900):245-49.

―――. "Economics and Jurisprudence." *Science* 8 (2 July 1886):14-19.

―――. "Relation of the State to Industrial Action." In *Two Essays by Henry Carter Adams,* edited by Joseph Dorfman, pp. 57-133. New York, 1969.

―――. "Review of Clark's Philosophy of Wealth." *Political Science Quarterly* 1 (December 1886):687-90.

―――. "Shall We Muzzle the Anarchists?" *Forum* 1 (July 1886):445-54.

―――. "Statistics as a Means of Correcting Corporate Abuses." *Publications of the AEA* 6 (1891):73-78.

―――. "The Labor Problem." *Scientific American,* Supplement, 22 (21 August 1886):8861-63.

―――. "The Position of Socialism in the Historical Development of Political Economy." *Penn Monthly* 10 (April 1879):285-94.

Adams, Thomas S. "Porto Rican Finance under the Spanish and American Governments―Discussion." *Publications of the AEA.* 3d Ser., 3 (1902):342-50.

"Affairs of the American Social Science Association." *Journal of Social Science* 6 (1874):16.

American Social Science Association. *Constitution, Address, and List of Members* [1865].

"American Social Science Association." *Journal of Social Science* 6 (1874):1-4.

Andrews, E. Benjamin. "Individualism as a Sociological Principle." *Yale Review,* o.s. 2 (May 1893):13-27.

―――. *Institutes of Economics.* Boston, 1889.

―――. "Political Economy, Old and New." *Andover Review* 6 (August 1886):130-38.

Bascom, John. *Political Economy.* Andover, Mass., 1859.

Bemis, Edward W. "Municipal Ownership of Gas in the United States." *Publications of the AEA* 6 (1891):287-472.

―――, et al. *Municipal Monopolies.* Boston, 1899.

―――. "Socialism and State Action." *Journal of Social Science* 21 (September 1886):33-69.

Bentley, Arthur. *The Process of Government: A Study of Social Pressures.* 1908. Reprint. Bloomington, Ind., 1949.

Blodget, Lorin. "Waste of Existing Social Systems." *Journal of Social Science* 4 (1871):8-18.

Board of Regents. *The Reorganization of the Kansas State Agricultural College.* Manhattan, Kans., 1897.

Board of State Charities of Massachusetts. *First Annual Report.* 1864.

Board of State Charities of Massachusetts. *Second Annual Report.* 1866.

Bowen, Francis. *American Political Economy.* Boston, 1870.

———. *Principles of Political Economy.* Boston, 1856.

Brandeis, Louis D. "The Incorporation of Trades-Unions." *Journal of Social Science* 41 (1903):16-21.

Brown University Trustees. *The Andrews Controversy.* Providence, R.I., 1897.

"Business and Debates of 1886." *Journal of Social Science* 22 (1887): xiii.

Butler, Nicholas Murray. "Ely's Labor Movement in America." *Science* 8 (15 October 1886):353-55.

Clark, John Bates. *The Distribution of Wealth: A Theory of Wages, Interest and Profits.* 1899. Reprint. New York, 1956.

———, and Giddings, Franklin Henry. *The Modern Distributive Process.* Boston, 1888.

———. *The Philosophy of Wealth.* Boston, 1886.

———. "The Scholar's Political Opportunity." *Political Science Quarterly* 12 (December 1897):589-602.

"Comment and Criticism." *Science* 8 (23 April 1886):361.

Commons, John R. *The Distribution of Wealth.* 1893. Reprints of Economic Classics. New York, 1965.

Cooley, Thomas M. "Arbitration in Labor Disputes." *Forum* 1 (June 1886):307-13.

"Current Record of the Association." *Journal of Social Science* 2 (1870):viii-ix.

"Current Record." *Journal of Social Science* 3 (1871):199.

Curtis, George William. "Opening Address." *Journal of Social Science* 6 (1874):33-38.

Dunbar, Charles F. "The Academic Study of Political Economy." *Quarterly Journal of Economics* 5 (July 1891):397-416.

———. "The Reaction in Political Economy." *Quarterly Journal of Economics* 1 (October 1886):1-27.

Eaton, John. "Scientific Method in the Common Affairs of Life." *Journal of Social Science* 21 (1886):ix-xxiii.

———. "Scientific Methods and Scientific Knowledge in Common Affairs." *Science* 4 (12 September 1884):246-48.

Eliot, Samuel. "An American University." *Journal of Social Science* 5 (1873):162-77.

———. "Civil Service Reform." *Journal of Social Science* 1 (1869): 112-19.

Ely, Richard T. *An Introduction to Political Economy.* New York, 1889.

———. "Ethics and Economics." *Science* 7 (11 June 1886):529-33.

————. "Fundamental Beliefs in My Social Philosophy." *Forum* 18 (October 1894):173-83.

————. *Labor Movement in America*. New York, 1886.

————. "On Methods of Teaching Political Economy." In *Methods of Teaching History*, edited by G. Stanley Hall, pp. 61-72. Boston, 1898.

————. "Political Economy in America." *North American Review* 144 (February 1887):113-19.

————. *Problems of Today*. New York, 1888.

————. "Recent American Socialism." *Johns Hopkins University Studies in Historical and Political Science* 3 (April 1885):231-304.

————. "Report of the Organization of the American Economic Association." *Publications of the AEA* 1 (March 1886):3-46.

————. *Social Aspects of Christianity*. New York, 1889.

————. *Socialism: An Examination of Its Nature, Its Strength and Its Weakness, with Suggestions for Social Reform*. New York, 1894.

————, and Finley, John. *Taxation in American States and Cities*. New York, 1888.

————. "The Economic Discussion in Science." *Science* 8 (2 July 1886):3-6.

————. "The Founding and Early History of the American Economic Association." Papers and Proceedings of the American Economic Association, Supplement. *American Economic Review* 26 (March 1936):141-50.

————. "The Past and Present of Political Economy." *Johns Hopkins University Studies in History and Political Science* 2 (March 1884):137-202.

Farnam, Henry. "Review of Ely's, The Labor Movement in America." *Political Science Quarterly* 1 (December 1886):683-87.

Fisher, Arthur F. *The Process of Government: A Study of Social Pressures*. 1908. Reprint. Bloomington, Ind., 1949.

Folwell, William Watts. "The New Economics." *Publications of the AEA* 8 (1893):19-40.

Garfield, James A. "The American Census." *Journal of Social Science* 2 (1870):31-55.

Giddings, Franklin Henry. "Sociology and the Abstract Sciences: The Origin of the Social Feelings." *Annals of the American Academy of Political and Social Science* 5 (March 1895):746-53.

————. *The Principles of Sociology*. 1896. Reprint. New York, 1899.

————. "The Relation of Sociology to Other Scientific Studies." *Journal of Social Science* 32 (1894):144-50.

————. "The Sociological Character of Political Economy." *Publications of the AEA* 3 (1888):29-47.

Giddings, Franklin Henry. "Utility, Economics and Sociology." *Annals of the American Academy of Political and Social Science* 5 (November 1894):398-404.

————. *The Theory of Socialization: A Syllabus of Sociological Principles.* New York, 1897.

Gilman, Daniel Coit. "Opening Address." *Journal of Social Science* 12 (1880):xxii-xxiv.

Godkin, E. L. "Legislation and Social Science." *Journal of Social Science* 3 (1871):115-32.

Goodnow, Frank. *Municipal Home Rule.* New York, 1895.

————. *Politics and Administration.* New York, 1900.

————. "The Work of the American Political Science Association." *Proceedings of the American Political Science Association* 1 (1904):35-46.

Gunton, George. "Liberty in Economic Teaching." *Gunton's Magazine* 18 (March 1900):231-32.

[————]. "Professor Bemis and the University of Chicago." *Public Opinion* 19 (11 November 1895):582.

Hadley, Arthur Twining. "Economic Laws and Methods." *Science* 7 (16 July 1886):46-48.

————. "Economic Theory and Political Morality—Discussion." *Publications of the AEA.* 3d Ser., 1 (1900):45-88, 287-88.

————. *Economics.* New York, 1896.

————. "Ely's 'Socialism and Social Reform.' " *Forum* 18 (October 1894):184-91.

————. "How Far Have Modern Improvements in Production and Transportation Changed the Principle That Men Should Be Left Free to Make Their Own Bargains? Part 1." *Science* 7 (5 March 1886):221-28.

————. "Jay Gould and Socialism." *Forum* 14 (January 1893):686-93.

————. "Review of Commons's The Distribution of Wealth." *Yale Review,* o.s. 2 (February 1894):439-40.

————. "The Relations between Economics and Politics." *Publications of the AEA.* Economic Studies, 4 (1899):7-28.

Hammond, W. G. "Legal Education and the Study of Jurisprudence." *Journal of Social Science* 8 (1876):165-76.

[Harper, William Rainey]. "The President's Quarterly Statements." *The Quarterly Calendar,* 4, Nos. 1 and 2. Chicago, 1895.

Harris, W. T. "Moral Education in the Common Schools." *Journal of Social Science* 18 (1884):122-34.

H[ill], [R. T.] "Cornell University." *Index* [of the Free Religious Association], 29 July 1886, pp. 51-52.

Hill, William. "State Railways in Australia." *Journal of Political Economy* 3 (December 1894):1-23.

Howerth, Ira W. "Present Condition of Sociology in the United States." *Annals of the American Academy of Political and Social Science* 5 (September 1894):112-21.

"Introductory Note." *Journal of Social Science* 1 (1869):1-2.

James, Edmund J. "Newcomb's Political Economy." *Science* 6 (27 November 1885):470-71.

———. "Relation of the Modern Municipality to the Gas Supply." *Publications of the AEA* 1 (1886):47-122.

———. "The State as an Economic Factor, Part 1." *Science* 7 (28 May 1886):485-88.

Jenks, Jeremiah W., et al. "Essays in Colonial Finance." Report of the AEA Committee on Colonies. *Publications of the AEA*. 3d Ser., 1 (1900):385-688.

———. *Great Fortunes: The Winning, the Using.* New York, 1906.

Knight, George. "The Political Science Association of the Central States." *Annals of the American Academy of Political and Social Science* 5 (March 1895):144-45.

Laughlin, J. Laurence. *The Elements of Political Economy.* New York, 1887.

———. "The Study of Political Economy in the United States." *Journal of Political Economy* 1 (December 1892):1-19.

Lieber, Francis. *Civil Liberty and Self Government.* New York, 1853.

Mathews, Shailer. "Christian Sociology. Part 4: The State." *American Journal of Sociology* 1 (March 1896):604-17.

Mayo-Smith, Richmond. "Methods of Investigation in Political Economy." *Science* 8 (23 July 1886):81-87.

———. "Review of Commons's The Distribution of Wealth." *Political Science Quarterly* 9 (September 1894):568-72.

———. "Review of Hadley's Railroad Transportation and Laughlin's History of Bimetallism in the United States." *Political Science Quarterly* 1 (March 1886):568-72.

Moses, Bernard. "The Nature of Sociology." *Journal of Political Economy* 3 (December 1894):24-38.

National Civic Federation. *Industrial Conciliation.* Report of the Conference held in New York, December 16 and 17, 1901. New York, 1902.

———. *Municipal and Private Operation of Public Utilities.* Report of the Commission on Public Ownership and Operation. 3 vols. New York, 1907.

———. *National Conference on Taxation.* New York, 1901.

Newcomb, Simon. "Aspects of the Economic Discussion." *Science* 7 (18 June 1886):538-42.

———. "Can Economists Agree upon the Basis of Their Teaching?" *Science* 8 (9 July 1886):25-26.

[———]. "Dr. Ely on the Labor Movement." *Nation* 43 (7 October 1886):293-94.

———. "Review of Ely's Outlines of Economics." *Journal of Political Economy* 3 (December 1894):106.

———. *Principles of Political Economy.* 1886; Reprints of Economic Classics, New York, 1966.

———. "The Problem of Economic Education." *Quarterly Journal of Economics* 7 (July 1893):375-99.

———. "The Two Schools of Political Economy." *Princeton Review,* n.s. 14 (November 1884):291-301.

"Newcomb's Political Economy." *Nation* 42 (14 January 1886):38-39.

"Notes." *Nation* 39 (24 July 1884):74.

"Organization of the American Sociological Society: Official Report." *American Journal of Sociology* 11 (January 1906):555-69.

Patten, Simon Nelson. "[David A.] Wells' Recent Economic Changes." *Political Science Quarterly* 5 (March 1890):84-103.

———. "The Failure of Biologic Sociology." *Annals of the American Academy of Political and Social Science* 4 (May 1894):63-91.

———. *The Premises of Political Economy.* Philadelphia, 1885.

———. "The Relation of Economics to Sociology." *Annals of the American Academy of Political and Social Science* 5 (January 1895):577-83.

———. "The Scope of Political Economy." *Yale Review,* o.s. 2 (November 1893):264-87.

Perry, Arthur Latham. *Elements of Political Economy.* New York, 1866.

"Preliminary Report of the Committee on Colonies." *Publications of the AEA.* 3d Ser., 1 (1900):283-86.

"Principal Objects of the American Social Science Association." *Journal of Social Science* 1 (1869):3-4.

"Progress in Economic Education." *Journal of Social Science* 1 (1869):139.

Reinsch, Paul Samuel. *Colonial Administration.* New York, 1905.

———. *Colonial Government: An Introduction to the Study of Colonial Administration.* 1902. Reprint. Freeport, N.Y., 1970.

"Report of the Anniversary Meeting, December 28, 1909." *Publications of the AEA,* 3d Ser., 11 (1910):107-9.

Ross, Edward Alsworth. *Social Control: A Survey of the Foundations of Order.* New York, 1901.

Sanborn, Frank B. "Address of the Chairman." *Journal of Social Science* 22 (1887):98-110.

————. "Aids in the Study of Social Science." *Journal of Social Science* 19 (1885):49-56.

————. "Past and Present Social Science." *Journal of Social Science* 43 (1905):1-21.

[————]. "Report of the General Secretary." *Journal of Social Science* 12 (1880):1-5.

[————]. "Report of the Secretary." *Journal of Social Science* 20 (1885):14-26.

————. "Society and Socialism." *Journal of Social Science* 33 (1895):20-28.

————. "The Commonwealth of Social Science." *Journal of Social Science* 19 (1885):1-10.

————. "The Social Sciences: Their Growth and Future." *Journal of Social Science* 21 (1886):7-12.

————. "The Work of Social Science in the United States." *Journal of Social Science* 6 (1874):36-44.

————. "The Work of Social Science, Past and Present." *Journal of Social Science* 8 (1876):23-39.

Seligman, Edwin R. A. "Changes in the Tenets of Political Economy with Time." *Science* 7 (23 April 1886):375-82.

————, Gardner, Henry, and Farnam, Henry. *Report of the Committee of Economists on the Dismissal of Professor Ross from Leland Stanford Junior University*. 1901.

————. "Sidgwick on Political Economy." *Index,* 16 August 1883, pp. 75-76.

————. "Review of Henry Sidgwick's The Scope and Method of Economic Science." *Political Science Quarterly* 1 (March 1886):143-45.

Shaw, Albert. "New Studies in Political and Social Science." *Dial* 6 (July 1885):72-74.

————. "Political and Economic Literature from the Universities." *Dial* 8 (July 1887):61-64.

————. "Recent Economic Works." *Dial* 6 (December 1885):210-13.

Small, Albion Woodbury. "Academic Freedom." *Arena* 22 (October 1899):463-72.

————, and Vincent, George E. *An Introduction to the Study of Society*. New York, 1894.

————. *General Sociology*. Chicago, 1905.

————. "Scholarship and Social Agitation." *American Journal of Sociology* 1 (March 1896):564-82.

[Small, Albion Woodbury]. "The American Sociological Society." *American Journal of Sociology* 12 (March 1907):579-80.

———. "The Era of Sociology." *American Journal of Sociology* 1 (July 1895):1-15.

———. "The Relation of Sociology to Economics." *Journal of Political Economy* 3 (March 1895):169-84.

———. "Discussion." *Publications of the AEA* 10 (1895):106-17.

———. "The State and Semi-Public Corporations." *American Journal of Sociology* 1 (January 1896):398-410.

Smith, Munroe. "The Domain of Political Science." *Political Science Quarterly* 1 (March 1886):1-8.

"Social Science Instruction in the Colleges, 1886." *Journal of Social Science* 21 (1886):xxxv-xlix.

Spalding, J. L. "Are We in Danger of Revolution?" *Forum* 1 (July 1886):405-15.

Stanford, Jane Lathrop. *Address on the Right of Free Speech.* Stanford, Calif., 1903.

Strauss, Oscar S. "Industrial Peace." *Journal of Social Science* 41 (1903):46-53.

Sumner, William Graham. "American Finance." *Journal of Social Science* 6 (1874):181-89.

———. *Collected Essays in Political and Social Science.* New York, 1885.

———. *Earth-Hunger and Other Essays,* edited by A. G. Keller. New Haven, Conn., 1913.

———. *Folkways.* Boston, 1906.

———. "Industrial War." *Forum* 2 (September 1886):1-8.

———. "The Challenge of Facts." In *Sumner Today,* edited by Maurice R. Davie, pp. 67-92. New Haven, Conn., 1940.

———. *What Social Classes Owe to Each Other.* New York, 1883.

Talbot, Emily. "Methodical Education in the Social Sciences." *Journal of Social Science* 21 (1886):13-21.

Taussig, Frank William. "The State as an Economic Factor, Part 2." *Science* 7 (28 May 1886):488-91.

"The American Association Meeting at Philadelphia." *Science* 4 (July-December 1884):189-90.

"The American Social Science Association." *Journal of Social Science* 6 (1874):1-14.

"The American Sociological Society." *American Journal of Sociology* 12 (March 1907):579-80.

"The Case of Professor James Allen Smith." *Industrialist* 23 (2 September 1897):180.

"The Case of Professor Ross." *Science,* N.S. 13 (8 March 1901):362-70.

"The Organization of the American Political Science Association." *Proceedings of the American Political Science Association* 1 (1904):5-12.

"The Social Science Association." *Popular Science Monthly* 5 (July 1874):367-69.

Tracy, Frank Basil. "Menacing Socialism in the Western States." *Forum* 15 (May 1893):332-42.

"Under False Colors." *Popular Science Monthly* 7 (July 1875):365-66.

United States War Dept. *The War of the Rebellion: A Compilation of the Official Records of the Union and Confederate Armies.* 128 vols. Washington, D.C., 1880-1901.

United States Industrial Commission. *Reports.* 19 vols. Washington, D.C., 1900-1902.

Veblen, Thorstein. "Industrial and Pecuniary Employments." *Publications of the AEA.* 3d Ser., 2 (1901):190-235.

———. "Professor Clark's Economics." *Quarterly Journal of Economics* 22 (February 1908):147-95.

———. "The Instinct of Workmanship and the Irksomeness of Labor." *American Journal of Sociology* 4 (September 1898):187-201.

———. *The Theory of Business Enterprise.* New York, 1904.

———. *The Theory of the Leisure Class: An Economic Study of the Evolution of Institutions.* New York, 1899.

Walker, Amasa. *The Science of Wealth: A Manual of Political Economy.* Boston, 1866.

Walker, Francis Amasa. "Recent Progress of Political Economy in the United States." *Publications of the AEA* 4 (1889):243-68.

———. *Wages Question.* New York, 1876.

Ward, Lester Frank. *Dynamic Sociology.* 2 vols. New York, 1883.

———. "The Place of Sociology among the Sciences." *American Journal of Sociology* 1 (July 1895):16-27.

———. *The Psychic Factors of Civilization.* Boston, 1893.

Wayland, Francis, et al. "Discussion of Papers of 1885." *Journal of Social Science* 21 (1886):xxvi-xxxiii.

———. *The Principles of Political Economy.* Boston, 1850.

Wayland, H. L. "Compulsory Arbitration." *Journal of Social Science* 31 (1894):lxii-lxxii.

———. "Has the State Abdicated?" *Journal of Social Science* 30 (1893):v-xviii.

———. "The State and the Savings of the People." *Journal of Social Science* 22 (1887):156-65.

Wells, Oliver E. "The College Anarchist." *Nation* 59 (12 July 1894):27.

White, Andrew Dickson. *History of the Warfare of Science with Theology in Christendom*. New York, 1896.

———. "Instruction in Social Science." *Journal of Social Science* 28 (1891):1-20.

Will, Thomas Elmer. "A Menace to Freedom: The College Trust." *Arena* 26 (September 1901):244-57.

Willoughby, Westel Woodbury. *An Examination of the Nature of the State: A Study in Political Philosophy*. 1896. Reprint. New York, 1911.

Willoughby, William Franklin. "State Activities in Relation to Labor in the United States." *Johns Hopkins University Studies in History and Political Science* 19 (April-May 1901):181-269.

———. *Territories and Dependencies of the United States: Their Government and Administration*. New York, 1905.

Wilson, Thomas Woodrow. *Congressional Government*. Boston, 1885.

———. *The New Freedom*. New York, 1913.

———. *The State: Elements of Historical and Practical Politics*. 1889. Rev. ed. Boston, 1898.

Wright, Carroll D. "Popular Instruction in Social Science." *Journal of Social Science* 22 (1887):28-36.

———. "The Growth and Purposes of Bureaus of Labor Statistics." *Journal of Social Science* 25 (1888):1-14.

———. "The Scientific Basis of Tariff Legislation." *Journal of Social Science* 19 (1885):11-26.

Of the secondary sources, Joseph Dorfman's five-volume analysis of *The Economic Mind in American Civilization* is indispensable for any study involving economists. More than an acute analysis of factors that influenced the thought of both major and minor figures, it also provides a useful summary of economic history and introduces an incredible range of sources. As a compendium on the major economic thinkers and social reformers of the period, Sidney Fine's *Laissez Faire and the General-Welfare State* must be consulted almost as frequently. On the history of the economics profession, the numerous articles by A. W. Coats are a significant contribution. L. L. Bernard and Jessie Bernard, *Origins of American Sociology: The Social Science Movement in the United States,* attempts a comprehensive survey of all the social thinkers, but it is so often marred by special pleading for the importance of academic sociology and by errors in fact that it must be used with great caution. There is no similar comprehensive study of political scientists, but Bernard Crick, *The American Science of Politics,* comes closest.

The standard source on academic freedom is Richard Hofstadter and

Walter P. Metzger, *The Development of Academic Freedom in the United States.* Benjamin Rader's *The Academic Mind and Reform: The Influence of Richard T. Ely in American Life* stands out among the intellectual biographies of social scientists. Of the university histories, Hugh Hawkins, *Pioneer: A History of the Johns Hopkins University, 1874-1889,* is a model study. Laurence Veysey, *The Emergence of the American University,* is a massively researched and intelligent effort to place the emerging university among the major social institutions of modern America. The most stimulating synthesis of the entire period is Robert Wiebe, *The Search for Order, 1877-1920;* its analysis of the way various groups of Americans responded—some defensively and others more creatively—to the disruptive forces of modernization, particularly by organizing around their occupations, is especially suggestive for this type of study. Of the growing literature on professionalization, a few sociological studies proved most helpful. The secondary works cited in this study, as well as others that were useful, are listed below:

Abbot, Charles G. "Simon Newcomb." *Dictionary of American Biography,* 13:452-54.

Barber, Bernard. *Science and the Social Order.* Glencoe, Ill., 1952.

Barclay, Thomas S. "J. Allen Smith: An American Scholar." *Missouri Alumnus* 19 (April 1931):234, 239, 241.

Beale, Howard K. *A History of Freedom of Teaching in American Schools.* New York, 1941.

Bell, John Fred. *A History of Economic Thought.* New York, 1953.

Bergquist, Harold E., Jr. "The Edward W. Bemis Controversy at the University of Chicago." *AAUP Bulletin* 58 (December 1972):384-93.

Bernard, Luther Lee, and Bernard, Jessie. *Origins of American Sociology: The Social Science Movement in the United States.* New York, 1943.

Black, R. D. Collison, Coats, A. W., and Goodwin, Craufurd D. W., eds. *The Marginal Revolution in Economics.* Durham, N.C., 1973.

Borneman, Alfred. *J. Laurence Laughlin.* Washington, D.C., 1940.

Brooks, Van Wyck. *New England: Indian Summer, 1865-1915.* Boston, 1940.

Brown, Bernard E. *American Conservatives: The Political Thought of Francis Lieber and John W. Burgess.* New York, 1951.

Bryson, Gladys. "The Emergence of the Social Sciences from Moral Philosophy." *International Journal of Ethics* 42 (April 1932):304-23.

Bucher, Rue, and Strauss, Anselm. "Professions in Process." *American Journal of Sociology* 66 (January 1961):325-34.

Carr-Saunders, A. M. "Metropolitan Conditions and Traditional Professional Relationships." In *The Metropolis in Modern Life,* edited by Robert Moore Fisher, pp. 279-88. New York, 1955.

Carr-Saunders, A. M., and Wilson, P. A. *The Professions*. Oxford, 1933.

Chuggerman, Samuel. *Lester F. Ward: The American Aristotle*. Durham, N.C., 1939.

Church, Robert. "The Development of Social Sciences as Academic Disciplines at Harvard University, 1869-1900." 2 vols. Ph.D. dissertation, Harvard University, 1965.

————. "The Economists Study Society: Sociology at Harvard, 1891-1902." In *Social Sciences at Harvard, 1860-1920*, edited by Paul Buck, pp. 18-90. Cambridge, Mass., 1965.

Coats, A. W. "American Scholarship Comes of Age: The Louisiana Purchase Exposition 1904." *Journal of the History of Ideas* 22 (July 1961):404-17.

————. "The First Two Decades of the American Economic Association." *American Economic Review* 50 (September 1960):555-74.

————. "The Origins of the 'Chicago School(s)?' " *Journal of Political Economy* 71 (October 1963):487-93.

————. "The Political Economy Club: A Neglected Episode in American Economic Thought." *American Economic Review* 51 (September 1961):624-37.

Cravens, Hamilton. "The Abandonment of Evolutionary Social Theory in America: The Impact of Academic Professionalization upon American Sociological Theory, 1890-1920." *American Studies* 12 (Fall 1971):5-20.

Crick, Bernard. *The American Science of Politics: Its Origin and Conditions*. Berkeley, Calif., 1959.

Curti, Merle, and Carstensen, Vernon. *The University of Wisconsin: A History, 1848-1925*. 2 vols. Madison, Wis., 1949.

Daniels, George. "Baconian Science in America, 1815-1845." Ph.D. dissertation, University of Iowa, 1963.

————. "The Process of Professionalization in American Science." *Isis* 58 (Summer 1967):151-66.

David, Henry. *The History of the Haymarket Affair*. New York, 1936.

Dewey, Davis R. "Francis A. Walker as a Public Man." *Review of Reviews* 15 (1897):166-71.

Donnan, Elizabeth. "A Nineteenth Century Academic Cause Celebre." *New England Quarterly* 25 (March 1952):23-46.

Dorfman, Joseph. *The Economic Mind in American Civilization*. 5 vols. New York, 1949.

————. "Edwin Robert Anderson Seligman." *Dictionary of American Biography,* Supplement 2, 22:606-9.

————, and Tugwell, Rexford. "Francis Lieber: German Scholar in America." *Columbia University Quarterly* 30 (1938):159-90, 267-93.

————. "The Role of the German Historical School in American Economic Thought." *American Economic Review* 45 (May 1955):17-28.

————. *Thorstein Veblen and His America*. 1934. Reprints of Economic Classics. Clifton, N. J., 1972.

Dyer, John P. *Tulane*. New York, 1966.

Elliott, Orrin L. *Stanford University, the First Twenty-Five Years*. Stanford, Calif., 1937.

Fetter, Frank A. "The Early History of Political Economy in the United States." *Proceedings of the American Philosophical Society* 87 (1944):51-60.

Fine, Sidney. *Laissez Faire and the General-Welfare State*. 1956; Ann Arbor, paperback edition, 1964.

Fishbein, Morris. *A History of the American Medical Association, 1847-1947*. Philadelphia, 1947.

Fox, Daniel M. *The Discovery of Abundance: Simon N. Patten and the Transformation of Social Theory*. Ithaca, N.Y., 1967.

Freidel, Frank. *Francis Lieber, Nineteenth Century Liberal*. Baton Rouge, La., 1947.

Genzmer, George Harvey. "Franklin Benjamin Sanborn." *Dictionary of American Biography*, 16:326-27.

Ginger, Ray. *Altgeld's America*. New York, 1958.

Goode, William J. "Community within a Community: The Professions." *American Sociological Review* 22 (April 1957):194-200.

————. "Encroachment, Charlatanism, and the Emerging Profession: Psychology, Sociology, and Medicine." *American Sociological Review* 25 (December 1960):902-14.

Goldman, Eric. "J. Allen Smith: The Reformer and His Dilemma." *Pacific Northwest Quarterly* 35 (July 1944):195-214.

Green, Marguerite. *The National Civic Federation and the American Labor Movement, 1900-1925*. Washington, D.C., 1956.

Greenwood, Ernest. "Attributes of a Profession." *Social Work* 2 (July 1957):45-55.

Gross, Neal, et al. *Explorations in Role Analysis*. New York, 1958.

Grossman, David Michael. "Professors and Public Service, 1885-1925: A Chapter in the Professionalization of the Social Sciences." Ph.D. dissertation, Washington University, 1973.

Gruber, Carol Signer. "Academic Freedom at Columbia University, 1917-18: The Case of James McKeen Cattell." *AAUP Bulletin* 58 (September 1972):297-305.

Haddow, Anna. *Political Science in American Colleges, 1636-1900*. New York, 1939.

Hadley, Morris. *Arthur Twining Hadley*. New Haven, Conn., 1948.

Hawkins, Hugh. *Pioneer: A History of the Johns Hopkins University, 1874-1889*. Ithaca, N.Y., 1960.

Herbst, Jurgen. *The German Historical School in American Scholarship: A Study in the Transfer of Culture*. Ithaca, N.Y., 1965.

Higham, John. *History: The Development of Historical Studies in the United States*. Englewood Cliffs, N.J., 1965.

Hinman, E. L. "E. Benjamin Andrews." In *The University of Nebraska, 1869-1919*, pp. 130-33. Lincoln, 1919.

Hofstadter, Richard, and Smith, Wilson, eds. *American Higher Education: A Documentary History*. 2 vols. Chicago, 1961.

————. *Anti-Intellectualism in American Life*. New York, 1962.

————, and Metzger, Walter P. *The Development of Academic Freedom in the United States*. New York, 1955.

————. *Social Darwinism in American Thought*. Rev. ed. Boston, 1955.

————. *The Age of Reform: From Bryan to F.D.R.* New York, 1955.

————. "William Graham Sumner, Social Darwinist." *New England Quarterly* 14 (1941):457-77.

Hoogenboom, Ari. *Outlawing the Spoils: A History of the Civil Service Reform Movement, 1865-1883*. Urbana, Ill., 1961.

Hoxie, R. Gordon, et al. *A History of the Faculty of Political Science, Columbia University*. New York, 1955.

Kennedy, David M., ed. *Progressivism: The Critical Issues*. Boston, 1971.

Kolko, Gabriel. *The Triumph of Conservatism: A Reinterpretation of American History, 1900-1916*. Glencoe, Ill., 1963.

Kuhn, Thomas. *The Structure of Scientific Revolutions*. Chicago, 1962.

Laughlin, J. Laurence. "Francis Amasa Walker." *Journal of Political Economy* 5 (March 1897):228-32.

Leiby, James. *Carroll Wright and Labor Reform: The Origins of Labor Statistics*. Cambridge, Mass., 1960.

Linton, Ralph. *The Cultural Background of Personality*. New York, 1945.

Lubove, Roy. *The Professional Altruist: The Emergence of Social Work as a Career, 1880-1930*. Cambridge, Mass., 1965.

Lynn, Kenneth S., et al. "The Professions." *Daedalus* 82 (Fall 1963):647-856.

MacIver, Robert. *Academic Freedom in Our Times*. New York, 1955.

Mann, Arthur. *Yankee Reformers in the Urban Age*. Cambridge, Mass., 1954.

Martindale, Don. *The Nature and Types of Sociological Theory*. Boston, 1960.

McCrea, Roswell C. "A Biographical Sketch of Simon Nelson Patten." *Annals of the American Academy of Political and Social Science*, Supplement, 107 (May 1923):346-54.

————. "Edward Atkinson." *Dictionary of American Biography*, 1:406-7.

Merriam, Charles E. "John William Burgess." *Dictionary of American Biography,* Supplement 1, 21:132-34.

Merton, Robert K. *Social Theory and Social Structure.* Glencoe, Ill., 1949.

————. *Some Thoughts on the Professions in American Society.* Brown University Papers, 37. Providence, R.I., 1960.

Metzger, Walter P. *Academic Freedom in the Age of the University.* New York, 1961.

Mohr, James C. "Academic Turmoil and Public Opinion: The Ross Case at Stanford." *Pacific Historical Review* 39 (February 1970): 39-61.

Mowry, George. *The California Progressives.* Berkeley, Calif., 1951.

Nichols, Jeanette P. "Francis Amasa Walker." *Dictionary of American Biography,* 19:342-44.

Normano, J. F. *Spirit of American Economics.* New York, 1943.

Nosow, Sigmund, and Form, William, eds. *Man, Work and Society.* New York, 1962.

O'Connor, Michael J. L. *Origins of Academic Economics in the United States.* New York, 1953.

Odum, Howard, ed. *American Masters of Social Science.* New York, 1927.

————. *American Sociology.* New York, 1951.

Opie, Redvers. "Frank William Taussig." *Economic Journal* 51 (June and September 1941):347-68.

Page, Charles Hunt. *Class and American Sociology: From Ward to Ross.* New York, 1940.

Payne, Charles E. "Jesse Macy." *Dictionary of American Biography,* 12:176-77.

Perlman, Selig. "John Rogers Commons, 1862-1945." *American Economic Review* 35 (September 1945):782-86.

Pound, Roscoe. *The Lawyer from Antiquity to Modern Times.* St. Paul, Minn., 1953.

Purcell, Edward A., Jr. *The Crisis of Democratic Theory: Scientific Naturalism and the Problem of Value.* Lexington, Ky., 1973.

Rader, Benjamin G. *The Academic Mind and Reform: The Influence of Richard T. Ely in American Life.* Lexington, Ky., 1966.

Reiss, Albert J., ed. *Cooley and Sociological Analysis.* Ann Arbor, Mich., 1968.

Rosenberry, Marvin B. "Henry Carter Adams." In *Michigan and the Cleveland Era,* edited by Earl D. Babst and Lewis G. Vander Velde, pp. 23-41. Ann Arbor, Mich., 1948.

Schumpeter, J. A., Cole, A. H., and Mason, E. S. "Frank William Taussig." *Quarterly Journal of Economics* 55 (May 1941):337-63.

Seager, Henry R. "Address." *Annals of the American Academy of Political and Social Science,* Supplement, 186 (May 1923):336-38.

"Simon Newcomb." *Proceedings of the American Philosophical Society* 49 (1910):iii-xviii.

"Sketch of William Graham Sumner." *Popular Science Monthly* 35 (June 1889):261-68.

Small, Albion Woodbury. "Fifty Years of Sociology in the United States." *American Journal of Sociology* 21 (May 1916):721-864.

Smith, Wilson. *Professors and Public Ethics: Studies on Northern Moral Philosophers before the Civil War.* Ithaca, N.Y., 1956.

Spencer, Joseph Jansen. "General Francis A. Walker: A Character Sketch." *Review of Reviews* 15 (1897):159-66.

Sproat, John G. *"The Best Men": Liberal Reformers in the Gilded Age.* New York, 1968.

Somit, Albert, and Tanenhaus, Joseph. *The Development of American Political Science.* Boston, 1967.

Starr, Harris E. *William Graham Sumner.* New York, 1925.

Storr, Richard J. *The Beginnings of Graduate Education in America.* Chicago, 1953.

Swanson, Richard Allen. "Edmund J. James, 1855-1925: A 'Conservative Progressive' in American Higher Education." Ph.D. dissertation, University of Illinois, 1966.

Taussig, F. W. "My Father's Business Career." *Harvard Business Review* 19 (Autumn 1940):177-84.

Thwing, Charles F. *A History of Higher Education in America.* New York, 1906.

Tugwell, Rexford. "Notes on the Life and Work of Simon Nelson Patten." *Journal of Political Economy* 31 (April 1923):153-208.

Unger, Irwin. *The Greenback Era: A Social and Political History of American Finance, 1865-1879.* Princeton, N.J., 1964.

Veysey, Laurence R. *The Emergence of the American University.* Chicago, 1965.

Vollmer, Howard M., and Mills, Donald L., eds. *Professionalization.* Englewood Cliffs, N.J., 1966.

Weinstein, James. *The Corporate Ideal in the Liberal State, 1900-1918.* Boston, 1968.

Wiebe, Robert. *The Search for Order, 1877-1920.* New York, 1967.

Williamson, Harold F. *Edward Atkinson: The Biography of an American Liberal, 1827-1905.* Boston, 1934.

Wilson, R. Jackson. *In Quest of Community: Social Philosophy in the United States, 1860-1920.* New York, 1968.

Znaniecki, Florian. *The Social Role of the Man of Knowledge.* N.Y., 1940.

Index

Abbott, Lyman, 75, 89 n, 172 n

Academic disciplines, emergence of, 241. *See also* Economics: emergence of; Political science: emergence of; Sociology: emergence of

Academic freedom, 7, 125-27, 126 n, 140, 209, 238; defense of, 7, 155, 242 n, 250, 261; limits of, 126, 156, 216-18, 240, 243, 251; meaning of, 126, 156, 163

Academic freedom cases: causes of, 143, 164, 205-6, 222; regional characteristics of, 209, 221, 227, 261; results of, 7, 257-59, 261

Academics. *See* Social scientists: academic; professional

Adams, Charles Francis, 66

Adams, Charles Kendall: in H. C. Adams case, 129, 134, 137, 138; in emergence of political science, 280, 281-82, 283; as supporter of Ely, 70, 155, 155 n, 162 n

Adams, Henry, 57

Adams, Henry Carter: academic freedom case of, 128-42, 163, 170, 208, 213, 234, 249, 257; in Andrews case, 214, 217, 217 n, 219, 222 n; in Bemis case, 192, 194, 197; career of, 57, 91, 101, 128-32, 139, 151 n, 161 n, 232 n, 260, 283; careerism of, 53-54, 128, 137, 160, 263-64, 307; in Commons case, 201; early life of, 49-52; on economics and jurisprudence, 101-2, 103, 104, 113; economic views of, 91, 100-103, 104, 130-34, 138-39, 149, 160 n, 169 n; on Ely, 90; in Ely trial, 154 n; as ethical economist, 49-53, 127-28, 130-31, 146; in founding of American Economic Association, 70, 72, 73, 74, 76, 78, 79; on government regulation, 52, 103, 104-5, 133, 149; on labor, 130, 134, 136; as major figure

in economists' compromise, 90-91, 100, 104-5, 107, 127; as moderate, 101-2, 104-5, 107, 138-39; in Political Economy Club, 67; in Political Science Association of Central States, 263-64; as progressive reformer, 140, 160 n, 267, 269, 271 n, 276; religious influence on, 49-52, 56; in removal of Ely, 116-19, 118 n, 121, 122, 122 n; in Ross case, 247, 249, 250, 255; in *Science* "Economic Discussion," 93, 94, 100-103, 103-5, 105 n, 106, 130; in Smith case, 223, 227; on socialism, 52, 130-31, 133-34, 136, 138-39

Adams, Herbert Baxter, 63, 75, 75 n, 89 n, 178, 283

Adams, Thomas S., 286

Addams, Jane, 224 n, 267

Advocacy: in conflict with objectivity, 121, 143-44, 183, 204, 211, 290-91, 322; conservative, liberal, and radical, 159; danger of, 101, 166; danger of in universities, 139, 155, 206-7, 210, 232, 235; defense of, 113-15, 211, 214, 241, 247, 271; defining limits of, 124, 126-27, 143-44, 205, 211, 213, 227-28, 229, 256, 257, 259; as inherent right, 156, 164, 214, 215; in platform of early American Economic Association, 73-76, 90; as professional liability, 119-20, 159; as professional responsibility, 47, 114, 164, 178-79, 217, 238, 251, 273; as right conferred by professional competence, 96, 112-15, 126, 155, 156, 157, 199, 210-11, 214, 246, 256, 322; as threat to scientific objectivity, 147, 159. Views on: of H. C. Adams, 100-103, 138, 141-42, 144, 201; of Ashley, 251; of Bemis, 164; of Commons, 164, 199, 273-74; of Dunbar, 112-13, 120-21, 155, 158;